East Asia in the World

From the *Foundations in Global Studies* series, this text offers students a fresh, comprehensive, multidisciplinary entry point to East Asia, with an emphasis on the globalizing processes the region is undergoing. After a brief introduction to the study of East Asia, the early chapters of the book survey the essentials of East Asian history and offer an overview of the region's languages, economic development, and global connections. Students are guided through the material with relevant maps, resource boxes, and text boxes that support further independent exploration of the topics at hand.

The second half of the book presents an interdisciplinary portrait of the region through a set of case studies that explore key aspects of the cultural, economic, and political life in specific countries, sometimes holding up a mirror to the region as a whole. Readers will come away from this book with an understanding of current issues that have particular relevance in East Asia as we know it today and of the larger globalizing forces shaping the region and beyond.

Anne Prescott is the director of the Five College Center for East Asian Studies in Massachusetts and a national director for the National Consortium for Teaching about Asia, a leading provider of professional development training on East Asia. Trained as an ethnomusicologist specializing in traditional Japanese music, she spent eight years in Japan. She has been an administrator at area studies centers since 2002.

Foundations in Global Studies
Series Editor: Valerie Tomaselli, MTM Publishing

The Regional Landscape

East Asia in the World: An Introduction
Editor: Anne Prescott, Five College Center for East Asian Studies at Smith College

The Middle East in the World: An Introduction
Editor: Lucia Volk, San Francisco State University

South Asia in the World: An Introduction
Editor: Susan Snow Wadley, Syracuse University

East Asia in the World

An Introduction

Edited by Anne Prescott

Routledge
Taylor & Francis Group

NEW YORK AND LONDON

First published 2015
by Routledge
711 Third Avenue, New York, NY 10017

and by Routledge
2 Park Square, Milton Park, Abingdon, Oxon, OX14 4RN

Routledge is an imprint of the Taylor & Francis Group, an informa business

Library of Congress Cataloging in Publication Data
East Asia in the world : an introduction / edited by Anne Prescott.
pages cm. — (Foundations in global studies)
Includes index.
1. East Asia. 2. East Asia—Civilization. 3. East Asia—Social conditions.
4. Globalization—East Asia. I. Prescott, Anne (Director), editor.
DS504.5.E263 2015
950—dc23
2014043225

ISBN: 978-0-7656-4321-6 (hbk)
ISBN: 978-0-7656-4322-3 (pbk)
ISBN: 978-1-315-71734-0 (ebk)

Typeset in Times New Roman
by Swales & Willis Ltd, Exeter, Devon, UK

Contents

About This Book

East Asia in the World: An Introduction—the third book in M.E. Sharpe's *Foundations in Global Studies: The Regional Landscape* series—provides a fresh, systematic, and comprehensive overview of East Asia. Including coverage of China (including Taiwan), North Korea, South Korea, and Japan, the East Asia considered here is cogent and diverse at the same time; the vast areas under this formulation share patterns of history and culture, but also diverge in dramatic ways across the broad reach of its geography. For instance, these East Asian countries are not only tied together by their physical proximity, but also by two prominent cultural bonds that originated in China: the first being Confucianism and the second being the use of Chinese characters in their writing systems. These regions, often considered under a separate rubric in the traditional area studies approach, are considered critical here in understanding how "East Asia" developed across the centuries and how it is defined today. And while the focus is on the more typical "core" East Asian countries rather than those in Southeast Asia, the globalized complexion of East Asia is made clear in our broader reach.

The exploration of globalizing processes is indeed the focus of *East Asia in the World*, and the series as a whole. As we examine a host of global patterns that are reflected in and that shape the region—money flows, diasporic movements, hybridity in language, political movements affected by worldwide media and movement of ideas—the "in the World" part of the title gets a full hearing. Indeed, the variations in this wide region's social, cultural, economic, and political life are explored within the context of the globalizing forces affecting *all* regions of the world.

In a simple strategy that all books in the series employ, this volume begins with an overview and foundational material (including chapters on history, language, and economic development), moves to a discussion of globalization, and then focuses the investigation more specifically through the use of case studies. The set of case studies exposes readers to various disciplinary lenses that bring the region to life through subjects of high interest and importance to today's readers. Among others, these topics include the new car culture in China; the use of the radio as new media and technology in colonial Korea; the effect that Japan's March 2011 Triple Disaster had on minorities; Confucianism in modern East Asia; and the growing effect of China's one-child policy on the country's urban daughters.

A deliberate attempt has been made to illustrate the connections between peoples and countries that make up East Asia, and to counter the contemporary media focus on turmoil in the region. The chapters in Part Two, on history and language, illustrate clearly, for instance, that the region is much more than the sum of its civil and regional conflicts.

In addition to her own contributions as author of the overview and fundamentals chapters, the editor, Anne Prescott, director of the Five College Center for East Asian Studies at Smith College, has assembled a team of specialists, primarily from the Five Colleges (Amherst College, Hampshire College, Mount Holyoke College, Smith College, and the University of Massachusetts Amherst) to contribute case studies to the volume. The team represents the full range of disciplines brought to bear in the study of East Asia, including, among others, anthropology, communications and media, geography and the environment, geopolitics and international affairs, history, linguistics, and political economy.

Resource boxes, an important feature of the books in this series, are included to preserve currency and add utility. They offer links that point readers to excellent sources—mostly online—on the topics discussed. The links, which include connections to timely data, reports on recent events, official sites, local and country-based media, and visual material, establish a rich archive of additional material for readers to draw on. The URLs included are known to be current as of July 1, 2014, and in the case of expired URLs, enough information has been provided for the reader to locate the same, or similarly useful, resources.

As with all books about regions with writing systems different than the Roman alphabet, we needed to determine the best way to transliterate "foreign" words. Our decision was to follow specific systems, but not to be dogmatic in their application. Specifically, the spellings of Chinese, Korean, and Japanese words were standardized with the use of, respectively, the *hanyu pinyin* (usually referred to simply as Pinyin), Revised Romanization of Korean (RR), and revised Hepburn transliteration systems. However, when the spellings prescribed by these systems went against legitimate, more commonly accepted alternatives, we usually decided to use the more prevalent spelling. In particular, the RR system was developed relatively recently. We chose to use it, however, because it is the one officially endorsed by the Republic of Korea (South Korea) and it lends itself well to computer input as it does not rely on diacritical marks. However, because the RR system was developed in 1995 and adopted in 2000, most resources do not yet use this system. We have assisted the reader, where necessary, by providing what are perhaps more familiar spellings of words, particularly Korean place and personal names. For example, the city of Pyongyang is Pyeongyang and former President Roh Tae-woo's name is No Tae-u in Revised Romanization.

PART ONE

Overview

1

Introducing East Asia

Anne Prescott

East Asia is geographically expansive, culturally diverse, economically vital, and the source of traditions both old and new. It is also often misunderstood. Indeed, the term "East Asia" conjures up many images: of Japanese cosplay ("costume play"—dressing up in costumes to represent a character, often from manga or anime), kung fu (*gongfu*), or kimchi (spicy Korean vegetables); of Kim Jong-un, Mao Zedong, or Ichiro Suzuki; and of the films of Miyazaki Hayao, the music of Psy, or the art of Ai Weiwei.

There is no single highway through the historical and cultural landscape of East Asia; each person approaches it from a different place on the map, and we can choose any number of roads to begin to learn about—and understand—this region in the western Pacific that is home to 20 percent of the world's population. Once distanced from much of the rest of the world by geographical barriers and long journeys, today technology has helped bridge the gap and allows us to interact with the people of East Asia, leading us to discoveries about how they have become part of today's global landscape.

This chapter briefly considers some of defining characteristics of the region as well as the geographical, historical, and cultural traits that distinguish each of the countries of East Asia. (See Table 1.1 for a statistical snapshot of East Asia.) It focuses on those characteristics critical to understanding the role these nations play in globalization, and on a number of the challenges they face, either individually or as a region. With this introduction, each reader will begin to discover the best route for traveling through the complexities of East Asia in today's world.

Defining East Asia

The countries of China (including Taiwan), North Korea, South Korea, and Japan are grouped together under the umbrella of "East Asia," based on their geographic proximity as well as historical and modern cultural and economic ties, particularly two prominent common cultural bonds originating in China. The first is Confucianism, an ethical and philosophical system that permeates deeply into East Asian societies. (See Chapter 12 for a discussion of Confucianism in East Asia today.) The second is the use of Chinese characters (called *hanzi* in Chinese) in

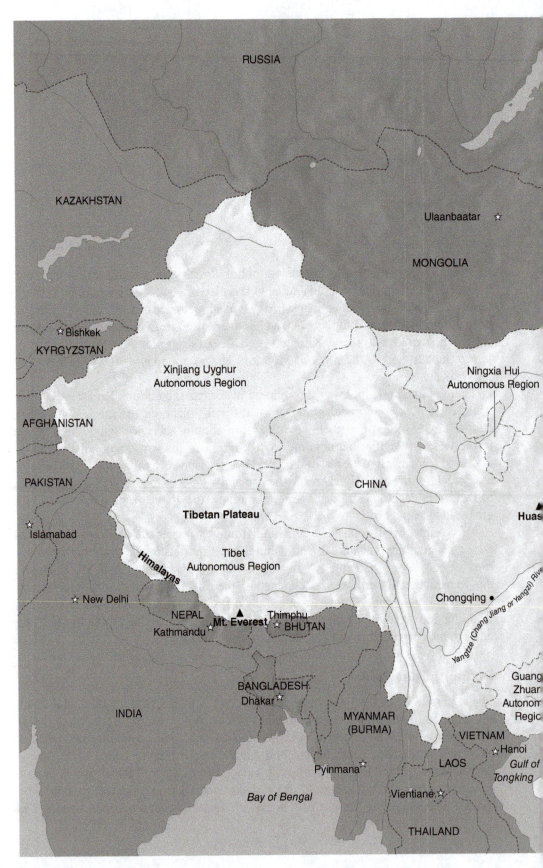

East Asia: China (including Taiwan), Japan, North Korea and South Korea, its neighbors, and the major geographical features and cities cited in this introduction.

their writing systems. Adopted centuries ago in Korea and Japan, the people in those countries continue to refer to this writing system as "Chinese characters" in their languages (*kanji* in Japanese, *hanja* in Korean). Examples of how the characters are used will be found in the chapter on languages. China, the Koreas, and Japan are also facing many of the same environmental, economic and cultural hurdles in the twenty-first century, some of which are the result of or exacerbated by an increasingly integrated global world.

Based on these criteria, Vietnam may also be considered a part of the greater sphere of Chinese influence, and, as such, some scholars include Vietnam in East Asia. Although Confucianism continues to be important in Vietnamese culture, Chinese characters are no longer used in its written language, and many scholars and scholarly organizations classify Vietnam as a Southeast Asian country. Mongolia is geographically just to the north of China, but neither Confucianism nor the Chinese writing system have played a role in the culture and society of that region. As a result, Mongolia is usually grouped with other Inner Asian (sometimes referred to as Eurasian) countries such as Uzbekistan, Turkmenistan, Tajikistan, Kyrgyzstan, and Kazakhstan. Scholars of Inner Asia may also study the people in the Xinjiang, Inner Mongolia, and Tibet regions of China.

> The Sinor Research Institute for Inner Asian Studies (http://www.indiana. edu/~srifias/) and the Inner Asian & Uralic National Resource Center (http:// www.indiana.edu/~iaunrc/), both at Indiana University, are good resources for understanding the differences between East Asia and Inner Asia.

Geography and Climate

The climates in East Asia range from subarctic in the north to tropical in the south, and are influenced by continental winds from the northwest, monsoon winds from the southwest, and typhoons that crawl up the coasts of China, Korea, and Japan. Long rivers traverse the continent, while much shorter rivers flow from the mountains to the sea on the Korean Peninsula and in Japan. Desert lands spread out in northwestern China, and the high Tibetan plateau is known as the "roof of the world." The Pacific basin is bordered by the Ring of Fire, a seismically active belt that spawns frequent earthquakes and volcanoes that affect East Asia. Mountains feature prominently in the history and culture of the region. Koreans consider Mount Paektu, on the border between China and Korea, to be the sacred place of their ancestral origin. Mount Fuji is one of the three sacred mountains in Japan, and in 2013 it was named a UNESCO World Heritage Site. The Himalayas, the tallest mountain range in the world, mark part of China's western boundary, and the Five Great Mountains—Taishan, Huashan, Hengshan (in Hunan Province), Hengshan (in Shanxi Province) and Songshan—are important landmarks in China.

Table 1.1

A Statistical Snapshot of East Asian Countries

	Area (km^2)	Arable land	Urbanization, 2011	Population, July 2014 est.	Cell phones	Life expectancy, 2014 est. (male and female)	Literacy
China (PRC)	9,596,961	11.62%	50.6%	1.36 billion	1.1 billion (2012)	m: 73.09 f: 77.43	95.1% (2010 est.)
Taiwan (ROC)	35,980	24.00%	NA	23.36 million	29.5 million (2012)	m: 76.72 f: 83.20	96.1% (2003)
Hong Kong	1,104	5.05%	100.0%	7.11 million	16.4 million (2012)	m: 80.18 f: 85.71	93.5% (2002)
Macau	28.2	0.00%	100.0%	607,500	1.6 million (2012)	m: 81.52 f: 87.59	95.6% (2011 est.)
Japan	377,915	11.26%	91.3%	127.10 million	138.4 million (2011)	m: 81.13 f: 87.99	99.0% (2002)
South Korea (ROK)	99,720	14.93%	83.2%	49.04 million	53.6 million (2012)	m: 76.67 f: 83.13	97.9% (2002)
North Korea (DPRK)	120,538	19.08%	60.3%	24.85 million	1.7 million (2012)	m: 65.96 f: 73.86	100% (2008 est.)

Source: Compiled from the CIA *World Factbook*, https://www.cia.gov/library/publications/the-world-factbook/wfbExt/region_eas.html, accessed May 16, 2014.

China

Historically, "China" referred to a collection of kingdoms and empires, commonly called dynasties. The area under dynastic rule changed over time as lands were conquered or lost in wars. Through much of history, the Chinese believed in the Mandate of Heaven, the idea that heaven gives the emperor (usually a male) the right to rule based on his ability to govern rather than his social status. Using this reasoning, even a commoner or a foreigner could be accepted as the ruler. Poverty and disaster were seen as signs from heaven that the ruling emperor was unjust and should be replaced.

Chinese Dynasties and Key Events

- Xia, ca. 2100–1600 BCE.
- Shang, ca. 1600–1050 BCE. Oldest written history dates from this dynasty.
- Zhou, ca. 1046–256 BCE. Longest-lasting dynasty in Chinese history.
- Qin, 221–206 BCE. Capital at Chang'an (Xi'an); created a unified state by imposing a centralized government; Qin emperor died in 210 and was buried with Terracotta Warriors.
- Han, 206 BCE–220 CE. Confucianism officially established as the basis for the Chinese state; the name of the dominant ethnic group in China, the Han, comes from the name of this dynasty, as does the name of the Chinese writing system, *hanzi* (literally "Chinese writing"). Silk Road began.
- Six Dynasties Period, 220–589 CE. Period of instability following the fall of the Han; Buddhism introduced to China.
- Sui, 581–618 CE. Reunification of China.
- Tang, 618–906 CE. Golden age of Chinese civilization. Chang'an (presently Xi'an) was the capital; at the eastern end of the Silk Road, it was the most populous city in the world at that time. The Tang Dynasty had great cultural influence on Korea, Japan, and Vietnam.
- Five Dynasties Period, 907–960 CE.
- Song, 960–1279 CE. Great economic and social changes occurred during this period.
- Yuan, 1279–1368 CE. Established by the Mongols under Kublai Khan; the Mongols reigned from Beijing over most of what we know as China today.
- Ming, 1368–1644 CE. Han reestablished rule.
- Qing, 1644–1912 CE. Manchus reigned from Beijing.

Source: Asia for Educators website, http://afe.easia.columbia.edu/timelines/china_timeline.htm.

A fun way to memorize the sequence of the Chinese dynasties is to sing them, as is shown in a YouTube video (http://www.youtube.com/watch?v=xJis9TSw1rE) sponsored by ChinaX, part of Harvard's edX online learning offerings.

Under pressure from reformers hoping for modernization and a republican-style government, the last Manchu emperor abdicated in 1912, and the Qing Dynasty ended. During the first half of the twentieth century, various forces struggled to establish the modern state of China, leading up to the Chinese Civil War, which ended in 1949 with the exile of the Nationalists on the offshore island of Taiwan and the Communists in control of the mainland. Today China can refer to the People's Republic of China (PRC), or mainland China, and the Republic of China (ROC) on Taiwan. Since 1949 both governments, separated by the narrow Taiwan Strait, have claimed to be the official representatives of the Chinese people. The United Nations acknowledged the PRC as the lawful representative of China in 1971. The United States recognized the ROC as the official representative of the Chinese people until 1979, at which time it recognized the PRC as the legitimate representative.

The People's Republic of China (PRC, or Mainland China)

The People's Republic of China is the fourth-largest country (in area) in the world (after Russia, Canada, and the United States), and with an estimated 1.35 billion people, it has the world's largest population (followed closely by India, with the United States a distant third). The population is primarily concentrated on the eastern coast, and with the exception of a few regional cities, the western and central sections of the country are relatively sparsely inhabited. The major urban areas of the country include the capital, Beijing, in the northeast; Shanghai, in the east; Chongqing, the former provisional capital of Chiang Kai-shek's government during World War II, in the southwest; and Shenzhen and Guangzhou, two important cities on the Pearl River Delta in the south.

The official name of the country today is Zhonghua Renmin Gongheguo (People's Republic of China), but the Chinese usually refer to their country as Zhongguo, which means "Middle Kingdom." Zhongguo has been used as the name of a collection of united provinces in the central plain for more than 2,500 years, and it reflects the Chinese idea that it resides at the center of the world. Given this name, it should come as no surprise that China shares borders with 14 countries.

China is not a homogenous nation. Han Chinese make up 91.6 percent of the population, with the remaining 8.4 percent, or nearly 115 million people, belonging to one of 55 ethnic minority groups recognized by the Chinese government (CIA *World Factbook*). These include Koreans, who live primarily in the region near the border with North Korea; Tibetans; Manchus; Mongols; and Uyghurs (also spelled Uighurs or Uygurs). Although the official language is Mandarin Chinese, other languages and regional dialects are spoken, and several autonomous regions have additional official languages. Regardless of the dialect—Cantonese or Mandarin, for example—the written language is the same. It is therefore not unusual in major cities to see two Chinese people who speak different dialects communicating with each other by writing words down. Minority issues, including those relating to domestic migrants, are thus very much a part of the reality of local, as well as global, exchanges and discourse. Increasingly, another set of minorities, foreign residents attracted to the burgeoning economic market, are an important part of the discussion of minority concerns.

Autonomous Regions in China

China has designated five regions as autonomous areas, established for ethnic minorities living within the Chinese state:

- Guangxi Zhuang Autonomous Region. Located in the south, established in 1958; home to the Zhuang people.
- Inner Mongolia Autonomous Region. Located in the north, established in 1947; home to the Mongolian people.
- Ningxia Hui Autonomous Region. Located in the north, established in 1958; home to the Hui people.
- Tibet Autonomous Region. Located in the west, established in 1965; home to the Tibetan people and the world's highest mountain, Mount Everest, or Chomolungma in Tibetan.
- Xinjiang Uyghur Autonomous Region. Located in the northwest, established in 1955; home to the Uyghur people.

Operating at the same administrative level as provinces of China, the autonomous regions have greater local control than do other provinces. In some cases, especially in the Tibetan and Uyghar regions, considerable political controversy exists regarding Chinese control over the regions.

Special administrative regions (SARs) have also been designated—one for Macau, once a Portuguese colony, and one for Hong Kong, once under the control of the United Kingdom. See below for more on these two SARs.

A list of the 55 ethnic minority groups in China can be found at "56 Ethnic Groups" (http://english1.english.gov.cn/2006-02/08/content_182626.htm), a web page of the Chinese government's Official Web Portal.

The waters to the east of China include the Korea Bay, East China Sea, South China Sea, and the Taiwan Strait, which separates the mainland from the island of Taiwan. The Diaoyu Islands (Senkaku Islands in Japanese), strategically located in the East China Sea northeast of Taiwan and southwest of Japan, are a source of controversy because they are claimed by the People's Republic of China, Taiwan, and Japan.

The Yangtze (also Chang Jiang or Yangzi) River is the longest river in China, and the Yellow (Huang He) River is the second longest; both play an important role in the history, culture, and economy of China. The Yellow River valley was the major population center and the source of early Chinese history and culture, and thus it is called the Cradle of Chinese Civilization. The Three Gorges Dam, the largest hydroelectric power station in the world, completed in 2012, is on the Yangzte River, which originates in the Qinghai–Tibet Plateau and empties into the East China Sea at Shanghai. The Yellow River, named for the color of the soil that washes down from the Loess Plateau in the north-central region of the country, runs through what was once the most prosperous region in China, which was the birthplace of ancient Chinese civilization. The Pearl River Delta, where the Pearl River flows into the South China Sea, includes the cities of Guangdong, Shenzhen, and Hong Kong, which is administered as a special autonomous region (SAR) of China. It is one of the most densely populated areas in the world and also one of the centers of great economic growth in contemporary China. In fact, more than half of all commerce conducted between the United States and China passes through Hong Kong.

Table 1.2

Population of Major Cities in China and Taiwan

City	Population (million)	Year of data
Shanghai, PRC	16.575	2011
Beijing, PRC	15.594	2011
Chongqing, PRC	9.401	2011
Shenzhen, PRC	9.005	2011
Guangzhou, PRC	8.884	2011
Hong Kong, PRC	7.112	July 2014 est.
Macau, PRC	0.588	July 2014 est.
New Taipei City, ROC	3.900	August 2011
Kaohsiung, ROC	2.777	no date available
Taichung, ROC	2.647	2010
Taipei, ROC	2.673	2012

Source: Compiled from the CIA *World Factbook*, https://www.cia.gov/library/publications/the-world-factbook/wfbExt/region_eas.html, accessed May 16, 2014; for the cities in the ROC, compiled from the official government websites (http://English.taipei.gov.tw; http://www.kgc.gov.tw; http://eng.taichung.gov.tw), accessed July 3, 2014.

Republic of China (ROC, or Taiwan)

The Republic of China (ROC), commonly referred to as Taiwan, was established by the Nationalist Party under Chiang Kai-shek on Taiwan in December 1949, following its defeat on the mainland in the civil war with the Communists under Mao Zedong. The strategic location of this small island in the East China Sea has made it a much-desired territory throughout history. It is less than 200 miles east of Fujian Province on the mainland, 69 miles from Yonaguni Island, Japan, and about 300 miles north of the Philippines across the Luzon Strait.

Taiwan was inhabited primarily by indigenous people until the seventeenth century, when settlers from the mainland began to migrate to the island. In the seventeenth century, the Spanish, Dutch, and Chinese all claimed it as their own at one time or another. The Portuguese named the island Formosa, or Beautiful Island, in 1544, and this name is sometimes still used today, particularly in the tourism sector. The Qing Dynasty conquered the island in 1683 and ruled through the nineteenth century. Japan occupied Taiwan for 50 years, from 1895, when it defeated the Qing Dynasty in the Sino-Japanese War, until the end of World War II. In 1945, Japan surrendered control of Taiwan to the Nationalist Party-led Republic of China (ROC), which was the ruling government of China. During this time of upheaval on the island, China was engaged in a civil war between the Communists, led by Mao Zedong, and the Nationalists, led by Chiang Kai-shek. The Communist victory over the Nationalists in 1949 resulted in the ousting of Chiang Kai-shek as the leader of the Republic of China on the mainland and his flight to Taiwan, where he reestablished the ROC. (At that point, the Communist mainland became the People's Republic of China.) Taiwan went through the process of democratization in the 1980s and 1990s and is now a multiparty democracy.

The population of Taiwan—with a land mass just about the size of the U.S. states of Maryland and Delaware combined—is 23.3 million. The capital of Taiwan is Taipei, and the largest city in terms of population, New Taipei City, surrounds Taipei. Located on the northern end of the island, their populations total over 6.6 million. The second largest city, Kaohsiung, is at the southern end of the island and has a population of over 2.7 million. About two-thirds of the island is rugged mountains, with flatter plains on the western end. Taiwanese, including Hakka, make up 84 percent of the population, while 2 percent are aboriginal people (Austronesian people who were living on the island before Han Chinese immigration began in the seventeenth century), and the remaining 14 percent are mainland Chinese (CIA *World Factbook*). Mandarin Chinese is the official language, but a significant number of people speak Taiwanese and Hakka dialects. One of the results of Japanese colonization is that many elderly people also speak Japanese. Taiwanese are free to practice any religion, with 93 percent, according to the *World Factbook*, following Buddhist and/or Daoist traditions.

Indigenous people in Taiwan actively promote their history and traditions, including through the following resources:

- Taiwan Indigenous Culture Park (http://www.tacp.gov.tw/tacpeng)
- Taiwan First Nations (http://www.taiwanfirstnations.org/)

Hong Kong Special Administrative Region of the PRC

Hong Kong (officially the Hong Kong Special Administrative Region, or Hong Kong SAR) has played an important strategic role in global trade for centuries. Hong Kong Island and the adjacent Kowloon Peninsula were claimed by the United Kingdom (U.K.) as colonies during the Opium Wars. Near the end of that era, in 1897, the New Territories, bordering the Kowloon Peninsula, were leased by China to the United Kingdom for 100 years. The United Kingdom controlled this valuable piece of land for more than a century, with the exception of a short period during World War II when Japan occupied the region, but as 1997 approached, the British government negotiated a peaceful return of the leased land and colonial territory back to China.

Hong Kong operates under the "one country, two systems" principle. This means that the Hong Kong SAR functions under a capitalist system and maintains control of most of its affairs, including political and economic systems, while the remainder of the mainland (PRC) follows a socialist system, with political and economic systems under the control of the central government in Beijing. Chinese and English are its official languages, and it has its own currency issued by Hong Kong banks. Hong Kong plays a vital role as a hub for global commerce; it is home to numerous international companies and banks, and is one of the busiest shipping ports in the world.

Macau Special Administrative Region of the PRC

Macau (Macau Special Administrative Region, or Macau SAR) was administered by Portugal from the mid-sixteenth century until its return to the People's Republic of China in 1999. As with Hong Kong, Macau also operates under the "one country, two systems" model and retains local control over most of its affairs. In recent years Macau has become a major gambling resort. Chinese and Portuguese are both official languages in this small area, which is less than one-sixth the size of Washington, D.C. It also has its own currency, and Portuguese culture is still very much evident.

Korean Peninsula

The Joseon (also romanized as Choson or Chosun) Dynasty (1392–1897), which controlled what are today North Korea and South Korea, was the last Korean dynasty and the longest-lasting Confucian dynasty in East Asia. Much of modern Korean etiquette and cultural norms, as well as the modern Korean spoken and written language, dates from this period. Other notable achievements of the Joseon Dynasty were the development of the *hanggeul* (*hangul*) syllabic writing system by King Sejong (ruled 1418–1450) and nearly 200 years of unbroken peace in the seventeenth and eighteenth centuries. In 1897, King Gojong (ruled 1863–1907) ended the Joseon Dynasty when he declared the founding of the Korean Empire, which he continued to rule until 1905. In that year Korea became a protectorate of Japan, and in 1910 Japan annexed Korea by force.

At the conclusion of World War II, in 1945, Japan's rule of the Korean Peninsula ended. The Soviet Union and the United States became trustees of the land, which was divided roughly along the 38th parallel into North Korea, overseen by the Soviet Union, and South Korea, which was under U.S. supervision. The Yalu River marks the northern boundary of North Korea with China, and the peninsula is separated from Japan by the East Sea, also called the Sea of Japan. The West Sea (known outside of Korea as the Yellow Sea) lies between the peninsula and China, and the South Sea (known outside of Korea as the East China Sea) is to the south. Since the 1950s, the two Koreas have evolved in very different directions. North Korea has been heavily influenced, both politically and culturally, by the former Soviet Union, while South Korea, which still has a strong U.S. military presence, has been influenced by the United States. The Demilitarized Zone (DMZ), a no-man's land separating the two countries, is jointly administered by the two Koreas and United Nations Peacekeeping Forces.

An age-old issue for Korea is its geographical and historical position as a "shrimp caught between two whales": the physical, cultural, and economic giant, China, to the west and its former colonizer and economic power, Japan, to the east. The period of Japanese colonization (1910–1945) left a deep cultural scar on the people. Although still in the shadows of its neighbors, South Korea is strongly asserting itself on a global stage, presenting its individuality through economic achievement and showcasing its cultural treasures.

Democratic People's Republic of Korea (DPRK, or North Korea)

North Korea is ruled autocratically by Kim Jong-un (given as b. 1983), the grandson of the founder "Great Leader" Kim Il-sung (1912–1994) and son of "Supreme Leader" (formerly known as "Dear Leader") Kim Jong-il (1941–2011). The official name of the country, which is slightly smaller than the U.S. state of Mississippi, is the Democratic People's Republic of Korea (DPRK), and its capital is Pyongyang. North Koreans informally refer to their country as Joseon (or Choson, the name of the last Korean dynasty to rule the peninsula). Kaesong is an important city for cross-border economic exchange with South Korea, and Rason is a Special Economic Zone bordered by the East Sea (Sea of Japan), Russia, and China.

There are no independent media outlets, and radios and televisions sold in North Korea are pre-tuned to the four official state-owned stations. Recent reports indicate that cell phones and smuggled DVDs are beginning to infiltrate the country, making it possible for citizens to learn about other countries. Although 19 percent of the land is arable, the country has been subjected to numerous droughts and flooding in recent years and has reportedly suffered from widespread famines.

Republic of Korea (ROK, or South Korea)

Known officially as the Republic of Korea (ROK), South Korea is commonly called Hangguk (or Hanguk) by the country's citizens. Roughly the size of the U.S. state of Indiana, South Korea is slightly smaller than North Korea. It also has less arable land than North Korea, but it supports about twice as many people. The southern half of the Korean peninsula is mostly hills and mountains, with coastal plains in the west and south. The largest city in this multiparty democracy is the capital, Seoul; other major cities include Busan (or Pusan), Incheon (or Inchon), Daegu (or Taegu), and Daejon (or Taejon). South Korea's industrial strengths are well known in the world, and it is a major player in the global economy. The diasporic community—as well as the large number of students, both at the secondary and postsecondary levels, who live in the United States—has been instrumental in raising awareness of the country's history and culture.

Following the June Democracy Movement in 1987, South Korea held its first democratic elections in December 1987, and the first democratically elected President, Roh Tae-woo, was inaugurated in February 1988. On February 25, 2013, Park Geun-hye became not only the first female leader of Korea, but also the first female leader in East Asia in modern times.

The people of South Korea are free to observe any religion they choose, and Buddhism, Confucianism, Christianity (divided into Protestantism and Catholicism) and Shamanism are all practiced there today. The growth of Christianity in Korea, particularly since World War II, is quite striking, with more than 31 percent of the population claiming to be Christians. Only slightly more than 24 percent are Buddhist, the next largest religious affiliation (CIA *World Factbook*). In addition, a number of new religions, including the Family Federation for World Peace and Unification (often known simply as the Unification Church) founded by the Reverend Sun Myung Moon, are active in Korea.

The island of Dokdo (Takeshima in Japanese) lies in the Korea Strait between South Korea and Japan, and is claimed by both countries. Each nation bases its claims on historical documents dating as far back as the sixth century. Dokdo comprises two small islets, which have been inhabited by a small number of South Koreans (mostly police and military) since 1965 and are valued for their fishing grounds and possible natural gas reserves.

South Korea and Japan both have websites in English presenting the rationale for their claims to the island of Dokdo (Takeshima in Japanese). The Korean side is presented on the Dokdo Research Institute's website (http://www.dokdohistory.com), and the Japanese case can be explored at the "Takeshima" page of the Shimane Prefectural Government's website (http://www.pref.shimane.lg.jp/soumu/takesima_eng).

Across the DMZ

Even though the border between the two Koreas is virtually impenetrable, attempts have been made to bridge the divide. South Korean companies have established a limited number of business ventures in North Korea, but political interference from North Korea has hindered their operations. In 1998 the Mt. Geumgang (or Kumgang, "Diamond Mountain") tourist region, known for its scenic beauty since ancient times, was established by a South Korean company, Hyundai Asan, for South Koreans. Originally accessible only by boat, a road across the DMZ eventually linked North and South, allowing 2 million South Koreans to visit the region until its closure in 2008. In order to obtain hard currency, North Korea required monetary transactions at the resort to be carried out in U.S. dollars. In July 2008, a South Korean tourist was shot and killed for allegedly wandering into a North Korean military site. Visits to Mt. Geumgang have been suspended since that time, and the South Korean–owned properties were seized by North Korea.

In 2003 the Kaesong Industrial Zone, largely financed by South Korea, was established in the city of Kaesong, which is six miles north of the Demilitarized Zone (DMZ) in North Korea. Operated jointly by North Korea and South Korea, it houses more than 120 South Korean companies that employ more than 50,000 North Koreans. Relations between the two countries deteriorated after Pyongyang conducted a nuclear test in February 2013, and the facility was closed for five months as the two countries negotiated its reopening.

Table 1.3

Population of Major Cities in Korea

City	Population (million)	Year of data
Seoul, ROK	9.794	2010
Busan, ROK	3.415	2010
Incheon, ROK	2.663	2010
Daegu, ROK	2.446	2010
Daejon, ROK	1.502	2010
Pyongyang, DPRK	3.255	2008
Kaesong, DPRK	0.310	2011

Source: Compiled from the Korean Statistical Information Service (http://kosis.kr) and the United Nations Statistics Division (http://unstats.un.org/unsd/demographic/sources/census/2010_PHC/default.htm), accessed July 3, 2014.

Japan

Japan consists of four main islands: from north to south, they are Hokkaido, Honshu, Shikoku, and Kyushu. South of Kyushu is the Ryukyu Island chain (in Okinawa Prefecture); many of those islands are closer to China than to the major cities in Japan. Over 91 percent of the people of Japan live in cities (CIA *World Factbook*), which are concentrated on the eastern coast of the main island of Honshu. Tokyo is the largest metropolitan area; other major population centers include the metropolitan region of Osaka-Kobe and the city of Nagoya on Honshu, the metropolitan area of Fukuoka/Kita-Kyushu on Kyushu, and the city of Sapporo on Hokkaido. The majority of people are ethnic Japanese (98.5 percent), but substantial numbers of Koreans, Chinese, and South Americans of Japanese ancestry also live in Japan. The Japanese call their country Nippon or Nihon (different pronunciations reflect regional pronunciations). Literally, this means "the base of the sun," and it is often translated as the Land of the Rising Sun.

The islands that make up Japan are long and narrow and stretch from approximately 46° latitude in the north to 20° latitude in the south. This results in climates as varied as the snowy northern island of Hokkaido (with its main city Sapporo) to temperate Tokyo and subtropical Okinawa. With the exception of Hokkaido, the country experiences a rainy season lasting about six weeks in late spring (in the south) and early summer (farther north). More than 50 percent of Japan is mountainous, and the highest peak is Mount Fuji (3,776 meters, or 12,388 feet).

The indigenous religion of Japan is Shinto, with Buddhism imported from China around the sixth century. Shinto and Buddhism play different roles in the spiritual life of the people: Shinto focuses on the here-and-now, while Buddhism is more concerned with the afterlife. It is common for people to follow practices of both Shinto and Buddhism, and to incorporate aspects of Christianity into their lives as well. For example, Shinto *kami* (gods) may be seen as buddhas in different stages of rebirth, rituals associated with the Christian marriage ceremony are common, and practicing Christians often have a small Buddhist altar in their homes to pay respects to their deceased relatives.

Table 1.4

Population of Major Cities in Japan (2009)

City	Population (million)
Tokyo metro area	36.51
Osaka-Kobe	11.33
Nagoya	3.26
Fukuoka/Kita-Kyushu	2.81
Sapporo	2.67

Source: Compiled from the CIA *World Factbook*, https://www.cia.gov/library/publications/the-world-factbook/geos/ja.html, accessed May 16, 2014.

Japan is a constitutional monarchy and the only country in the world today with an emperor. Theoretically, the imperial lineage can be traced back from the current emperor, Akihito, in an unbroken line to the first, Jimmu, who ruled from 660–585 BCE. For much of Japan's history, however, the country was not controlled by the emperors, but rather by military commanders called *shogun*. At the beginning of the Meiji Restoration, the emperor was restored to the throne and the country underwent significant changes, including a shift from a feudal society to a market economy, land reforms, accelerated industrialization, and the abolishment of the four divisions of society (samurai, peasants, artists, and merchants), which were important in the preceding Edo period (1600–1867).

The indigenous people of Hokkaido, the Ainu, are unrelated to the majority Japanese and have their own language and traditions. Today they have largely been assimilated into the Japanese population, but in recent years there has been a movement among the Ainu to reclaim their culture. The native people of the Ryukyu Islands also have their own language and traditions, and they have been heavily influenced by the cultures of China and Southeast Asia. The Ryukyu Kingdom was established in 1429 and formally annexed by the Meiji government of Japan in 1879.

Current and Future Challenges

In the twenty-first century China, Japan, and Korea are facing many challenges as individual countries, as a region, and as global citizens. Because these challenges, including environmental problems, territorial disputes and national security, and aging populations, nearly always impact other countries, the causes and solutions are best understood from the broader perspective of global awareness.

Issues of Sovereignty and Rights in China

The status of the Uyghur and Tibetan minorities in their respective autonomous regions is a major issue for China, as is the level of rural-to-urban migration. Both of these concerns affect China's political and economic relations with other countries. The Uyghurs are ethnic Turkic people, mostly Muslim, who live in the Xinjiang Autonomous Region in western China, which is their historical homeland. Since 1949 an influx of Han people into the region has changed the dynamics in Xinjiang. This has led to a strong separatist movement, and clashes between the Uyghur separatists and the ruling government have occasionally become violent. Tibetans, who practice Tibetan Buddhism, live mainly in the Tibet Autonomous Region in western China. Like Xinjiang, the area has been under nominal Chinese rule for generations, but since 1951 the region has been subject to increased control from the central government. In 1950, after the Chinese Civil War, the Chinese government took firm control of the region, and the Dalai Lama, Tibet's religious leader, went into exile during the 1959 Tibetan Rebellion. Both the Uyghur and Tibetans are harnessing media and technology to tell their stories, and both have supporters throughout the world, creating global interest in these domestic situations.

The rights of migrants who have been moving in droves from rural areas to urban cities, usually in search of work, have also posed challenges to China's system of social and economic control. Under the *hukou* system of household registration created in 1958, Chinese citizens are only allowed to reside in the locality where they are registered. Therefore, large and growing settlements are home to illegal domestic migrants who are not registered in the city where they reside, thus rendering them ineligible for basic services such as access to education, health care, and social services. Despite this lack of access to services, these workers play a vital role in the economic success of the cities where they live. Indeed, the global economy would be impacted negatively without their labor. Therefore, pressure to change the *hukou* system, or in some way allow for the rights of internal migrants, continues to build.

Japan's Aging Population

Population aging is a challenge facing many countries in the world with declining birth rates, and Japan is among the most severely impacted. The economic and cultural effects are felt beyond the immediate world of the elderly. In Japan, one of the most pressing problems related to the growing number of elderly persons is a shortage of health-care professionals. To address this issue, the Japanese government is allowing highly skilled workers, primarily from Southeast Asia, to enter the country and seek employment in this field.

This has necessitated the modification of immigration laws, special Japanese language training programs, and the creation of licensing programs that can accommodate workers who are not yet fluent in Japanese. It has also generated frank discussions on cultural integration issues, both for the care workers, who may struggle with unknown cultural practices, and for their patients and employers, who are likely unfamiliar with the customs of the caregivers.

Environmental Degradation

Environmental degradation is one of the most pressing issues across the region, and in recent years air pollution originating in China has been one of the most visible examples. A number of factors have produced choking levels of air pollution in cities across the country, including Chinese dependence on coal as a major energy source for industry and home heating and the rapid increase in private car ownership (see Chapter 9). Air pollution originating in China extends beyond national borders as winds carry particulates to Korea, Japan, and even as far as the United States.

The United States and other countries contribute to the problem when manufacturing is outsourced to China, since increased industrial production is partly responsible for the rise in air pollution. In addition, goods manufactured in China must be shipped to their destinations, which results in additional pollutants from the transport vehicles. In effect, one of the prices we pay for cheap consumer goods is poor air quality, which results in global health issues and added economic burdens due to lost productivity.

Heavy industry, such as the coal and steel production plants in Benxi in eastern China, contribute significantly to air pollution in the country. *(WikiMedia Commons, Andreas Habich, http://tinyurl. com/k8ehx65).*

Intraregional—and International—Security Concerns

A regional issue that can elicit strong feelings of national loyalty and often colors sentiments on a wide range of matters involves territorial disputes over islands in the waters between China, Japan, and Korea. Although most of the islands concerned are uninhabited or sparsely settled, legal possession of these islands comes with fishing and mineral rights as well as visibility in strategic locations. These disputes cause tension in the region, occasionally leading to protests and minor acts of violence by private citizens. The territorial assertions have also found their way into school textbooks as each country works to cement its version of history in the minds of younger generations. Some of these disputes impact the United States, which is bound by treaty to provide military support to Japan, South Korea, and Taiwan should one of them face aggression from other countries. Although solutions, such as submission of the claims to the Permanent Court of Arbitration, have been suggested, no such actions have been taken to date, and these disputes are likely to continue well into the future.

The disputed territories are:

- Senkaku (in Japanese)/Diaoyu (in Chinese) Islands. Claimed by Japan, China, and Taiwan. The islands were administered by the United States from 1945 to 1972, when they reverted to Japanese control (along with Okinawa).

- Nansha (in Chinese)/Spratly Islands. Claimed by China, Taiwan, Vietnam, Malaysia, Brunei and the Philippines.
- Dokdo (in Korean)/Takeshima (in Japanese)/Liancourt Rocks. Claimed by South Korea and Japan, currently inhabited by South Korea.
- South Kuril Islands. Claimed by Russia and Japan, currently inhabited and administered by Russia.
- Huangyan Dao (Chinese)/Scarborough Shoal. Claimed by China and the Philippines.

Protests in 2013 in Japan over the conflict with China concerning the Senkaku (in Japanese)/ Diaoyu (in Chinese) Islands. *(WikiMedia Commons, Alper* Çuğun, *http://tinyurl.com/na7pff7).*

Information and documents on the U.S. treaties with South Korea, Japan, and Taiwan that dictate actions the Unites States will take to protect the interests of those countries are available from the following websites:

- Mutual Defense and Status of Forces Agreements between the United States and South Korea (http://www.usfk.mil/usfk/sofa)
- Status of Forces Agreement between the United States and Japan (http:// www.mofa.go.jp/region/n-america/us/security/agree0009.html)
- Taiwan Relations Act (http://www.ait.org.tw/en/taiwan-relations-act.html)

Japan's Current Pacifism and Past Militarization

Global security is often viewed as a responsibility to be shared among the countries of the world. Japan is increasingly being asked to step up and provide trained military personnel to peacekeeping missions around the world. Such requests have stirred a passionate response in a country that, according to Article 9 of its Constitution, has renounced the right to wage war:

> Aspiring sincerely to an international peace based on justice and order, the Japanese people forever renounce war as a sovereign right of the nation and the threat or use of force as means of settling international disputes.
>
> In order to accomplish the aim of the preceding paragraph, land, sea, and air forces, as well as other war potential, will never be maintained. The right of belligerency of the state will not be recognized.

In fact, Japan does have trained military troops, the so-called Self-Defense Forces (SDF), which were established under the Self-Defense Forces Law of 1954. According to this law, the actions of the SDF are limited to defending the country against attacks. In 1957 the Basic Policy for National Defense allowed Self-Defense Forces to assist in domestic emergencies, such as the 1995 Great Hanshin Earthquake and the 2011 Triple Disaster—an earthquake, tsunami, and nuclear meltdown—that struck the Tohoku region. Since 1992 the SDF has supplied UN Peacekeeping Missions with Self-Defense personnel, who are limited to non-combat humanitarian and support roles. At the request of the United States, the SDF also deployed noncombat troops to assist in Iraq. Both the 1992 and 2004 overseas deployments triggered much debate as the Japanese people dealt with the competing demands of the limits of Article 9 of the Constitution and being an equal partner in international support and collaboration.

Japan's actions during the Pacific War (1937–1945) continue to present serious obstacles to regional integration. These activities included expansion and colonization under the Greater East Asia Co-Prosperity movement, mass killings (e.g., the Nanjing Massacre in China in 1937), human medical experiments conducted on civilians and prisoners of war in China (e.g., Unit 731); forced labor and forcing women (in both cases, mostly Koreans) to serve as sexual slaves, or "comfort women," for military personnel. Memories of these atrocities are brought to the forefront by Japanese elected officials' visits to the Yasukuni Shrine in Tokyo, often occurring around the August 15 anniversary of the end of the Pacific War. Japan's wartime dead, including Class A war criminals, are enshrined as *kami*, or gods, at this Shinto shrine. These visits are interpreted by many as government approval of the atrocities committed against the nations and people of the region during the war, and apologies by the Japanese government to China and Korea for wartime atrocities are seen as insincere or rendered meaningless by visits to the Yasukuni Shrine.

The Divided Peninsula

The division of the Korean peninsula has created a number of critical challenges. One of these is defending against North Korean military incursions across the DMZ, while another involves the breakup of families who were separated when the peninsula was divided.

Since the division of the peninsula, the North has attempted on numerous occasions to infiltrate the South, including four tunnels discovered between 1974 and 1990 that had been dug under the DMZ as military invasion routes. North Korean missile tests threaten not only South Korea but Japan. In addition, the DMZ is under the joint control of North Korea, South Korea, and United Nations Peacekeeping Forces, so actions there impact not only Koreans but have potential consequences for the rest of the world as well.

When the Korean Peninsula was divided in 1945, many families were separated, causing emotional hardships in a society that values regular visits to hometowns to pay respects to ancestors and visit relatives. Occasionally, North Korea allows elderly South Koreans to visit the North for highly controlled reunions. Displaced North Koreans and South Koreans cut off from their ancestral origins often resort to visiting sites on the edge of the DMZ, such as Imjingak, a park where they can carry out ancestor rites at Mangbaedan, a monument with tablets representing the provinces of North Korea. Many also tie ribbons, flags, or strips of paper with written messages for relatives in the North on a chain-link fence that marks the boundary of the DMZ.

View from a road leading to the southern boundary of the Korean Demilitarized Zone. (WikiMedia Commons, SPC 4 Long/Defenseimagey.mil, Wikimedia Commons, http://tinyurl.com/od9g27v).

South Korea is looking forward to the day when the peninsula will be reunified, and the Ministry of Unification works on related issues. With the slogan "A New Era of Hope and Happiness," the ministry's four main objectives are building a foundation for national unification, creating a thriving culture, ensuring ROK citizens' welfare, and economic revival. If, or when, the peninsula is reunified, the new Korea will face daunting issues of integration, social support, infrastructure development, and economic stability.

The South Korean Ministry of Unification website (http://eng.unikorea.go.kr) contains a wealth of information, not only on the Ministry's work but also on current affairs in North Korea. The Ministry also has an English-language Facebook page (https://www.facebook.com/unikorea.eng).

References and Further Research

Central Intelligence Agency (CIA). *The World Factbook*. https://www.cia.gov/library/publications/the-world-factbook.

Gale, Alastair. "Pyongyang Threatens to End Venture." *Wall Street Journal*, April 8, 2013. http://online.wsj.com/news/articles/SB10001424127887323550604578410010892971052.

Harden, Blaine. 2012. *Escape from Camp 14: One Man's Remarkable Odyssey from North Korea to Freedom in the West*. New York: Penguin.

Kang Chol-hwan, and Pierre Rigoulot. 2005. *The Aquariums of Pyongyang: Ten Years in the North Korean Gulag*. Translated by Yair Reiner. New York: Basic Books.

"Koreas Restart Operations at Kaesong Industrial Zone." *BBC News*, September 16, 2013. http://www.bbc.com/news/world-asia-24104774.

Lipman, Jonathan, Barbara Molony, and Michael Robinson. 2012. *Modern East Asia: An Integrated History*. Boston: Pearson.

2

East Asian Studies: History, Careers, and Resources

ANNE PRESCOTT

The roots of East Asian Studies can be found over a century ago, linked to the history of international exchanges in the region. Today, similar globalizing forces shape vibrant career paths for people with specialties in the field, and there is a wide range of sources available to help in their investigations.

History of the Field

Scholarly interest in East Asia (as well as South and Southeast Asia) has its roots in colonization by European powers. The first formal organization devoted to Asian Studies, the Royal Asiatic Society of Great Britain and Ireland, was established in 1823, and the *Journal of the Royal Asiatic Society*, founded in 1834, is still published today. In addition to scholars, missionaries became active in China, Japan, and Korea after restrictions on their activities were eased or lifted in the nineteenth century. Along with the promulgation of their religious teachings, American missionaries also established health care and educational institutions in East Asia. Like the scholars of the Royal Asiatic Society, missionaries played an important role in raising interest in and awareness of China, Japan, and Korea in two ways. First, upon their periodic home visits to the United States, they brought stories of the people with whom they worked. Second, they nurtured academics by creating language dictionaries and systems for writing Chinese, Japanese, and Korean in the Roman (Western) alphabet (a process called Romanization, with such systems including McCune-Reischauer for Korean and Wade-Giles for Chinese).

Books written by Europeans and Americans who traveled to East Asia in the late nineteenth and early twentieth centuries further contributed to interest in that part of the world. The works of Lafcadio Hearn, Isabella Bird, and Pearl Buck were widely consumed, and to this day they continue to be important resources for learning about early interactions between Westerners and Asians, as well as the cultures of China, Japan, and Korea in the late nineteenth and early twentieth centuries.

Table 2.1

Books by Lafcadio Hearn, Isabella Bird, and Pearl Buck

Lafcadio Hearn	*Kwaidan: Stories and Studies of Strange Things*
	Glimpses of Unfamiliar Japan
	Out of the East: Reveries and Studies in New Japan
	Japanese Fairy Tales
Isabella Bird	*Unbeaten Tracks in Japan*
	Among the Tibetans
	Korea and Her Neighbors
	The Yangtze Valley and Beyond
	Chinese Pictures
Pearl Buck	*East Wind, West Wind*
	The Good Earth
	Dragon Seed
	Pavilion of Women
	Peony

By the mid-nineteenth century, many colleges and universities in the United States had begun offering courses in East Asia, with a primary focus on China and the Chinese language. In 1834, Wesleyan University in Connecticut established the Missionary Lyceum, a "society having for its principal object the benefit of the missionary cause," according to the East Asian Studies section of the Wesleyan University website (http://www.wesleyan.edu/mansfield/about/earlyhistory.html), and within a year the organization began to focus on China. In 1872 Edward Tompkins established one of the first academic departments devoted to the study of Asia, at the University of California at Berkeley. Chinese was taught at Harvard University beginning in 1879, and in the 1890s the University of Chicago proposed to create a faculty position in Chinese language. In 1881, students from the Oberlin Graduate School of Theology began mission work in Shanxi, China, and the Oberlin Shansi program, which continues today, was founded in 1908. Columbia University established a program in Chinese studies in 1901 and appointed its first professor of Chinese studies in 1902.

At the end of the nineteenth century, graduates of colleges and universities in the United States were instrumental in establishing schools, including institutions of higher learning, in East Asia. This led to the development of exchange programs between their U.S. alma maters and the newly established institutions in East Asia, and some of those programs continue to this day.

Japanese language and studies were added to college and university curricula in the early twentieth century. The Japanese program was established at Stanford University in 1913, while at Columbia University the Japanese library collection was begun in 1929 and language classes were added in 1938. Harvard began teaching Japanese in 1931, and in 1939 John King Fairbank and Edwin O. Reischauer started teaching a course titled History of East Asian Civilization, which is still taught.

Korean studies came to U.S. institutions much later: in 1942, Berkeley became the first institution to offer courses in the Korean language.

When the United States entered the Pacific War in 1941, it became apparent that there was a lack of East Asia expertise in this country. The U.S. government established military language schools to help fill this need, and by the end of the war, in 1945, the United States had a small but growing number of experts trained in the history, cultures, and languages of China, Japan, and Korea. The postwar occupation of Japan (1945–1952) and the Korean War (1950-1953) added not only more experts, but also greater numbers of men and women who had served in the U.S. military in East Asia and who had firsthand experience and interest in the region. In response to this demand, many colleges and universities established departments of East Asian studies in the early postwar years. Scholars who had been trained at the military language schools, people from missionary families, and alumni who had established schools in East Asia were the foundation on which the first departments of East Asian studies were built in the United States.

The global implications of the launch of Sputnik 1 by the Soviet Union during the Cold War prompted the U.S. government to recognize the need for more specialists in area studies. In response to this need, the National Defense Education Act of 1958 was passed, followed by the Higher Education Act of 1965, which provided funding for National Resource Centers (NRCs) at universities throughout the United States. Commonly referred to as Title VI NRCs (named for the section of the act under which they were authorized), these area studies centers continue today, providing training for college students as well as funds for outreach programs for educators, elementary and secondary school students, and the general public.

A current list of the federally funded East Asia National Resource Centers is available on the website of the National Resource Centers for Foreign Language, Area & International Studies (http://www.nrcweb.org/nrcList.aspx). The site includes descriptions of the individual centers that summarize their history, offerings, and contact information.

Another institution largely responsible for the promotion of learning about East Asia is the U.S.-based Association for Asian Studies (AAS). Founded in 1941 as the Far Eastern Association, the original purpose of the organization was to publish the *Far Eastern Quarterly*. In 1948 it was renamed the Association for Asian Studies and became an active scholarly organization, with the Sinologist and missionary Arthur W. Hummel Sr. as its first president. At the association's inception, "Far East" included East and Southeast Asia, but today it has expanded to include South Asia as well, and its membership includes 8,000 Asia specialists in a variety of disciplines. The AAS divides East Asia into two subregions: Northeast Asia, comprising Korea and Japan; and China and Inner Asia. Members are primarily academics at postsecondary schools, but outreach personnel (people who plan programs for K-12 students and teachers as well as the general public), K-12 educators, and others are also members. The AAS publishes the *Journal of Asian Studies* (*JAS*), *Education About Asia* (established in 1996), and a number of monographs.

In the late twentieth century, East Asian studies was bolstered by the establishment of ASIANetwork, a consortium primarily comprising small liberal arts colleges. With funding from the Luce Foundation, the Freeman Foundation, and others, this organization offers faculty members and students at its member schools research, programmatic, and short-term study abroad opportunities that might not be viable if run by a single institution.

The website of the Association for Asian Studies (https://www.asian-studies. org) provides additional information about the association and the region.

The ASIANetwork website (http://www.asianetwork.org) has a list of the member institutions, as well as the programs it sponsors, along with other information about the consortium.

In the early 2000s, East Asian studies at the undergraduate level was greatly enhanced through the Freeman Foundation Undergraduate Asian Studies Initiative, which provided seed funding for faculty appointments, short-term study abroad programs, course creation, and other programming for the purpose of enhancing education about Asia at the postsecondary level.

Careers in East Asian Studies

East Asian linguistic and cultural fluency are vital as globalization continues to transform the world. In an October 30, 2013, *CNN Money* article by Annalyn Kurtz titled "The Hottest Job Skill Is. . .," the lead sentence reads, "The Army, NYPD, and State Department can't get enough workers with this job skill. Neither can Fortune 500 companies, hospitals, local courts, and schools. What is it? Fluency in a foreign language." People with training in East Asian languages and cultures, regardless of their major, find employment in many sectors, from academia to government to the private sector, and the article's author notes that there is particular demand for those who specialize in legal, medical, technical, or scientific knowledge.

People with advanced academic degrees find a range of employment opportunities in academia—not only in East Asian languages and literatures and East Asian Studies departments, but also in history, anthropology, religion, teaching, art, and music. East Asia specialists are even employed in the sciences, including the fields of infectious diseases, nutrition, and medicine, as well as in agriculture, business, and finance. Indeed, almost any discipline one can think of has a need for individuals with such knowledge. Library and media specialists may also focus on a geographic region, and they undergo the same rigorous training as those in other disciplines.

There are also East Asia specialists in academia who are not professors. Study abroad advisors whose portfolios include East Asia are most likely trained in East Asian studies, speak an East Asian language, and have studied abroad in an East Asian country. Outreach personnel are key members of university area studies centers, and most have advanced degrees and speak one of the languages of their target areas. Both of these careers can be rewarding for people who would prefer something other than teaching.

Working for the U.S. government is another common career path, and federal government scholarships may be available for students who are interested in doing so. The most obvious placements are in the State Department, either domestically or as a Foreign Service Officer overseas. The Central Intelligence Agency employs those with fluent language skills to monitor media from East Asian countries, or to take on other assignments that require linguistic fluency. The Federal Bureau of Investigation and the National Security Agency also have positions for area specialists. Other federal agencies such as the Department of Commerce and even the National Endowment for the Arts need employees who understand the cultures and languages of other countries. The State Department has programs and scholarships to encourage students to study East Asian languages and cultures. Scholarships range from support to study abroad as a high school or college student all the way to full tuition scholarships.

There are people with East Asia expertise among our elected and appointed government officials. Kirsten Gillibrand, a U.S. senator from New York, majored in East Asian studies and studied abroad in China, and she serves on the Committee on Foreign Relations, including the Subcommittee on East Asian and Pacific Affairs. The former Utah governor, ambassador to China, and one-time presidential hopeful Jon Huntsman speaks Chinese. Sabrina McKenna, an associate justice of the Supreme Court of Hawaii, majored in Japanese as an undergraduate. Timothy Geithner, the former secretary of the treasury, studied government and Asian Studies and earned an MA in international economics and East Asian studies. Jay Rockefeller, a U.S. senator from West Virginia, majored in Far Eastern studies, studied in Japan for three years, and currently serves on the Senate Committee on Finance Subcommittee on International Trade, Customs, and Global Competitiveness.

Museums employ curators and educational specialists who have training in East Asian studies. For example, the Children's Museum of Boston, the Andy Warhol Museum, and the Field Museum in Chicago all have staff members who are specialists in East Asia and use those skills on a daily basis in curating collections, developing exhibits, and planning programs for teachers, children, and the general public.

Foreign government consulates, embassies, and other agencies based in the United States need U.S. citizens to support their activities in the United States.

Consulates and embassies need Americans who can assist citizens of East Asian countries living in the United States, as well as Americans wishing to visit those countries. Linguistic and cultural training is essential for these positions, and it can be difficult to find Americans who have the proper backgrounds. Renay Loper, a program officer for the Japan Foundation in New York City, says, "The beauty of my role working for a Japanese organization based in the US is that I have the best of both worlds: promoting and supporting the exploration and study of Japan and Japanese culture (in particular) to American universities, nonprofits, and communities; while simultaneously liaising for my Japanese colleagues and Japan-based organizations and bridging the cultural gaps, misunderstandings, and stereotypes that exist about the U.S. and Americans" (personal communication).

Some of the most successful journalists have backgrounds in area studies. Mike Chinoy earned his BA in Chinese studies before embarking on a career in journalism, including a stint as CNN's Senior Asia Correspondent. His training and linguistic skills served him well as he reported from Tiananmen Square during the pro-democracy protests in 1989. NPR's Anthony Kuhn uses his knowledge of China to report on developing stories in that country. Sheryl WuDunn, who reported from Beijing for the *New York Times* in the 1980s, used her fluency in Chinese to gain access to places other journalists could not go. She and her husband, Nicholas Kristof, won the Pulitzer Prize for their reporting on the 1989 Tiananmen Square protests. Their stories are documented in the 1995 book *China Wakes: The Struggle for the Soul of a Rising Power*.

East Asian studies majors are in the private sector too. Joe Mallahan, a management consultant and former senior vice president at T-Mobile USA, says, "My studies of East Asia early in my career helped broaden my perspectives and sharpen my skills around communication, economic analysis, organizational development, and strategic thinking in ways that I can't imagine I could have obtained from other fields of study. I developed unique analytical 'muscles' that I used in my business pursuits in ways that went well beyond just applying my regional subject matter expertise" (personal communication).

Even the sports and entertainment fields need people who have studied East Asia. The Boston Red Sox and other baseball teams with Japanese players hire people as interpreters, translators, and coordinators to assist their Japanese players and their families with their adjustment to life in the United States. Jerome White (known as Jero), who studied Japanese at the University of Pittsburgh, is bridging U.S. and Japanese cultures as a recording artist in Japan, singing a popular Japanese song style called *enka*.

In conclusion, as one can plainly see from this discussion, there is a place for those with language skills and cultural knowledge in almost any employment sector. Consulting companies, law firms, manufacturers, health-care providers, and numerous other employers require individuals with such knowledge, and this need is not likely to diminish in the future.

Tools for Studying East Asia

There are numerous resources for students wishing to pursue Chinese, Japanese, or Korean studies, particularly with the large increase in electronic resources available online since the late twentieth century. Governments, private and professional organizations, and colleges and universities provide resources such as face-to-face lectures, exhibits, and classes, as well as online courses, databases, webinars, and more. College and university East Asian library and media specialists often have the most comprehensive knowledge of resources, and they have created various resource pages designed for students.

Sharon Domier, East Asian Studies Librarian at the University of Massachusetts, Amherst, specializing in East Asian studies, creates course and subject guides for students at her institution. These guides can be accessed on the library's website (http://guides.library.umass.edu/eastasian). Websites of other institutional libraries provide similar useful guides, which are also available online.

The primary East Asia professional organization is the Association for Asian Studies (https://www.asian-studies.org). Most members are academics, but anyone with an interest in Asia, including students, is welcome. There are also discipline-specific organizations, such as those listed here:

- Chinese Oral and Performing Literature, or CHINOPERL (https://chinoperl.osu.edu)
- Manchu Studies Group (http://www.manchustudiesgroup.org)
- Society for Asian Music (http://asianmusic.skidmore.edu)
- Society for East Asian Anthropology (http://www.aaanet.org/sections/seaa)
- Society for East Asian Archaeology (http://www.seaa-web.org)
- Society for the Study of Chinese Religions (http://isites.harvard.edu/icb/icb.do?keyword=k7027)
- Society for the Study of Japanese Religions (https://sites.google.com/site/ssjrhome/home)

Most of these organizations have their own publications and welcome the active participation of students at their conferences and other events. Students often enjoy low (or no) membership fees and substantial discounts at conferences. An Internet search will lead to additional information on how to join these and other similar groups.

Humanities and Social Sciences Online, or H-Net (http://www.h-net.org), hosts discussion groups that are open by subscription to all who are interested. H-Asia, H-Japan, and H-Northeast Asia are the groups that are relevant to East Asianists.

Information on new publications, meetings and conferences, special lectures, and job openings—mostly academic, but occasionally outside academia—are posted on these discussion boards. They are also good places to ask questions about research topics. Go to the H-Net website to read archived messages or to subscribe to a list.

Since the late 1950s, the U.S. government has funded East Asia National Resource Centers (NRCs) at universities throughout the country. NRC programs include lecture series, films, conferences, and other events of interest to students. NRCs may also have information on study abroad (including short-term) programs and exchanges as well as scholarships.

The National Resource Centers website (http://www.nrcweb.org/) features a list of all the NRCs, including those for East Asia (click on the "World Area" drop-down menu for the NRCs for various geographic areas).

The U.S. Department of Education established National Foreign Language Resource Centers (http://www.nflrc.org) in 1990 for people who speak foreign languages. The National East Asian Languages Resource Center (NEALRC) at Ohio State University (http://nealrc.osu.edu) offers a variety of training programs, including multimedia-based online materials.

The governments of China, Taiwan (represented in the United States by the Taipei Economic and Cultural Office [TECO]), South Korea, and Japan often have research or lending libraries, hold classes, sponsor events, and provide networking opportunities. They also provide information on study abroad opportunities and scholarships. In addition, the consulates and embassies of each country provide various resources. Other government-funded organizations include the following:

- Confucius Institutes (http://www.chinesecio.com)
- Japan Foundation (http://www.jpf.go.jp/e)
- Japan Information Centers

  o Washington, DC (http://www.us.emb-japan.go.jp/jicc)
  o Chicago (http://www.chicago.us.emb-japan.go.jp/jic.html)
  o New York (http://www.ny.us.emb-japan.go.jp/en/b/01.html)

- Japan National Tourism Organization (http://www.jnto.go.jp/eng)
- Korea Foundation (http://en.kf.or.kr)
- Korea Tourism Organization (http://www.visitkorea.or.kr/intro.html)

Private organizations such as the Asia Society, Korea Society, Japan Society, and Japan-America Society have many of the same functions as the organizations listed above. There are countless local organizations as well, from Sister Cities International groups to foreign resident associations, religious organizations, music groups, and more. Most welcome anyone with a sincere interest in learning about the countries and cultures they represent. Information on these groups can be found at stores and supermarkets that cater to foreign residents from China, Japan, and Korea.

Foreign newspapers, in English or in Chinese, Japanese, and Korean, both free and by subscription, can be easily accessed on the Internet. They are helpful for research, language practice, and staying up-to-date on the latest news.

> English-language translations of official press releases from the Korean Central News Agency of the DPRK (http://www.kcna.co.jp/index-e.htm) are available online. Comparing reports from other countries on the same story provides interesting insights into North Korea (the Democratic People's Republic of Korea, or DPRK).

Students interested in East Asian film will find the Asian Educational Media Service (AEMS) helpful. Housed at the University of Illinois, AEMS (http://www.aems. illinois.edu) has an online searchable annotated database of films on Asia, and it also publishes an online newsletter with film reviews.

Study Abroad and Learning the Language

Living and studying abroad is the best way to learn the language and culture of China, Japan, or Korea. Identifying a quality program can be confusing and time-consuming. College and university study-abroad advisors can recommend appropriate placements based on a person's goals. Many institutions have their own exchange programs, which are administered by resident faculty members from the United States and may provide coursework in English and intensive language training. Increasingly, institutions are creating exchanges through which students from the United States and the target country switch places, with each one paying tuition at their home institution.

Scholarship programs are available for domestic and overseas language study. The U.S. government considers some languages to be critical to its interests, and it provides special support to study them. Chinese, Japanese, and Korean are all designated as such. Some of the government scholarship programs require a term of government service after graduation, and preference is usually given to candidates who indicate an interest in pursuing government work.

Listed below are some of the language study opportunities available from both government and private organizations. Some are only open to students at universities that have been chosen through a competitive application process, while some are open to any student who meets the application criteria. Study abroad offices, National Resource Centers, and East Asian studies departments are all good resources for available opportunities.

- Foreign Language and Area Studies (FLAS) Fellowships offer support for both academic year and summer language training. FLAS funding is available for the study of Chinese, Japanese, and Korean. Information is available from the U.S. Department of Education (http://www2.ed.gov/programs/iegpsflasf/index.html).
- The Critical Language Scholarship (CLS) Program (http://www.clscholarship.org) also offers funding for Chinese, Japanese, and Korean.
- Boren Scholarships (http://www.borenawards.org/boren_scholarship) include funding for Cantonese, Mandarin, Japanese, and Korean.
- The 100,000 Strong Foundation (http://100kstrong.org) provides funds for students to study in China.
- The Benjamin A. Gilman International Scholarship Program (http://www.iie.org/Programs/Gilman-Scholarship-Program) provides funding for U.S. undergraduates who are receiving Federal Pell Grant funding at a two- or four-year college or university.
- The Foundation for Global Scholars (http://www.fgscholars.org) is an independent granting organization that prioritizes providing support to traditionally underrepresented students.

The following organizations maintain lists of scholarship providers for international study:

- NAFSA: Association of International Educators (http://www.nafsa.org)
- Earlham College (Japan Study) (http://japanstudy.earlham.edu/study-japan/scholarships)
- National Foreign Language Center at the University of Maryland (http://www.nflc.umd.edu/support_college#.UtsfetIo5ko)

Opportunities for language study in the United States, particularly in the summer, also exist. Middlebury College's summer language program (http://www.middlebury.edu/ls) is well known for its rigorous courses. STARTALK Chinese programs are intensive, federally funded summer programs held at various universities. An Internet search will return information on current programs.

Information on government-sponsored scholarships to study in South Korea, China, or Japan is available at the following government websites:

- For South Korea, go to the government-run Study in Korea website (http://www.studyinkorea.go.kr/en/sub/overseas_info/korea_edu/edu_scholarship.do).
- For Taiwan, visit the Taipei Economic and Cultural Office website (http://www.edutwny.org/index.html).
- For Japan, go to the Japanese government's Study in Japan site (http://www.studyjapan.go.jp/en).

PART TWO

Fundamentals

3

Modern East Asia: A History

Jerry P. Dennerline

History is not just a factual account of what happened in the past, nor is it simply background information for the present or, perhaps, the future. Historians, standing in the present as they view the past, construct narratives with the advantage of hindsight. The historical actors themselves, whether emperors, diplomats, students, mothers, working women, farmers, or soldiers, were "outcome blind." They could not write the narratives in which historians place them, nor could they imagine the perspectives from which historians write. Yet neither can historians, with the advantage of hindsight and the help of generations of scholars and researchers who preceded them, imagine the perspectives of their successors in generations to come. Historians construct narratives, consciously revising those of their predecessors, and knowing full well that these narratives will also sooner or later be revised. This brief narrative will draw attention to significant themes that emerge from the many stories about what has happened, not just in one country or in the specific relations between or among countries, but across the region sometimes called "East Asia" over the past 120 years.

A Geopolitical Perspective

Korea in the Middle

In the spring of 1894 a religious sect in Korea rose in rebellion against the king. The Korean kingdom, known as Joseon (also romanized as Choson or Chosun), had emerged along with the Ming Empire in the fourteenth century after the massive civil wars that expelled the Mongols from China. With Ming protection, Joseon had survived an invasion by Toyotomi Hideyoshi, the unifier of Japan, in the 1590s. It had survived the collapse of the Ming and the Manchu conquest of China 50 years later. It had avoided conquest and colonization by Western powers in the 1800s. The Tonghak Uprising of 1894, however, proved to be its undoing, not because the rebels succeeded—their aim was to remove the modernizing reformers from the Joseon court and drive the foreigners out of the kingdom—but because the court's two foreign protectors, China and Japan, fought between themselves. The ensuing war between the modernizing armies of China's Qing Empire, heirs of the Manchu conquest, and the already modernized armies of the new Meiji emperor of Japan ended in a decisive victory for Japan. With the Treaty of Shimonoseki in 1895, the sun had begun to rise on a new East Asian world order.

In the old East Asian world, the Qing emperor had presided as "Son of Heaven," with the active acceptance of tributary kingdoms, such as Joseon, the tacit approval of others, such as Vietnam, and the more disinterested tolerance of peripheral rulers, such as Hideyoshi's successors, the Tokugawa shoguns in Japan. For at least a century before the Treaty of Shimonoseki, this China-centered sun had been setting. Foreign powers had arrived with gunboats and with a hunger for markets that could serve their expanding economies and their colonial interests. In response, the old regimes were forced to accept "unequal" treaties with the foreign powers and open special "treaty ports" in which the foreigners claimed "extraterritorial rights" that exempted them from local laws. Progressive advisors to these regimes launched self-strengthening reforms, applying technologies and techniques they learned from the intruders. The Tonghak rebels were just one among many new religious sects across this changing world that mobilized believers to rid it of what they felt was a new evil.

There were other resisters to the modernizing effort. Over the decade before 1894, while the Qing and Meiji governments were launching their self-strengthening efforts, the regent who spoke for the child-king Gojong had already put down one Tonghak uprising and driven the sect underground. But he had also presided over the killing of Christian missionaries and resisted retaliatory incursions by French and German gunboats. The regent's faction at court sought to reaffirm the Confucian orthodoxy that had prevailed since Ming times, which had itself enabled a number of pragmatic social and political reforms in recent decades. The regency had also rejected a diplomatic mission from the new Meiji government because it claimed equal status for Japan as a nation—with an "emperor" —under Western rules of international engagement. Once Gojong succeeded to the throne and began to speak

The Korean Emperor Gojong in an 1884 photograph. *(Wikimedia Commons, Percival Lowell, http://tinyurl.com/olsqbm2.)*

with his own voice, the Joseon court embarked on its own self-strengthening program. Relying heavily on the military and diplomatic advice of the Qing reform leader Li Hongzhang and wary of Japanese belligerence, Gojong's regime had to deal with the regent's conservative faction as well as progressives who were actively supported by Japanese diplomats. With the Treaty of Shimonoseki, Korea was declared independent of the Qing, leaving the Korean factions to fight among themselves as Japanese influence prevailed.

The Korean story underscores the general key themes in East Asian history during this period. The old East Asian world had depended on loyalty to sovereigns within a world system that placed the highest value on stability. In Confucian terms, this value was called world peace. In Korea, loyalty to the sovereign had also enabled reformers to negotiate with local communities to limit corruption, provide for a functional distribution of revenues, and ensure a degree of social justice within the parameters of Confucian ethics. The same was true for China and Japan. Commercial development, new products, new crops, and improvement of agricultural techniques had long been a central part of this system. The gunboats and unequal treaties destabilized it, and the very different ethics and religious beliefs of the newly influential outsiders inspired religious resistance, pragmatic adaptation, and enthusiastic innovation in varying degrees. Conflicts escalated. By the time they came to a head in Korea, the Japanese experience suggested the direction of events to come.

For an overview of Confucianism in East Asia, read *Confucius in East Asia: Confucianism's History in China, Korea, Japan and Việt Nam* by Jeffrey L. Richey, published in 2013 by the Association for Asian Studies. It is available through libraries or for purchase from AAS Publications (https://www. asian-studies.org/publications/cart/Members.aspx?Action=ServiceDetail& productID=428).

The Meiji Miracle

What were the Japanese solutions? In 1889 the "oligarchs" of the Meiji regime, under the leadership of Itō Hirobumi, unveiled a new constitution. In it the emperor was declared sovereign, and the Diet, modeled on the Prussian institution that had served to legitimize the new German Empire in the previous decade, provided the space in which the people's voice could be heard. There was a Lower House of representatives, elected by 1 percent of the male population, and an Upper House of peers, to which members of the newly titled nobility were appointed. Cabinet ministers were responsible only to the emperor himself. The point of the constitution was twofold. First, it would ensure that the Meiji regime would be recognized by foreign powers as the legitimate government of the Japanese nation, enabling it to negotiate revisions of the unequal treaties. Second, it would channel the opposition and overcome the resistance of conservatives and populists to the oligarchs themselves. In brief, the new constitution promised stability in one state, reaffirming the value of loyalty to the sovereign and limiting popular resistance, while it also enabled a new powerful leadership to identify, direct, and command the national interest.

> To read the full text of the Meiji Constitution of 1889 in English, go to the "Text of the Constitution and Other Important Documents" section (http://www.ndl. go.jp/constitution/e/etc/c02.html) of the Japanese National Diet Library website.

While the new Japanese system provided a model for a new East Asian world, it also revealed certain legacies that were unique to the Japanese experience. First of all, the Meiji oligarchs were a very special class of leaders. They had themselves emerged from the lower ranks of the samurai, combining their forces to overthrow the Tokugawa shoguns, whose power depended on the personal loyalty of military chieftains called daimyo in widely scattered domains. They agreed to call on the young emperor, whose inherited position as the blood descendent of Japan's patron deity had long since been ritualized, to authorize their new government with a "charter oath." They were young men, from strong ethical and military traditions, who had few vested interests but firm patriotic goals. Second, as a group they were consensus builders and centralizers who reacted decisively to deflect internal opposition. One member left the coalition and raised a serious rebellion from his home province in 1877 because the oligarchy had not used force against Korea when the regent had rejected the Meiji diplomatic mission. The oligarchs rallied to crush the challenge while reaffirming the commitment to revise the unequal treaties as their primary goal.

In addition, the ferment that led the oligarchs to seize power in the first place had already produced a variety of popular new religions, as well as divisions among vested interests across the country. The oligarchs themselves were forming political parties in anticipation of a national assembly. Popular demands for representative government led to a consensus among them that an assembly was necessary for developing the national interest and ensuring legitimacy, but that vested interests must not be allowed to obstruct or deflect the self-strengthening effort. Armed with this pragmatic and authoritarian point of view, they designed a constitution that would allow popular engagement but limit populist power. While the Lower House had the power of the purse, if it should become deadlocked and fail to approve a budget, the previous year's budget would apply by default. To deal with the issue of religious conflict, the oligarchs led the Diet to affirm separation of religion and state, while also defining reverence for the emperor, whose divinity could not be challenged, as a national obligation that transcended private religious belief.

Underlying the new Japanese polity was an economic infrastructure that had grown at record-breaking speed on the backs of a new working class, predominantly rural women, who had been under the oligarchs' management since 1868. The Meiji reformers had mounted a national campaign to support the study of natural sciences, medicine, technology, engineering, and industrial organization. Beginning in the early 1870s, they rejected the English model of free markets and found resonance in the newer German model of state-led development. Building on a healthy agrarian economy, the industrial policy planners took advantage of Meiji social and administrative reforms to finance development. The stipends due to samurai whose superiors were dispossessed by the political transformation were converted to interest-bearing bonds, reducing government costs. Scientifically augmented agricultural production and heavy land taxes paid for investment in silk and cotton factories, copper and coal mines, and tea plantations to build an economy that leapt into the global marketplace.

While patriarchal authority commanded the young workers to put up with low wages and miserable working conditions, the rapidly accumulating capital funded the large conglomerates known as *zaibatsu*. The still familiar names of Mitsui, Mitsubishi, and Sumitomo graced the firms that engaged in banking and international shipping as they competed in the newly opened treaty ports of China and the industrial development of Korea. Under this regime, as the population grew along with food production, a national railway system blossomed and Japan's urban population began to swell. This was the world over which the oligarchs managed to keep control.

Reformers in Korea and China studied the Japanese solution. After the Treaty of Shimonoseki in 1895, they actively pursued it. But the Japanese experience was both admirable and frightening. It was admirable for the resolute application of state policy and power to industrial development. It was frightening in that it built on uniquely Japanese conditions, including seizure of power from the old regime, and required a concentrated national commitment to self-sacrifice and ruthless pursuit of economic power.

Imperialism

What made the ruthless pursuit of economic power frightening by 1895 was the rapid expansion of military force that was also required. Competitive military expansion in the pursuit of both markets and resources was the hallmark of the age of imperialism. The cost of expansion was high, and the cost in turn drove the demand for more access and more control. As Japan entered into this competition through Korea, it unwittingly joined in the cycle of increasing costs and benefits, which would in turn raise the demands for the personal sacrifice and patriotic commitment of the Japanese people.

For China, the Treaty of Shimonoseki, negotiated by Itō Hirobumi and Li Hongzhang, was the latest in a series of blows to the Qing self-strengthening effort. The unequal treaties that had begun with the British victory in the Opium War (1839–1842) created a chain of foreign concessions in treaty ports all across China. Each new treaty came with a "most favored nation" clause, which meant that whatever concession was granted to one foreign power was also granted to all the others. In this case the Japanese won the right for all the foreign powers to

Itō Hirobumi (left) and Li Hongzhang (right). *(Wikimedia Commons, Underwood & Underwood, http://tintyurl.com/l6ke7w2; Wikimedia Commons, Peabody Essex Museum, http://tinyurl.com/l72xmg2).*

build their own factories in China. In addition they won for themselves control of the Liaodong Peninsula in southern Manchuria, where they planned to develop a new port and a railway to the north, paralleling those they would build in Korea. France collaborated with Russia and Germany to intervene, since Russia wanted railway rights in Manchuria, and Germany was eyeing similar rights in Shandong to the south. As a consolation for this indignity, Japan was offered Taiwan, which it quickly colonized and began to develop as well. With that, a "scramble for concessions" in China was on.

In contrast to Japan, the Qing self-strengthening effort was hampered by a different set of legacies. Li Hongzhang and other leaders of the effort emerged not from a power seizure but from a massive and protracted civil war against rebels of many stripes across the subcontinent. The self-strengtheners had joined with local leaders to raise militias, recruit young scholars as civil officials, and support the Qing to restore a stable order on the old model, reviving Confucian ethical values in the process. As many as 20 million people died and much land was laid waste. The foreign powers, led by the British, responded first by demanding new revisions of their treaties, which the Qing court rejected, and then by occupying the imperial capital at Beijing, burning and looting the classic eighteenth century summer palace before they left. Later, they sided with the Qing to protect the foreign concessions, but they also prevailed on the Qing to allow foreign embassies in Beijing and set up a new office for management of foreign affairs. In addition they imposed indemnities for their military costs. The Qing efforts at self-strengthening resulted only in a string of costly losses at the hands of imperialist powers. The Treaty of Shimonoseki also imposed a large indemnity on the Qing, which was another nail in the coffin.

The Japanese entry into the scramble for concessions had another effect as well. It inspired a new generation of political activists in China to learn from Japan. If the Meiji reformers had first seized power with the help of the young emperor, pursued constitutional legitimacy, and streamlined the government to implement its industrial policy, then the progressives of China's scholar-official class should appeal to the new young reform-minded Emperor Guangxu to follow suit. The effort moved forward in 1898 but fell victim to factional intrigue and a coup by Empress Dowager Cixi, who had recently stepped down as regent and who feared that the hovering Japanese, the young reformers, and the New Army commander Yuan Shikai were themselves about to gain control of the emperor. After a brief setback, the constitutional movement was revived and the Qing sent thousands of students to Japan to prepare for its ultimate success.

In the meantime, however, the foreign powers turned one more page in East Asia. With the United States now joining the imperialist game with the occupation of the Philippines and winning a concession to build half of the main north-south railway in China, another religious uprising threatened the foreign powers directly. The Boxer Rebellion (or Boxer Uprising), as it was known in English because of the martial arts training on which it drew, first targeted Chinese Christians in the flood-damaged, drought-plagued Shandong Province. In the spring of 1900 the seemingly leaderless mass of young peasant men, many claiming possession by angry spirits, spread northward toward Beijing, killing Chinese Christians and calling for Qing support. When the Empress Dowager gave up on quelling the uprising and the foreign powers collaborated to send troops to Beijing, she declared war on them instead. Yuan Shikai, then governor of Shandong, and other more progressive governors in the south stood aside. The result was another humiliating Qing defeat, this time at the hands of the "Eight Powers," including Japan (as well as the United States, Britain, Germany, and others), acting in concert. The Eight Powers then imposed another heavy indemnity, relating to their costs in the war, on the Qing in an agreement called the Boxer Protocol.

The Boxer Protocol of 1901, a "Peace Agreement between the Great Powers and China," involved China, Japan, the United States, and nine European nations. A link to it can be found on the University of Southern California's US-China Institute "Resources" web page (http://china.usc.edu/Resources21.aspx).

Yet it was also clear that the foreign powers were desperate to avoid a real war with an enraged and religiously motivated Chinese peasantry. Already in danger of falling into war with one another, they needed a stable Qing Empire, in which they were now deeply and competitively invested. The foreign troops wreaked bloody vengeance on the villages of North China, doing nothing to improve the Western image there. The shared stance of the foreign powers on the side of stability and the American "Open Door Policy" remained unchanged until the Great War (World War I) in Europe brought this chapter in their story in East Asia to an end. The Japanese would then stand alone, caught up in the vicious imperialist cycle they had so willingly joined.

Republican Revolution in China

By 1903, East Asia seemed back on the path to a new order. There would be three sovereign nations under modern constitutional governments with Japan in the lead. Clear signs of the new direction emerged from the Chinese students in Japan, when imperial Russia refused to withdraw the troops it had sent to Manchuria in the wake of the Boxer Rebellion. The Qing had sent the students to their eager Japanese teachers in hopes of building a common East Asian front against the foreign powers. The Qing reformers were now focused on ending the highly selective system of civil service examinations that had cemented the social networks among communities across China for hundreds of years. To pass these exams, the young Chinese men who strove to serve as officials across the empire studied Confucian classics, Chinese history, literature, and statecraft. In Japan, thousands of Chinese students now studied science, medicine, business, and law, as well the civics and ethics of what should become the new "East Asian" world order. Many studied in military and police academies, while others prepared for a new type of civil service, modeled on the one that was making the Japanese bureaucracy an effective new tool of modernization.

But the Chinese students also experienced the authoritarian force of the Japanese state as its diplomats and officials implemented policies urged by the Qing to suppress political activism. The more radical students shared a sense of outrage with like-minded young Japanese, giving rise to an even more radical brand of political action. While international influences such as socialism, feminism, and anarchism spread among them, the call for a new Chinese nationalism and revolution against the Qing regime rang the loudest among the Chinese. The call was for an armed revolution to overthrow the entire ancient imperial state system, sweeping away the Manchus, who refused to fight the Russians for their own homeland, and lead the long-oppressed Chinese nation. As the more moderate Chinese students continued to hope for a stable constitutional monarchy on the Japanese model, it was the Japanese armed forces that drove the Russians away.

The Treaty of Portsmouth that ended the Russo-Japanese War in 1905 was a milestone on the way to the Russian Revolution and the rise of Communism 12 years later. For the Japanese, it was both a step toward the exploitation of Manchuria's bountiful resources and a lesson in the financial and human costs of continuing warfare. While many beleaguered Japanese peasant households suffered from military conscription and the loss of male children, Chinese students in Japan formed a Revolutionary Alliance with the rising leader of Chinese revolutionaries overseas. Sun Yat-sen, a physician of peasant background educated in Hawaii and Hong Kong, had been raising funds and winning supporters among Japanese pan-Asianists and Chinese business communities in Southeast Asia. With his international reputation as an advocate of republican government, he persuaded the students that he could win the neutrality of the foreign powers. The fragile new alliance struggled to design a political strategy and a party platform as the Qing government sent emissaries to the West to study other constitutional regimes.

The Portsmouth Peace Treaty website (http://www.portsmouthpeacetreaty. com), run by the Japan-America Society of New Hampshire, is an online museum that includes primary source documents, newsreel footage, and more.

Adding to the Chinese nationalist fervor in 1905 was the legislative and judicial tightening of regulations under America's racially discriminatory Chinese Exclusion Act of 1882. A broad popular movement rose up in the Chinese treaty ports and Chinese communities of Southeast Asia to boycott American goods. The Revolutionary Alliance drew on this movement and on the proliferation of civic organizations authorized by the Qing to develop Chinese commerce, combat opium addiction, and prepare for local self-governance under constitutional law. As provincial assemblies made up of educated elites and reformers spawned financial groups to recover railway rights from foreign investors, young Japanese-educated New Army officers took up their positions within the provincial commands. Arguments for revolution now included strong racialist rhetoric, mirroring the racialist polemics of the Western powers. The arguments blamed the Qing ruling house, as Manchus, for oppressing the Chinese "Han" race and allowing the superior foreign powers to humiliate them. The ancient Chinese imperial system, with its authoritarian Confucian ideology, was the tool the Manchus used to deny Chinese equality in the world.

When Emperor Guangxu and Empress Dowager Cixi both died in 1908, a new generation of young Manchu regents gave credence to these claims by dismissing key Chinese reformers like Yuan Shikai, floating new foreign loans, and ordering the nationalization of the railways under Qing control. On October 10, 1911, New Army officers who had joined the Revolutionary Alliance sparked a military revolt that inspired all the southern provinces to secede from the empire. Sun Yat-sen returned from fund-raising in America and accepted the position of provisional president of the new Republic of China (ROC) that was offered him by the Revolutionary Alliance commanders. By then, representatives of the revolutionaries and the constitutional reformers had already brokered a peace settlement with Yuan Shikai in return for his promise of winning the abdication of the Manchus. Finally, to secure both domestic peace and the neutrality of the foreign powers, Sun stepped down from the presidency in favor of Yuan Shikai. The Republic was born and the Chinese nation, for the moment, was preserved.

Japanese Imperial Expansion

The Great War in Europe (1914–1918) brought down the Russian, German, Austro-Hungarian, and Ottoman Empires. The Versailles Peace Conference (also called the Paris Peace Conference) in the spring of 1919 promised to use international diplomacy to end imperialism and foster independence around the globe. In East Asia, what could this promise mean? By this time the Chinese Republic had disintegrated as regionally based "warlords" contended for control of a bankrupt and powerless regime in Beijing. In Tokyo nascent political parties in the Diet struggled to make their voices heard by the imperially appointed cabinet and the increasingly autonomous military command. Korea was under the thumb of a Japanese military governor-general who reported only to the Japanese emperor himself. Somewhere, it seems, East Asia had taken a wrong turn.

One military faction in Japan favored taking unilateral action and expanding the empire in East Asia. For them the Treaty of Versailles meant that Japan could claim rights to former German concessions in Shandong and expand direct Japanese control from Korea to Manchuria. For less aggressive imperial advisors, the promise of Versailles meant that they should loosen controls in Japan and Korea and gain domestic popular support with long overdue social policies. For the Japanese imperial command in Korea, these opposing alternatives meant either increasing or loosening control with the same ends in mind. For the politically astute educated class in Japan, the promise of the treaty meant that they should amplify the voices of working people, poor farmers, women, and intellectuals. For political parties in the Diet, this meant extending voting eligibility to the entire male population and appointing government ministers from the parties themselves. For Korean nationalists across the sea, it meant public demonstrations, popularly termed the March First Movement, for on that day in 1919 they made an open declaration of Korean independence and were crushed. For the disenfranchised Chinese, it meant launching a massive public campaign, beginning with a storm of telegrams, escalating to student demonstrations on May 4, and culminating in a general strike in Shanghai. The Beijing regime had declared war on Germany in August 1917 in hopes of regaining control of German concessions in Shandong, but the warlords had also signed contradictory secret agreements with Japan. The aim of the May Fourth protests was to stop Chinese diplomats from signing the Treaty of Versailles, which would hand the concessions over to Japan instead.

The patriotic May Fourth Movement in China in 1919 not only forced the Beijing regime to reject the treaty and forgive the students who raised the protest, it also inspired widespread cultural activism and educational missions to the countryside by advocates of what was called the New Culture. At the same time, democratic forces in Japan made headway against the militarists as the developing industrial economy across East Asia stimulated additional activism among industrial entrepreneurs and a burgeoning new working class.

Students freed after their arrest during the May Fourth Movement in China, 1919. *(Wikimedia Commons, http://tinyurl.com/lnd8mb4).*

With this flurry of new political activism, three new approaches to organizing and directing social forces appeared across East Asia. The first grew from traditional ways of negotiating among interests, maintaining stability, and guaranteeing an equitable distribution of welfare in the old agrarian-based societies. This "corporatist" approach would establish the rights and obligations of different interest groups, such as managers and workers within factories, while maintaining state control. The idea was to prevent antagonistic relations between different classes that might spread from one distinct social unit to another. The second approach, which involved securing rights for associations and unions that represented competing or conflicting interests under the protection of the law, was imported from the West along with capitalist enterprise and constitutional law. This new approach drew on liberal and social democratic ideas and practices. After the success of the Russian Revolution in 1917 and the advent of the Soviet Union, an explicitly communist approach added one more element to the mix. These three approaches identified differing political agendas. The state-makers, or political leaders who were heirs to the "self-strengtheners" of the previous century, sought to use them to the advantage of their states.

The state-makers in China emerged not from Beijing but from the southern coastal city of Guangzhou (Canton), where the Soviet Union and the arm of international Communist movement known as the Comintern sent money and personnel to help Sun Yat-sen build a new Chinese Nationalist Party. The new party, which included members of the nascent Chinese Communist Party, was highly centralized and compartmentalized, using the model developed by Lenin to seize power in Russia. The military arm of the new party launched a northern expedition against the warlord regimes in 1927. At the head of this army was Jiang Jieshi, better known in English as Chiang Kai-shek, whose corporatist sympathies and distrust of Communists after their success in organizing labor unions led to his bloody suppression of them in Shanghai. After that, the Communists moved to the countryside and the expansionist wing of the Japanese imperial army in Manchuria prepared to intervene.

The interventionist Kantōgun (Kwantung Army) first offered the northernmost Chinese warlord, who was retreating from Beijing, an alliance in Manchuria, and then assassinated him en route. Strengthening their position in defense of the growing Japanese corporate interests around the South Manchurian Railway system, they also succeeded in destabilizing domestic politics in Japan. The expansionist faction asserted its influence in a period of "politics of assassination" in Tokyo as the Kwantung Army continued to provoke military incidents in Manchuria, finally taking control of the region in September 1931. East Asia's tragic wrong turn had led to a new period of international conflict that ultimately ended in the region's most catastrophic total war.

War in East Asia

The war in Asia was a complex series of nested conflicts. It began not as a front in what is conventionally called World War II, but with the Nationalists' northern expedition against the warlords in 1927, when Chiang Kai-shek purged his party of Communists, driving them deep into the countryside to organize a resistance. At this time the Japanese forces in North China moved to protect their special interests there. The three-way war escalated with the Japanese Kantōgun (Kwantung Army) occupation of Manchuria in 1931, after which Japan rejected European diplomatic intervention and established a new puppet state called Manchukuo, with the last Manchu emperor as sovereign. With the Chinese populace demanding that Chiang suspend his war against the Communists to form a new United Front against the Japanese, Japan attacked North China and Shanghai in July 1937, driving the Nationalist government and armies to the mountains of Chongqing in the west.

When the war broke out in Europe in September 1939, the Japanese were freed from defending Manchukuo and Inner Mongolia against the Russians, whose attention was diverted to the European conflict, and they adopted a "southern strategy" of expansion into Southeast Asia. The goal was to secure vital resources for the continuing campaign in China, but the strategy led eventually to conflict with the United States and the disastrous Pacific War. After destroying the U.S. fleet at Pearl Harbor, Japan went on to capture the Philippines and the British, French, and Dutch colonies of Southeast Asia. By 1945 the United States had liberated the Philippines and was negotiating plans for the end of the East Asian war with the Soviet Union and the other Allied Powers. It was agreed that Manchuria and Taiwan would revert to Chinese sovereignty, but also that Russia would enter the war against Japan belatedly and occupy Korea, while the United States would occupy Japan. After the U.S.

atomic bombing of Hiroshima in August 1945, with the European war at an end, Russian troops entered Manchuria and the Chinese Communists' People's Liberation Army (PLA) went to reclaim Chinese sovereignty there. The war between that army and the severely weakened Nationalist forces for control of the Chinese mainland continued until the Communist victory in 1949 sent Chiang Kai-shek and the remnants of the Nationalist regime to Taiwan and established the People's Republic of China (PRC). Peace, however, did not settle over East Asia until well into the next decade, and the resulting messiness—from expedient compromises and convenient resolutions—has left much unresolved.

The Chinese Communist Party had built its army in the hinterlands during the war. After Chiang Kai-shek's purge of his party in 1927, Mao Zedong and other Communist leaders succeeded in organizing several rural soviets—mass-based but party-controlled local regimes—in South China. They began carrying out peasant-based land reforms while Chiang Kai-shek was extending his regime from the centrally located Nationalist capital in Nanjing. Losing out to Chiang's military campaigns in 1934, the Communists abandoned these soviets and undertook their famous "Long March" through the southern and western mountains, while under constant siege by the Nationalist armies, to Yan'an in the northwest. The survivors of this ordeal accepted Mao Zedong as the leader of their party, which was now a lean and experienced community of devoted revolutionaries. In Yan'an, Mao developed a new set of strategies and tactics for combining Leninist authoritarian politics,

Mao Zedong voting, ca. 1950. Image from *Quotations from Chairman Mao. (Wikimedia Commons, The People's Republic of China Printing Office, http://tinyurl.com/ptu5tb5).*

peasant mobilization, guerrilla warfare, and national resistance. As patriotic students and urban intellectuals joined the movement, it grew in size and scope. After the Japanese invasion in 1937, Communist units across North China began to challenge the legitimacy of the absent Nationalist regime. By the time the tide turned against the Japanese in the Pacific War, the Communists had built a highly disciplined, centrally controlled army and a loyal bureaucracy. They began to carry out land reform, eliminating landlords and supporting agricultural cooperatives in the areas under their control across the north from Yan'an to Manchuria.

The U.S. decision to end the Pacific War by dropping atomic bombs on Hiroshima and Nagasaki had enormous consequences. Nuclear holocaust became a reality in Japan, and the American demand that Japan surrender unconditionally—and that the emperor personally broadcast the surrender order to his subjects at home and abroad—shattered the myth of imperial invincibility that had legitimized Japan's mission in Asia. The American General Douglas MacArthur, as supreme commander of the Allied Powers in Japan, oversaw the demilitarization of Japan and the implementation of a new constitution before the Japanese restored independent native rule with a newly elected government in 1952.

In the meantime, the American occupation government subjected a large number of wartime leaders to trials for war crimes by the International Military Tribunal in Nuremberg. Critics wondered why there was only "victor's justice," and why no question was raised about the use of atomic bombs on whole cities as a war crime as well. In addition, the American occupation of Korea cut short the efforts of Korean nationalists to form an independent regime of their own based on hastily organized People's Committees. Instead, the Allied Powers' occupation of the south was matched by Soviet Russian support for the Communist regime of Kim Il-sung in the north. Kim had organized a guerilla resistance with Chinese Communist protection in Manchuria during the war. Once it was clear that his party was in control within Korea north of the 38th parallel, the United States stood firmly behind the right-wing Korean party that had prepared itself in the United States under Syngman Rhee in the south. With little political support inside Korea, Rhee's regime purged the domestic Communists who were released from prison in the south. As the civil war unfolded in China and the United States applied itself to the immediate rebuilding of Japan, the Cold War began on Asian soil.

Cold War

In East Asia, the beginning of what Europeans and Americans called the Cold War was not at all cold. Nor can the resurgence of violence on the Korean peninsula be explained as just an early episode in the global divide between the communist East and the democratic West. With the "liberation" of China in 1949, Mao had announced that the PRC would have to "lean to one side" in the Cold War. In the struggle between the surviving Western imperialist powers and the rising Socialist bloc, he claimed, there could be no middle ground. The PRC proceeded to collectivize agricultural production, realizing significant growth in the process. Soviet aid to China came in the form of scientific, technological, and military expertise. China repaid the Russians with propaganda support and grain. By 1950 Kim Il-sung and his Korean Workers' Party had carried out land reforms and nationalized the heavy industries left by the Japanese in the North. For them, reunification and independence on the Chinese model seemed within reach. Stalin promised material support, and Mao promised solidarity. The American occupation had not won popular support in the South, and Syngman Rhee's Republic of Korea (ROK) looked like a cross between Japan's old Manchukuo puppet regime and the prewar Japanese colonial administration. Kim Il-sung's Korean Liberation Army launched its conquest of the South in June of 1950, occupying Seoul in a few days and restricting the ROK to the southeastern "Pusan perimeter" by summer's end.

As Kim's Korean Workers' Party reinstated People's Committees in the South and began to carry out land reform there as well, the United States petitioned the UN Security Council, in the temporary absence of the Soviet Union's delegate, to launch a "Police Action" in support of the ROK. In the months that followed, General MacArthur led a massive U.S. invasion that first turned the tide against the North, then provoked China to enter the war on the side of the North, which ended with a "truce" in 1953 that marked the 38th parallel as a Demilitarized Zone (DMZ) between two separate Korean regimes. Millions of Koreans, some 900,000 Chinese soldiers, and 55,000 Americans died, with nothing but the near total destruction of both North Korea's industry and the South's capital city of Seoul to show for it.

The Cold War era of containment and proxy wars, pitting the United States against the Soviet Union—along with the allies and client states on both sides all across the globe—would continue for decades, obscuring the progressive social goals that were shared across the divide. Indeed, land reform had been the first item on the social agenda that the American occupation imposed on Japan. In addition, the new American-imposed constitution of 1947 envisioned equal rights for women and new marriage laws to enforce these rights. The People's Republic of China passed a similar law in 1950, and it was redistributing land to the peasants as well.

The American need for material support in the Korean War provided the initial stimulation for the recovery of Japan's devastated industries. The new Japanese constitution denied it a standing army, making it dependent on the United States for defense, but also enabling it to focus its national economy on the global consumer market. In the PRC the war confirmed Communist leaders' suspicions that the United States was just the latest in a string of imperialist powers against which the Chinese, as well as the Koreans, had been struggling for the past century. As if more confirmation were needed, the U.S. extended its power from new military bases in Okinawa to the defense of the remnant Nationalist government on the island of Taiwan. Under this U.S. umbrella, Chiang Kai-shek secured Nationalist control of Taiwan, denying the recently liberated populace a political voice. Chiang's regime survived on the pretense that it was the legitimate government of China, and it continued to represent the nation in the United Nations for another 20 years.

The focus of the Cold War in East Asia then shifted to Vietnam, where a hot war of independence was still raging. The Vietnam Independence Party, or Viet Minh, which was aligned with the Communist bloc, defeated the colonial French forces at Dien Bien Phu in 1954, bringing that part of the conflict to a pause. After the Geneva Conference that underwrote the continued division of both Korea and Vietnam that year, the PRC began to assert itself diplomatically among the emerging postcolonial nations of South and Southeast Asia, Africa, and the Middle East.

China was still "leaning to one side," yet even as the United States supported Chiang Kai-shek's call to retake the mainland, the European-educated premier of the PRC, Zhou Enlai, was charming European diplomats in Geneva and "non-aligned" Third World leaders at their conference in Bandung, Indonesia, the following year. By 1956, with the onset of anti-Stalinist revisionism in Russia and resistance movements against Soviet control in Eastern Europe, Mao and the new Soviet leader, Nikita Khrushchev, publicized their mutual distrust. Over the next few years the "friendship alliance" between the PRC and the USSR broke down. China had its own nuclear bomb, the war in Vietnam heated up, and the Communist Party in China, now firmly under Maoist control, entered onto a radical new revolutionary path.

The End of War and Revolution

Mao had begun formulating a new version of Communism at Yan'an during the war of resistance against Japan in the 1930s. Drawing on the experience of the Russian Revolution, he adapted the theory and practice of Marxism-Leninism to Chinese conditions. Marxism had sprouted in Europe in the 1840s with the idea that industrialization under "bourgeois," or capitalist, control produced a broad class of dispossessed working people who, through labor unions and international political association, could gain control of the means of production and distribute the benefits more equitably by socialist means. With the expansion of the imperialist powers by 1900, Lenin added the idea of centralized Communist Party authority and a party-led military force to serve as a "vanguard" for socialist revolution. In China in the 1930s industrial development was in its infancy, a weak Nationalist government faced escalating Japanese encroachment, and a growing but increasingly impoverished peasantry remained disengaged from national politics. Mao's idea was to implement strict Leninist-style control within the Chinese Communist Party (CCP), using it to mobilize poor peasants as soldiers to resist Japan while attacking the problem of rural disengagement with centrally organized land reform. The key to implementing this idea was to educate party members in socialist theory, create a regime of propaganda that could adapt the thinking and the language of illiterate peasants to national resistance and revolution, and transform the "class bound" habits and attitudes of educated cadre and rural peasantry alike into a new radical revolutionary mentality.

The CCP applied this ideology during the war of resistance against Japan, but once it was in power it followed the more bureaucratic Soviet model of development, stressing state-owned heavy industry and collective farms. With the old owners and managers forcefully removed and the socialist system in place, Mao began to press the party to return to his revolutionary strategy to attack the massive bureaucracy that was settling into place. After a campaign to mobilize popular criticism of bureaucratic entrenchment and encourage creative solutions led unexpectedly to vocal resistance, the party cracked down on the critics in a broad purge called the "anti-rightist" campaign in 1957. Undaunted by this setback, Mao then drove the Party to implement large-scale rural communes in a "Great Leap Forward," toward the utopian goal of communism without enduring capitalist economic development first. When this experiment led to greater problems of mismanagement and ultimately a disastrous famine in north and central China, Mao stepped aside to allow more pragmatic leaders to restore socialist order. Yet the constantly recurring rituals of ideological "rectification"—demanding that party members purge themselves of old habits and old attitudes—would not fade away.

In 1966 Mao drew on his own political charisma to regain control of the party and appeal to the nation's youth to launch a Great Proletarian Cultural Revolution against what he called the "capitalist roaders" who he claimed had captured control of the party and the nation itself. Authorities within the universities, secondary and primary schools, and middle schools (as well as local governments and military and police units) were ordered to stand aside. Students of all ages, organized as "Red Guard" units, first challenged teachers and administrators, then attacked local leaders and intellectuals, and finally divided into factions to fight among themselves. Party leaders soon resorted to military intervention to end the worst of the violence, but the Maoists remained in control for a decade. The revolution in China ground to a halt as the most radical idealists presided over a nation with little appetite for further change. Meanwhile, Maoist ideas of continuing revolution, populist mobilization, and "People's War" spread around the world, influencing Third World independence movements and opposition movements in the developed world as well.

While the Maoists were continuing to make revolution in China, leaders of the dominant Liberal Democratic Party (LDP) in Japan were adapting to the new global power structure with a different innovative approach. While the new constitution had guaranteed civil and political rights to opposition political parties, autonomous business corporations, labor unions, and women and minority ethnic groups, the American occupation had left large portions of the old *zaibatsu* conglomerates and old political leadership on the civilian side intact. In 1955 a coalition of political leaders formed the LDP, which would maintain its cohesion by consensus as it provided incentives and security for corporate growth and global economic expansion.

This restructuring of political authority around consensus succeeded in limiting efforts by labor unions, the faction-ridden Socialist Party, and a smaller Communist Party to gain a share of the power. Under these conditions, university students in Japan who were opposed to U.S. hegemony organized student strikes and protests against Japan's compliance with the growing American military involvement in Vietnam. Key targets of protest included American military bases in Okinawa, the potential of harboring nuclear weapons on Japanese soil, and the renewal of the U.S.-Japan

Security Treaty in 1960 and again in 1970. By the time of the second renewal, many Japanese students were thoroughly engaged in the global student protest movement in which Mao's idea of continuing revolution and People's War played such a visible part. In Japan, where the LDP consensus held sway and the Socialist opposition split along ideological lines, the struggle was increasingly ritualized to fit into the new pattern of state-managed global economic engagement. This pattern produced annual double-digit economic growth with nearly full employment being guaranteed by the large corporations that participated in it.

The effectiveness of the Japanese model was obvious to both the citizenry and the military government of South Korea, but the DMZ between North and South continued to shape strategies there. The extremely unpopular Syngman Rhee was reelected president among reports of widespread fraud in 1960. A student-led popular uprising and the regime's bloody crackdown led the ROK army and the United States to withdraw their support, forcing Rhee's resignation. A new National Assembly took power, only to be shut down by a military coup led by General Park Chung-hee. This new military dictatorship, with U.S. support, launched another authoritarian strategy for development, combining strong state-supported conglomerates like those in Japan, called *chaebol*, while suppressing the labor unions along with students and popular opposition. This regime achieved economic results that matched the Japanese, but without shaping an equivalent political consensus. In an environment plagued by North Korean military threats and active assassination squads alongside American-supported anti-Communist propaganda from the South Korean generals, a disenfranchised and discontented middle class continued to grow.

Emerging East Asia

During the 1970s, East Asia was emerging from the Cold War ahead of the two superpowers. By the end of the decade the world was wondering at the degree of stability and economic success in the "Four Little Dragons" or "Asian Tigers"—South Korea, Taiwan, Hong Kong, and Singapore—that had followed Japan in export-led engagement with the global economy. In 1971 a string of events signaled that the PRC was ready to join in this emergence. With the Maoists apparently in charge, the aging chairman's chosen successor, the head of the People's Liberation Army (PLA) and chief advocate of the radical leftist line, died in a plane crash while attempting to flee to the Soviet Union. The public accusation that Lin Biao had tried to carry out a coup against Mao brought an end to the widespread faith in Mao's wisdom. Almost immediately the old party leadership, with Mao in agreement, reached out to an eager U.S. president, Richard Nixon, who sought to lead the United States out of the Vietnam War by playing "the China card."

In the "Shanghai Communiqué" of 1972, the United States and China agreed to leave the fate of Taiwan to the future and launch friendly trade relations across the Cold War divide. Left out of the negotiations, Japan recognized the PRC and began to compete with Europe and the United States for investment opportunities there. The

United States ceased blocking China's entry into the United Nations, and in 1974 an emerging new leader, Deng Xiaoping, addressed the world from there, announcing that China would ally itself with the underdeveloped Third World, leaving the two superpowers and the developed nations of Europe to their post-imperialist fate. Japan and the Asian Tigers had found their own way to economic growth and independence; now China was no longer "leaning to one side."

The 1972 Shanghai Communiqué marked a very important point in Sino-American relations. Read the full text in the U.S. State Department's "History" section (http://history.state.gov/historicaldocuments/frus1969-76v17/d203).

In Taiwan, martial law had prevailed since 1947. A class of native Taiwanese leaders, deprived of a political voice under Japanese rule, responded to the new regime's promise. Some of them hoped for independence, and all of them hoped for political rights, but they were violently suppressed in the wake of a popular protest against corruption and abuse by the new occupying ROC regime. But the Nationalists managed to carry out land reform by offering shares in new export-oriented industries in return for agricultural land, which was sold at controlled prices to the farmers. This policy of returning land to the tillers was consistent with the original platform of the Nationalists in the 1920s. It was also consistent with the postwar reforms in Japan, both Koreas, and China, and the relative political stability and access to foreign markets that came with American military protection made it possible. Suddenly, in 1972, the "China card" deprived the ROC of its fictional status as the government of all of China, legitimized by its place on the Security Council of the United Nations. When Chiang Kai-shek died in 1975, a new generation of Nationalist Party leaders began to emerge under the leadership of the generalissimo's son, Chiang Ching-kuo. With the death of Mao Zedong and Zhou Enlai the following year, Chinese on both sides of the Taiwan Strait began to anticipate a lessening of tension and, perhaps, reconciliation as well.

Unfortunately, tensions in South Korea under Park Chung-hee escalated right along with the economic success. In 1974, the year Deng Xiaoping addressed the United Nations, Park's suppression of popular unrest among the increasingly urbanized populace was rewarded with an assassination attempt that succeeded in killing his popular wife. The political conflict intensified until rivals assassinated Park himself in 1979. The perpetrators released well-known opposition leaders from prison, but a new dictator emerged to crush a student uprising in Kwangju, the memory of which became the rallying cry of the opposition for the decade that followed, rivaling the March First Movement of 1919 in the annals of Korean history. As the military dictatorship in the South continued to claim legitimacy with its anti-Communist security stance, the economy of North Korea, under the weight of

Statues of Korean leader Kim Il-sung and his son and successor Kim Jong-il on Mansu Hill in Pyongyang. *(Wikimedia Commons, J.A. de Roo, http://tinyurl.com/mkfa4al).*

its heavy industry, began to stagnate, an effect magnified by the silencing power of the rising personality cult of the "Great Leader" Kim Il-sung. Just as the rest of East Asia seemed to be on a new track, the Cold War's DMZ line across the Korean peninsula seemed to drive the military regimes on both sides to increasingly oppressive extremes.

The most dramatic changes of the next decade occurred in China. Deng Xiaoping formally claimed leadership of the Chinese Communist Party (CCP) and the state in 1978, promising a new era of pragmatic reforms. Suddenly, students and intellectuals who had been denounced or sent to the countryside for reeducation returned to engage in the public discourse, applying posters to what became known as the "Democracy Wall" in Beijing. Soon there were new journals and an array of voices calling for progressive change. Nothing like liberal democracy resulted, but by 1981 the CCP had put the Maoist era to rest, accepting responsibility for following Mao after he started making "mistakes" and reclaiming its roots in the pragmatic policies of the past.

The new policies would focus on economic and scientific "modernization," on higher education and international educational exchange, and on learning how to engage the global economy rather than fighting it. Ideology gradually gave way to pragmatic successes. New cities arose as Special Economic Zones, where foreign and Chinese investors would share in the profits. Market incentives and private household enterprises reappeared. While the party retained sole rights to political power, the official policy was now to develop "socialism with Chinese characteristics," in what the new premier called "the early stages of socialism." What this meant was that China would find its own way to invest in, support, and manage a capitalist economy without abiding the political influence of an independent capitalist class. It would join the East Asian innovators in the global economy as they continued to keep the foreign imperialists at bay.

Most dramatic of all was the emergence of privately and collectively owned enterprises in rural areas, where the communes and collective farms were disbanded. In contrast to Japan and South Korea, the vast rural population of China had not been displaced by urban manufacturing. In the 1950s the CCP had collectivized agriculture everywhere in order to regulate the food supply and prevent mass migration to the cities, where opportunities for work were insufficient. In the 1980s the poorest rural communities demanded that the farms be divided up among the local households, giving them more options for production and for allocating their labor. Villages that were better off then shifted their collective resources to more profitable nonagricultural enterprises, engaging directly in domestic and international trade.

For more than a decade these enterprises and the proliferating opportunities that grew from them fueled China's economic expansion. Some rural households were becoming rich, some villages were managing to attract migrant workers and skilled managers, and, at the same time, many poorer rural households began sending members to work in towns and cities farther and farther from home. This grassroots economic mobilization was, indeed, uniquely adapted to Chinese circumstances and to the historical moment. By the time the collapse of the Communist regimes in Eastern Europe signaled the end of the Cold War, China had already joined with the rest of East Asia—the two Koreas excluded—in moving beyond it.

New World

Most American and European historians, along with international affairs commentators, view the end of Soviet control of Eastern Europe and the collapse of the Soviet Union between 1989 and 1991 as the end of a world-defining era. Almost immediately the global focus turned to ethno-religious and international conflicts from the Balkans, across the Arab world, to Iraq, Iran, Afghanistan, and Pakistan. For the people of East Asia, the focus was split between the ongoing economic development of the whole region and the newly developing popular culture that followed the extensive influence of digital technology around the globe. Governments in East and Southeast Asia continued to deal with the effects of the Cold War and worry themselves over the new geopolitical fault lines, but pragmatic economic issues and shared popular culture were now shaping the interests of the populace.

East Asia's authoritarian political cultures adapted to the emerging new world in various ways. Perhaps the most dramatic adaptation occurred in Taiwan. Chiang Kai-shek's son and successor, Chiang Ching-kuo, had managed to negotiate what most citizens agreed was an inevitable shift to multiparty democracy. Before his father's death in 1975, and preceding the U.S. recognition of the PRC in 1979,

Chiang was already overseeing the rapid economic development recognized as the "Taiwan Miracle." In 1987 he formally ended the martial law in Taiwan that had begun in 1947, having already allowed the opposition to organize a political party. Chiang's death in 1988 was followed by an orderly transition. His elected successor, Lee Teng-hui, who was the new leader of the Nationalist Party but also a native Taiwanese, offered a formal apology for the massacre that had led to martial law and eventually spoke in favor of Taiwan's independence. Since then, the opposition has won and lost national power by election, while the system has remained stable. Yet Taiwan remains an island state without independent status among nations. The initial shift to multiparty democracy in 1987, on the other hand, led political reformers in the PRC and international observers of China to hope for a similar reform there, but this was not to be.

Instead, the new pragmatic leaders in China argued over what kind of participatory political reform was suitable to Chinese conditions as economic growth accelerated. The growing and increasingly ambitious student population, disgruntled with the corrupt manipulations of privilege by well-connected CCP officers and their offspring, demanded more freedom of expression. As progressive party leaders loosened the reins in order to amplify progressive voices in leadership circles, students began to advocate autonomous student associations, democratic elections, and transparent grievance procedures on their campuses. When the campus-bound movements began to boil over into public protests, Deng Xiaoping joined party elders in clamping down. Hu Yaobang, the younger progressive general secretary of the party, was removed without a vote early in 1987. His death in the spring of 1989 provided the occasion for protesting students from all the universities of Beijing to occupy the massive open space of Tiananmen Square, the physical and symbolic center of the nation.

The Tiananmen demonstrations continued for six weeks, marring the party's reception for Mikhail Gorbachev, the Soviet reformer and first Soviet leader to visit Beijing since Khrushchev did so in 1959. Citizens and established intellectuals supported the students' outcry, and workers joined them and began to organize their own autonomous unions, but as the more pragmatic student leaders retreated to their campuses and the government declared martial law, no one could persuade the rest to abandon their hold on this space. Finally, after much popular intervention, as well-disciplined but poorly prepared army troops ploughed through the throngs to take control of the Square, hundreds of citizens lost their lives. The experiment with participatory democracy came to a tragic, bloody end. After a brief period of settling down, during which the Communist parties of Europe and the Soviet Union lost their power, the CCP restarted its economic development program, with its promise of expanding material benefit for the populace under continuing authoritarian rule.

The story in Japan was different. The LDP had managed to stay in power since 1955 by maintaining a consensus among contending factions within and splitting the opposition without. The carefully managed economic policy was so successful that Japan's trade advantage with the United States led to both the emulation of the world's business classes and the resistance of populist politicians. By the 1980s the combination of these two responses was producing excessive global investment in Japanese stocks and excessive Japanese purchasing of U.S. debt, along with fearmongering and Japan-bashing abroad. Even as the Asian Tigers and China absorbed more and more Japanese investment and increased trade with Japan, memories of Japanese imperialism and suspicions of its leaders' designs colored international relations and recurrent popular protests. In China, student protests had charged political leaders with corruption, gullibility, and incompetence in accepting Japanese exploitation. Right-wing nationalists in Japan charged the LDP with not standing up to the United States and with undermining Japan's martial tradition while Chinese and Koreans inflated their claims against Japanese wartime atrocities.

At the same time, corruption and factional divisions within the LDP further undermined its support in the increasingly urbanized population. When economic recession finally hit Japan in 1990, LDP factions and opposition parties that had been gaining strength began to realign themselves. Finally, in 1993, as political reconciliation and multiparty democracy blossomed in Taiwan and the authoritarian model began to produce new spectacular growth in China, a coalition of LDP breakaway factions, socialist parties, and the Buddhist-inspired Clean Government Party formed the first non-LDP government in Japan since 1955. The LDP breakup did lead to a decade-long series of weak coalition governments, but the new coalition succeeded in reforming the electoral system that had practically guaranteed a single-party monopoly for 40 years. As the political leaders sought new approaches to revive the national economy and engage with the changing world, women, workers, minority ethnic groups, and social and environmental activists increased their political voice.

Under the weight of military dictatorship after the Kwangju incident in 1980, South Korean activists found their voice in grassroots cultural revivals. As rural communities in China developed their township and village enterprises, Chinese university students experimented with democracy on their campuses, and the more conservative of urbanized Japanese citizenry waxed nostalgic over their disappearing rural roots. Students and intellectuals in South Korea, however, turned nostalgia into professional activism. The appeal of core cultural values and the revival of uniquely Korean characteristics cut across class divisions in the mostly urbanized society. As in Japan, the new middle class, workers, and social activists joined in support of opposition political leaders.

Park Chung-hee's successor, Chun Doo-hwan, had tried to implement social reforms, but had never become popular. He had groomed as his successor Roh Tae-woo, who would have to appeal to the electorate under constitutional law in 1988. In 1987 widespread strikes and labor protests brought on another crackdown, but it was the last. American pressure joined with popular protests and political realignment to force the military leadership to compromise. The following year the constitution was rewritten, allowing for direct election of the president, ending 30 years of military rule. During his brief presidency, Roh competed with the opposition for popular support, allowing new rights for women and giving more freedom to the press. He redirected South Korean foreign policy, opening relations with China and the Soviet Union. By the time of the Soviet collapse in 1991, the new popularly elected president, Kim Young-sam, was dismantling the institutions that had maintained the military dictators and overseeing their trials, even as the new government presided over slowing economic growth. The most popular and longest-persecuted political leader, Kim Dae-jung, was pressing for open negotiations with the North. Only North Korea remained mired in Cold War legacies.

Bridge to the Twenty-First Century

Kim Dae-jung had led the opposition to Park Chung-hee in the National Assembly of South Korea ever since the 1961 coup, with near unanimous electoral support from his district. Under military rule he had been locally elected, removed, reelected, arrested, kidnapped, and exiled. After 1988 he returned to prominence, and in 1997 he was elected president. By that time, North Korea's "Great Leader," Kim Il-sung had died, and the centrally planned economy had collapsed. His son Kim Jong-il succeeded him as "Dear Leader." The world hoped this was the chance for change. After 1997 all of Asia was struggling with a severe recession brought on by the collapse of Thailand's currency and the resulting financial crisis, sending South Korea to the International Monetary Fund (IMF) for a bailout. North Korea was scarcely connected to the global capitalist economy, but it was already hard hit by the demise of its Soviet and Eastern European trading partners. Agricultural production had dropped precipitously. In 1995–1996 a disastrous famine struck the North. Under these conditions, in 1998 Kim Dae-jung launched an outreach program labeled the "Sunshine Policy." Japan, China, and the United States had already contributed to famine relief, and the new policy was intended to foster reconciliation and exchange across the DMZ without antagonizing the North with an agenda for reunification. Some South Korean industrialists were supportive, whereas conservative politicians reacted with the argument that the South was offering much needed relief and foreign exchange to the North, while the latter pursued a policy of "military first." Subsequent administrations have altered, opposed, or revived the effort, for which Kim Dae-jung was awarded the Nobel Peace Prize in 2000.

As of 2013, South Korea had its first woman president, Park Geun-hye, a conservative who is also the daughter of Park Chung-hee. In North Korea, the equally new regime of Kim Jong-il's son, the young Kim Jong-un, stubbornly pursued the North's military goals, including nuclear weapons, to the point of shutting down exchanges with the South entirely. Most observers have said that the policy could shift dramatically at any time. By August 2013 new cross-border interactions were under way.

The 1997 financial crisis affected Southeast Asian economies more than those of East Asia, but the general trend was an immediate reduction in exports. The authoritarian government of Singapore managed the crisis well, and by this time China was

Korean President Park Geun-hye (left) and Chinese President Xi Jinping during a joint press conference on June 27, 2013, at the Great Hall of the People in Beijing, China. *(Wikimedia Commons, Korea.net/Korean Culture and Information Service [Cheong Wa Dae], http://tinyurl.com/pnk4bor).*

following the Singapore model of joint venture investments, currency management, and exports. China's decision to spur rapid growth but limit political participation outside the Communist Party enabled the government to weather this financial storm and the next one, in 2008, as well. The Chinese reallocated investments and labor to state-owned industries, supported Chinese currency by buying U.S. debt, and building infrastructure. On the one hand, the government has accelerated the building of the world's most comprehensive high-speed rail system. On the other, the shift to more state-owned firms without nonparty public oversight or an independent judiciary has exacerbated the abuse of privileges, corruption, and bribes.

A new constitution in China has imposed limits of two consecutive five-year terms on the offices of president and premier, ensuring regular changes in leadership. To counter the effects of limiting nonparty political opposition, the CCP adopted new rules for membership, inviting private entrepreneurs and recruiting among the newly educated, many of whom studied abroad. Recognizing the need and the value of investigative reporting, legal training, and critical voices at the grassroots level, the party adopted changes in the language of governance. Protests against corrupt local officials have proliferated, with journalists reporting such abuses, which often leads to removal or prosecution by higher authorities. Contested local elections are becoming the norm in rural areas, and urban activists press for recognition of constitutional rights to free speech and assembly, and for an independent judiciary. As of the spring of 2013 the newly elected president and premier have promised to reduce support for state-owned industries and to reduce restrictions on rights, but signs of actually loosening control are still few. The idea of radical constitutional change remains politically sensitive, as is evident with the imprisonment of Liu Xiaobo, who was awarded the Nobel Peace Prize in 2010 for his role in drafting and winning thousands of signatures from intellectuals and professional people for a liberal proposal called "Charter 08."

In matters that the CCP leaders consider not to be politically sensitive, social action and popular culture in China is vibrant. Rapid economic growth has led to a massive mobilization of migrant workers among a populace that was recently pinned down by local household registration that determined access to jobs, health care, and education. Nongovernmental organizations (NGOs) and religious organizations, often with foreign or multinational affiliations, have taken on these social services, as well as environmental watchdog functions, with the government's blessing. Controls still abound, but the activity nonetheless expands. Increasingly, the experience of such organizations in Korea, Japan, and Taiwan is brought to bear on China. In better-off rural areas, local collectives and the charity of local entrepreneurs adds to this brand of civil society. The flow of people and information, now enhanced by cellular and digital technology, is also shaping it across local and regional boundaries within China. Future developments in the political culture are certain to reflect the influence of this new technology.

The hit-and-miss development of civil society under authoritarian governments in East Asia, from imperial and colonial times through total war and postwar readjustment, has been a major theme of this chapter. The other major theme has been the development and the limits of national identities and nation-states. The shift of Japanese focus from Western influence to military dominance and imperialism, to defeated nation, to recovery without a military presence, to renewal of engagement in East Asia is one story. The Chinese focus on developing wealth and power under the Qing, to the disintegration of the Republic, to civil war and foreign occupation, to independence and experimentation with radical alternatives to capitalism, to a uniquely Chinese engagement with capitalist globalization is another. The contested status of Taiwan, the division of Korea, and the engagement of South Korea and Taiwan in the rapidly developing economy of China is yet another. All of these stories have unfolded under the influence of Western expansion and the peculiar forms of international conflict, cooperation, and law that accompanied it.

Family and Social History

Having examined this history, it is interesting to return to the beginning and see what happens if the story is viewed from a different perspective—from the viewpoint of the daily lives of the people across the region. Between the spring of 1894, when the Tonghak rebellion unfolded, and the signing of the Treaty of Shimonoseki the following year, a 28-year-old maid by the name of Ning was engaging in a drawn-out struggle for dignity with her mistress in a small Qing administrative city not far from a major naval base on the Shandong coast across from Korea. She had taken her young daughter and left her opium-addicted and abusive husband to go begging in the streets, eventually finding employment with a military family there. Her own life story, as told to a sympathetic listener 40 years later, tells how she and the cook, tailor, mistress, local missionaries, and others she knew dodged the shrapnel from incoming Japanese fire one day that winter. She also describes reactions to the Boxers in 1900, superstitions about missionaries that were belied by her own experience, her young son's fear of having his pigtail cut off as required after the revolution in 1911, and her granddaughter's academic success and commitment to national liberation in 1935. But her own story is less about these events than it is about food, family, work, and faith in the fundamental values and life-cycle rituals that sustained her through the massive dislocations that punctuated her life.

Ning Lao T'ai T'ai's story is told in the book *A Daughter of Han: The Autobiography of a Chinese Working Woman* (1945, reprinted 1967). It was written by Ida Pruitt, as told to her by Ning.

Apart from her personal story, Ning describes a world in which people moved from village to town, from town to city, and from Shandong to Manchuria in search of work. Amid this increasing mobility, she describes family traditions in rapid decline at all levels of society and new opportunities created by rapidly shifting markets and new-style schools. By focusing on such personal life stories, especially the stories of women's lives, and placing them in time and space, historians construct narratives of social change that differ from national histories. From this perspective the intentions, the decisions, and the actions of progressive reformers, generals, and revolutionaries take a back seat to those of mothers, wives, and workers whose values and life choices chart courses of their own. While there is no denying that the old societies of East Asia have changed dramatically over the past 150 years, the precise nature, the pace, and even the direction of the change has rarely matched the ideas that social planners and national historians had of it.

In this limited space, only the tip of the iceberg can be examined. To begin with, in 1895 the population of Japan, Korea, and China combined was about 440 million. Most people lived in farming villages then, but global commerce and manufacturing were changing that. The Japanese population, which had been comparatively stable over the previous century, had increased by about 25 percent to a total of 41 million. Rapidly increasing numbers of young men became soldiers as well as workers, while women also joined the industrial workforce. These patterns, which challenged traditional family life as they imposed new market forces on land, staple products, and labor, were already familiar in Europe and North America. In China, where families had always divided their property among heirs and carefully allocated their labor to agricultural and handicraft products, the population had doubled to some 390 million over the previous century. While Korea's population of ten million paled in comparison, the pressure on the land was no less than it was in China. Under these conditions, the open spaces of Manchuria and, to a lesser extent, the frontiers below the mountains in Taiwan became targets not only for entrepreneurship and exploitation of resources, but for migration and settlement as well. Between 1900 and 1945, under economic and political conditions that varied as described before, some 25 million Chinese, one million Japanese, and 800,000 Koreans found temporary or permanent homes there.

Of course, the Manchurian case is just one example of what drives this narrative. In Japan, industrialization came in the late nineteenth century, and following that, the primary forces over time were urbanization, then militarization, and finally the growth of consumerism. In China in the mid-twentieth century, the socialist state halted migration to the cities and encouraged population growth, but it finally reversed this course in the 1980s. A general trend is revealed in these histories: in fits and starts, large numbers of people moved, taking with them the identities and values that had been shaped by family traditions. As total war, revolution, and military dictatorships continued to bombard these families, personal obligations and corresponding life choices have often inspired resilience and enabled the survivors to thrive. At the same time, the personal liberation from patriarchal authority that has gradually unfolded for women, sometimes by their own agency and sometimes by conditions imposed on them, has not erased the power of family ties or the gendered hierarchy in work and politics.

It was clear from the outset that markets and mobility would challenge the social order at its core. In Meiji-era Japan, the slogan "good wife, wise mother" became the standard to which educated women should judge themselves. The slogan resonated with the Western ideal of the modern bourgeois, or middle-class, family and traditional Confucian ideals of feminine virtue. Many Chinese women who were educated by Christian missionaries or in Japan or America before the 1920s understood the ideal as consistent with the goal of national liberation. Women's liberation would not come first. For less fortunate villagers and urban working women, finding work might involve breaking away from family control or even from ideals of virtue by working as waitresses, entertainers, or prostitutes, or it could involve following family orders to work as maids or in factories. In either case, women's social roles and status would both change.

After World War II, the American-imposed constitution changed the legal status of women in Japan, while socialist legislation gave women total equality in China and North Korea. In contrast, postcolonial South Korean family law restored precolonial patriarchal authority while military dictatorship delayed the change in legal status for women until the 1990s. Changing the legal status in Japan provided new opportunities and new protections for women, but it could hardly transform deeply rooted gender biases or the social structures in which families were at the core. As the LDP developed Japan's new economic policy, it staved off labor unrest by maintaining nearly full employment while leveling wages and limiting competition in the labor market. Women set off to work in positions that were mostly gender-specific with little chance for advancement. In socialist China, where there was no market at all, men and women workers in the cities whose households (*hukou*) were permanently attached to production units were equally secure and equally immobile. Eighty percent of the population, which grew to one billion by 1982, lived in rural households that were attached to collectives. Under this radical socialist restructuring, women were said to "hold up half the sky." Still, with work, food, and housing allocated to households and women moving from a father's household to a husband's at marriage, the opportunity to change gender biases in rural family and village life was limited.

Since the 1980s, China's decollectivization, market reforms, and rapidly increasing demand for urban labor has made much of the economy dependent on some 200 million migrant workers who remain attached to rural households. This demographic flux and 35 years of strictly enforced birth control policy have altered the balance within families and between urban and rural society, but the *hukou* system continues to identify rural households with native villages and to determine where individuals may receive social benefits. Until this changes the impact of market reforms on gender bias may remain unclear. In Japan an increasing demand for educated workers in the 1980s did little to change the gender balance in the workplace, while the increasingly affluent younger generation increasingly delayed marriage and limited childbirths. By 2013 the population of Japan, Korea, and China combined was about 1.44 billion, 3.3 times that of 1895, but the fertility rate across the region was the lowest in the world. This story continues to unfold.

Cultural History

The Tonghak Uprising of 1894, with which this chapter began, also serves as a window into one more set of issues in the history of modern East Asia—the complex tapestry of religious life, popular culture, and political change. Unlike the European story, with its struggle between sacred and secular, or church and state, in East Asia, before the impact of modern change was felt, popular beliefs and practices tempered, and were tempered by, social and political institutions without drawing this sort of line. In Japan under the Tokugawa regime, Buddhist temples had offered prayers and performed funeral rites for families in their communities while keeping population registers that determined the distribution of taxes and duties levied by the local daimyo and their military overlords, the shoguns. Shinto priests had mediated between the populace and the spirits that inhabited the landscape around them. Buddhism thrived in Korea as well, while local shamans mediated with the spirits, but in Korea, as in China, the central bureaucracy controlled taxes and other duties with the loyal cooperation of local elite families who were bound by Confucian obligations to the ruler. In China the system of Confucian education and official recruitment by examination had tolerated popular beliefs in the earthly interventions of gods, ghosts, and ancestors from a distance, allowing rulers to officially recognize local shrines and temples, with their diverse and colorful array of deities, spirit mediums, seasonal fairs, and ritual processions.

Folk temple rituals were usually performed by professional Daoist priests, while classical Confucian rituals prevailed in family affairs. In Chinese religious life, Buddhism provided relief for individuals through prayer, the chanting of scriptures, and personal acts of selfless compassion.

Christianity had entered this world with Jesuit missionaries in the sixteenth century. Despite some success in converting local people, Christianity was generally attacked by the ruling authorities as destabilizing, and the papal authorities rejected Jesuit proposals to compromise. In the nineteenth century the new wave of Protestant missionaries, while devoted to saving souls, also brought modern education and medicine as well as new notions of personal and civic virtue. Progressives across East Asia saw that Christianity could be a useful tool for self-strengthening and nation-building on Western models, but as patriots they also saw that it could threaten the cultural integrity on which modern nation-states depended for cohesion. At the same time, however, local communities could find conversion helpful in seeking privileges or protection as the old states began to fail. Alternatively they could form new alliances against native Christians with the cohesion provided by popular religious traditions and beliefs. The Tonghak Uprising in 1894 was one example of how changing religious life, popular culture, and politics could have serious and unpredictable consequences. The Boxer Rebellion six years later was another.

The 1889 Meiji constitution reflected the oligarchs' awareness of the problem, which had been openly discussed in the new print media: should Japan be identifying with Asia or with the West? Needing to ensure cultural coherence and at the same time show the world that theirs was a nation that adhered to the rule of law, the oligarchs and their parliamentary advisors established freedom of religious choice as a private matter. At the same time, in public life, the constitution demanded absolute loyalty to the emperor as a sovereign of divine descent. Under these rules, Buddhism, Shinto, Christianity, and an array of syncretic "new religions" of Japan survived within their own separate spheres into the postwar era, reforming their practices to suit the demands of a sometimes blindly loyal and sometimes alienated and despondent populace. Over the decades, as peace endured and the economy thrived, these reformed and newly invented religions of Japan came to fill important cultural roles.

In colonized Korea and Taiwan, where loyalty to the emperor of Japan was strictly enforced but never a matter of faith, Christianity was welcomed by many. In recent decades Christian beliefs and practices have unfolded there in ways that are remarkably parallel to those of modern Buddhism. The ethics and personal regimens are similar, for youth groups proliferate in each, and believers participate in similar charitable and relief activities. In China, on the other hand, early twentieth-century reformers inherited the classical Confucian distaste for "superstitious" beliefs and what they considered exploitation of uneducated people by monks, priests, and shamans. Revolutionaries then blamed Confucian aloofness for the ubiquitous spread of folk beliefs and practices that kept the people ignorant, poor, and divided. Some, especially those who attended mission schools or studied abroad in Europe and America, turned to the universality of Christian belief in the hope that over time it could help to build a popular base for coherence around civic virtue. Others turned to the utopian promise of communism, rejecting all religions as exploitative elaborations of superstition and ignorance. Within the Communist Party under Mao, faith in the communist vision resonated remarkably with the classical Confucian vision of one common, peaceful world, while practices of self-criticism and compliance with shared social goals paralleled Confucian methods of self-cultivation. Just as remarkably, popular beliefs and practices, challenged but not eliminated by socialist education and reform, have emerged in all their diversity to temper the demands of a rapidly changing social world. In China today they exist and interact with a swiftly growing Christian community in defiance of the law but in concert with the official will to foster harmony, encourage private involvement in social services, and counter bureaucratic corruption.

One piece of the cultural story remains to be told. Before the arrival of telegraphic communication, radio, film, and the commercial press, popular culture throughout East Asia unfolded in urban theaters, teahouses, elite homes, temple fairs, and on the streets around itinerant storytellers. Comic and tragic characters—including military commanders, civil officials, noble ladies, scholars, merchants, courtesans, monks, beggars, and charlatans—came to life in these venues. The stories and songs drew heavily on long-familiar themes of martial virtue, scholarly arrogance, romance, greed, and ghostly retribution. Some cultural clues and deeper meanings were shared across East Asia as part of a common literary heritage. Others were strictly local or specific to a native regime. But as popular media, often with religious overtones, they all reinforced fundamental moral and social values with their inherent critique of the abuses of wealth and power. By the 1930s, new technologies and new media had brought dramatic changes to popular culture throughout East Asia. Commercial newspapers and pulp fiction thrived. The music, drama, and film worlds of Shanghai, Seoul, and Tokyo were inextricably linked to those of Singapore, Bombay, London, and New York. Global popular culture, emerging from Europe and America, was the lifeblood of the new East Asian middle class, while authoritarian regimes censored the content and adapted the forms to serve as propaganda. What, then, has happened to the old popular culture, and what is the place of global culture in East Asia today?

Everywhere in East Asia, as in other parts of the world over the past few decades, nostalgia has played a role in reviving cultural traditions, preserving cultural heritage, and tempering the social and economic effects of globalization. While religious revitalization, quite apart from nostalgia, has led to some renewal of popular art forms, government sponsorship, tourism, new opportunities for creative exploration, and the expansion of communication and curiosity in the digital age have had other unexpected effects. Popular culture is now truly global, and the influences within it are multidirectional. At the same time, as heritage sites proliferate, performers of traditional popular arts reappear in certain venues. The view from 2013 is dramatically and unexpectedly different from that of 50 years ago, and the story will change as the future unfolds.

The East Asian World Today

In the realm of international relations, this brief history may not help in answering the pressing questions about the future that planners and experts want to raise. But it will end with the questions that only the history itself can bring to the fore. To what degree have the legacies of Western expansion dominated international relations in this region? To what degree do these legacies determine what is happening now? In 2013, China and Japan were facing off over a string of uninhabited rocky islets north of Taiwan. Beneath the sea lies oil, but on the surface the issue is unsettled claims from the end of the war, some 70 years ago. While the status of Taiwan remains undefined in terms of international law, this legacy of Japanese colonization and postwar American intervention has not prevented an increasingly cordial flow of people, money, and goods across the Taiwan straits. Some native Taiwanese call themselves Chinese, with natural affinities to the speakers of their common southern Fujian dialect, while some feel their Taiwanese roots define them differently.

In 1997, Hong Kong reverted to Chinese sovereignty to begin a 50-year trial as China's only "Special Autonomous Region." Many people there feel a natural affinity with other speakers of the Cantonese dialect but distinguish between Chinese sovereignty and the legitimacy of the CCP. Tibet and Xinjiang, sparsely populated by people whose cultures and languages have deep roots beyond traditional Chinese ones, are defined by China as "Autonomous Regions" with special administrative characteristics. China's claims have historical bases, but autonomy and incumbent rights are not honored, while governments in exile make alternative claims to sovereignty. A new, troubling stream of ethnically and politically charged suicides among Tibetans continues. "Charter 08" proposed autonomous status for these regions in a new Chinese federation. Are legacies of the pre-Western East Asian order, with one large, central power and autonomous but respectful peripheral states, at all visible in this changing world?

Much will depend on how the states and the people who are peripheral to China continue in their developing relations with the state and the people in China. In Japan, the renewal of LDP strength since 2003 and the vociferousness of right-wing conservatives have led to tensions with China, but the correctives that have emerged from the very different civil societies of both countries have minimized the effects. Leading the LDP resurgence as Japan's popular prime minister from 2001 to 2006, Koizumi Junichiro deployed Self-Defense Forces units to Iraq and made much of his visits to the Yasukuni Shrine, where wartime Japanese soldiers are honored without reference to their role in China and Korea. Chinese reactions were especially strident, but with Koizumi's retirement the tensions have lessened. Currently, trade, tourism, and popular culture flow freely across the region despite religious, linguistic, and administrative boundaries. As the one remaining superpower, the United States continues to defend its interests and to claim a role in the defense of South Korea, Japan, and Taiwan. Yet its role increasingly appears peripheral as well.

In the early 2010s, only the Korean Workers' Party and the people of North Korea seem to lack a clear path for integrating into this changing East Asian world.

Historical narratives never really end. After all, they are shaped by a present beyond which one cannot clearly see. This particular narrative began in 1894, with the questions raised when a religious sect rose in rebellion against the Korean king and the progressive reformers who advised him. It ends with the questions raised by the North Korean predicament today. The story of change in East Asia from then to now has been bumpy, diverse, dramatic, and never predictable. The story itself will change as the future unfolds.

References and Further Research

Armstrong, Charles K., Gilbert Rozman, and Samuel Kim, eds. 2006. *Korea at the Center: Dynamics of Regionalism in Northeast Asia*. Armonk, NY: M. E. Sharpe.

Conrad, Sebastian, and Prasenjit Duara. 2013. *Viewing Regionalisms from East Asia*. Regions and Regionalisms in the Modern World. Washington, DC: American Historical Association.

Cumings, Bruce. 2005. *Korea's Place in the Sun: A Modern History*. Updated ed. New York: W. W. Norton.

Dower, John. 1999. *Embracing Defeat: Japan in the Wake of World War II*. New York: W. W. Norton.

Gordon, Andrew. 2009. *A Modern History of Japan: From Tokugawa Times to the Present*. 2nd ed. New York: Oxford University Press.

Lipman, Jonathan, Barbara Molony, and Michael Robinson. 2011. *Modern East Asia: An Integrated History*. Boston: Pearson.

Perry, Elizabeth J., and Mark Selden, eds. 2010. *Chinese Society: Change, Conflict, and Resistance*. 3rd ed. New York: Routledge.

Pruitt, Ida. 2011. *A Daughter of Han: The Autobiography of a Chinese Working Woman*. Eastford, CT: Martino Fine Books.

Schell, Orville, and John Delury. 2013. *Wealth and Power: China's Long March to the Twenty-First Century*. New York: Random House.

Spence, Jonathan D. 2012. *The Search for Modern China*. 3rd ed. New York: W. W. Norton.

4

East Asian Languages

ANNE PRESCOTT

Language plays a large role in the formation of national identity, and learning a language offers unique insights into the history and culture of the people who speak it. Languages are constantly changing, and by examining the changes a language undergoes one can also learn about changes within the society that speaks that language. In recent years the technologies enabling globalization, particularly the Internet, have added new and interesting developments to languages and their roles in culture, trade, and beyond.

Much as Latin was once the common language of Europe, for hundreds of years people in China, Japan, and Korea (and until the late nineteenth century, Vietnam) have used Chinese characters for written communication. This common written language united a vast geographical region and enhanced trade and cultural exchange. The spoken languages of these countries, however, are unique and unrelated. Structural differences in the languages meant that when Korea and Japan adopted the Chinese writing system it had to be modified to accommodate the unique aspects of their specific languages.

East Asian languages have another commonality that can provide insight into how the societies are structured. The primary social identifier for speakers of Chinese, Japanese, and Korean is the family unit rather than the individual. In language this is expressed in name order: the family name precedes the given name, and while the family name may be used alone, the given name is normally not used alone except within the family and with close friends. Titles (the equivalents of Professor, Dr., Mr., Mrs., etc.) are also commonly attached at the end of names (and are sometimes used instead of names) to indicate relationships between a speaker and listener, or to indicate the subject of the conversation. This linguistic practice illustrates the fact that the family unit is more important than the individual, and that hierarchical relationships between people, based on age, profession, education, social status, and kinship ties, are also important social components of language.

Chinese Characters

The oldest known examples of Chinese writing are found on ox bones and turtle shells, called oracle bones, which were used in fortune-telling. Questions about the

This sign in Japan says "welcome" in Japanese (top), English, Korean *hanggeul* (middle right), simplified Chinese characters (bottom left), and traditional Chinese characters (bottom right). *(Photo courtesy of Jenny Matsui)*

weather, crop planting, military campaigns, future prospects for the royal family, and other important matters were carved onto the bones using a special script. The bones were heated until they cracked, and fortunetellers used the patterns created by the cracks to make predictions. Their prophecies were then carved on the same bones. The majority of oracle bones with carved writing still in existence are thought to date from the end of the Shang Dynasty, around 1200–1050 BCE.

Chinese characters (called *hanzi* in Chinese, *kanji* in Japanese, and *hanja* in Korean) are broadly divided into two types: pictographs and ideographs. Pictographs are stylized "pictures" of the objects they represent, such as sun (日), mountain (山), and person (人). Ideographs represent an abstract idea, such as up (上), down (下), or one (一). Aggregate compounds combine one or more simple characters. A tree (木) behind the sun (日) means east (東), and two trees become a forest (林). Characters are composed of parts, called radicals, which often offer hints about the meaning. Characters with the sun radical (日) often have something to do with the sun or light: 明 (light, bright), 旭 (the morning/rising sun), 早 (early, fast), and 昭 (bright, clear).

Hanzi have been altered and simplified over the years. Today the People's Republic of China (PRC) uses simplified characters, which were developed in the mid-twentieth century to increase literacy. Traditional characters continue to be used in Taiwan, Hong Kong, and many immigrant communities throughout the world.

Chinese characters are written with individual lines, or strokes. The order in which the strokes are written is not random and must be memorized. In general, left to right strokes are written first, then top to bottom strokes. Radicals are usually written as a single entity on the side, at the top, or on the bottom of an aggregate character.

Table 4.1

Examples of Traditional and Simplified Chinese Characters

English meaning	Traditional	Simplified
east	東	东
electric	電	电
father*	父	父
mother*	母	母
music	音樂	音乐
parent	親	亲
talk	話	话
telephone	電話	电话
university	大學	大学

*These are the same in each system.

Source: Compiled by the author.

Chinese character dictionaries can be organized in one of two ways. The first is by the number of strokes (separate lines) in the character. For example, the character 早, meaning "early," is written using six strokes, so in this type of dictionary one would search through a list of all the characters written with six strokes, of which there may be hundreds. The second type of dictionary is organized according to the radical, the primary building block of the character. The character 早 is composed of the four-stroke radical for sun (日) plus two strokes. To look it up by the radical, one first goes to the section for four-stroke radicals, finds the sun radical, and then searches within the section for the sun radical plus two strokes.

The website Chinese Characters and Culture (www.Zhongwen.com) is a great tool for learning Chinese characters.

Chinese can be romanized (written using the Latin alphabet) as well. Several systems of romanization have been developed that use the alphabet to approximate the pronunciation of Chinese. The official romanization today in the PRC and Taiwan is *hanyu pinyin* (usually simply referred to as Pinyin), which was developed in the 1950s. Prior to 2009, Taiwan used the Wade-Giles system of romanization, which was developed in the 1860s by Thomas Francis Wade and revised in 1912 by Herbert Allen Giles. Resources published in Taiwan prior to 2009, as well as most Taiwanese personal names, are romanized using this system. In Taiwan a non-Latin transcription system of 37 phonetic symbols and four tone marks, called *zhuyin fuhao* (more commonly referred to as "bopomofo," the first phonetic syllables in *zhuyin*) is also used to transcribe Chinese. It was introduced in Taiwan in 1910 and is still widely used to teach Chinese and for computer input.

Table 4.2

Names of Famous People and Places Romanized in Wade-Giles and Pinyin

Wade-Giles	Pinyin
Mao Tse-tung	Mao Zedong
Chou En-lai	Zhou Enlai
Teng Hsiao-p'ing	Deng Xiaoping
Sinkiang	Xinjiang
Chungching	Chongqing
Pei-ching	Beijing

Source: Compiled by author.

Computer input is done on a standard alpha-numeric keyboard with the operating system configured for Chinese, either traditional or simplified characters, using Pinyin or another system of romanization. Once a word is entered on the keyboard, all of the characters that are pronounced with that sound appear in a dropdown menu, and the user selects the appropriate character. For example, if the user enters "ma," the dropdown menu presents more than 20 choices from which to select. If the user wishes to input the "ma" meaning "mother," she selects 母. If the intended meaning is horse, she selects 馬. The system typically lists the characters from most to least frequently used, making it fairly fast and easy to find the character that represents the romanization entered.

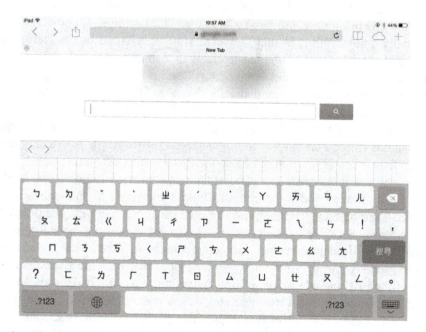

Screenshot of a *Zhuyin fuhao* (Bopomofo) computer keyboard.

Screenshot of a computer keyboard with *ni hao* (hello) in Pinyin and the various possibilities that appear. The first choice (on the far left) is *ni hao*; the other single characters are all read as *ni*.

Spoken Chinese

People in the PRC and Taiwan speak not only Chinese, in one of its many dialects, but other languages as well. In fact, there are several hundred dialects or languages written not only in Chinese, but also in Arabic and Latin scripts. Some of the dialects are mutually unintelligible, in that they cannot be understood by speakers of other Chinese dialects. This should not be surprising in a country with 1.35 billion people. Chinese is also spoken in other countries in Southeast Asia, including Singapore, Myanmar (Burma), Malaysia, and the Philippines. There are also large Chinese-speaking communities in Canada, England, and the United States.

What we call "Mandarin Chinese" is based on the Beijing dialect of spoken Chinese and is called *Putonghua* (common speech) or *Hanyu* (Chinese language) in Chinese. This is the official language in the PRC (with a few exceptions), and the one that is taught in schools. The official language policy in Hong Kong is biliterate (the ability to read and write in both Chinese and English), and trilingual, with Mandarin, Cantonese, and English the accepted spoken languages. The official languages in Macau SAR are Cantonese and Portuguese. The Autonomous Regions also have additional official languages, including Tibetan in Tibet, Mongolian in Inner Mongolia, and Uyghur in Xinjiang. Other languages that are widely spoken in some regions of the PRC include Korean, Vietnamese, and Russian. In Taiwan, Mandarin is the official language, but Taiwanese Hokkien is widely spoken.

Mandarin Chinese and the other Chinese dialects are tonal languages, and the tone (pitch) gives syllables their specific meanings. Mandarin has four tones: tone one is

Coca-Cola in simplified Chinese (read from the bottom of the can to the top). *(Photo courtesy of Jenny Matsui)*

high, tone two is rising (the pitch starts low and ascends), tone three falls and then rises, and tone four is falling (starts high and descends). The most famous example of the difference tone makes in understanding Chinese is the syllable "ma." When spoken with tone one, it means mother; with tone two, it means hemp; with tone three, horse; and with tone four, scold. The Cantonese spoken in Hong Kong has six tones, but in nearby Guangzhou it has seven. In a language where tone is so important, it is easy to see how different dialects might be mutually unintelligible.

Chinese contains foreign loanwords that have been adopted from various countries at different times in history. These words are written with Chinese characters that are usually chosen for their pronunciation rather than their literal meaning. However, meaning plays a part in choosing the character. For example, Coca-Cola is 口可口樂, meaning, roughly, "to allow the mouth to rejoice."

Written Chinese serves as a linguistic unifier in a country with so many dialects. Nationally broadcast TV programs are subtitled in Chinese characters, which enable all Chinese, regardless of the dialect they speak, to understand what is said. This characteristic of Chinese television also makes it a very useful tool for students of Chinese language.

Written Korean

Koreans also have a long history of writing with Chinese characters, which they call *hanja*. Prior to modern times, only the ruling elite learned to write. In 1446 King Sejong oversaw the creation of a phonetic alphabet called *hanggeul* (or *hangul*), which consists of 14 basic consonants and ten basic vowel sounds, which can be combined for an additional 11 vowels. The 24 basic vowels and consonants are grouped together in syllabic blocks. Each block always includes at least one vowel and one consonant, and each may contain up to five vowels and consonants. For example, the one-syllable word *mal* (말), meaning "language," consists of three parts: ㅁ (m), ㅏ (a) and ㄹ (l). The placement of the individual *hanggeul* syllables within a block are governed by specific rules, with some *hanggeul* considered to be "horizontal" and some "vertical" in terms of their placement within the block. Just as there is a correct stroke order for writing Chinese characters, there is an accepted order for writing the strokes for a given *hanggeul*—in general, top to bottom and left to right. The blocks are written left to right horizontally across the page, or top to bottom and right to left vertically on the page. There is a specific "dictionary order" for *hanggeul*, which corresponds to alphabetical order in English.

With only 24 basic *hanggeul* characters, the written language adapted relatively easily to the computer keyboard. Korean-language keyboard overlays for use on a standard English-language keyboard can easily be found by searching the Internet. With the Korean language option enabled, the user simply inputs the desired *hanggeul* character as it appears on the keyboard overlay.

With the creation of *hanggeul*, even commoners could learn to read, but *hanja* continued to be used by educated people until the late nineteenth and early twentieth centuries. *Hanggeul* was adopted for use in official documents in 1894, in elementary school textbooks in 1895, and it was used in newspapers for the first time in 1896. Until then, literature and official documents did not use *hanggeul* except for native Korean words, so all educated people learned to read and write both *hanja* and

Screenshot of a Korean *hanggeul* computer keyboard.

hanggeul. Today, North Korea uses *hanggeul* exclusively, and *hanja* is in limited use in South Korea. South Korean newspapers use *hanja* in parentheses to clarify abbreviations or homonyms. For example, all of the following words are pronounced *sudo* in Korean: 囚徒 (prisoner), 水稲 (wetland rice), 修道 (spiritual discipline), 首都 (capital city), 水道 (drain, rivers). Using *hanja* assists the reader in understanding which "*sudo*" is the one intended.

Hanja are also used in academic writing and novels by older authors, who are more likely to have learned *hanja*. Most family and given names can be written in *hanja* (e.g., Kim金) but are ordinarily written in *hanggeul* (e.g., Kim김). Some parents give their children "pure" Korean names, which are never written in *hanja*.

Korean has been romanized using several systems, including Yale, McCune-Reischauer (MR), and the recently approved (2000) South Korean government standardized system called Revised Romanization of Korean (RR). All official documents, signs, and so on in South Korea must now use the RR system. One of the benefits of RR, the system generally followed in this book, is that it does not include diacritical (or accent) marks and does not use apostrophes, which makes it easier for computer use.

Spoken Korean

Korean is not only spoken in North Korea and South Korea, but it is also one of the official languages in the Yanbian Korean Autonomous Prefecture in China. Some Korean residents of Japan, descendants of those who were brought forcibly to Japan during its colonial rule of Korea, still speak Korean today, as do Koreans in diaspora communities. Most scholars consider the Korean language to be unrelated to any other language in the world, while a few think that it belongs in the Altaic language family, along with Turkic and Mongolic languages. There are regional dialects within Korea, but for the most part speakers of one dialect can understand speakers of another. The standard spoken language in South Korea is the Seoul dialect, and in North Korea it is the Pyongyang dialect.

The Korean language reflects the relationships between the speaker or writer, the audience she is addressing, and the person she is discussing. To show respect, speakers and writers use honorifics, which include special nouns and different verb endings, when talking or writing about people of a higher social status than they are, such as older people, employers, teachers, and customers. Contemporary spoken and written Korean uses a simpler system of honorifics, and young people are less likely to adhere strictly to the traditional levels of formality. Nonetheless, honorifics remain an important part of the language and culture of Korea.

The online *Korean Multimedia Dictionary* (http://www.indiana.edu/~koreanrs/kordic.html) is an excellent resource for learning more about how to speak Korean.

Spoken Korean uses words with Chinese origins, native Korean vocabulary, and, increasingly, loanwords from English. Loanwords use a pronunciation that is easier for Korean speakers. In principle, one-syllable words become two syllables, with the second syllable ending in "u." For example, box becomes *bakseu*, and hamburger, *haembeogeo*. The meanings of loanwords may also be different from the original English. The word *meeting* (using a Korean pronunciation) means a blind date.

Since the Korean War, differences in pronunciation, verb inflection, and vocabulary have developed between the spoken languages in North Korea and South Korea. While loanwords in South Korea are likely to come from English, loanwords in North Korea often come from Russian. Even when the same English loanword is used in both North and South, it may be pronounced differently because of dialectical alterations. North Koreans are more likely to create a "native" word using Korean language roots and endings rather than borrowing from a foreign language. There are also transformations due to differences in the political system and social structure.

Written Japanese

Japanese is usually written with a combination of Chinese characters, called *kanji* (adopted in Japan from China around the fourth century CE), and one of two *kana* syllabaries, *hiragana* and *katakana*. Each *hiragana* and *katakana* character represents one spoken syllable, with a total of 48 *kana* in each system (five vowels, one singular consonant, and 42 combinations of a consonant followed by a vowel). Japanese can be written without *kanji*, and any word can be written in either *hiragana* or *katakana*, but it is more difficult to read without *kanji*, because there are many homonyms. Historically, it was more socially acceptable for women to write in *kana*, and the famous novel *Tale of Genji*, by Lady Murasaki, was written in *kana*. Today *hiragana* is used to write native Japanese words and grammatical particles (syllables that have no meaning other than to mark parts of speech, such as the subject or object), and *katakana* is used to write foreign loanwords (called *gairaigo*), including personal names (e.g., Obama オバマ), location names (e.g., Massachusetts マサチューセッツ), and other words adopted from foreign languages that have become a part of the Japanese language, sometimes replacing the native Japanese word (if any). *Katakana* may also be used as a visually distinctive way to emphasize native Japanese words, particularly in advertising.

Each *kanji* typically has at least two readings (ways to pronounce it). The *on-yomi* is the Chinese pronunciation of the character as perceived by the Japanese when *kanji* were imported into Japan. The *kun-yomi* is the indigenous Japanese pronunciation of the word. For example, the *on-yomi* for 水 (water) is *sui* (*shui* in Chinese) and the *kun-yomi* is *mizu*. The *on-yomi* is often (but not always) used when two characters are combined: *suisha* (水車) is water wheel. Some characters, particularly names of places and people, have unusual readings that must simply be memorized. Today, some characters are read using a better-known foreign language word. For example, even though there is a way to pronounce 頁(meaning "page," as in page in a book) in Japanese (*ketsu*) it is nearly always read as *peiji* (page) today.

Japanese language learners find that online dictionaries such as *Denshi Jisho* (http://jisho.org/) facilitate learning.

There are several romanization systems used in Japan. The three most common are modified Hepburn, Kunrei-shiki, and Nihon-shiki. The Hepburn system is the most widely used by English speakers. All Japanese elementary school students learn the Roman (Western) alphabet, and romanization is used with computers, which recognize any of the romanization systems and immediately transliterate them into *kana* and/or *kanji* as appropriate, in the same way as described earlier for inputting Chinese language.

Table 4.3

Examples of Written Japanese

Kanji	水	水車	水道	下水道
Hiragana	みず (すい)*	すいしゃ	すいどう	げすいどう
Katakana	ミズ(スイ)*	スイシャ	スイドウ	ゲスイドウ
Romanization	*mizu (sui)**	*suisha*	*suidou*	*gesuidou*
English meaning	water	waterwheel	water supply	drain

*on-yomi (kun-yomi)

Source: Compiled by author.

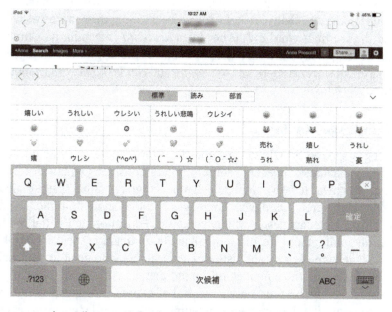

Japanese computer input (in *romaji*) for the word *ureshii* (happy). In addition to the choices using *kanji* (嬉しい), *hiragana* (うれしい), and *katakana* (「ウレシイ 」), many emoticons also appear.

Spoken Japanese

The Japanese language reflects relationships between people, and like Korean, the language includes honorifics, which are used when talking or writing about people who are of a higher or lower social status than the speaker or writer. For example, younger siblings do not use older siblings' given names, but address them as *onii-san* (older brother) or *onee-san* (older sister). Older siblings typically address their younger brothers and sisters by their given names, but omit the honorific "san" (roughly equivalent to Mr., Mrs. or Ms.), which is attached to names by people from outside the family. Television news typically uses neutral language, with a few exceptions—the most noticeable, perhaps, is in stories about the emperor and his family, when honorifics are used.

Japan is a mountainous country, and in the past the high peaks and deep, narrow valleys made visits to neighboring towns difficult. This contributed to the development of many regional dialects. Since 1945 the Tokyo dialect has been the standard spoken language and is taught in schools and used in broadcast media. Most dialects can be understood fairly well by people from outside the region where it is spoken, but some are more challenging. Perhaps the most widely recognized dialect is the Kansai dialect (*Kansai-ben*), which is spoken in the Kansai region of western Japan. Public figures often speak *Kansai-ben* when they want to emphasize their identity with that region. Since the March 11, 2011, Triple Disaster (earthquake, tsunami, and nuclear accident), Tohoku dialects have become an important tool in maintaining awareness of the continuing needs in that region. Similarly, dialects are used in catchphrases for the tourism industry.

As with Korean, the pronunciation of loanwords (*gairaigo*) must be adapted to fit the Japanese language. For example, hamburger becomes *hanbāgā* (a dash [macron] over a vowel indicates that it is held for twice the length of a vowel without the dash), and the German word *arbeit* becomes *arubaito* (meaning part-time work in Japanese). Some *gairaigo* are shortened versions of the original word. *Depātomento sutoa* (department store) is shortened to *depāto*, and *rimōto kontororu* (remote control) is simplified as *rimokon*.

Other Languages in Japan

The languages spoken by Okinawans and the Ainu people of Hokkaido cannot be understood by Japanese speakers. Some scholars consider Okinawan (the primary language of Okinawa) to be a completely distinct language rather than a dialect. There are also several different Okinawan languages and dialects within the islands of the prefecture. Although Japanese is the language of education and is the primary language used in public, there are still more than 900,000 native speakers of Okinawan, and it is the language used by activists and entertainers who want to emphasize their heritage. In Hokkaido, the language of the indigenous Ainu is linguistically distinct from Japanese. Today there are only a handful of native Ainu speakers left, but there are efforts to revitalize the language, including radio Ainu language courses for the general public.

References and Further Research

Chang, Raymond, and Margaret Scrogin Chang. 1978. *Speaking of Chinese: A Cultural History of the Chinese Language*. New York: W.W. Norton.

Frellesvig, Bjarke. 2011. *A History of the Japanese Language*. Cambridge: Cambridge University Press.

Kindaichi Haruhiko. 1978. *The Japanese Language*. Translated by Umeyo Hirano. Rutland, VT: Charles E. Tuttle.

Lee, Ki-Moon, and S. Robert Ramsey. 2011. *A History of the Korean Language*. Cambridge: Cambridge University Press.

Stanford Program on International and Cross-Cultural Communication (SPICE). 1995. *Demystifying the Chinese Language*. Stanford, CA: Stanford Program on International and Cross-Cultural Communication.

There are many no- or low-cost apps available for mobile devices that teach how to speak Chinese, Japanese, or Korean, and how to write Chinese characters, Japanese *katakana* and *hiragana*, or Korean *hanggeul*. Dictionaries for all levels of language learners are also available online and for mobile devices.

PART THREE

The Global Context

5

East Asian Economies in a Globalizing World

Thomas Gottschang

Although the countries of East Asia are linked by strong cultural and historical threads, wide differences in their economies and income levels exist. By 2013 the three major East Asian economies, those of China, Japan, and South Korea, had reached distinctly different levels of economic development.

For the purpose of this discussion, "economic development" refers to improvement in an economy's ability to provide the goods and services that allow the people of the country to meet their needs and achieve their desires. As reflected in gross domestic product (GDP) per person (per capita), measured in comparable prices (purchasing power parity, or PPP), Japan is near the top of the development ladder and has one of the highest standards of living in the world. Its overall economy is third in the world in size, despite having a population of only 127 million. China has the world's second largest economy, after that of the United States, but, with a population of over 1.3 billion people, is still a relatively poor country in terms of individual income levels, despite its massive size and recent high rate of growth. South Korea's economy is only around one seventh as large as China's in absolute size, but its per capita GDP is nearly as high as Japan's and its population has the living standards of a fully industrialized country.

Table 5.1

Statistical Portrait of East Asia's Major Economies

	Population, 2014 est. (million)	Median age, 2014 est.	GDP per capita, 2013 (PPP)
China	1,349	36	$9,100
Hong Kong	7	45	$50,700
Japan	127	46	$36,200
South Korea	49	40	$32,400
North Korea	25	33	$1,800*
Taiwan	23	39	$38,500
Vietnam	92	29	$3,500

* North Korea GDP per capita estimate is for 2011.

Source: Compiled from the CIA *World Factbook*, https://www.cia.gov/library/publications/the-world-factbook/, accessed June 30, 2014.

China

China's rapidly growing economy is the result of over 100 years of turmoil. Before the establishment of the People's Republic in 1949, most of the economy was pre-modern, with the great majority of the population living in the countryside and working in non-mechanized agriculture. Some industry had been established in major urban centers, particularly Shanghai, Hong Kong, Wuhan, Tianjin, Beijing, and the Northeast (Manchuria), but modern growth had been hindered by years of warlord conflict from 1916 to 1927, by Japanese invasion and war from 1932 to 1945, and by the civil war that lasted from 1945 to 1949.

Following the defeat of the Nationalist (Guomindang) forces under Chiang Kai-shek (Zhang Jieshi) and their retreat to the island refuge of Taiwan, the Communist government, under the leadership of Chairman Mao Zedong, began the effort to create a new economic system that would be modern, efficient, and socialist. After stabilizing the war-ravaged economy in the early 1950s, the new government adopted a centrally planned economic system similar to that of the Soviet Union. Nearly all industry was government owned and controlled, as were the banking system and the country's natural resources, communications, and transportation. By the 1960s, agriculture was organized in large collectives called communes, which ranged in size from around 15,000 to 30,000 people. Each commune was composed of several production brigades, each the size of a small town, and each production brigade was made up of several production teams, which were usually based on pre-socialist villages.

Farm families earned income working in collective fields and workshops, and they were each allotted a small private plot where they could grow their own produce and raise chickens or pigs. Under the Maoist economy, joblessness, homelessness, and class privilege were largely eliminated. The rigidities of the planning system,

Shanghai, China, 2006. *(Photo by Jakob Montrasio, https://www.flickr.com/photos/yakobusan/ 278128338/, licensed under Creative Commons Attribution 2.0 Generic [https://creativecommons. org/licenses/by/2.0/])*

however, coupled with the nearly complete absence of market institutions, restrained specialization, investment, and innovation, resulting in a very slowly rising level of economic output per person after the 1950s.

Two major upheavals interrupted development in this period and raised doubts about the country's trajectory in the minds of many Chinese people. The Great Leap Forward of 1958–1961 was a hugely ambitious restructuring of the economy that was intended to propel it forward into modernity, but instead resulted in declining output and widespread famine. The Great Proletarian Cultural Revolution of 1966–1976 (often shortened to the Cultural Revolution) was Mao's final effort to eliminate social stratification. He called on the youth of the country to attack and reject the vestiges of the old society, setting off years of chaos and violence—particularly in the cities—with stability returning only after his death in 1976.

The website Chinese Posters: Propaganda, Politics, History, Art (http://chinese-posters.net) features Chinese poster art, including images from the Great Leap Forward and the Cultural Revolution, from the collections of the International Institute of Social History (IISH), in Amsterdam, and Stefan R. Landsberger, a professor at the University of Amsterdam and Leiden University.

The centrally planned economic system that was developed under Mao was largely successful at stabilizing the economy, virtually eliminating unemployment, providing the basic necessities of life, and creating the foundations of modern industry. By the time of Mao's death, however, many leaders realized that the economy showed little growth on a per capita basis, and that China's standard of living was falling far behind those of several of its neighbors, including Japan, Taiwan, and Hong Kong. Under the leadership of Deng Xiaoping, the Chinese Communist Party decided in December 1978 to allow rural collective units to experiment with market-based reforms, including a return to family farming, greatly increased access to markets, and higher prices for agricultural products. By the early 1980s these reforms had spread throughout most of the countryside and had dramatically increased the quantity, quality, and variety of food available to the Chinese population.

Bloomberg's web page "China's Economy" (http://topics.bloomberg.com/china's-economy) offers links to articles, photos, videos, and interviews devoted to economic news for China.

Following this initial success, market-based reforms were introduced in most aspects of the economy, including foreign trade and investment. The slogan of the time was *gaige, kaifa,* or "reform and opening." As markets became available for food, clothing, and housing, barriers to internal migration were largely removed, setting the stage for an enormous flood of workers moving from the low-income countryside to the higher wages of urban and industrial jobs.

Although the pace of reform slowed briefly in the aftermath of the harsh suppression of the Tiananmen Square incident on June 4, 1989, the economy grew at a rate of nearly 10 percent per year during the 1980s, 1990s, and early 2000s. This remarkable record of growth was made possible by two aspects of the economic system that existed under Mao. First, the centrally planned system operated on a largely self-sufficient basis, with little contact or trade with most advanced industrial countries. As a result, the level of technology in China had fallen far behind that of the developed world by the late 1970s. Once the reforms began and China opened its markets to the rest of the world, it was able to rapidly import new technology, rather than having to develop it gradually. Second, the economic system that evolved under Mao effectively prevented unauthorized population and labor movement by means of a household registration system known as the *hukou*. As a result, by the early 1980s there was an enormous pool of underemployed, low-income labor in the countryside. Once the emergence of markets made migration possible, tens of millions of workers travelled from the countryside to the cities to find higher-paying jobs. This huge supply of low-wage labor enabled many Chinese firms to produce goods for world markets at prices lower than those of competitors in countries with higher incomes.

Example of a household registration certificate required under China's *hukou* system. *(Photo by Micah Sittig, https://www.flickr.com/photos/msittig/4100896968, licensed under Creative Commons Attribution 2.0 Generic [https://creativecommons.org/licenses/by/2.0/])*

Is China Socialist or Capitalist?

When Americans and other Westerners visit China, they see much about the economy that is familiar. China has stock markets, supermarkets, home improvement stores, huge banks, and many privately owned automobiles. Indeed, capitalist elements do exist in the Chinese economy, in the sense that many firms and productive resources are privately owned. On the other hand, the government is still essentially an arm of the Communist Party of China, which asserts that China is a socialist country and that the economy is a "socialist market economy."

What this means is that while the vast majority of economic activity takes place through open markets that determine most prices, the state retains either ownership or control over key elements of the economy, notably land and other natural resources, much of transportation and communications infrastructure, and, importantly, the banking system. The core of the banking system still consists of the "big four" commercial banks, all of which have sold large numbers of stock shares, but in which the state holds a controlling interest. This system has allowed China to benefit from much of the efficiency and dynamism of a market economy, while at the same time the state has retained a greater ability to guide the economy than in most capitalist systems.

Foreign Trade and Investment

Trade grew rapidly beginning in the 1980s, providing jobs, new technology, and the competitive pressure that forced Chinese firms to meet international standards in quality as well as price. In recent decades, much of China's export trade has been based on international supply chains, with firms in neighboring countries like South Korea making components of a product, then shipping them to China, where they are assembled for final export.

An important milestone for China's international trade was its accession to the World Trade Organization (WTO) in 2001, resulting in reduced tariffs and other trade barriers for both imports and exports. The process of qualifying for WTO membership required China to clarify its legal code, adopt modern international accounting standards, and eliminate opaque and arbitrary trade practices, all of which benefited the Chinese economy. In addition, the conditions for entry required that China open some of its previously closed markets to international competition, notably banking and the automotive industry, resulting in powerful incentives for domestic firms to modernize their operations, often by means of joint ventures with major international firms.

The World Trade Organization (WTO) is run by its member governments, and its agreements cover goods, services, and intellectual property. More information about China's involvement and activities as a WTO member can be found on the organization's web page "China and the WTO" (http://www.wto.org/english/thewto_e/countries_e/china_e.htm).

Expanding Domestic Markets

An interesting thing happened in China when the United States and most of Europe plunged into recession in 2009: the growth rate of the economy barely slowed. The Chinese economy continued its rapid rise, despite sharp declines in the incomes of its major trade partners. This resilience during the worldwide recession was largely due to the momentum of consumer spending by the country's newly affluent middle class. A telling statistic, in fact, is that China became the world's largest producer of automobiles in 2009, and of the 16 million cars produced that year, all but a few hundred thousand were purchased by people in China.

Environmental Crises

China has nearly the same land area as the United States, but almost four times as many people and far less inhabitable terrain. While large parts of the country have little or no population— particularly the Tibetan plateau, home to the Tibetan minority population and making up one of China's Autonomous Regions, and the great deserts of Xinjiang in the far west, the site of another autonomous area home to the Uyghur people—massive population is densely crowded along the eastern seaboard and the Yangtze River system of central China.

This concentration of people has exerted enormous pressure on natural resources and the environment for centuries. The electric power required for expanding industrialization has been generated primarily by coal, with which the country is well endowed. The government has long struggled to restrain the pollution of air, water, and soil, but the need for millions of new jobs each year has resulted in ever-rising levels of contaminants, and Chinese cities have become dangerously polluted.

> The website of the PRC's Ministry of Environmental Protection (http://english.mep. gov.cn) offers information on state-run programs to tackle environmental issues.

Special Places: Hong Kong and Taiwan

The small island of Hong Kong was turned over to Great Britain as a result of China's defeat by British forces in the Opium War of 1839–1842. It was then governed as a colony of the United Kingdom until its return to Chinese sovereignty in 1997. As a British colony and China's most important port, Hong Kong enjoyed great commercial success, with income levels and living standards far higher than those of the rest of China. When Hong Kong returned to Chinese control, the Chinese government agreed to allow it to retain its own form of government, its own economic system, and its own currency and banking system. This commitment has been honored, and Hong Kong, while part of China, holds a unique status that in many ways is similar to that of an independent entity, such as Singapore.

Taiwan, a large island off the southeast coast of China, has historically been popu-lated almost entirely by Chinese people, many from the nearby province of Fujian. At the end of the Chinese Civil War, in 1949, the defeated Nationalist forces under Chiang Kai-shek retreated to Taiwan, where they were protected by the U.S. Navy. The government of the People's Republic of China has always considered Taiwan a renegade province and has arrayed significant military forces across the strait that separates the island from the mainland. By the late 1980s, however, investors from Taiwan's rapidly developing capitalist economy were increasingly involved in invest-ment projects in China, taking advantage of its lower wages and its enormous domestic market. By 2013, although the military standoff continued and Taiwan had not been formally reunited with China, the two economies had become closely integrated, with growing trade supported by increasing numbers of direct flights and shipping routes.

Hong Kong, Taiwan, and the Southeast Asian city-state of Singapore, at the south-ern tip of Malaysia across the South China Sea, are sometimes referred to in China as the "China Circle."

Japan

Japan experienced two periods of extraordinary growth in the modern era. The first began in the late nineteenth century, when an exceptional group of leaders under the auspices of Emperor Meiji (reigned 1868–1912) abruptly brought an end to the country's

銀座・鉄道馬車　明治後期　東京　Ginza Street with horse-drawn trolley, Tokyo, ca.1910

The Ginza district in Tokyo, ca.1910, during the modernization program instituted under the Meiji empire. *(Photo by Danny Choo, https://www.flickr.com/photos/dannychoo/5278569009/, licensed under Creative Commons Attribution-Share Alike 2.0 Generic [https://creativecommons.org/licenses/by-sa/2.0/])*

traditional social, economic, and political structures and systematically set out to import and promulgate the elements of a modern industrial nation. By the 1930s the material success of this effort had created the military power that Japan employed in its efforts to seize large parts of East and Southeast Asia, and that in turn resulted in the Pacific portion of World War II.

Japan's second period of remarkable economic growth occurred in the decades following its crushing defeat at the end of the World War II. From the mid-1950s through the 1970s, Japan moved from restoring its war-ravaged industries to become a major exporter of increasingly advanced manufactured products. Gross domestic product initially grew at over 9 percent per year, then slowed during the international oil crisis of the mid-1970s, but continued at around 5 percent per year through the 1980s. Much of this growth has been attributed to the efforts of the Ministry of International Trade and Industry (MITI), which supported industries that it believed had the potential to become internationally competitive by means of protective tariffs, subsidies, and informal coordination of investment and research. Another unusual aspect of the rapidly growing Japanese economy was the central role of large conglomerates of firms, known as *keiretsu*, which continue to be major influences in Japan's economy. *Keiretsu*, such as Mitsui, Mitsubishi, and Toyota (Tokai), typically consist of 20 or more firms, grouped around a bank and a trading company. Coordination of efforts within a *keiretsu* can speed up decision making and facilitate the close communications required for the highly efficient provision of inputs that has characterized the operations of some of Japan's most successful firms, such as Toyota. On the other hand, critics of the system argue that it can hinder competition and that it has resulted in a two-tier, or dualistic, economy, in which roughly half of the labor force works for smaller firms that do not enjoy the high incomes and job security provided by firms in the *keiretsu*.

The Economist's web page "Japanese Economy" (http://www.economist.com/topics/japanese-economy) offers links to its print articles, blog posts, and other features on the Japanese economy.

By the end of the twentieth century, Japan had the second-largest national economy in the world, smaller only than that of the United States, with high personal incomes, and one of the best health-care outcomes in the world in terms of high life expectancy and low infant mortality. The economy entered a period of prolonged stagnation, however, in the 1990s. High savings rates and strong export performance, which vastly increased capital used for domestic investment, contributed to very high real estate prices in the 1980s, creating a serious price bubble. In the 1990s the bubble burst and real estate prices plummeted, causing a huge loss of wealth for investors and initiating a decline in consumer demand that resulted in deflation—persistently falling prices—and interest rates that fell to effectively zero. In the 1990s and early

The Akihabara electronics district, Tokyo, Japan. *(Wikimedia Commons, Richard Cornish, http://tinyurl.com/kfbpzlo).*

2000s, the government attempted to invigorate the economy by supporting failing banks and firms and engaging in numerous public works projects, such as roads and bridges, but demand failed to recover. Shinzo Abe, elected prime minister in December 2012, announced an ambitious plan to restore the economy and end deflation through a combination of stimulative fiscal and monetary measures. As of the end of 2013, the economy showed encouraging signs of growth, including a rise in GDP and in the stock market.

The 2011 Earthquake, Tsunami, and Nuclear Crisis

On March 11, 2011, the most powerful earthquake to ever strike Japan occurred off the northeast coast of the Tohoku region, causing tsunami waves of up to 40.5 meters in height that devastated coastal towns. In addition to the destruction of buildings, roads, ships, railways, and power lines, the tsunami catastrophically damaged nuclear reactors at the Fukushima Daiichi Power Plant, which suffered explosions and partial meltdowns and released radioactive contamination into the surrounding air and water. Damage to buildings and infrastructure and loss of electric power sharply reduced production by Japanese industries in the months following the earthquake. The overall economy had largely recovered from the disaster by mid-2013, but many Japanese remained displaced, and the Fukushima plant was still dangerously unstable at the end of the year.

A Paradox

The Japanese economy of the early twenty-first century presents a puzzling image. It is one of the most technologically advanced countries in the world, its people enjoy excellent health and high living standards, and it is home to some of the most successful and respected international firms, including Toyota, Sony, and Nikon, to name only a few. But the economy has struggled unsuccessfully to achieve sustained growth for two decades, the population is declining, and the government seems unable to gain firm control of some basic problems, including resolution of the Fukushima nuclear crisis.

Korea

Historically, Korea was a single nation, although invaded at times by China and Japan. In 1905 it was occupied by Japan, and it was formally annexed by that country in 1910. It remained under Japanese administration until the end of World War II. After Japan's defeat by the Allied forces, Korea was divided roughly in half, with the North governed by a Communist state, the Democratic People's Republic of Korea (DPRK) under Kim Il-sung, supported by the Soviet Union. The South was governed by the Republic of Korea (ROK), supported by the United States. In 1950 the North invaded the South, resulting in the bitter and bloody Korean War, which ended in 1953 with an armistice—an agreement to stop fighting—but no peace treaty. Since that time the Demilitarized Zone (DMZ) between the two states has been heavily fortified, and armed clashes have occurred sporadically. In November 2010, for example, forces of the DPRK fired artillery at a small island held by the South.

North Korea

Throughout the history of the DPRK, its government has shown little interest in developing the country's economy, focusing instead on military technology. Since its establishment under Kim Il-sung, the DPRK has followed a policy known as *juche*, or "self-reliance." Before 1991, North Korea depended heavily on the Soviet Union for economic assistance. After the collapse of the Soviet Union in that year, the DPRK's only substantial economic relationship was with China, whose leaders repeatedly encouraged its government to pursue the kind of market-based reforms that China was following. The DPRK instead continued to employ a tightly controlled policy of central planning, while lacking many of the inputs required for effective economic activity, including energy resources. The 1990s saw declining GDP per capita, crop failures, and repeated years of famine. In the early 2000s, modest steps toward reconciliation with South Korea and the United States, under Kim Il-sung's son, Kim Jong-il, were negated by the DPRK's development and testing of nuclear weapons and long-range missiles.

By the end of 2013, the country's new leader, Kim Jong-un, the son of Kim Jong-il, who died in 2011, continued to issue provocative statements and to develop nuclear weapons. In December 2013 he publically removed from office and then executed the country's second most powerful official, who was also his uncle, raising international concerns about the stability of the regime. Efforts by South Korea to provide food aid to the North and to establish rudimentary economic cooperation programs, along with humanitarian moves to enable communication between separated families, have borne some fruit, but have usually been rebuffed by the DPRK. Although a single nationality and culture, North and South Korea have been separated for so long and have taken such different economic paths that the two economies today have little in common.

North Korean economic initiatives, *juche*, and more are explained on the official website of the DPRK (http://www.korea-dpr.com).

South Korea

In contrast to the DPRK, in the years after the end of the Korean War, South Korea developed a vibrant capitalist market economy, aided by close ties with the United States and by trade and foreign investment from Japan. An authoritarian government emerged in the 1950s and guided the economy into internationally important industries, including ship building, heavy equipment, automobiles, and electronics. The South Korean economy developed growing numbers of high-level manufacturing industries, in many cases working through joint ventures with Japanese firms. A national emphasis—almost an obsession—on education generated a labor force that supported the dramatic success of manufacturing firms that are among the most successful in the world.

Since the 1960s the economy has been dominated by large family-controlled industrial conglomerates, or groups of allied firms, known as *chaebol*, which worked closely with the government and with the banking system. The leading *chaebol* include names that are recognized around the world, such as Samsung, Hyundai, and LG. The partnership between the *chaebol* and the government resulted in powerful growth, but also created flaws that became apparent in the Asian financial crisis of 1997. Because of their privileged status, *chaebol* were able to borrow large amounts of funds from major banks without adequate scrutiny or reserve backing. When the Asian financial crisis erupted in the summer of 1997, instigated by the collapse of a commercial building boom in Thailand, international investors sold off assets of other Asian countries whose financial markets were suspected of weakness. The lax lending standards of some South Korean banks came to light as a number of *chaebol* collapsed and devastated financial markets when they could not cover their debt obligations. The South Korean economy dropped into a sharp recession, as the US dollar exchange rate for the South Korean currency, the won, and South Korea's GDP both fell by more than a third between the summer of 1997 and the summer of

1998. Banking practices and the *chaebol* were reformed following the crisis, and the South Korean economy quickly regained the ground it had lost and has grown rapidly in the succeeding years.

The Economist's web page "Korean Economy" (http://www.economist.com/topics/korean-economy) offers links to its print articles, blog posts, and other features on the Korean economy.

Export-Oriented Growth

South Korea, like Japan, is a leading example of a country that has achieved rapid growth in real GDP, incomes, and living standards by following a strategy focused on developing export industries. The development of exports benefits a country by introducing technology that is advanced enough to enable products to compete in international markets. Not only is income generated by the jobs in the exporting industries, but the new technology also becomes part of the productive capacity of the country's domestic economy. Expansion of exporting industries was also a way to overcome Korea's deficiencies in natural resources and to make use of its relatively dense population. The strategy's success is reflected in South Korea's standing as the sixth-largest exporting nation in the world (as of 2012), despite ranking 26th in population size. At the same time, it is the seventh most important importing nation, indicating a healthy trade balance and strong domestic markets. South Korea's most important trade partner is China, which accounts for roughly a fifth of its imports and exports, followed by Japan and the United States, each accounting for about 10 percent of the total.

South Korea's exporting industries include some that are among the most important in the international market. Its largest export sector, making up around a quarter of all exports, is electronics, including semiconductors, wireless communication devices, LCD devices, and electronic components. Another major export sector is shipbuilding, in which it is the world leader, with slightly over half of the international market. Major shipbuilding firms include Hyundai Heavy Industries and Samsung Heavy Industries. Automobile manufacturing grew rapidly beginning in the 1980s, and as of 2012 South Korea ranked fifth among the world's producers, with an output of 4.5 million vehicles, closely following Germany, and around half the output of Japan. The largest South Korean auto producer is Hyundai-Kia Automotive Group.

Vietnam

Although Vietnam is considered part of Southeast Asia, it abuts China's southeastern border and shares deep cultural and historical ties with China. After the end of World War II, Vietnam followed China in establishing a Communist state and a socialist economy; at the end of the 1980s—after a grueling Cold War–based conflict between

Hyundai Heavy Industries shipyard, Ulsan, South Korea, 2013. *(Photo by Sarah Tz, https://www. flickr.com/photos/120420083@N05/13898498821/, licensed under Creative Commons Attribution 2.0 Generic [https://creativecommons.org/licenses/by/2.0/])*

the north and south of the country fueled by international involvement, including major participation on the side of South Vietnam by the United States—it again followed China's lead in turning to a market-based economic system, while continuing to adhere to Communism in the political realm.

Although much smaller than that of China, Vietnam's population today is well over 90 million, making it a significant presence among states in the region. Like China, it has a relatively young and well-educated population and a relatively low average income level, resulting in a labor force that is attractive to many international firms. In recent decades, as incomes in China have grown, Chinese firms have also turned to Vietnam as an attractive investment site.

Regional Themes

The countries of Asia are divided by differences in languages, writing systems, political ideologies, and historic and current frictions and grievances. Their economies, however, share important trends, including increased levels of urbanization, growing numbers of elderly people, and the challenges presented by migration.

Urbanization

East Asia is well on its way to becoming an overwhelmingly urban region. When a country's economy becomes more modern, workers move from farming in the countryside to higher-paying industrial jobs in the cities. As a population becomes more urban, the birth rate goes down, due to smaller living spaces, better health care, and fewer opportunities for children to help their families by working. At the same time, urban adults live longer, and the overall result is that there are fewer young people and more elderly, causing a rise in the dependency ratio (the number of nonworking people for each worker).

Japan was the first Asian nation to modernize and industrialize, and by the late twentieth century its population was overwhelmingly urban, like those of the mature industrial economies in Western Europe and the United States. Today over 90 percent of Japanese people live in cities.

China lagged behind its neighbors in economic development during the years of Mao Zedong's leadership (1949–1976), but since the early 1980s the growth of industry has been accompanied by rapid expansion of the country's cities and a massive movement of population out of the countryside. By 2011 just over half of the population lived in cities, with the proportion rising by nearly 3 percent each year.

South Korea lies between Japan and China in its level of urbanization, as well as in other economic measures. By the end of 2013, around 84 percent of South Korea's population lived in cities, which were still growing, but at a very slow pace.

Aging Populations

In all three of the major East Asian economies, as in other countries around the world, increased urbanization and higher income levels have led to longer average life spans and lower birth rates, and thus to a rising share of older people in the population. Here again, the three countries' different levels of development are reflected in their different shares of people over the age of 65.

Japan's population has one of the highest proportions of elderly people in the world, at nearly 25 percent in 2013. It also has the world's highest life expectancy, at nearly 84 years of age, and a birth rate that is far below the level required to maintain the size of the population, which is declining by around 0.1 percent each year.

In China, around 10 percent of the population is over 65, but the proportion is expected to rise quickly in the coming years, due in part to the country's controversial policy of allowing only one child for most families since the mid-1970s. As of 2013 the population was growing at a very slow pace of around half a percent each year.

In South Korea around 12 percent of the population is elderly, and here, too, the proportion is rising rapidly as young urban families concentrate on providing excellent education for a few children rather than on having multiple children.

All three countries face a future in which the number of young workers entering the labor force will decline and each worker will have to support a growing number of nonworking elderly people and children.

Migration

Population movements, both internal and international, have played major roles in the economic development of all the major East Asian countries. Differences in income levels create powerful incentives for people to move from regions or countries with lower incomes to those with higher incomes. In the early twentieth century, the populations of Japan, China, and Korea were all overwhelmingly rural. Over the course of the century, the growth of industry fueled a migration from the countryside into the cities in all three countries.

China experienced huge internal population movements in the twentieth century. In the early decades economic growth, led by railway expansion in the three provinces of the Northeast (Manchuria), attracted millions of workers from the North China provinces of Shandong and Hebei, even when the region was occupied by Japanese forces from the early 1930s until the end of World War II. Further population shifts took place during the Maoist era, largely for the purpose of opening new agricultural lands in remote areas, including Heilongjiang (northern Manchuria), Inner Mongolia, and Xinjiang. Since China's opening to international markets in the 1980s, many young Chinese have gone abroad to study and remained in the countries where they pursued their educations, particularly the United States, Europe, and Australia, especially in the aftermath of the Tiananmen Square protests in 1989. The rise in incomes, job opportunities, and living standards in China in the twenty-first century, however, has increasingly drawn foreign-trained Chinese back to China. This trend has also attracted small but growing groups of migrants from countries as diverse as the United Kingdom, Russia, and Nigeria.

An informative exploration of the influx of labor migrants from Africa to China can be found in Adams Bodomo's 2012 book *Africans in China: A Sociocultural Study and Its Implications on Africa-China Relations*.

When Japan began the process of modernization in the late 1800s and early 1900s, large numbers of Japanese were recruited as labor, mainly for agriculture, in Hawaii, the western United States and western Canada, and South America (particularly Brazil). These transplanted populations formed the basis for enduring cultural and commercial ties that continue to the present. As Japan became a leading economic power in the late twentieth century, Japanese students and business people spent time abroad and foreign workers from countries such as China, the Philippines, Nepal, and Brazil came to Japan in search of opportunities. Despite Japan's declining population and need for additional labor, however, cultural and social attitudes have resulted in relatively few foreigners remaining on a permanent basis, and in the early twenty-first century they accounted for less than 1 percent of the population, less than in any other major industrialized country.

In the first half of the twentieth century, when Korea was occupied by Japan, Koreans were moved to support the goals of the Japanese Empire. Hundreds of thousands of Korean farmers were settled in eastern Manchuria (Northeast China), while nearly two million Koreans were taken to Japan to labor in the factories that supported Japan's military expansion. Following the end of World War II, most—though not all—of these involuntary migrants returned to Korea. In the decades after the Korean War, as South Korea recovered from the wartime devastation and began to lay the foundation of a modern industrial economy, many South Koreans left their homeland to seek work. In the 1970s and 1980s, tens of thousands of Korean workers went to the Middle East and other countries as contract workers for Korean construction and engineering firms. Since the 1990s, growing labor demand and rising incomes at home have largely ended this movement, and in recent years workers from lower income countries in Asia have flowed into South Korea. In 2008 the number of workers entering the country from abroad reached 550,000. Another aspect of international movement has been migration for marriage. Since the end of the Korean War, the United States has permanently stationed around 30,000 troops in South Korea, and around a tenth of them have returned home with Korean wives. Since the early 1990s there has been a rising movement of migrants into South Korea to marry rural people who have not been able to find spouses. By 2007 the number of marriage immigrants was nearly 105,000. Although most are foreign women coming to marry Korean men, around a third are foreign men marrying Korean women.

References and Further Research

Bodomo, Adams, 2012. *Africans in China: A Sociocultural Study and Its Implications on Africa-China Relations*. Amherst, NY: Cambria Press.

Chung, Young-Iob. 2007. *South Korea in the Fast Lane: Economic Development and Capital Formation*. Oxford: Oxford University Press. A comprehensive examination of the policies and history of the rapid rise of the South Korean Economy.

Clark, Donald. N. 2012. *Korea in World History*. Ann Arbor, MI: Association for Asian Studies. A concise and readily accessible history of Korea.

Flath, David. 2005. *The Japanese Economy*. New York: Oxford University Press. A solid textbook on the economy of Japan.

Lin Yifu, Fang Cai, and Zhou Li. 2003. *The China Miracle: Development Strategy and Economic Reform*. Rev. ed. Hong Kong: Chinese University Press. Explains China's economic development from the perspective of leading Chinese economists.

Naughton, Barry. 2007. *The Chinese Economy: Transitions and Growth*. Cambridge, MA: MIT Press. An excellent textbook.

Park, Yung Chul, and Hugh Patrick, eds. 2013. *How Finance is Shaping the Economies of China, Japan, and Korea*. New York: Columbia University Press. Discusses the recent evolution of the Japanese economy in comparison with those of China and Korea.

Rosser, J. Barkley, Jr. and Marina V. Rosser. 2004. *Comparative Economics in a Transforming World Economy*. 2nd ed. Cambridge, MA: Massachusetts Institute of Technology. Includes an analysis of each of the major East Asian economies from the point of view of comparative economic systems.

Journals and Websites

China Daily, China's official English-language newspaper, is published six days a week and is available online at http://www.chinadaily.com.cn/. Articles cover stories on economic issues as well as political, social, cultural, and human-interest topics. The website has a searchable data base of past issues and links to a wide range of information sources on China.

Current History (http://www.currenthistory.com/) is published nine times each year; the September issue is always devoted to useful overview articles that review recent developments in the countries of East Asia.

Education About Asia (https://www.asian-studies.org/eaa/), published three times a year by the Association for Asian Studies, often contains articles by specialists on the economies of the countries of East Asia. It also provides valuable information about teaching materials for Asia.

The *Korea Times* is one of several English-language daily newspapers published in South Korea. It is available online at http://www.koreatimes.co.kr.

The Korean Statistical Information Service (KOSIS) website (http://kosis.kr/eng/index/index.jsp) provides online access to official data for South Korea (Republic of Korea). It can be searched and is regularly updated.

The *Mainichi* is an English-language website of *Mainichi Shimbun* (*Daily News*), one of several major Japanese newspapers that operate an English-language website.

The National Bureau of Statistics of China website (http://www.stats.gov.cn/english/) contains official economic data, reports, communiqués, and links to the annual *Statistical Yearbook*, among other sources.

The Statistics Bureau of Japan, part of the Ministry of Internal Affairs and Communications, has a website (http://www.stat.go.jp/english/index.htm) that contains a wealth of official data and useful links to other resources.

The World Bank website (http://www.worldbank.org/) provides access to the data and research reports of the largest international organization devoted to economic development. It includes economic data and development evaluations for all the major East Asian economies.

The World Factbook (https://www.cia.gov/library/publications/the-world-factbook) is an online reference of the Central Intelligence Agency of the United States. It is a useful source that presents key data on all the economies of the world and is regularly updated.

6

Globalization in East Asia

ANNE PRESCOTT

Globalization is a process of international integration that results from the exchange of commodities, ideas, and cultures. The outcomes of this process include increased economic and cultural interdependence, along with the genesis of new cultural hybrids. Although the term globalization only came into vogue in the late twentieth century, the practice of regional exchange and integration has been around much longer. In earlier times, this was a slow process, since it relied on travel by beasts of burden and ships, and on written correspondence. Later, the tempo of change quickened with the advent of trains, planes, the telegraph, and the telephone. At the beginning of the twenty-first century, fax machines, the Internet, smartphones, and other technological advances have further accelerated the speed of globalization and the ease with which people can communicate with others around the world.

Very often, globalization, particularly cultural expressions of the phenomenon, means Westernization or, to Americans, "doing things our way." Reports on cultural and economic globalization in the United States very often focus on the diffusion and impact of American culture and goods—pop music, McDonald's, basketball, etc.—on the rest of the world. Indeed, music in the Euro-American tradition, whether Beethoven or Bono, has permeated nearly every country on earth, McDonald's has restaurants in more than 100 countries around the world, and star NBA player jerseys are worn by young people far from the United States. However, globalization is a two-way street, and Hello Kitty and PlayStation, products of Japan, and Gangnam Style, a cultural export of South Korea, have been embraced outside of their countries of origin and are equally a part of the globalization phenomenon.

Media outlets in the United States report on the effects of economic and cultural globalization every day. In general, the outcomes of cultural integration are likely to be viewed as positive developments unless they are seen as destroying native cultural practices. Economic globalization news, however, tends to focus on events and actions that negatively impact the United States and other Western countries. In the 1980s, Japan's economic strength was blamed for woes in the U.S. market, but in recent years collective attention in the United States has shifted to China, and issues such as the transfer of manufacturing to China and other countries are often cited as blows to the U.S. domestic economy. Very little is said about any positive effects of these economic processes. For the United States, income is earned by American companies operating in East Asia, and American consumers have the advantage of lower-cost imports manufactured in China. Also often overlooked is the increased earning power of the Chinese, who can now afford to purchase products exported to China from the United States.

The exchange of commodities, ideas, and culture among societies—in effect, globalization writ small—has existed as a more regionalized phenomenon for millennia. This chapter expands the common Western-centric view of globalization by examining diffusion from East Asia. In the process, it explores specific historical and contemporary examples of interdependence and hybridity that have resulted from regional and global integration.

East Asia at the Center

More than two millennia ago, China was a regional center for the exchange of goods, technology, learning, philosophies, religions, and more. The very name for the Chinese state, "Middle Kingdom" (Zhongguo), reflects the notion that its inhabitants saw themselves at the center of the world as they knew it. As Warren Cohen argues in *East Asia at the Center: Four Thousand Years of Engagement with the World* (2000), viewing globalization through an East Asia–centered lens can be very helpful in understanding the ever-shifting dynamics of global interaction. In addition, studying both contemporary and historical examples from geographically and culturally distant countries, without the emotional baggage of familiarity, can help us examine the pluses and minuses of globalization from a more neutral viewpoint.

From a historical perspective, the Silk Road— a network that enabled trade and exchange to flourish across a broad region—is a prime illustration of earlier instances of globalizing forces. From the second century BCE through the sixteenth century CE, it was not a single road, but a collection of routes, over land and sea, connecting Europe, Africa, China, and points in between—a "network" by definition. Eventually Silk Road goods made their way from the terminus in the Chinese city of Chang'an (now Xi'an), to the eastern borders of China and beyond to Korea and Japan. While not all of the interactions on this ancient system of roads were beneficial to the people or had positive outcomes—for instance, diseases such as the bubonic plague were spread via the Silk Road routes—myths and stories, food traditions, and the transmission of religious beliefs and rites are all attributed to Silk Road exchange.

The British Library's International Dunhuang Project (http://idp.bl.uk/) provides information about Silk Road history, artifacts, cultures, languages, and religions. In photos and text, it chronicles modern Silk Road explorations. It also provides links to digital resources around the world.

Sponsored by the Stanford Program on International and Cross-Cultural Education (SPICE), the SPICE Interactive "Silk Road" (http://virtuallabs. stanford.edu/silkroad/index.html), a collaboration between SPICE and Stanford's Virtual Labs, has a host of resources, including interactive maps and a Jeopardy game.

Today, museums are filled with artifacts that provide evidence of an early form of globalization along the Silk Road, including figurines of Europeans riding on camels, musical instruments adopted in regions far from their original homes, fabrics dyed with nonindigenous substances, and more. The famous Gion Festival of Kyoto, Japan, first held in 869 CE, features huge floats with gigantic tapestries hung on the sides. Some of the tapestries were made in China, Mongolia, Persia, Korea, and even as far away as Belgium, and they depict scenes from Asia, the Middle East, and Europe.

The Araretenjin Yama float in Kyoto's Gion Festival is decorated with replicas of sections of a sixteenth-century Belgian scroll depicting scenes from Homer's *Iliad*. Naginata Hoko, the most famous and prominent float in the festival, is decorated with tapestries from Persia, China, Mongolia, and Korea. An Internet search will reveal photos of these tapestries, and more information on the festival and floats is available on these links:

- Official website of the Gion Matsuri Yamahoko Rengōkai (Association of Gion Matsuri Floats) (http://www.gionmatsuri.or.jp/yamahoko/). Although primarily in Japanese, there are short descriptions of each of the floats as well as a summary of the festival history and events in English.
- "Gion Matsuri" on The Samurai Archives/SamuraiWiki (http://wiki.samurai-archives.com/index.php?title=Gion_Matsuri).

Even the English names "China," "Japan," and "Korea" are by-products of interactions between Europe and East Asia. The name Korea is derived from outsiders' understanding of the pronunciation of the Korean kingdom of Goryeo (918–1392). Europeans first used the name China, based on the Sanskrit word for the region, Cina, in the sixteenth century. There are a number of theories on the origin of the word Japan. It may be based on the Shanghai dialect pronunciation of the Chinese characters for Nippon (the Japanese name for their country), Zeppen; the Malay word for the country, Zepang; or the early Mandarin Cipan. When the Chinese word for country, *guo*, is appended to Zeppen, it becomes Zeppenguo, or "Zipangu" in Japanese, a term that has undergone "reverse import" and is now used in Japanese manga and anime. Another theory is that the Portuguese Yat-pun, which is based on a southern Chinese pronunciation of the country name, morphed into the English word Japan (the written "Y" in Dutch is pronounced as "J").

Broadening the Sphere of Exchange

Once trade had been established over the Silk Road, connections continued and expanded both by land and sea. As Europeans and East Asians became more familiar with each other's goods, consumer demand ensured that these ties not only endured but grew, and cultural interdependence became even more important. Compared to the rapid pace of global exchange today, this was "slow-motion" globalization, but it is part of the continuous path to today's interconnected world.

Commodities and ideas from East Asia eventually made their way beyond the continents of Europe and Asia to North America, where they have played an important role in economic and cultural trade since colonial times. Long sea journeys were difficult, as ships had to travel either east around the Cape of Good Hope at the southern tip of Africa or west via Cape Horn at the far end of South America, but goods from China, Japan, and Korea were prized in colonial America. In those days, commerce was further complicated by trade restrictions in East Asia, as foreigners were allowed to trade through only a limited number of ports. Despite these obstacles, by 1776 and the founding of the United States, sea trade with East Asia and demand for tea, porcelain, silk, and other wares had grown so much that most people had at least one or two items in their homes that were imported from the region.

One of the primary ports for ships traveling to and from East Asia was Salem, Massachusetts. The Peabody Essex Museum in Salem has an impressive collection of Asian artifacts specifically connected with that trade. An overview of the collection can be found at the museum's "Asian Export Art" web page (http://www.pem.org/collections/9-asian_export_art).

As demand for goods from East Asia grew in the nineteenth century, Europeans and Americans forced China, Japan, and Korea to open more ports and ease trade restrictions in those countries in order to broaden commerce and exchange. Higher levels of business and cultural interaction resulted, and all parties found new outlets for their products. One example of this increasing cultural exchange was the discovery by Westerners of Japanese decorative arts. Ukiyo-e, the iconic woodblock prints familiar to many in the West, were eagerly collected in Europe and North America, and artists such as Henri de Toulouse-Lautrec, James Abbot McNeill Whistler, Vincent van Gogh, and Claude Monet were influenced by the techniques and aesthetics of ukiyo-e, which led to cultural hybridity as they experimented with these new methods of expression.

In this Chinese room at Lichtenwalde Castle in Niederwiesa, Germany, both the items and the manner of decoration demonstrate the Chinese influence typical of the chinoiserie style. *(Wikimedia Commons, Geisler Martin, http://tinyurl.com/nwpdgts)*.

In music, composers such as Camille Saint-Saens, W. S. Gilbert and Arthur Sullivan, and Giacomo Puccini wrote operas with Japanese story lines or themes. China, too, was an inspiration for artists who combined Chinese and European styles, aesthetics, and techniques to create what is called chinoiserie, a style particularly prominent in the baroque and rococo interior design styles of the seventeenth and eighteenth century. Even ordinary people became enamored with East Asia; at one time the amount of porcelain from China ("china") one owned was an indicator of one's social status.

The Dutch artist Vincent van Gogh was strongly influenced by Japanese ukiyo-e, as is seen in these two works: a comparison of Van Gogh's *The Bridge in the Rain (after Hiroshige)* to Ando Hiroshige's Ōhashi *Atake no Yūdachi* (Evening shower at Atake Great Bridge) can be seen on Wikimedia Commons (http://tinyurl.com/my2sour).

Learn more about theories of cultural hybridity in Chapter 1 of Marwan M. Kraidy's book *Hybridity, or the Cultural Logic of Globalization*, available online from Temple University Press (http://www.temple.edu/tempress/chapters_1400/1770_ch1.pdf).

Taking the Lead in Globalization Today

In the late twentieth and early twenty-first centuries, new technologies have had a huge impact on the way we interact with people both near and far. On the Silk Road, it often took weeks and months to travel one of the many routes, and people had ample direct interaction with other cultures. Today, not only can we travel great distances more easily and in greater comfort, but technology also allows us to travel "virtually" at very little or no cost. Instead of spending weeks on a boat traveling from North America to Asia, an airplane covers the distance in less than a day. A letter that took a week to reach the other side of the world can now be sent instantly by e-mail; expensive trans-Pacific phone calls have been replaced by free Skype calls; and online translation tools, as unreliable as they sometimes are, assist in communicating with those who do not speak our language. These technologies—plus radio, movies, television, audio recordings, and more—allow us to easily exchange ideas with others in distant places, which then leads to increased international integration.

As much as technological innovations have enabled greater economic exchange, they have also had a profound effect on the spread of culture. Popular culture is an extremely effective means of bringing people together. The seeming omnipresence of McDonald's is often used to represent the globalization of culture, but China, Japan, and Korea have also produced cultural phenomena that have spread around the globe. Hello Kitty, the fictional character introduced by the Japanese company Sanrio on various consumer products, may have been brought to life in Japan, but the icon has been embraced around the world. Manga and anime, particularly the works of Miyazaki Hayao, are also wildly popular globalized cultural forms, and ones that have come full circle, for comic papers were first introduced into Japan from Europe and the United States in the late nineteenth and early twentieth centuries. This art form inspired a generation of Japanese artists, and now Japanese artists are capturing the world's attention with their masterpieces.

Christine Yano, in her 2013 book *Pink Globalization: Hello Kitty's Trek across the Pacific* (Durham, NC: Duke University Press) examines Hello Kitty's journey to becoming a global phenomenon. The introduction is available on Google books (books.google.com/books?isbn=0822353636).

Food is another powerful globalizing force. Chinese cuisine has long been a favorite in the United States, for example. Beyond the ubiquitous Chinese buffets, many Americans have learned to differentiate regional Chinese cuisines, and Mongolian hot pot and dim sum are no longer exotic dining styles. Japanese sushi has hooked the interest of many Americans, and there is now an American version of the popular Japanese cooking show *Iron Chef.* Korean food is well represented in the popular food trucks that cruise urban areas, and kimchi and bibimbap are now well known to the many fans of that country's food. Even as the cuisines of East Asia have spread beyond the region, Westerners have embraced that food, or hybridized it, by merging local tastes with East Asian tradition. This has resulted in dishes such as crab Rangoon, California rolls, fortune cookies, and other "authentic foods" that are unknown in their supposed homelands.

Sports, music, film, and visual arts are also popular global cultural commodities from East Asia. The Korean Wave (*hallyu*), which includes music, film, and television, first washed over Korea's neighbors in Japan, China, and Southeast Asia. Launched in the late 1990s, *hallyu* dramas such as *Winter Sonata* (*Gyeoul Yeonga*) were responsible for much of its regional (and eventually global) spread. Beginning around 2009 the Korean Wave lapped onto the shores of Europe and North America, laying the groundwork for the arrival in 2012 of Gangnam Style, by South Korean musician Psy. *Hallyu* cast a spotlight on Korea, resulting in increased interest not only in Korean popular culture, but also in the country's language, traditions, and history.

The Korean TV program *Arirang Today* produced the report "Hallyu Takes the United States by Storm!"—available on the progran's YouTube channel (http://www.youtube.com/watch?v=hsnVitJ5Vvw) to document the Korean Wave in the United States.

Challenges in a Globalizing East Asia

Global exchange has also produced global problems. Pollution, the by-product of industrialization, which in turn was enabled by the sharing of technology across countries and regions, now impacts regions beyond the locality of an industry. China's reliance on coal for energy production impacts air quality as far away as the west coast of the United States, and decreases in global oil production in the 1970s had a serious economic effect on Japan, which depends on imported oil. The March 11, 2011, Tohoku Triple Disaster (earthquake, tsunami, and nuclear disaster) in Japan, which triggered a meltdown of three of the six reactors at the Fukushima Daiichi Nuclear Power Station, had both domestic and international consequences. Domestically, nuclear power contributed as much as 30 percent of the energy used in the country at the time of the disaster. Popular resistance to the continued use of nuclear energy immediately after the meltdowns at Fukushima Daiichi led to all of Japan's nuclear power plants being taken off-line (those that were operating at the time) or being kept off-line (those that were shut down for maintenance). In mid-2014 the government continued to struggle with the question of whether or not to restart them. The disaster also prompted other countries, particularly in Europe, to reexamine their nuclear power policies, and Germany and Switzerland have decided to phase out nuclear power by 2022 and 2034, respectively (Kottasova 2014).

The Triple Disaster of March 11, 2011, released a barrage of man-made industrial debris, which was carried as far as the western coast of the United States. In 2013, a boat from Takata High School in Rikuzentakata, Iwate Prefecture, a small village that was almost completely destroyed by the tsunami, washed up on a beach in Crescent City, California, a fishing town that was nearly destroyed by a tsunami in 1964 and experienced a small tsunami from the disaster. Through social media, students at Del Norte High School were able to find the owners of the boat and return it to them in February 2014. The video *Recovering Hope* (http://vimeo.com/88625751) tells the story of turning disaster into friendship.

As Western cultural icons such as Mickey Mouse have infiltrated markets in East Asia, legal issues such as copyright have become sticking points, and countries must now deal with conflicting views on the ownership and use of intellectual property. In some cultures, using ideas and designs that originate with others is seen as a respectful act, but in North America and Europe the appropriation of original work without permission is illegal. Prior to the advent of social media, many instances of copyright infringement went unnoticed or unreported, but with an increasingly mobile population and widespread use of social media, these transgressions are easily, instantly, and widely disseminated.

Human rights issues, including human trafficking, child custody rights, refugees, and the death penalty, among others, also complicate mutual understanding and impact exchange. Different views on how society should operate and what constitutes "human rights" are often at the root of international disputes. In East Asia, the death penalty is one example. In cultures where the good of the collective society is prioritized, such as those in East Asia, capital punishment may be seen as a way to ensure harmony among the general population. Indeed, the use of the death penalty is often cited as an example of an individual right that is sacrificed for the benefit of the group. In fact, all of the countries in East Asia have the death penalty, though a moratorium against it has been in place in South Korea since 1998 (Bright 2012).

Another example is childhood custody. Japan does not typically recognize joint custody of children in cases of divorce. Full custody is given to one parent, and the other parent usually has no contact with the children. An increase in the number of international marriages that have ended in divorce has resulted in some controversy. There have been a number of high-profile cases in which one spouse has taken physical custody of the children in Japan in violation of a court-mandated joint custody decree in another country. Without the cooperation of the custodial parent, the noncustodial parent has no legal recourse in Japan to see their children. The 1980 Hague Convention on the Civil Aspects of International Child Abduction was instituted to govern international cases such as these, but Japan did not sign it until April 1, 2014, and the country is still struggling with internal laws to address various custody situations.

The Hague Conference on Private International Law was first convened in 1893. It negotiates and drafts multilateral treaties and conventions, including the 1980 Hague Convention on the Civil Aspects of International Child Abduction, the text of which is available on its website (http://www.hcch.net/index_en.php?act=conventions.text&cid=24).

Immigration and minority issues present another human rights challenge. These issues are magnified as the number of immigrants, both legal and illegal, and the diversity of their origins have increased in response to changes resulting from economic globalization. Domestic migration within China for employment purposes puts an extra strain on already overcrowded Chinese urban areas. In addition, people from Africa are increasingly seeking business opportunities in China (as are Chinese in Africa), particularly in the Pearl River Delta cities on the country's southern coast. In the early twentieth century, Japanese immigrated in large numbers to South America to escape poverty at home. Today, their descendants return to the land of their ancestors to find work. These individuals look physically the same as the Japanese, but they encounter a culture that is substantially different from the one they grew up with in South America. South Korea, meanwhile, is coping with a small stream of North Korean refugees who are suddenly confronted with ideas and consumer goods from around the world that they have never encountered previously. This can be overwhelming to them, and it can result in difficulties when they integrate into the global society.

It is vital to examine globalization concerns not only from Western perspectives, but through an East Asia–centered lens as well. Chinese, Japanese, and Korean viewpoints on globalizing processes, and on the issues arising from these processes, are critical elements in the contemporary study of the region. As the twentieth century dawned, how the three cultures influenced each other was perhaps the most critical element in defining the political and social forces that shaped these societies. Now, at the opening of the twenty-first century, the spheres of influence are opened and the theater of study is no longer East Asia in isolation but East Asia in the world.

References and Further Research

Allen, Matthew, and Rumi Sakamoto. 2006. *Popular Culture, Globalization and Japan*. New York: Routledge.

Andrea, Alfred J. 2014. "The Silk Road in World History: A Review Essay." *Asian Review of World Histories* 2, no. 1 (January): 105–127. http://www.thearwh.org/journal/arwh_2-1_andrea.pdf.

Armstrong, Charles K. 2013. *The Koreas*. 2nd ed. New York: Routledge.

Bentley, Jerry H. 1993. *Old World Encounters: Cross-Cultural Contacts and Exchanges in Pre-modern Times*. New York: Oxford University Press.

Bright, Arthur. 2012. "India Uses Death Penalty: 5 Other Places Where It's Legal but Rare." *Christian Science Monitor*, August 29. http://www.csmonitor.com/World/Asia-South-Central/2012/0829/India-uses-death-penalty-5-other-places-where-it-s-legal-but-rare/South-Korea.

Chang Yun-Shik, Hyun-Ho Seok, and Donald Baker, eds. 2011. *Korea Confronts Globalization.* Reprint. New York: Routledge.

Cohen, Warren. 2000. *East Asia at the Center: Four Thousand Years of Engagement with the World.* New York: Columbia University Press.

Guthrie, Doug. 2012. *China and Globalization: The Social, Economic and Political Transformation of Chinese Society.* 3rd ed. New York: Routledge.

The International Dunhuang Project: The Silk Road Online. http://idp.bl.uk/.

Iwabuchi Koichi. 2002. *Recentering Globalization: Popular Culture and Japanese Transnationalism,* Durham, NC: Duke University Press.

Kim, Samuel D. 2000. *East Asia and Globalization.* Lanham, MD: Rowman & Littlefield.

Kottasova, Ivana. 2014. "Interactive: How Fukushima Changed World's Attitudes to Nuclear Power." CNN, March 12. http://edition.cnn.com/2014/03/12/business/nuclear-power-after-fukushima/#index.

Kraidy, Marwan M. 2005. *Hybridity, or the Cultural Logic of Globalization.* Philadelphia, PA: Temple University Press.

Liu, Xinru. 2010. *The Silk Road in World History.* New Oxford World History. New York: Oxford University Press.

Watson, James. 2006. *Golden Arches East: McDonald's in East Asia.* 2nd ed. Stanford, CA: Stanford University Press.

Yano, Christine. 2013. *Pink Globalization: Hello Kitty's Trek across the Pacific.* Durham, NC: Duke University Press.

7

Debunking the Myths

ANNE PRESCOTT

An irony of globalization is that, even as images and ideas become accessible more quickly across national and cultural boundaries, stereotypes of peoples and societies persist. In fact, these stereotypes may emerge stronger in this environment. The dissemination of popular culture, transmitted across the globe, may have something to do with this, since mass media outlets often offer surface portrayals of peoples and cultures. Yet deeper knowledge of other countries and societies is certainly possible, and direct connections and interactions among individuals of different cultures are on the rise through travel, educational exchange, and virtual communities.

Indeed, stereotypes of the United States and Americans are often expressed in other countries, including China, Japan, and Korea. Among these is that everyone in the United States has a gun; Americans eat steak every day; Americans are loud, tall, and fat; and there are lots of cowboys in the United States who look like they just stepped out of a John Wayne movie. Stereotypes of other Western societies exist, purporting that British food is terrible, French are chic, or Canadians apologize for everything. Likewise, simplistic ideas about East Asians, some of which are examined in this chapter, abound. While there may be a kernel (or more) of truth to some of these images, they are generally recognized as sweeping generalizations.

In examining the nature as well as the roots of the ideas some people hold about East Asia and East Asians, we learn not only about China, Japan, and Korea, but about ourselves as well. As with many myths and misconceptions, some of the preconceived ideas that Westerners have about China, Japan, and Korea have their roots in cultural practices, real or perceived, in the region. Some may even be endorsed, at least unofficially, by a nation or its citizens to promote a desired image on the national or international stage. Such efforts are enabled in a globalized media environment through movies, television, and advertising.

Common Myths

Let's begin with the broadest myth: "All East Asians are alike." The truth is, of course, that they are no more alike in their physical looks or actions than any other national or cultural group. In fact, if one believes much of the media produced in East Asia (or even the United States), all Westerners are "alike" in that they are fit, wear trendy clothing, and drive expensive cars. These gross generalizations about what people are—or are not—are no more true about the people of China, Japan, and Korea than they are about the people of Europe and the United States. As discussed in previous chapters, there are many ethnic groups in East Asia, particularly China, and they have their own traditions, religious practices, and social customs. There is also diversity in physical traits. In cities and regions of China with large numbers of people who trace their roots to Central Asia, it is not unusual to see people with blue eyes and curly brown hair.

Another common misconception is that "all East Asians are smart." There is no special "intelligence gene" in East Asia, but parents, students, and society in general commonly have a high level of regard for education and teachers, an attitude supported by Confucian traditions. Children generally are expected to study diligently and reach their full intellectual and academic potential, whatever that may be. Students rarely have part-time jobs until they get to college—studying is their "job." It is typical for parents to support their children with the tools they need to succeed, at least as much as their resources and social circumstances allow, including access to the best teachers and study materials possible, a comfortable place to study, and high expectations. Exceptions exist, of course, and conditions can mitigate against high achievement, and opportunities for it. For instance, children of migrants (mostly from rural China) who live illegally in Beijing cannot attend public schools there because they do not possess the proper residency documents.

An often-repeated misbelief is that East Asians are not innovators but simply copy Western inventions. According to a 2013 article by Bruce Upbin in *Forbes* magazine, however, 16 of the 100 most innovative companies in the world are in East Asia. Japan's Sony Corporation has long been a world leader, with many innovative audio and electronic products, including the first pocket transistor radio (1958), the first portable tape player (Walkman, 1979), the CD player (1982), the first portable CD player (1984), and PlayStation (1994). Lesser-known companies are also innovative. For instance, the Chinese pork producer Henan Shuanghui (which recently acquired the American pork producer Smithfield Foods) maximizes output through computerization of the entire pork production process.

The belief that East Asians are incapable of innovation is often attributed to the centralized school curricula, which places an emphasis on rote learning and through which all students progress at the same pace through the same lessons in the same order. The Confucian respect for the teacher as the ultimate standard of excellence also helps to account for this belief. But perhaps a more culture-centric bias undergirds this myth: if a given innovation from China, Japan, or Korea is not applicable to or valued in Western cultures, the innovation and its usefulness to the people who created it may be invisible. QR (Quick Response) Codes are an example of an original product that was widely used in East Asia before it was known in the United States. Developed in Japan in 1994 for use in keeping track of components in automotive manufacturing, QR codes were then adapted for uses in other industries such as telecommunications and advertising. Although slow to catch on in the United States and

Europe, the growth in the use of cell phones with cameras has contributed to the broad application of this technology, first in East Asia and now increasingly in the West.

Food is an important cultural component in every society. Many Westerners who travel to East Asia expect to find that sweet and sour pork dominates the Chinese diet and that Japanese consume sushi daily, but in fact the diets of the people in East Asia are diverse and reflect local geography, history, and global integration. Millions of Chinese live too far from the sea or major rivers to eat fish, and rice is not the primary crop in northern areas of the region. In northern China, wheat noodles and dumplings are as ubiquitous as pasta and bread are in the United States. In Korea, kimchi (a spicy dish made of fermented vegetables, often napa cabbage) is the national dish, and in recent years the average consumption has been 20–24 kilograms (44–53 pounds) per person per year. Rice consumption is dropping in Japan, so much so that a new kind of bread, made with rice flour, is being promoted to support rice farmers. And although East Asians traditionally eat many foods with chopsticks, they regularly use knives, forks, and spoons as well, and many use these utensils more frequently than they do chopsticks.

The Korean Tourism Organization website (http://english.visitkorea.or.kr) has information on the history of kimchi, and on how to make it.

Exaggeration or misinterpretation of historical facts may also take on mythical qualities at times. One prime example is the notion that Japan was "closed" during the Edo (Tokugawa) period (1603–1867). It is true that Western residents of Japan were expelled in the early Edo years in reaction to their efforts to spread Christianity, which the rulers saw as a threat to their power. But trade between the Japanese and others continued, albeit under strict controls and from a limited number of ports. Chinese and Koreans continued to travel to and trade with Japan in the greatest numbers, but the Dutch, acting as agents for other European nations, also traded with Japan from the island of Dejima, located just offshore from the southern port city of Nagasaki.

Take a virtual historical tour of Dejima on the City of Nagasaki website (http://www.city.nagasaki.lg.jp/dejima/en).

Ideas About Gender

Gender-based stereotypes, primarily regarding women, also abound. The controlling mother dedicated solely to the educational success of her children is one such generalization. Japanese *kyōiku mama* (education moms), Korean mothers of "wild geese" (children who live with their mothers apart from their fathers to pursue better educational opportunities), and Chinese "tiger moms" are often credited with the success of their children, pushing them to the limits in curricular and extracurricular studies; but certainly not all East Asian mothers take such domineering roles in their children's educational careers.

Another gender-based stereotype is that of the subservient woman—the Asian wife walking three steps behind her husband. The apparent lack of strong female role models in business or international affairs supports this image, but the truth is that among the approximately 750 million women in Asia, there are (and have been, throughout history), many female leaders. From Hua Mulan, the legendary ancient Chinese girl who took her father's place and fought in the army for 12 years to the Japanese diplomat Sadako Ogata who, among other distinguished positions, was the United Nations High Commissioner for Refugees from 1991 to 2001, and South Korean president Park Geun-hye, in office since 2013, women are positive, active participants in East Asian society.

Perhaps one of the most insidious stereotypical images of Asian women, specifically Japanese women, is that of the geisha. Thought to be women of loose morals, geisha are not, by definition, prostitutes, though the association developed after World War II, when prostitutes adopted the title of "geisha" to attract patrons from the occupying military forces. In fact, the term *geisha*, or "art person," refers to a woman who is highly trained in traditional dance and music, and it refers to females of any age who are trained in and perform these arts.

Stereotypes About Martial Arts

The idea that most, or at least many, East Asians practice one or more of the martial arts is also prevalent with outsiders. Perhaps this comes from the popularity of martial arts movies and the global-star status of Bruce Lee, Jackie Chan, and others. The martial arts of kung fu (*gongfu*), wushu, karate, taekwondo, and others do have a long history in East Asia. They are practiced for many reasons, among them self-defense, competition, physical health, and spiritual development, and are an important part of the cultures of China, Korea, and Japan. But the story of martial arts movies stars is more complex. Many of them were in fact trained as acrobats for traditional Chinese opera. Before mass media were so readily available, traveling theater troupes circulated through towns and cities in China, presenting historical and mythical dramas as a popular type of entertainment. Acrobatic skills, in this context, are important in conveying the stories of warlords fighting in battles, as well as tricksters escaping from difficult situations. By the mid-twentieth century, with the advent of movies and radio, followed by television, the demand for traditional live theater was on the decline. Many of the actors trained in acrobatics found work in the film industry where their skills transferred easily to the popular martial arts genre.

Classical Training for Martial Arts Films

The China Drama Academy in Hong Kong trained young boys in the arts of Peking Opera, including acrobatics. The elite performing troupe, which was active in the 1950s and 1960s, was known as the "Seven Little Fortunes." Members of that group who became martial arts film stars include Jackie Chan, Sammo Hung, Yuen Biao, Corey Yuen, and Yuen Wah.

Finally, a popular and once pervasive myth is that the Great Wall of China is the only man-made structure that can be seen from the moon. If this is true, then you should be able to see Interstate 70 as it crosses the mountains in Colorado. It is wider than the Great Wall (30 feet at its widest) and "closer" to the moon—the highway is nearly three times higher in elevation than the highest point on the Great Wall. The truth is that the Great Wall cannot be seen from the moon. Government-certified Chinese tour guides and others repeated this myth as part of their standard narration for many years, but now they specifically point out that this is not true. Still, the myth endures, prolonging an image of a China as a massive power, with a past of powerful empires, great technical knowledge, and the ability to carry out monumental engineering projects.

There are many other myths about East Asia, its people and its cultures, and, taken as a whole, they form a certain picture to outsiders who are looking for sound bites that capture what "they" —the people of China, Japan, and Korea—are. Global integration provides outsiders with unprecedented access to deeper and more nuanced understandings, allowing one to separate the strands of truths, half-truths, and unfounded suppositions.

References and Further Research

Davies, Roger J., and Osamu Ikeno. 2002. *The Japanese Mind: Understanding Contemporary Japanese Culture*. Boston: Tuttle.

Mair, Victor H., Sanping Chen, and Frances Wood. 2013. *Chinese Lives: The People Who Made a Civilization*. New York: Thames and Hudson.

Rohlen, Thomas P., and Gerald K. LeTendre. 1999. *Teaching and Learning in Japan*. Cambridge: Cambridge University Press.

Shah, Angilee, and Jeffrey N. Wasserstrom, eds. 2012. *Chinese Characters: Profiles of Fast-Changing Lives in a Fast-Changing Land*. Berkeley: University of California Press.

Suzuki, David, and Keibo Oiwa. 1999. *The Other Japan: Voices Beyond the Mainstream*. Golden, CO: Fulcrum Publishing.

Upbin, Bruce. 2013. "The Ten Most Innovative Companies in Asia," *Forbes Magazine*, August 15. http://www.forbes.com/sites/bruceupbin/2013/08/15/the-ten-most-innovative-companies-in-asia/.

Wasserstrom, Jeffrey N. 2013. *China in the 21st Century: What Everyone Needs to Know*. 2nd ed. New York: Oxford University Press.

Zha, Qiang, ed. 2013. *Education in China: Educational History, Models, and Initiatives*. Great Barrington, MA: Berkshire.

PART FOUR

Case Studies

8

Introduction to the Case Studies

Anne Prescott

The case studies in this volume present a wide range of issues that have shaped or are shaping contemporary East Asia. The authors represent different primary academic disciplines, but each of them draws on a range of fields in their works. Societies do not exist in a single dimension, and the issues that affect societies are best understood as the result of intersecting planes of influence. As a result, any description or analysis of a particular issue, culture trait, or historical event is greatly enhanced when viewed through the lens of multiple disciplines. In order to utilize primary source documents and native informants, the scholars of these case studies speak and read the language(s) of the country where they do their primary work. Most also have at least some knowledge of another East Asian language.

The anthropologist Beth Notar examines the change from bicycle mobility to auto-mobility in China, looking at the impact that transformation has on space, place, and public health. As she notes, "cars do not simply enter a landscape, they transform it." She uses anthropological fieldwork strategies such as open-ended interviews and participant observation, a research methodology in which the researcher becomes closely involved with the cultural practices being investigated and uses his or her observations in answering research questions. Notar's fieldwork, conducted primarily in the city of Kunming, was carried out at auto expos, car dealerships, and drag racing events. She combines interviews with car owners and her own participation in car-related events to gain insight into the impact automobility has not only in China, but in the rest of the world as well.

Jina Kim examines the introduction of the radio into Korea through a literary lens. She begins by commenting that South Korea today is seen as a "technologically savvy, hyper-wired place," but then asks how Korea got to this point. She interprets the recent advances in technology and social media as the continuation of a century of technology and now-traditional media influencing people and society, beginning with the radio. Using Ch'ae Man-Sik's satirical 1938 novel *Peace Under Heaven* as the focus, her narrative includes not only the history of early radio in Korea, but also the influence of Japan's colonization of Korea on the introduction of radio in the country, as well as the role of women in Korean radio broadcasting, notably the economic impact it has had on them. She also examines the close relationship between print and broadcast media.

Joshua Roth takes an unusual approach in his anthropological case study that examines minorities in Japan. Roth collaborated with Mariko Sikama, a Japanese-Brazilian who has lived in Japan for many years, and together they paint a complicated and nuanced picture of one minority group in Japan, Brazilians of Japanese ancestry. They chose a specific point in time, the March 11, 2011, Triple Disaster in the Tohoku region, as the focus of their analysis. (For historical context, the authors reference the case of another minority group in Japan, Koreans, at the time of a similar disaster, the September 1, 1923, Great Kanto Earthquake.) Using social media posts and interviews, they discuss the consequences the Triple Disaster had on this sometimes marginalized and often fragile group, who are a part of the community by virtue of their Japanese heritage, yet are also removed from it because of their identification as Brazilians culturally. Focusing on this specific case helps the reader to identify universal topics surrounding minorities in a global world.

Confucianism is one of the elements that unites East Asia as a region, but the historical role of this philosophical tradition differs from its place in contemporary societies. Jeffrey Richey discusses Confucianism from its historical roots as the source of authority for East Asian governments to its place in modern-day East Asian societies. He first focuses on China, where the government is now using Confucianism to enhance its international image. He then discusses Confucianism in Korea, which outwardly appears to be the most Confucian society in East Asia today. Japan may be the least visibly Confucian today, but the core of the society reveals solid Confucian moorings that are still present. Finally, Richey suggests likely directions that Confucianism will take in these countries in the next few decades as they continue on a path to greater global integration.

Jacques Fuqua draws on many years as a U.S. military officer working on East Asia security issues in his writing on the Korean peninsula and global security. He summarizes key points in the recent history of the region, including the Japanese colonial period, the division of the Korean peninsula in 1948, and the Korean conflict from 1950 to 1953. These become the basis for explaining the role that other countries in the region, as well the United States, have played and continue to play in current events on the Korean peninsula. He introduces the North Korea political philosophy of self-reliance, called *juche*, in his discussion of the history of the North Korean regime and its actions today. Finally, he outlines the consequences for South Korea, the United States, China, Japan, and Russia of various scenarios that might play out in the Koreas in the future.

The ethnomusicologist Junko Oba uses the interdisciplinarity of her field, which combines musicology and anthropology, to examine not only the sonic sensation we call "music" but also musical activity—the who, when, where, and why of music making—surrounding the Japanese national anthem. Ethnomusicologists often examine living traditions or current musical activities, conducting fieldwork, analyzing recordings (both video and audio), and using written materials, including printed, online, and social media resources, in their research on music and music-making activities. Oba's case study on the Japanese national anthem, "Kimigayo," examines the nonmusical, social effects of this song, including the nationalistic meaning of the lyrics and the legislation dictating how, when, where, and by whom it must be sung. She considers the effects of group singing of the national anthem on the individual singers and those who are listening. This includes broader geopolitical implications, since the lyrics and usage of the national anthem are sometimes perceived by Koreans, Taiwanese, and people of other nations as symbols of the painful colonization period at the beginning of the twentieth century. Legislating how, when, and where "Kimigayo" should be sung leaves some to wonder if the era of Japanese dominance has really ended.

The anthropologist Maris Gillette's case study weaves together an examination of porcelain manufacturing in Jingdezhen, China, and international trade from the fifteenth century to today. Once a powerful global player in ceramic manufacturing, as a result of domestic politics and competition from European and American porcelain products, the Chinese porcelain trade in general, and the city of Jingdezhen in particular, faced a disastrous decline by the beginning of the twentieth century. Today, Jingdezhen is working to reverse its fortunes in an increasingly interconnected world, and those efforts are impacted—both positively and negatively—by globalization. Gillette utilizes historical and contemporary documents as well as fieldwork in Jingdezhen to present the story of the people and products of the city.

Bruce Baird examines the story of the twentieth-century Japanese theatrical dance form butō (also romanized as butoh), which grew out of the turbulence of postwar Japan. Butō artists have created new body languages, and the art was—and continues to be—molded by geopolitical pressures brought about by contact with other cultures around the world. In response to these forces, butō artists have created new body languages that express emotions which are at once beautiful and raw. Although Japan is the birthplace of this artistic form, today it is truly a global one, as it continues to be strongly influenced by traditions from outside Japan and practiced by artists around the world. As Baird states, "this dance form has taken its place among the most important developments in performing arts in the latter half of the twentieth century."

In the West, China's one-child policy is often seen purely as a human rights issue. But the issue is more complex in a society where boys have historically been preferred over girls by families, and where they have been given greater freedom and advantages than girls. The anthropologist Vanessa Fong examines how girls who were born after the one-child policy was implemented in 1979 are helping to change gender norms. She does this through a combination of fieldwork centering on a girl in the city of Dalian, and through a survey of larger groups of singleton (only-child) girls and their families. As she states, "because they have had more support from their parents than previous generations, singleton daughters have unprecedented freedom to challenge gender norms. At the same time, however, their freedom is limited by a system that remains structured by socioeconomic and gender inequalities." Her work clarifies the changes in domestic roles, education, work, marriage, and other areas of Chinese society, and she discusses the remaining limits to their power in a society impacted by the one-child policy.

9

From Flying Pigeons to Fords: China's New Car Culture

Beth E. Notar

From Flying Pigeons to Fords

It is difficult to believe now, but I used to bike all over Beijing. After graduating from college, and working a summer job, I moved to China's capital city to study at Beijing University, the country's top educational establishment. Not long after arriving on campus, I visited a state-run department store (there were no private stores back then) and picked out a black (well, all the bikes were black) Flying Pigeon brand classic cruiser. My Flying Pigeon was a men's bike, but since it had a 22-inch frame, smaller than the standard 28-inch frames, it suited me. As a foreign student I was able to buy a bike directly from the store without having to wait for a ration permit. This was in 1985, six years into China's reform era and the shift from a centrally planned economy to a global market economy.

Riding my bike home that day, I learned that I had to dismount when passing through the university gates so that campus security could see who was coming and going. I observed that the Chinese students swiftly dismounted by swinging a right leg over the back book rack, took just a few short steps through the gate, then placed a left foot on the pedal, swung the right leg over the frame, and were quickly off again. I began to do the same.

Every day after classes were over, and on weekends, I would hop on my Flying Pigeon and, sometimes with classmates, sometimes by myself, ride onto Haidian Road. There, I would join the city's millions of other cyclists in a great river of black and blue and white and green. The bicycles were all black, and the people were all dressed in the revolutionary-era style of the time, wearing either blue cotton pants and jackets or olive green army surplus pants and white shirts.

There were very few cars in Beijing then. The center lanes of broad avenues such as Haidian Road would be largely empty except for a few chauffeured Red Flag limousines allocated for the use of high-ranking officials, some taxis for foreigners, and public buses. The side lanes belonged to those of us on bicycles.

Haidian Road had large, tall trees planted along both sides. These trees sheltered the avenue from the sun and created a dappled pattern of sunlight and shadow. My classmates and I would join the other cyclists along this shady avenue, cruising at a moderate speed to keep pace. Amazingly, given the number of bicycles, I observed very few collisions. People used their bicycle bells—"ting, ting" —to warn others around them of their presence. Being part of the flow of humanity—on bicycles, going neither too fast nor too slow, with the sound of bells all around—was something I'd never experienced before, and it was exhilarating.

Sometimes my classmates and I would bike out to one of the former imperial summer palaces—Yuanmingyuan, which had been burned and looted by American, British, and French troops in 1860 and again in 1900, or Yiheyuan, with its famous marble boat, considered a symbol of the decadence of the dowager empress and marking the decline of the last Chinese dynasty, the Qing, which fell in 1911. Sometimes we would bike to the center of Beijing to see the former imperial palace, the Forbidden City, and Tiananmen Square, with its large portrait of Chairman Mao Zedong, the man who led the Chinese Communists to victory over the Nationalists in 1949, the year that marked the founding of the People's Republic of China. My classmates and I would leave our bikes at designated parking lots presided over by fierce older women who would charge us one *mao* (ten Chinese cents, the equivalent of one U.S. cent then) for the privilege of parking.

Learn about the history of the Flying Pigeon bicycle and check out the models being sold today at the company's website (http://www.flying-pigeon.eu).

Of course, biking could be tough, too. In the winter, sandstorms would sweep in from the Mongolian steppes and the strong winds would make me feel as if I were riding in place. Also in the winter, the omnipresent coal dust discharged from furnaces would leave a film on my hair and skin. Like many other Beijingers, I took to wearing a cotton face mask in the winter in order to keep this dust out of my nose and lungs.

Yet if I sound nostalgic about biking in Beijing it is because, when I return there now, it is almost impossible to remember that I ever did so. Beijing has become notorious for traffic jams, some lasting up to nine days. Nor am I the only one has these fond memories of cycling in China. In his book *As China Goes, So Goes the World*, the historian Karl Gerth similarly remembers fondly buying a black bike as a student in China in 1986 and hearing the sound of bicycle bells, instead of the car engines and horns one hears now. In a recent article titled "The Good Old Days on China's Erba Che [28 inch bikes]," a Chinese author describes her fond memories of the old black bikes—how her father eventually bought one for the family, how he lovingly maintained it, how he had a little wooden seat built for her, and how he would give her rides to school or to visit relatives. At the end of the article the author includes a recent photograph. On the left hand side is a dense traffic jam with at least three lanes of cars stuck bumper to bumper; on the right, cordoned off from the heavy traffic, is a lane with a lone male cyclist, and no other bicycles—or cars— in sight. In 1986 it was almost impossible to imagine that Beijing would become a city of traffic jams. Now, it is almost impossible to remember that bicycles used to dominate the streets there.

The article "The Good Old Days on China's Erba Che [28 inch bikes]" is posted at the China Daily Forum (http://bbs.chinadaily.com.cn/thread-853800-1-1.html), an online resource hosted by *China Daily*, a Chinese-based, English-language news conglomerate. The photo of the lone bicycle rider alongside the massive traffic jam is on the last page of the article (http://bbs.chinadaily.com.cn/thread-853800-3-1.html).

In 1986, during my second year in China, the Flying Pigeon bicycle factory sold a record three million bicycles. Twelve years later, in 1998, the company sold only 200,000. That year, it fired most of its 7000 workers and moved to a smaller factory (Rocks and Wu 2004, n.p.). Conversely, in 1987, during my third year studying in China, there were only ten private cars in Beijing; there were over five million in 2013 (Chen 2013). Nationwide, private car ownership in China rose 500 percent between 2003 and 2011 (Whitely 2011; Chen 2013). In 2009, new vehicle sales in China surpassed those in the United States. By 2013, China had broken the world record for the most car sales in any one country—over 20 million—and the top-selling car was the Ford Focus, with nearly 403,000 sold (Kennedy 2014). China is now also the hottest market for high-end cars. For example, Lamborghini sales rose 150 percent between 2010 and 2011, and Jaguar sales jumped 71 percent between 2011 and 2012. It is estimated that by 2020 China will surpass the United States as the largest world market for luxury vehicles.

Table 9.1

Sales Figures of Luxury Vehicles in China from 2012 to 2013*

Luxury car brand	2012 sales	Change from previous year	2013 sales	Change from previous year
Audi	405,838	29.60%	492,000	21.2%
BMW	326,444	40.40%	390,700	19.7%
Mercedes-Benz	196,211	1.50%	228,000	16.0%
Jaguar, Land Rover	73,347	74.00%	95,100	30.0%
Volvo	41,989	−10.90%	61,100	45.5%
Total sold	1,043,829	26.07%	1,266,900	21.0%

*This chart does not include the very highest-end cars, such as Bentley, Ferrari, Lamborghini, and Rolls Royce.

Sources: Li Fangfang, "Volvo Sales Drop Defies Surging Luxury Sector," *China Daily*, January 18, 2013, http://www.chinadaily.com.cn/business/2013-01/18/content_16136859.htm; Ash, "Luxury Auto Brands Continue to Dominate in 2013," *China Car Times*, January 20, 2014, http://www.chinacartimes.com/2014/01/luxury-auto-brands-continue-dominate-2013/; "Jaguar Land Rover China Roars into 2014," *China Daily*, January 15, 2014, http://www.china.org.cn/business/2014-01/15/content_31192588.htm.

How did this shift from a society characterized by localized bicycle mobility to one characterized by globalized automobility occur? What does it mean for people in Beijing and other places in China to drive a global-brand car instead of riding a China-brand bicycle? What are the implications for China's entry into a global "system of automobility" for Chinese ideas about space and place, public and private, urban and rural, mobility and status, and work and leisure? What new kinds of social relations arise from such a change?

People who grew up in the United States may consider it "normal" for people to own a car, to travel mostly by car, and for the government to subsidize the automobile industry and its infrastructure. But there is nothing normal about this. Part of the task of an anthropologist is to familiarize the strange and question the familiar: as an anthropologist of China, I ask certain questions: What does it *mean* for a society to transform itself from one dominated by walking, biking, and taking public transport to one dominated by automobiles? What does it mean to have millions of new vehicles and millions of new drivers enter the landscape in the span of a few years?

Below, I briefly provide some background on the political and economic factors that have shaped China's global transformation from a society characterized by bicycle mobility to one characterized by automobility. Then I discuss some of the profound changes that can be observed in space, place, and public health, after which I explore some of the less obvious temporal transformations of China's shift to an automobile society. I show that, in addition to being stuck in traffic jams, people in China are spending time doing things they never did before, such as shopping for cars and car accessories, taking road trips, and even drag racing. It is these status-enhancing and pleasure-seeking activities that help explain why cars are so popular in China, despite their negative impact on other aspects of urban life.

Globalizing China

After China's paramount revolutionary-era ruler, Mao Zedong, died in 1976, and Deng Xiaoping (formerly purged by Mao) came to power in 1978, the Chinese Communist Party decided to depart from its more "leftist" policies and follow a path of "reform and opening" (*gaige kaifang*). This meant implementing market reforms and "opening up" to foreign trade and direct investment. As part of these reforms, China began to move away from its centralized, planned economy. Communes were disbanded, many state-run factories were closed, and college graduates were no longer guaranteed jobs. Instead, the country began to move toward a system where foreign companies could set up joint ventures, private businesses such as shops and restaurants were allowed to open, and graduates would have to compete for jobs. Whereas the previous system had emphasized collectivism and worked by allocation, the new system started to highlight individualism and began to work in part through market competition and consumption.

As the reform era has proceeded, China has become more integrated into the global economy. In his book, Karl Gerth provides an excellent overview of some of the structural reasons why integration into the global economy has pushed China to become an automobile society. In the 1990s, when China decided to join the World Trade Organization (WTO) in order to gain access to global markets, it was required to open its borders to more foreign imports. Predicting that this would mean pressure to import foreign cars, China decided to simultaneously develop both foreign-domestic joint ventures and its own auto industry.

As the history and anthropology of the global rise of car cultures have shown, cars do not simply enter a landscape, they transform it. A huge infrastructure is needed to support a society dedicated to automobility. Not only do there have to be places to refuel cars and places to purchase and repair cars, but there also have to be places to drive them and park them.

City streets in China—once dominated by bicycles—have been rebuilt to accommodate cars. This has meant the demolition and reconstruction of the old urban centers of most Chinese cities (often done with low-cost immigrant labor) to create highways, ring roads, and overpasses. This has happened in other times and places—such as the 1950s in New York, when the urban planner Robert Moses undertook massive development projects—but the speed and scale of the transformation of Chinese cities is unprecedented. It would be as if most of the old neighborhoods of Boston, New York, and Washington, DC, were demolished and rebuilt within ten years, along with those of Chicago, Atlanta, Dallas, Houston, Phoenix, Denver, Seattle, and San Francisco. When I return to Beijing, there is little about the city that I recognize from my student days, except for the area around the Forbidden City. A few years ago, when a friend told me to meet her at a coffee shop, I had no idea that I was next to Haidian Road where I used to bike—until she told me. There was nothing I could see that I remembered.

During the Mao years, under the "work-unit" (*danwei*) system of urban planning, a city dweller was allocated housing according to where he or she worked, usually somewhere near the factory, school, or office. In the reform era, many people no longer live in work-unit housing. Moreover, since old urban neighborhoods have been demolished to make room for new roads and new construction, people have had to relocate to the suburbs. In the 1999 film *Shower* (*Xizao*), the Chinese film director Zhang Yang humorously and poignantly depicts the demolition and displacement of an old Beijing neighborhood. This detachment of residency from workplace, as well as the growth of the suburbs, has led to a perceived "need" for car transport, at least until (or if) public transport fully connects the suburbs.

But it is not just within Chinese cities that new car-friendly roads have been built. Thomas Campanella, in *The Concrete Dragon*, writes that "into the late 1980s, China's highway system consisted of less than 200 miles of modern high-speed, limited-access motorway," but "by 2006 the National Trunk Highway System spanned 25,480 miles, making it second in length only to that of the American interstates" (2008, 222). In other words, in just 20 years, China developed a national highway system that rivals that of the United States.

Yet one could say that China is *returning* to Nationalist founding father Sun Yat-sen's 1922 dream of "one car per every person." In the 1920s, China already had started to embark on the global road to an automobile society. In the early twentieth century, as elites in China began to purchase imported automobiles (and as metropolitan areas began to use public buses for the masses), new urban roads were constructed. City walls were torn down to "open up" and "modernize" cities, and the old bricks were used for new roads. Old neighborhoods were also demolished to make way for new roads as well. For example, in 1935, the southwestern city of Kunming demolished 2000 houses to expand roads (Dikötter 2006, 81–82).

This journey toward becoming an automobile society was stalled during the Mao years (1949–1976), when private cars were banned. If the Communist revolution had not happened in 1949, China might have proceeded along the road to an automobile society without having first become a predominantly bicycle-oriented society. However, the transition would probably have proceeded more gradually. Now, the rush toward automobility has not only rapidly transformed all urban places, but it has also had a sudden, dramatic impact on public health.

To view Chinese versions of various models of major U.S. and European car manufacturers, and how the manufacturers market the cars visually, use the following links:

- Chevrolet (www.chevrolet.com.cn)
- Buick (www.buick.com.cn)
- BMW (www.bmw.com.cn)
- Volvo (www.volvocars.com/zh-cn)
- Toyota (www.toyota.com.cn)
- Honda (www.honda.com.cn)
- Jaguar (www.jaguar.com.cn)

As one might envision, the public health consequences of shifting from a bicycle society to an automobile society have been huge. In 2007, China overtook the United States as the biggest emitter of carbon dioxide. The air quality of major Chinese cities has deteriorated, prompting elites in Beijing to invest in expensive air filters for their cars and offices.

As people bike less and drive more—and participate in the kind of consumption practices that have gone along with global car culture, such as going to a McDonald's drive-through for fast food—obesity in China has been on the rise. In 1985 the only overweight people I encountered in China were officials. In urban areas, rice, wheat, and meat were rationed, with work units distributing ration coupons. Now people who can afford it can indulge in elaborate banquets, as well as fast food, and it is common to see extremely overweight children.

Most disturbingly, a shift to an automobile society has severely affected mortality. According to a 2011 *China Daily* report, "traffic accidents are the leading cause of death for people age 45 and younger in China." While data on traffic fatalities is disputed, according to the medical journal *The Lancet*, between 81,000 and 221,000 people now die in traffic accidents in China each year (Alcorn 2011).

China Daily's full report on traffic deaths, "Study: China Traffic Deaths Higher Than Police Say," from July 1, 2011, can be found on the paper's website (http://www.chinadaily.com.cn/china/2011-01/07/content_11808453.htm).

Given the negative consequences of a shift to an automobile society in terms of public health—decreased air quality, increased obesity, increased traffic fatalities—one might ask what the *appeal* of cars is. The sociologist Jack Katz has called cars "naturally seductive instruments." Anthropologists would argue that no technology is "naturally" seductive, but technologies can certainly be culturally seductive. What is it about cars?

Cars Are Not Just Cars

As anthropologists have long pointed out, things are not just things. Things take on special symbolic significance depending on who uses them and how they are used. Moreover, cars are a special kind of thing, one that the anthropologist Pierre Lemonnier has called a "strategic object" that communicates "*key values or fundamental characteristics of particular social relations*" (2012, 12; italics in original).

During the Mao years, while political elites lacked disproportionate purchasing power, and while available consumer goods were limited, elites *were* allocated preferential access to goods and services based on rank. One of the ways in which political rank was clearly manifested was in the kind of vehicle to which one had access. Although political elites are no longer the only ones to have access to cars, they are still a key marker of status. Since 1994, when private car consumption began to be allowed, businessmen, entrepreneurs, and even professors have been buying, or hoping to buy, cars. Cars may be thought of as the primary form of what the economist Thorstein Veblen, in *The Theory of the Leisure Class* (1899), termed "conspicuous consumption."

The full text of Thorstein Veblen's *The Theory of the Leisure Class* (1899) is available online through Project Gutenberg (http://www.gutenberg.org/files/833/833-h/833-h.htm).

While it is clearly observable that the shift to an automobile society has had negative consequences for place and public health in China, it may be less obvious that this shift has also transformed how people spend their time. People now spend time stuck in traffic jams, for one thing, and the ways people choose to spend their leisure

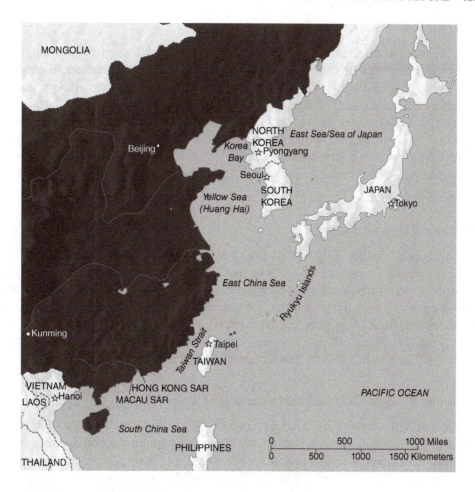

time has also changed. As discussed below, this can involve attending auto shows, decorating a new car, drag racing, and auto-club trips. Important to understanding the pleasure in these activities is the status that cars convey.

Research in Kunming

In 2008, I lived in the southwestern Chinese city of Kunming, the provincial capital of Yunnan Province, which borders Myanmar (Burma), Laos, and Vietnam. I had previously studied in Kunming in the mid-1990s (when I also biked everywhere), and had conducted research there for my first book on the impact of ethno-tourism inspired by representations in popular culture (guidebooks, movie musicals, and martial arts novels). It was during this earlier research that I became aware of the growing number of traffic accidents and became interested in studying China's new car culture.

(continued)

(continued)

In order to research new car consumption and use in and around Kunming, I engaged in what might be considered standard "fieldwork" methodology for cultural anthropologists: I conducted open-ended qualitative interviews (often lasting an hour or more) and engaged in "participant-observation"—participating in what people were doing, but also observing their activities, in order to better understand their point of view within their cultural context. While my methods were standard for anthropologists, my research sites were somewhat unconventional: auto expos, car dealerships, and drag racing strips.

Leisure Time and Cars

Kunming is a "smaller" city by Chinese standards, with a metropolitan area of 6.43 million persons. Despite this, Kunming, like Beijing, has demolished its old city and rebuilt it in a new car-friendly way. Interestingly, Kunming has also had the second-highest rate of car consumption in China, next only to the southeastern boomtown of Shenzhen. Four of the people I interviewed in Kunming—"Lonewolf," Prof. Li, John, and Mr. Wang (all pseudonyms)—exemplify changes in how China's new globalized automobile culture shapes how people spend their time.

"Lonewolf": Auto Shows and Dreaming of Cars

I first met "Lonewolf"—the English name he chose for himself—on a flight from Beijing to Kunming. I had just attended the Beijing International Automotive Exhibition, known as "Auto China," and noticed that the young man sitting next to me on the plane was looking at photographs of the exhibition on his laptop. We started talking about the auto show and spent the rest of the flight looking at the dozens of photographs that he had taken.

Lonewolf, a skinny guy in his twenties, with spiky hair, worked for an airplane parts company and had been attending another trade show in Beijing for a few days. When he finished his work at his trade show for the day, he would go to the auto show to look at the hundreds of cars on display.

The first auto expo in China was held in a series of bamboo sheds in Shanghai in 1921 (Campanella 2010 [2008], 223–225). However, during the Mao years (1949–1976), when private car consumption was banned, there were no auto shows. After Mao died in 1976, auto shows returned to China as part of reform and opening. The first small-scale auto show in post-Mao China occurred in Guangzhou (also known as Canton) in 1980, almost a decade and a half before people could purchase private cars. The first larger-scale auto show in reform-era China was the Shanghai Auto Show, held from July 3 to July 9, 1985, almost a decade before people could purchase private autos. A total of 328 enterprises from 22 countries exhibited, and attendees could see that there were more cars in the world than "the Red Flag limousines that ran the streets" ("First Shanghai Auto Show" [Diyi jie Shanghai chezhan]. 2005. Xinhua, April 21. http://news3.xinhuanet. com/auto/2005-04/21/content_2860274.htm; accessed August 21, 2014).

The Beijing International Automotive Exhibition was first held from July 3 to July 8, 1990, at the China International Exhibition Center. According to China's Car Net (Zhongguo qiche jiaoyi wang 2010), approximately 100,000 people came to see the 216 cars shown (China's Car Net [Zhongguo qiche jiaoyi wang] 2010). By the time I first attended the show in April 2008, over 800 vehicles were being shown. In April 2010 the Beijing show had 780,000 visitors and 990 vehicles on display (Auto Channel 2010); by April 2012 over 800,000 people attended and over 1,100 vehicles were being shown; and in April 2014 over 850,000 attendees could see 1,134 vehicles on display ("2010 Beijing International Automotive Exhibition [Auto China 2010] Concluded Successfully." 2010. PR Newswire. May 10. http://www.prnewswire. com'news-releases/2010-beijing-international-automotive-exhibition-auto-china-2010-concluded-successfully-93260824.html; accessed August 21, 2014; "Great Success of 2014 Beijing Automobile Exhibition." 2014. China Auto Show. April 30. http://www.China-autoshow.com/en/news/exponews/2014/0430/499.html; accessed August 21, 2014.) In its size and scale, the Beijing Auto Expo has come to rival some of the top auto expos in the world, including those in Paris, Frankfurt, Los Angeles, and Detroit (see http://www.theautochannel.com/news/2010/05/10/476857.html; accessed Aug. 6, 2013).

See what's new at the current Beijing International Automotive Exhibition at the English-language version of Auto China's website (http://autochina. auto-fairs.com/).

Lonewolf had just started working and had not yet saved enough money to buy a car, even a low-end Chery (Qirui) QQ hatchback, which sells for less than US$5,000. But he spent much of his free time dreaming about which kind of car he might eventually buy.

Later, when I interviewed Lonewolf, I asked him what he did with all of the photos he had taken at the Beijing Auto Expo. He told me that he e-mailed them to friends and colleagues, who would then share their photographs with him. They would spend much time comparing photographs of and reactions to the different cars on display, as well as the beautiful young women models posing with the cars.

The way Lonewolf and his friends spent time looking at cars and dreaming of getting a new car (as well as a beautiful girlfriend) is similar to that of many young American men. Yet some of the other ways in which people are spending their free time in China, at least as it relates to cars, differs markedly from the ways Americans enjoy their cars, as explored below.

Beijing International Automotive Exhibition, 2008. *(Beth E. Notar)*

Prof. Li: Auto Nanny and Car Decorating

I first met Prof. Li, a short, lively woman in her fifties, through another professor who told me that Prof. Li had just bought a new car, and suggested that she might be willing to talk with me. Prof. Li not only agreed to let me interview her and showed me her new car, but she also accompanied me to the shop where she had bought the decorations for her car, and, later, even went with me one night to a drag racing strip on the outskirts of town.

Prof. Li, who taught at one of the universities in Kunming, had purchased a bronze, four-door Chery (Qirui) sedan, and the decoration inside the car was just as important to her as the car exterior—as is the case for many new car consumers in China. Like most of the new car purchasers I interviewed, she had bought leather seats—"they're more durable and easy to clean," she explained. In addition, she, like many others, had bought seat covers. Prof. Li's were made of real sheepskin, but there were many other kinds available. When Prof. Li took me to the large auto accessories store called Auto Nanny (Che Baomu), I saw that it was also possible to order seat covers in woven bamboo, silk brocade, or shag carpeting, and in a variety of colors and patterns. In addition, Prof. Li had bought a steering wheel cover, a tissue box cover for the box of tissues in the back seat, and a dash pad for her cell phone.

Learn more about Qirui (Chery) automobiles on the company's international and domestic websites (www.cheryinternational.com and www.chery.cn, respectively).

Curiously to me, Prof. Li, as well as most others I interviewed, had paid for black tinted film to be placed on the windows, ordered from the America's Tint company. Although it was advertised as "American," I told Prof. Li that in the United States very few people had tinted windows, except for gangsters and politicians. Prof. Li said that she thought that the popularity of black window tints in China had to do with people modeling their cars on those of Chinese officials, who all had such window tints so that no one could see inside.

While Prof. Li's interior decoration was rather fancy by most American standards, I noticed at the Auto Nanny store that even more elaborate decorations were available. For example, there were seat belt covers with pink Hello Kitty designs, gearshift covers with Snoopy or other motifs, and holders for cups and keys and CDs. One could buy various objects to hang from the rearview mirror, like the clichéd fuzzy dice sometimes seen in the United States. These might be images of the Buddha, Chinese characters to promote longevity, or, more surprisingly, Chairman Mao as a kind of protector or god to ward off evil. One could also buy many different kinds of bumper stickers or decals, some meant to replicate luxury cars—for example, a silver Ferrari logo to place on one's low-end Chery QQ hatchback.

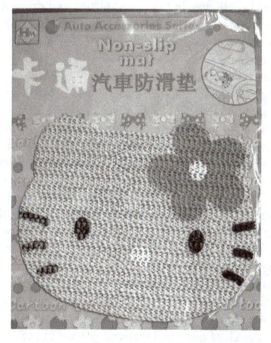

Interior decorations for cars can include nonslip mats with particular themes, such as this "Hello Kitty" version. *(Beth E. Notar)*

Lonewolf, like many Americans, spends time dreaming of buying a new car, but few Americans spend as much time as Prof. Li and other new car consumers in China shopping for and decorating their car interiors. What might be the explanation for this? It seems not only that people are modeling their cars on those of officials, as Prof. Li explained about the window tints, but also that cars now might have the same, or even higher, status for the Chinese consumer than for the U.S. consumer. In the mid- to late-1980s, when I first went to China, before a man asked a woman to marry him, he and his family ideally should have acquired a bicycle, a sewing machine, and a watch. Now, 20 years later and 20 years into China's booming economy, a man and his family should ideally have acquired a house and a car. Since a car is second only to a house in status as a kind of "strategic object," the care going into decorating a car is similar to that of decorating a house. Moreover, as the name of the store Auto Nanny indicates, for most Chinese urban families with only one child, the addition of a car is almost like adding a new member to the family.

Yet even Prof. Li's interior car decorations and the decorations I saw at the Auto Nanny store pale in comparison to those who are decorating their cars for a new form of car-related leisure activity in China: drag racing and drifting.

John: Drag Racing and Drifting

I first met John—the English name he had given himself—when I struck up a conversation with him about his car, a silver sports coupe, which was parked outside my family's apartment. He was in his early thirties and dressed in business attire: a button-down shirt and tie, gray slacks, black leather shoes. What struck me about John's car was not only that it sported different decals, but also that it had dynamic colored stripes painted on it.

John and his car were my first introduction to the world of modified cars, drag racing and "drifting" in China. Inspired by Japanese popular graphic novels (called manga in Japan) and animated movies (anime), such as *Initial D* and *Tokyo Drift*, young men in China have started to modify, drag race, and "drift" cars. To modify a car is not only to decorate it, as Prof. Li did with her car interior. It usually involves some elaborate paintwork—to indicate to others that it is modified—as well as more substantial modifications such as a new engine, exhaust system, and tires.

Sometimes men—and it is overwhelmingly men who are engaged in this activity— will do the modifications themselves, and sometimes they will ask a mechanic to do it for them. In John's case, he hired a mechanic to install a "turbo" engine, elaborate sound system, and under-body violet lights that made the car appear to float above the pavement at night.

John had his car modified not simply to show it off on the streets of Kunming, but primarily to drag race it with friends. Drag racing involves two cars competing side by side to see who can get to a finish line first. In Kunming, John and his friends raced at night on a stretch of new road that was not yet in use. Two guys would line up their cars, and a third guy would stand in the middle and say "One, two, three, drive!" Whoever got to the finish line first won the race.

Modified cars, Kunming, China. (*Beth E. Notar*)

Before, after, and during the races there was much revving of turbo engines, playing of loud music and flashing of lights. When the cars were not racing, or zipping back around to get into race position, they were parked to the side, where they could be shown off and admired—who had the nicest paint job, the best lights, the most powerful engine.

Drag racing was prohibited in Kunming (as in the rest of China) but the drivers played a game of cat-and-mouse with the police. John told me that he and his friends would send out a text message to each other: "When?" Then they would all meet and race until the police showed up, whereupon they would scatter. One night, Prof. Li asked to go see the drag racing with me. Since I did not have my own car, and since in the past I had ridden to the site with John and his girlfriend, Prof. Li's husband offered to drive us over. We were watching the racing, when, suddenly, I began to see guys jump into their cars and speed away. Then I noticed a police cruiser driving up and urged Prof. Li's husband to drive us away quickly, but he was not as fast as the other drivers. We were the only car stopped by the police that night. When Prof. Li's husband told the police officer that we were just there to watch—their car was clearly not modified or prepped for drag racing—he let us off with a warning and told us not to return. I was mortified that I had almost gotten Prof. Li and her husband into trouble. However, Prof. Li, if not her husband, seemed to find the whole night exciting.

In addition to drag racing, some of John's friends also engaged in "drifting" (*piaoyi* in Mandarin). Drifting is a technique invented by young Japanese men on the mountainous roads around Tokyo. It involves sliding through sharp curves so that one appears to "drift" around the curve. Drifting is dangerous. If a driver does not do it skillfully, he can slide off the road. Since Kunming, like Tokyo, has mountainous roads nearby, drifting has caught on there.

In the United States, people often associate car modification and drag racing with working-class or more marginalized young men. As anthropologists of American culture have found, in U.S. communities in Texas and California, Chicano, Latino, and Asian American men have used car modification and drag racing as a way to challenge and resist the strictures of a structurally racist and classist society.

In China right now, however, it is only elite young men who can afford to purchase and modify their own cars. John, for example, had an excellent white-collar job working for a bank. When John found out that my husband's rebel cousin had been part of a Mazda racing team in Japan, he asked if he could help him order a new engine to be shipped from Japan—a very expensive proposition. In contrast to the U.S. case, John and his friends' modification, racing, and drifting represents a flaunting of their elite status—even in front of the police—rather than any form of resistance.

Mr. Wang: Auto Club Tripping

In addition to drag racing, John and his friends would also go on road trips together, driving in a convoy to scenic towns north of Kunming, such as Dali, Lijiang, and Zhongdian (recently renamed "Shangri-La" to attract more tourists). The phenomenon of the "road trip" has caught on in China, but it differs from the classic American family or buddy road trip in that it is often done in a convoy of cars, with each driver using his or her own car. Called a "self-drive tour" (*zijia you*), these trips are organized by car dealers, car clubs, or groups of friends. I never went on a "self-drive tour" with John and his friends, but I did go on an auto-club trip organized by a Chery car dealership.

I first met Mr. Wang when a Chery car dealership in Kunming invited me to go along on one of their self-drive tours. The dealership had organized the trip for new owners of Chery "Tigo" SUVs, and Mr. Wang and his wife were new consumers.

Tire rolling during an auto-club trip. *(Beth E. Notar)*

On the morning of the tour, Mr. Wang and the other drivers met at a Sinopec gas station located on one of Kunming's ring roads. Since I did not have my own vehicle, I took a taxi to the gas station. Once there, the Chery dealer who was hosting the tour distributed flags, t-shirts, and stickers to each of the drivers (and to me, as a souvenir). Prominently brandishing the Chery logo, we followed the dealer out of town and drove on the new highway to the town of Yuxi, about 50 miles (80 kilometers) south of Kunming. After a multicourse banquet lunch, we drove to a parking lot by a park, where the dealer engaged Mr. Wang and the other drivers in a series of competitions—tire changing, tire rolling, and car decorating.

I realized that this auto-club trip represented a kind of "coming out" party for the new car owners; in a similar way to debutantes, their new SUVs and their new skill as drivers were making a first appearance before a larger public. The auto-club trip, as well as the t-shirts, stickers, and other objects with Chery logos, also served to foster brand recognition and identification among drivers like Mr. Wang and their families.

Conclusion

A few weeks after the auto-club trip, I bumped into Mr. Wang on a pedestrian overpass over a ring road in Kunming. He was pushing an old bicycle. "Mr. Wang," I asked, surprised, "what happened to your new SUV?" "Oh," he laughed, "since my office is not too far from my home, and since traffic has gotten so bad, I just bike to work."

Does Mr. Wang's return to riding a bicycle signal a potential return of a bicycle society in China? Most likely not. Given the current boom of car consumption in China, and the status associated with driving one's own car, China, like the United States, seems "carjacked," and it is difficult to imagine that China will return to the days of streets dominated by bicycles. Bicycles are seen as second best to cars—some are even named after car brands, such as Mercedes or BMW—and are also now more of a leisure item. When I was in Kunming during the summer of 2013, I saw for the first time groups of men outfitted in Lycra shirts and shorts, as if for the Tour de France, riding road bikes on the city outskirts.

Still, given rising concerns about air quality in Chinese cities, rising obesity rates, and rising numbers of traffic fatalities, perhaps there will be more people like Mr. Wang who will start biking again, and Chinese urbanites may once more hear the sounds of "ting, ting."

References and Further Research

Alcorn, Ted. 2011. "Uncertainty Clouds China's Road Traffic Fatality Data." *The Lancet* 378, no. 9788: 305–306. http://www.thelancet.com/journals/lancet/article/PIIS0140-6736(11)61153-7/fulltext.

Auto Channel. May 10, 2010. "2010 Beijing Automotive Exhibition (Auto China 2010) Concluded Successfully." http://www.theautochannel.com/news/2010/05/10/476857.html.

Barmé, Geremie R. 2002. "Engines of Revolution: Car Cultures in China." In *Autopia: Cars and Culture*, edited by Peter Wollen and Joe Kerr, 177–190. London: Reaktion Books.

Bourdieu, Pierre. 1984. *Distinction: A Social Critique of the Judgement of Taste*. London: Routledge & Kegan Paul.

Campanella, Thomas J. 2008. *The Concrete Dragon: China's Urban Revolution and What It Means for the World*. Princeton, NJ: Princeton Architectural Press.

Chappell, Ben. 2010. "Custom Contestations: Lowriders and Urban Space." *City & Society* 22, no. 1: 25–47.

Chen Aizhu. 2013. "Beijing to Slap Tougher Emission Standards on Vehicles: Xinhua." Reuters, January 23. http://www.reuters.com/article/2013/01/23/us-beijing-emission-idUSBRE90M10R20130123.

China Council for the Promotion of International Trade, Automotive Industry Commission. 2012. "The Relevant Data of the 2012 Beijing Auto Show." Beijing: China Council for the Promotion of International Trade, May 14. http://www.auto-ccpit.org/hyxwen/936.jhtml.

China Outpaces US in Monthly Auto Sales. 2009. China Daily. Feb. 10. http://www.chinadaily.com.cn/China/2009-02/10/content_746215.htm, accessed 10 Feb. 2009.

Conover, Ted. 2006. "Capitalist Roaders." *New York Times Magazine*, July 2. http://www.nytimes.com/2006/07/02/magazine/02china.html?pagewanted=all.

Croll, Elisabeth J. 2006. "Conjuring Goods, Identities and Cultures." In *Consuming China: Approaches to Cultural Change in Contemporary China*, edited by Kevin Latham, Stuart Thompson and Jakob Klein, 22–41. London and New York: Routledge.

Davis, Deborah. 2000. "Introduction." In *The Consumer Revolution in Urban China*, 1–22. Berkeley, CA: University of California Press.

Dikötter, Frank. 2006. *Exotic Commodities: Modern Objects and Everyday Life in China*. New York: Columbia University Press.

Gerth, Karl. 2010. *As China Goes, So Goes the World: How Chinese Consumers Are Transforming Everything*. New York: Hill and Wang.

Hessler, Peter. 2010. *Country Driving: A Journey Through China from Farm to Factory*. New York: Harper.

Jankowiak, William. 1993. *Sex, Death, and Hierarchy in a Chinese City*. New York: Columbia University Press.

Katz, Jack. 1999. *How Emotions Work*. Chicago: University of Chicago Press.

Kennedy, Bruce. 2014. "China Breaks World Record for Car Sales in 2013." CBS Moneywatch, January 31. http://www.cbsnews.com/news/china-breaks-world-record-for-car-sales-in-2013/.

Lemonnier, Pierre. 2012. *Mundane Objects: Materiality and Non-verbal Communication*. Walnut Creek, CA: Left Coast Press.

Lutz, Catherine, and Anne Lutz Fernandez. 2010. *Carjacked*. New York: Palgrave Macmillan.

Miller, Daniel. 2000. "Driven Societies." In *Car Cultures*, 1–33. Oxford: Berg.

Notar, Beth E. 2006. *Displacing Desire: Travel and Popular Culture in China*. Honolulu, HI: University of Hawai'i Press.

———. 2012. "'Coming Out' to 'Hit the Road': Temporal, Spatial and Affective Mobilities of Taxi Drivers and Day Trippers in Kunming, China." *City and Society* 24, no. 3 (December): 281–301.

Rocks, David, and Chen Wu. "A Phoenix Named Flying Pigeon." 2004. *Bloomberg Businessweek*, September 19. http://www.businessweek.com/stories/2004-09-19/a-phoenix-named-flying-pigeon.

Seiler, Cotton. 2008. *Republic of Drivers: A Cultural History of Automobility in America*. Chicago: University of Chicago Press.

Sun Yat-sen. 1929 [1922]. *The International Development of China*. 2nd ed. New York: Knickerbocker Press.

Urry, John. 2004. "The 'System' of Automobility." *Theory, Culture & Society* 21, no. 4–5: 25–39.

Wang, Shaoguang. 1995. "The Politics of Private Time: Changing Leisure Patterns in Urban China." In *Urban Spaces in Contemporary China*, edited by Deborah S. Davis, et al., 149–172. Washington, DC: Woodrow Wilson Center Press.

Whitely, Patrick. 2011. "Foot off the Brake." *China Daily*, June 1. http://www.chinadaily.com.cn/bizchina/2011-06/01/content_12623001.htm.

Zhangjudy. 2013. "The Good Old Days on China's Er Ba Che Bike." *China Daily Forum*. http://bbs.chinadaily.com.cn/thread-853800-1-1.html

Zhang, Jun. 2009. "Driving Toward Modernity: An Ethnography of Automobiles in Contemporary China." PhD diss., Yale University.

Zhang, Li. 2006. "Contesting Spatial Modernity in Late Socialist China." *Current Anthropology* 47, no. 3: 461–484.

Zhongguo qiche jiaoyi wang中国汽车交易网 [Auto 18 China's Car Net]. April 13, 2010. "Diyi jie Beijing chezhan jingxin choubei chenggong chuangban" 第一届北京车展精心筹备成功创办 [The first Beijing Auto Show is meticulously prepared and successfully set up]. http://news.auto18.com/html/2010-04-13/news_20100413173589.html

Films

Shower (*Xizao*). 1999. Directed by Zhang Yang. Beijing, China: Imar Film.

10

New Media and New Technology in Colonial Korea: Radio

JINA E. KIM

One of the dominant images of South Korea in the twenty-first century is that of a country that is technologically savvy, a hyper-wired place where almost every household has access to the world through high-speed, broadband Internet connectivity. South Korea has become a global leader in the information technology (IT) industry, certainly, as evidenced by both mobile phone production and usage. Smart phones made by Samsung and LG—both Korean companies—take up a large market share around the world, successfully competing side by side with Apple's iPhone. What's more, as the country plans for the 5G era in 2014, the number of mobile phones long ago surpassed the country's population of 48 million, meaning many people have more than one cell phone.

Researchers and journalists writing about South Korea's meteoric rise as an economic and technological power in the world have often cited South Korea's IT industry as a measurement for the country's rapidly globalizing society. It is typical to find scenes in Korea, especially in the large metropolitan areas like Seoul, where almost everyone is glued to their mobile screens, engaged in a vast range of activities—from streaming videos and listening to music to social networking, shopping, reading, and playing online games. These new mobile media and the technologies associated with them are altering the way South Koreans, and individuals across the globe, experience and interact with the world and people in the early twenty-first century.

Koreans encountered similar experiences of globalization with new media and new technology in the early twentieth century when they were introduced to radio. While it is obvious that the early twentieth-century radio and the early twenty-first century mobile media are not entirely equivalent, the ways they work to bring what is distant into our intimate spaces by collapsing time and space must have created similar experiences of wonder and a sense of possibilities, as well as confusion and danger. In this case study, I examine one of the new media technologies of the early modern period, the radio, to see how Koreans experienced it and what new possibilities it opened up. At the same time, since radio was part of the material culture of Japanese colonialism from the time it was introduced in Korea, I will also discuss how Koreans used the radio on their own terms despite colonial controls and restrictions.

A Satirical Representation of the Radio in a Modern Korean Novel

In Ch'ae Man-sik's satirical novel *Peace Under Heaven* (1938), the main character, Master Yun, appropriately nicknamed Toad for his large stature and unseemly appearance, is obsessed with money, status, young girls, his health, the Festival of Great Singers, and the radio. This absentee landlord lives a life of leisure listening to the radio and attending music performances in Gyeongseong (also Kyeongseong; later Seoul), all the while collecting rent from his family's land amassed in the most fertile region of Korea—the Jeolla province located in the southwestern part of the peninsula. Although live performances of traditional Korean ballads from the south are Master Yun's true love and longing, radio broadcasts of these songs are the best substitute, and he listens in religiously:

> And so he set up a little radio on the table next to where he slept. To master Yun, this radio with three lights on its face was as precious as gold or jade. The sounds of the south wafted to him from the transmitters in the broadcasting studio. Lying comfortably on quilted cushions, the stem of his long pipe in his mouth, he listened constantly to the sweet music, muttering, "Good!" (Ch'ae 1993, 13)[1]

Despite the extreme pleasure he takes from listening to the radio, Master Yun is completely ignorant when it comes to understanding what the radio is and how it functions. Taebok, who is entrusted with the responsibility of operating the radio, receives endless tirades from Master Yun whenever his songs are not available. Because Master Yun does not understand that there are radio stations, program arrangements, and on-air and off-air times, he expects a constant flow of southern music to enjoy endlessly. And when his music is not available, he harangues Taebok:

> "Law? What the hell is this dogshit about law? …What goddamn kind of sound is it that comes out fine until last night and then suddenly today is cut off or no reason? That's what I say. Have all *kisaeng* and the other performers dropped dead overnight?" (13–14)

Master Yun's fixation with the radio and his absolute lack of knowledge merge to create a highly comedic narrative in this extraordinarily satirical novel about the changing face of urban culture lived out by a pseudo–petty bourgeoisie in colonial Korea.

Ch'ae Man-sik is one of the most important and prominent Korean novelists of the early twentieth century. He was born on June 17, 1902, and died from tuberculosis on June 11, 1950. His novel *Peace Under Heaven* (*Taepyeong cheonha*) was serialized in *Jogwang*, one of the most popular variety magazines of the day, from January to September 1938.

A translation by Chun Kyung-ja, from which I quote in this chapter, was published by M. E. Sharpe in 1993 and can be purchased at the publisher's website (http://www.mesharpe.com/mall/resultsa.asp?Title=Peace+Under+Heaven%3A+A+Modern+Korean+Novel). A review of this translation can be found at Korean American Readings (http://bookoblate.blogspot.com/2008/10/peace-under-heaven-by-chae-man-sik.html). In addition, a preview of it can be found online by accessing it on Google Books (books.google.com) and typing in the title in the "Researching a Topic" box.

Though Ch'ae Man-sik's comical sketch is a fictional depiction of an early twentieth-century Korean's encounter with the radio, this is probably not an inaccurate portrayal of the general population. Although the first formal radio broadcasting in Korea began on February 16, 1927, the Government General of Korea (GGK) began testing it as early as 1924. According to a 1926 article in the popular magazine *Byeolgeongon* (The other heaven and earth), many experienced a similar "confusion" whereby some described their first encounter with the radio as "magic" or "a ghost's trick." Even after formal broadcasting began, many were still perplexed by the seemingly "magical" wireless box that would transmit sound. But as Ch'ae's novel depicts, although many people were still unaware of the detailed technical aspects of the radio, by the 1930s this new medium had become a commonly used technology, and one that Korean people were increasingly relying on for their information and entertainment. It had also become a medium through which an "imagined community" could be constructed. That is, as the political scientist Benedict Anderson theorized in his 1983 book *Imagined Communities*, the radio created a sense of being linked to others with shared experiences and through a common language.

The Birth and Development of Radio in Colonial Korea

The advent of radio broadcasting can be dated to 1897, when Guglielmo Marconi, an Italian inventor, obtained a patent for a radio receiving and transmitting device. By the 1930s, interest in both radio broadcasting and listening surged to unprecedented heights all over the globe, and Korea was not an exception. The radio became not only a viable site for numerous commercial, information, and government activities, but also a major center around which listeners could gather for leisure and entertainment. In the East Asian region, official radio broadcasting in Japan began on March 22, 1925, by the Tokyo Hōsō Kyoku (Tokyo Broadcasting Stations), which later was incorporated with Osaka (June 1, 1925) and Nagoya Hōsō Kyoku (July 15, 1925) to become the Nihon Hōsō Kyōkai (NHK-Japan Broadcasting Corporation) under the call sign JOAK. NHK was and still is a public broadcasting company under the jurisdiction of the Ministry of Communication of the Japanese government. Although official radio broadcasting began in 1925 in Japan, wireless communication, namely wireless telegraphy, was being used by the postal system and the military as early as 1897. It was not until the latter half of the Taishō period (1912–1926), however, that wireless telephony (radio) really began its ascendancy through research and development, technology import, and official testing.

For a short history of Nihon Hōsō Kyōkai (NHK-Japan Broadcasting Corporation), see the "History" page of the company's website (http://www. nhk.or.jp/bunken/english/about/history.html).

For Japan, the early twentieth century was also its age of empire. By 1925, Japan's colonial rule was firmly established in Taiwan (1895), Southern Sakhalin (or Karafuto, 1905), and Korea (1910); Japan also embarked on a swift control over various treaty ports throughout East Asia and Southeast Asia. When the Japanese army invaded Manchuria in 1931 and established the puppet state of Manchukuo, it also came under Japanese occupation. Moreover, Japan occupied, to different degrees, other parts of China, such as Port of Dalian, and maintained its own foreign concession in Shanghai until 1937, when the Japanese military took over the entire city. The Japanese then kept control over Shanghai until Japan's surrender at the end of World War II in 1945. Japanese occupation also reached deep into the islands on the Pacific South Seas.

In the process of empire-building, Japanese officials faced the crucial task of maintaining an expeditious flow of information and control between its colonies and the metropole. Radio, then commonly called *musen denwa* (無線電話), or a wireless telephone, became one such tool. Not only was the radio seen as a practical technological tool in governance and administration, but Japanese colonial officials also perceived it as an exceedingly effective tool in disseminating Japanese culture and values to its colonized subjects. Through broadcasting educational and news programs in Japanese, the colonizer aspired to bring together the various geographically and culturally scattered locals under the linguistic hegemony of Japan. It also used its various radio programs to advance its cultural assimilation policy. While many scholars have identified Japan's aggressive imperial assimilation policy (forced name change, prohibition of native language usage, and so forth), initiated in 1937, as part of Japan's wartime mobilization, the intricate deployment of radio broadcasting and radio programming by the Japanese colonizers, and the even more complicated relationship the colonized had had with the radio, begs one to reconsider the function of radio in a colonial setting. In effect, as the above example from

Ch'ae Man-sik's novel shows, although the radio was a product of colonialism, it was also significantly redefined and reshaped by the colonized users. Thus, as Michael Robinson, writing on broadcasting in colonial Korea rightly points out, Korean colonial radio did construct a culture of its own that in some aspects undermined Japan's original intent (Robinson 1998, 359–60).

To Listen or Not to Listen: Radio Dilemmas

Significantly, the colonized Koreans' construction of their own culture of radio was, in fact, set in motion even before formal radio broadcasting began in February 1927. Print media, such as newspapers and magazines in particular, actively participated in introducing the radio as a new form of civilization to the general population. In the July 23, 1920, edition of the *Chosun ilbo* (*Korea Daily News*), a brief article entitled "New Civilization: Transmission of Music through Wireless Telephone" reported on various radio broadcasting activities taking place in the United States. Interestingly, the *Chosun ilbo*'s first report on the radio preceded the famous first broadcasting by KDKA, a radio station in East Pittsburgh, Pennsylvania, on November 2, 1920. According to George Douglas, KDKA was the first radio station licensed by the U.S. government to operate a broadcasting service on U.S. soil (although other stations had begun regular broadcasting earlier than November 1920). Thus, not only did much broadcasting activity in the United States exist prior to the official establishment of KDKA, but many Koreans also had an interest in radio, as the *Chosun ilbo* article attests, prior to the commencement of testing in their own country. When official testing began in 1924, the number of feature articles in newspapers increased as well, which served as attractive free advertising for the GGK's Ministry of Communications. The coverage also helped increase the sale of newspapers: in addition to featuring articles and pictures about the radio, newspapers printed free admission tickets to the various demonstration events.

One headline read "One of the Most Important Intrigues of Modern Science" (*Chosun ilbo*, December 17, 1924). This article highlighted the importance of understanding modern science and technology, and it urged readers to actively seek knowledge and information from the radio demonstration to be held the next day. Two days later, the same reporter described the scene, in which an enormously successful public demonstration took place. Apparently it was being held in a Seoul public meeting hall where an unexpectedly large crowd had gathered:

> The crowd started to congregate around 6 o'clock. There were suited gentlemen and housewives as well as laborers. The elderly were also present. I felt as though Seoul citizens from all sectors of society were gathered there. The crowd that had assembled could not possibly all be accommodated, so the doors had to be closed shut in order to command some order. The meeting hall was so full of people that it was about to burst. (*Chosun ilbo*, December 19, 1924)

These demonstrations substantially raised the public's interest and curiosity about the marvels of radio, and for some the radio even presented the possibility of "spreading" Korean culture and "sounds of [Korean] language" outside the peninsular boundaries (*Chosun ilbo*, January 12, 1927).

After two years of testing, Kyeongseong Broadcasting Corporation (or the Korean Broadcasting Company, KBC), under the call sign JODK, began its formal programming on February 16, 1927. The initial broadcasting used a Marconi Q-type one-kilowatt transmitter at 690 KHz, by which the range of transmission was limited to central Seoul, where the station was located, and its near surroundings. The first KBC broadcasting station was located in central Seoul in Jeongdong and was housed in a two-story brick building owned by Yi Wangjik. The station occupied both floors and the basement and was flanked by two towering antennas. Despite the many successful pre-opening demonstrations, however, KBC did not experience a surge of subscriptions to the broadcasts upon its formal establishment. Nor did sales of receivers increase drastically during the initial phase of broadcasting. In the early stages, though the radio generated an enormous level of curiosity, the general public was reluctant to invest in purchasing a receiver and subscribing monthly to listen to the broadcasts. According to the April 20, 1926, edition of *Chosun ilbo*, a radio for private home use (for one person with headphones) cost between 10 and 15 won, and a monthly subscription fee cost two won. The same article lists the price of a crystal radio with a capacity of up to ten listeners (without headphones) to be about 100 won. In 1927 a crystal radio set with antenna was being sold for 6 to 15 won, while a vacuum tube radio went for 40 to 100 won (*Chosun ilbo*, April 21, 1927). Considering that an average monthly wage for a low-ranking office worker in the 1920s and 1930s ranged between 10 and 22 won, these costs were high for most people. Recognizing that the two won registration and monthly subscription fees were too high for Korean listeners, KBC reduced the fee to one won per month in hopes of attracting more subscribers.

Rich landowners like Master Yun in *Peace Under Heaven* were from a new, wealthy class that had the means to purchase a radio for "seventeen *wŏn* . . . plus one *wŏn* per month in listening fees" (Ch'ae 1993, 14). With about 100,000 won in capital on deposit in his bank, and annual rent of 10,000 bags of rice (a bag of rice on the average sold for about four won a bag in those days), Master Yun could certainly enjoy listening to the radio in the privacy of his own room, unlike most people, who were likely to have listened in public spaces, such as restaurants, cafes, department stores, train stations, or the streets. These public spaces, however, were also spaces predominantly inhabited by the new bourgeoisie and intelligentsia classes. Hence the radio represented at once a democratizing cultural artifact that could spread sound and culture to a broad populous, as well as a class-reifying artifact that reinforced the deepening class division in colonial Korea. But, oddly enough, even people like Master Yun, to whom the cost was insignificant, were still reluctant to part with their money for the privilege of having the radio "tease" them (Ch'ae 1993, 15). (As illustrated earlier, Master Yun believes that the radio is "teasing" him by providing his programs on some days and not on other days.) For example, in the novel, every month when the time comes to pay his fees, Master Yun undoubtedly complains, "What do they think the damn thing is? Does it entitle them to shake me down for cash every month?" (Ch'ae 14). The radio, in spite of delivering much satisfaction to listeners like Master Yun, was also a site of contention and frustration, especially since one had to pay for it.

While Ch'ae masterfully establishes Master Yun as a penny-pinching scrooge throughout the novel, the radio episode in particular draws attention to the triangulated relationship among the new bourgeoisie, technology, and colonialism. Through these explorations, Ch'ae Man-sik presents a social critique of the radically transformed social structure in colonial Korea. We are told that in the days of Master Yun's father, the family had come to amass wealth, but bandits constantly thieved and government officials extracted bribes, never granting the family a day of peace. But luck and timing bring "peace under heaven" to Master Yun. Japanese colonialism and Japan's land survey projects effectively alter Master Yun's life, and as a result he is able to accumulate even more land and move his family to Seoul, the capital, while maintaining his country estate and collecting rent as an absentee landlord. Although social class distinctions were "legally" dissolved during the late Joseon (Choson) Dynasty through the enactment of the Kabo Reforms, thereby freeing slaves and eliminating the literati social-class (*yangban*—the highest social-class), social customs and practices were still very much intact even during the Japanese colonial period, when power relations unequivocally disrupted (but did not eliminate) the thousand-year-old social structure.

The Daehan Jeguk Period

The period between 1897 and 1910, before the formal annexation of Korea by Japan in 1910, is generally called the Daehan Jeguk period, or the Period of the Great Han Empire, in which Korea was "independent" and no longer a tributary state of China. This status, however, came about in the aftermath of the Ganghwa Treaty, an unequal arrangement that Japan forced on Korea in order to open its ports to Japan and allow Japan to hold direct diplomatic relations with Korea. This can be seen as one of the first steps in Japan's move toward imperialism.

For Master Yun's family, and others like them who could not boast of an illustrious *yangban* family lineage, their newly gained wealth could buy a prominent genealogy, which Master Yun promptly does. With his newly purchased *yangban* genealogy, he also marries his son and grandsons to families of *yangban* origin, thus cementing the Yun's social class as hailing from the highest of the literati social classes. Just as he can buy his genealogy and status, Master Yun is amply capable of purchasing the newest technology—a technology that was as much a product of broader Western imperialism and Japanese colonialism as it was a product of the science and progress so important in the colonial metropole (Japan) as well as in the colonies (in this case, Korea). In many aspects, creating Master Yun as the protagonist of this novel helped to express the underlying tensions of colonialism—those questioning both the possibilities and the impossibilities that colonialism necessitates—and the impact of those tensions on the formation of colonial identity and subjectivity.

In addition to the exorbitant cost of radio, another frustrating obstacle experienced by both the broadcasters and listeners of radio was programming in two languages. During the first six years of broadcasting, KBC practiced a dual-language policy where the language breakdown ratio was roughly 30 percent Korean and 70 percent Japanese. Complaints by Korean listeners, however, resulted in an increase of Korean programs to 40 percent by July 1927. As one might surmise, this policy frustrated both Korean and Japanese listeners, whose programs were constantly being interrupted by the program in the other language. Newspapers published detailed schedules of the day's broadcasting program, but this neither alleviated the confusion nor lessened the complaints. KBC, under the jurisdiction of the GGK's Ministry of Communication, did experiment with various programming schedules. For example, the station alternated the same program in Japanese and Korean, and also alternated Japanese and Korean programs every other day. As depicted in *Peace Under Heaven*, however, the confusion Master Yun encounters upon learning that his program is on one night but not the next night appears to be not far from the truth. Furthermore, Ch'ae Man-sik's depiction of the dejected and desperate Taebok, who has to furnish Master Yun with his favorite programs, would likely also resonate with listeners who stridently wrote to the station with their complaints and requests:

> For some time the radio station had been receiving anonymous letters, dozens of them, all beseeching that southern music be broadcasted every day. These anguished letters were dispatched by Taebok who composed them in tears, literally, after bearing the full brunt of Master Yun's undue recriminations. (Ch'ae 1993, 14)

Various efforts to work within the dual-language broadcasting system, however, were largely considered failures. In the first six years of operation, KBC did not reach the anticipated number of registered subscribers, nor were the subscription fees adequate to cover the cost of operation.

Once again, Japanese officials had to make significant concessions in order to broadcast in Korea. It was announced in 1931 that opening a second station, an all-Korean-language station, was planned, and in 1933, KBC Station 2 began broadcasting in Korean with a more powerful transmitter (Han'guk Pangsong Kongsa 1977, 30–35). And in April 1937, when KBC Station 2 was able to broadcast with a 50-kilowatt transmitter, a far wider geographical range was achieved. In addition, the GGK began to launch regional broadcasting stations; the first was in September 1936 in the city of Busan, a southeastern coastal port city with a large Japanese settler population. Another station was established in Pyongyang, the current-day capital of North Korea, in April 1936. The Pyongyang station simultaneously launched an all-Korean-language station along with a Japanese-language station. All of these expansion activities were financed by Japan's NHK. In 1931, NHK provided a loan of 430,000 won to KBC to build facilities, and in 1935 an additional 543,000-won loan was added for establishing regional broadcasting stations. Ironically, as Michael Robinson astutely notes, it was the Japanese radio listeners in the metropole as well as those in the colonies who paid for and supported the Korean broadcasting system.

While broadcasting technology was advancing and expanding, one of the most crucial aspects for the success of radio listening continued to be its programming, the content of the daily radio program. Although the colonial regime made concerted efforts to use new media technology and programming to cement its cultural hegemony, Korean listeners did not always fall victim to the system of control or to the assimilation strategies. Rather, consumers learned to use, and indeed used, the radio for their own pleasure and entertainment. This appears to be the case, especially after the establishment of a separate Korean language broadcast system in 1933 in which 16 hours of radio broadcasting filled with news, education, and entertainment were carried per day. Seo Jaegil's 2007 study on colonial Korean radio charts the ratio of news, education, and entertainment content to be roughly 3:3:4 between 1929 and 1936. As shown in Ch'ae Man-sik's *Peace Under Heaven*, music was indeed one of the most popular types of programming, but radio dramas, novels, and dialogues also occupied a large portion of the schedules, which attests to the genre's popularity among the listeners.

To learn what KBS broadcasts today, in English and Korean, visit the KBS website (http://english.kbs.co.kr).

The establishment of the all-Korean-language station promoted the proliferation of radio sales and broadcast subscriptions throughout the 1930s. But more importantly, this station contributed to the development of Korean radio programs. An article in *Jogwang* variety magazine lists the programs aired on KBC Station 2, providing a glimpse of the variety of programs available to listeners. According to the article, radio programs can be largely divided into music, entertainment, education, and news (Jongwang, December 1935). The author goes on to describe the various things that can be heard under these different categories. For example, in terms of music programming, they aired popular Korean songs, *pansori* (which is Master Yun's favorite), and other music, such as Japanese music (in particular, *naniwabushi*) and Western music (mostly classical music). Another highly popular category was entertainment, which included radio dramas, radio novels, film stories, and comedy shows. News and weather reports certainly occupied an important position in radio programming as well. Additionally, lectures and information programs, children's programs, and sports filled the airwaves. The radio virtually provided everything that anyone would like to hear. In fact, the next month's *Jogwang* appropriately ruminates that "anyone who has experienced listening to the radio becomes so hooked [to it] that they won't last a day without being curious about what is on the radio."

Korean *pansori* and Japanese *naniwabushi* are sung narratives that were highly popular forms of musical performance. Much of these musical forms were disappearing as popular songs gained prevalence. Examples of both *pansori* and *naniwabushi* (also called rokyoku) can be found on YouTube.

Making Radio Work and Working for the Radio

For many, listening to the radio remained a form of entertainment. But for others, the advent of radio paved the way for new work and for the professionalization of work. At the time of KBC's first broadcast, the organisation employed about 50 people, of which only a handful were Korean. No Changseong and Han Deokbong were employed as technicians, while Ma Hyeongyeong and Yi Okgyeong were the first two female radio announcers. Ma and Yi, in particular, are noteworthy, because these two were the very first to be called "announcers," a new category of work.

Interestingly, for this position, the broadcasting company was specifically hiring women. A classified advertisement appearing in *Byeolgeongon* lists the required qualifications as follows: "Graduate of at least a girls high school; Age between 16-40." Besides listing the wanted qualifications, the ad also describes the pay and the kind of work that will be performed. "An apprentice's starting salary is 30 won per month. Upon becoming a full time announcer, salary will increase between 50 won to 60 won a month." Considering that low-ranking, male, office workers were paid 22 won a month, even the apprentice-level salary shows that female announcers were being paid handsomely. The ad goes on to say that "although this job is physically and mentally exhausting, the work is a very rewarding one because an announcer's single word can reach the ears of thousands of people around the world" (*Byeolgeongon*, March 1927).

Professional working women were still rare in Korea, so a combination of the first radio broadcasting and female announcers roused a great stir in the print media. Newspapers carried interviews with the newly hired announcers, and magazines began to publish roundtable transcripts regarding working women. Through radio broadcasting, the early twentieth-century *kisaeng* (female entertainers highly trained in the arts) also took on new roles, becoming active participants in modern urban technology. They were not only singing on public stages, but also performing for various radio programs. For a society that once believed "silence" in women was a virtue, a woman projecting her voice to be aired to "reach the ears of thousands of people around the world" marked a radical shift.

Yun Paeknam (1888–1954), a prominent pioneering film director, novelist and playwright of the colonial period, was an ardent advocate of radio and identified it as a critical medium for entertainment and information. He held important editorial positions in various newspapers and journals (several of which he was a founding member of). In 1917 he established the Yun Production Company and began his career as both producer and director. He was also a leading figure in the new drama movement and established his own drama troupe. With the establishment of KBC Station 2, Yun advocated for the radio becoming familiar technology to be used on daily basis (*Chosun ilbo*, January 15, 1933). In particular, he suggested that the radio should become so commonplace in the home of Koreans that it could be used for educational purposes as well as developing people's interests and tastes. The Korean word he and others used in this context is *chwimi* (趣味). In contemporary everyday parlance, this is often translated as "hobby." However, this is a neologism that came into use during the early twentieth century. The two Chinese characters used for this word are 趣 (*chwi*), meaning "mind" "intention" or "idea," and 味 (*mi*), meaning "taste." Early twentieth-century thinkers and artists, such as Yun Paeknam, used this word to mean "taste" in the aesthetic sense, which is also linked to the idea of self-development. For Yun and others, radio became a medium through which one could cultivate the self and engage in new kinds of work; as a new medium, it encouraged innovation in producing new kinds of programs most appropriate for the radio.

Although music was popular on the radio, radio dramas were even more popular. Writing for the radio became not only an important new career, but also a means for Koreans to debate and theorize on the potentials of the radio. One of the most daunting dilemmas for those writing for the radio, however, was the matter of how to compensate for visual cues and directions in a medium that relied on the oral and aural. Rather than reading texts and watching theatrical performances, the listener had to rely only on her or his hearing to understand and imagine the story being presented. While sound and hearing are central to the listening experience in radio dramas, as Tim Crook rightly points out, listening to radio dramas does not preclude visual realities, the theatrical, or the spectacle. In other words, radio drama is a form of storytelling transmitted through sound. Indeed, sound is so central to storytelling on the radio that it cannot be completely "separated from image based narratives," for it "exists as a dramatic storytelling form communicating action as well as narrative" (Crook 1999, 7). In essence, Crook is arguing that there is a very visual component to the psychology of listening. Ears see, he asserts. Crook's claims pointedly move toward the intermedial qualities of visualizing while listening to the radio, and toward how these intermedial qualities are achieved through writing for the radio.

Seo Jaegil's study on the development of the broadcasting arts, especially radio dramas, in colonial Korea clearly outlines the stages the genre underwent to distinguish itself from other genres, particularly that of stage theater. Seo shows how, in its early phase, radio dramas borrowed heavily from theatrical, filmic, and novelistic texts. That is, without adapting the existing texts specifically for the radio, many of the works were transferred to the radio to be performed (or, more accurately, to be read). In its scripted form, therefore, early Korean radio dramas differed little from stage scripts, which often included stage directions (e.g., place markers) and acting directions (e.g., affect, gesture, movement) invisible to the listeners when performed by voice actors in the radio station. As a result, early radio performances were wanting in various aspects. As many critics, including Seo Jaegil, have noted, these dramas lacked the aesthetics of radio dramaturgy. It was not until the mid-1930s that original radio dramas were written specifically for radio broadcasting by such writers as Yu Chijin, Yi Seogu, and Kim Unjong, to name just a few.

It appears that critics began seriously considering the art and theory of radio dramas only after radio became a popular medium in colonial Korean society, which was, as mentioned earlier, after the establishment of Korean-language broadcasting. In their writings on the radio, critics such as Han Sangjik, Yang Hun, and Yi Seokhun took up theorizing on radio dramas as a way to analyze the larger media phenomenon of the radio. In doing so, these critics began to postulate more specific methodologies for composing radio dramas that would pay close attention to the various aural aspects, including the special effects that could be produced through the mechanism of the radio; ways of enlivening the listeners' imagination via sound; usage of music for narrative and tone; and the construction of dialogue in ways that would replace simple, straightforward, descriptive narratives. This critical analysis entailed comparisons to the other media that were, in a sense, in competition with radio at the time. While they realized that the radio was an aural medium, they also recognized the importance of the qualities it shared with film, stage theater, and the serialized novel. Thus, writers and critics actively applied or rejected methods from the stage, film (especially the talkie), and the novel to find the most appropriate means of expression for the radio medium.

Korean television dramas continue the radio drama tradition and are still popular today. Many examples, with English subtitles, can be found on YouTube or other Internet sites. The KBS (Korean Broadcasting System) World TV channel (https://www.youtube.com/user/kbsworld) is a good place to begin.

Conclusion

As was the case with print media, radio did not escape being monitored by the Japanese colonial state. Restrictions and censorship tightened during the late colonial period, especially after the Second Sino-Japanese War began in 1937, when Japan decreed the *hwangminhwa/ kominka* (imperialization) movement. Paper shortages and censorship during wartime eventually led to the closing of *Chosun ilbo* and

Donga ilbo, the two major privately owned Korean-language newspapers, in 1940, leaving only the *Maeil sinbo*, the official organ of the Japanese colonial government, operating. At a time when the majority of Korean-language publications had been terminated, Korean-language broadcasting continued until 1944, albeit limited in its programming. Korean-language lessons and lectures were eventually banned altogether by 1941. Only those programs that voiced support for the imperialization and the *naisen ittai* (Japan and Korea as one) movements were permitted to be aired. Indeed, propaganda materials were effectively placed within mass media, such as the radio, to control and discipline the colonized subjects.

Yet, despite the loss of sovereignty and the censorship and suppression of the freedoms of press and speech, the case of radio in colonial Korea shows that Korean cultural producers and consumers were not mere victims of colonial repression or passive consumers of radio. Rather, Korean listeners demanded to use this new medium and new technology for their own pleasures, creative outlets, and educational purposes, among other uses. Furthermore, radio gave rise to new everyday spatial practices, leading to formations of new imagined communities connecting listeners, both those close to each other and those separated by great distances. After all, radio listening was taking place simultaneously across the country, dependent on a set programming schedule. And since the cost of owning a radio and subscribing to broadcast programming were expensive, radio listening became more or less a communal activity rather than strictly private. In these ways, the role of radio in the early twentieth century resembles our twenty-first century new media experiences, in which various mobile devices have come to reshape our everyday practices and social interactions, giving us a sense that we are instantly connected to the world outside our immediate circle.

Note

1. Quotations from *Peace Under Heaven* are taken from Chun Kyung-ja's English translation. Unless otherwise notated, all other translations are the author's.

References and Further Research

Anderson, Benedict. 1983. *Imagined Communities: Reflections on the Origin and Spread of Nationalism.* London: Verso.
Byeolgeongon (no longer in print).
Ch'ae Man-sik. 1993. *Peace Under Heaven*. Translated by Chun Kyung-ja. Armonk, NY: M.E. Sharpe.
Chosun ilbo (http://english.chosun.com/).
Crook, Tim. 1999. *Radio Drama: Theory and Practice.* London: Routledge.
Donga ilbo (http://english.donga.com/).
Douglas, George H. 1987. *The Early Days of Radio Broadcasting.* Jefferson, NC: McFarland.
Douglas, Susan J. 1999. *Listening In*. New York: Random House.
Han'guk Pangsong Kongsa [Public Office of Korean Broadcasting]. 1977. *Han'guk Pangsongsa* [History of Korean broadcasting]. Seoul: Han'guk Pangsong Kongsa.
Jogwang (no longer in print).
Nihon Hoso Kyokai. 1977. *Hoso Gojunenshi* [Fifty year history of broadcasting]. Tokyo: NHK.

Robinson, Michael. 1998. "Broadcasting in Korea, 1924-1937: Colonial Modernity and Cultural Hegemony." In *Japan's Competing Modernities: Issues in Culture and Democracy, 1900-1930*, edited by Sharon A. Minichiello, 358–378. Honolulu, HI: University of Hawai'i Press.

Robinson, Michael. 1999. "Broadcasting, Cultural Hegemony, and Colonial Modernity in Korea, 1924–1945." In *Colonial Modernity in Korea*, edited by Gi-Wook Shin and Michael Robinson, 52–69. Cambridge, MA: Harvard University Press.

Seoul Museum of History. 2003. *Geundae daejung yesul: Soriwa yeongsang* [Modern popular arts: sound and image]. Seoul: Seoul Museum of History.

Seo Jaegil. 2007. "Hangguk geundae bangsong munye yeongu" [A study on the modern Korean broadcast literature]. PhD dissertation, Seoul National University.

Takahashi Yuzo. 2000. "A Network of Tinkerers: The Advent of the Radio and Television Receiver Industry in Japan." *Technology and Culture* 41, no. 3: 460–484.

Tsugawa, Izumi. 1993. *JODK kieta kōrusain* [JODK, The call sign that was extinguished]. Tokyo: Hakusuisha.

Yang, Daqing. 2011. *Technology of Empire: Telecommunications and Japanese Expansion in Asia, 1886-1945*. Cambridge, MA: Harvard University Press.

Yoshimi, Shunya. 1995. *"Koe" no shihon shugi: denwa, rajio, chikuoniki no shakaishi* [The "sounds" of capitalism: a social history of telephone, radio, and record player]. Tokyo: Kōdansha.

Yun, Geumseon. 2010. *Radio punggyeong, soriro deuneun drama* [Landscapes of radio: Drama by ear]. Seoul: Yŏngŭkgwa Ingan.

11

Interpreting Minority Experiences of Japan's March 2011 Triple Disaster

Joshua Hotaka Roth and Mariko Sikama

Anthropological writing about cultural groups is the product of the encounter between researchers and particular interlocutors. Indeed, it's not a stretch to say that anthropological knowledge is produced collaboratively. But anthropologists rarely make this collaborative process visible, nor do they often fully share the credit for the interpretations that result. This is unfortunate, for it ends up producing a false impression of authoritative knowledge, when in fact knowledge is arrived at tentatively, and in some cases multiple contending interpretations may possess their own truths.

In recognition of these considerations, this chapter is the collaborative product of discussions between longtime friends, the anthropologist Joshua Roth and Mariko Sikama, a Japanese Brazilian who has resided in Japan for the past twenty-odd years. Its format—deliberately unconventional, with extended reflections, dialogues, and multiple interpretations— aims to lay bare the process by which anthropological knowledge is collaboratively produced. Rather than writing about minorities in Japan in the abstract, we focus on a specific moment, for it is in actual encounters at particular times that knowledge is produced. The moment we focus on is not typical. We consider the Triple Disaster of March 2011—a devestating earthquake, tsunami, and nuclear meltdown—in an effort to show that moments of crisis may reveal underlying perspectives on identity and belonging that in normal times go unstated, or even unexplored.

March 11, 2011, and its Aftermath

On March 11, 2011, the Pacific plate shifted violently westward and down into the subduction zone 60 miles off Japan's northeast coast, sending huge tsunamis crashing over fishing villages, carrying ships high up onto dry land, and washing people, cars, and all kinds of debris out to sea. The total number of confirmed dead was 15,887, with an additional 2,612 missing (National Police Agency 2014).

The tsunamis also topped the sea wall meant to protect the Fukushima Daiichi Nuclear Power Station, flooding the diesel-powered backup generators and leading to meltdowns (the severe overheating of the nuclear fuel, leading to a breach of the

A gymnasium in Sendai Municipal Nakano Elementary School on April 6, 2011, showing destruction not uncommon across the region struck by the Triple Disaster of March 2011. *(Wikimedia Commons, Cpl. Patricia D. Lockhart, Defenseimagery.mil, http://tinyurl.com/mymq37l).*

reactor core) in three of the six nuclear reactors (the other three were offline at the time). The Japanese government ordered an evacuation for everyone within a three-kilometer (1.6-mile) radius on March 11, and all those within ten kilometers (6.2 miles) were told to stay indoors. On March 12 the government extended the evacuation order to 20 kilometers (12.4 miles) for the Daiichi Power Station and ten kilometers for the Daini Power Station, located about ten kilometers south of the Daiichi plant. On March 15 an explosion at the Daiichi station released radiation into the air, prompting the government to recommend that those within 30 kilometers (18.6 miles) of Daiichi stay indoors to avoid exposure. Many people beyond these official zones decided to evacuate.

The U.S. government initially advised all U.S. citizens within a much broader 50-mile (80 km) radius to evacuate, but a month later reduced the evacuation zone to 25 miles (40 km). In many cases, local residents were torn about whether to abandon their homes and hometowns to seek refuge elsewhere. In the days following the meltdowns, the foreign staff of multinational corporations in Tokyo (more than 150 miles away) seemed to vanish, leaving their Japanese counterparts to run the offices on their own. Some foreigners married to Japanese also decided to leave Japan because of the uncertainty about radiation, with differing degrees of understanding on the part of their Japanese relatives. The decision to stay or leave Japan seems to have raised questions of allegiance to Japan, or at least of the commitment to a life there.

Brazilian migrants of Japanese descent who had been living and working in Japan also left in large numbers. Japanese Brazilians (the children and grandchildren of

Japanese migrants who went to Brazil from 1908 through the 1960s) started going to Japan in large numbers in the late 1980s, when the Brazilian economy was experiencing hyperinflation and before the Japanese economy entered its long recession. The Japanese government allowed overseas Japanese (known as *nikkei*) who could prove that they had at least one Japanese grandparent to apply for special visas without work restrictions. The number of Brazilians in Japan peaked at 312,582 in 2008. But the worldwide financial crisis that year caused many Brazilians to leave, and their numbers had dropped to 230,552 by 2010. The 2011 disasters motivated still more to leave, so that by the end of 2012 the numbers had declined to 190,581 (Ministry of Justice 2006–2013). Some of those who stayed criticized those who left as self-centered. If those who left were seen in some ways as abandoning Japan, some of those who decided to stay in Japan felt moved to profess their love for the country.

In the days after Japan's Triple Disaster, Japanese Brazilians made use of social networking sites to check in on each other and inquire about conditions in various parts of Japan. On March 18, Luís, another Japanese Brazilian friend of Joshua's and acquaintance of Mariko's living in Hamamatsu, 300 miles southwest of Fukushima, went far beyond those informational inquiries and posted a statement on his Orkut social networking page (which is no longer active) that is worth reproducing here in full:

> LONG LIVE THE JAPAN OF SOLDIERS, firefighters, paramedics, rescue workers who, out of obedience and solidarity, go with hope to encounter lives or bodies which have gone to live with GOD.

> LONG LIVE ALL THOSE WHO LEAVE THEIR HOMES, FAMILIES, sons, pregnant wives, grandparents, brothers and sisters, parents in order to serve a nation in a difficult moment, for those who have lost everything, APART FROM THEIR DIGNITY.

> LONG LIVE THE JAPANESE SOLDIERS AND FIREFIGHTERS AND THE RESCUE WORKERS FROM ALL THE WORLD for their enormous mission.

> LONG LIVE the doctors, nurses, the exhausted volunteers who take care of those lives that have not been lost.

> LONG LIVE THE VICTIMS who suffer so much, but who still know how to play with their sons, daughters, grandchildren, LONG LIFE AND HOPE to each person wherever they are.

> LONG LIVE THE SOLDIERS AND FIREFIGHTERS, technicians and specialists who put their lives and health in danger so that the RADIATION does not negatively affect us too much.

> LONG LIVE GOVERNMENT WORKERS who, for all their faults, DO NOT LET GO OF POWER and who take responsibility and get results so that we can be HAPPY.

> LONG LIVE GOD FOR GIVING UNDERSTANDING to TECHNICIANS SO THAT IN THIS SPRING OF THE MOST BEAUTIFUL CHERRY BLOSSOMS we can celebrate EASTER. THE RESURRECTION OF JESUS AND the resurrection of JAPAN!!!!!!!

> LONG LIVE EASTER!!!!!!!!!!!!!!!!

> I LOVE JAPAN AND SHE WILL OVERCOME AND CONTINUE HELPING MANY COUNTRIES!

This post celebrates those participating in the rescue efforts, expresses sorrow for the victims of the disasters, and ends with a declaration of love for Japan. These are sentiments that any number of people may have felt, given the scale of the tragedies that had just occurred. Yet disaster and crisis can reveal unspoken or unconscious assumptions that people have about their place within society. Luís's posts, and the reactions of many Japanese Brazilian migrants to these disasters, may tell us something about the place of minorities in Japan more broadly.

Many articles on the 3.11 Triple Disaster in Japan, written by scholars in various disciplines, can be found on the website of *The Asia-Pacific Journal: Japan Focus* (http://www.japanfocus.org/site/show_list/id/329).

One point of reference for thinking about disaster and minority experience in Japan is the 1923 Great Kanto Earthquake in Tokyo. At the time, false rumors were spread that Korean residents had set the fires that destroyed much of the city, poisoned wells, and committed other malicious acts. Bands of Japanese vigilantes, police, and military, some of whom were responsible for spreading the rumors in the first place, used them to justify the massacre of hundreds, if not thousands, of innocent Korean residents.

The SPICE (Stanford Program on International and Cross-Cultural Education) program at Stanford University develops educational materials on East Asia, including an overview of Koreans in Japan published in the Fall 2012 *SPICE Digest* newsletter (http://iis-db.stanford.edu/pubs/24465/Koreans_inJapan.pdf).

The 2011 disasters were not followed by any comparable tragedy of ethno-national hatred. Yet in recessionary Japan, minorities have been targeted for harassment by certain newly formed right-wing groups, according to Tomomi Yamaguchi (2013) and other observers. The discussion of allegiance to Japan that arose in the wake of 3.11 (or 3/11, as the tragedy is often referred to) raises some interesting questions. Minorities, whose legitimate place in Japan is sometimes called into question in everyday life, may feel even less secure during a crisis situation, because people may interpret decisions to leave, complain, or criticize as forms of abandoning Japan in its time of need. This is the context in which Luís expressed not just his solidarity with Japan, but also his love for his adopted home. Given the context, one may wonder whether his post expressed an underlying anxiety that he was not as accepted in Japan as he would like to be, or even that he could be the target of hatred.

Many commentators see globalization as leading to more widespread economic prosperity and the gradual spread of democratic ideals. Others, however, emphasize the possibility of negative outcomes, such as as environmental destruction on a global scale and the loss of local cultural identities. Both positive and negative perspectives share the understanding, however, of globalization as an inevitable process of increasing flows (of people, objects, finance, technology, ideas, and the like) that ever more tightly connect people and places around the world. This growing interconnectedness suggests that people will shed their parochial identities in favor of new hybrid or cosmopolitan identities.

The International Labour Organization (ILO) website contains links to publications about migration in the Asia Pacific region, which can be found at the
organization's "Asia-Pacific Migrations Publications" page (http://www.ilo.
org/asia/areas/labour-migration/WCMS_242020/lang—en/index.htm).

The Migration Policy Institute website has information on a variety of issues
on its "Asia and the Pacific" page (http://www.migrationinformation.org/
regions/Asia.cfm).

Recently, however, some have argued that globalization is not an inevitable process,
but a contingent one. Further, it does not always gather steam, but goes in fits and
starts. Anna Tsing (2004, 4) suggests that rather than the metaphor of global flows,
we think in terms of friction, of "the awkward, unequal, unstable, and creative qualities of interconnection across difference." The numbers of foreign migrants in Japan
might reinforce an assumption that globalization leads to more people in motion,
living and working in places other than where they started. But a closer look at the
actual encounter of peoples in workplaces, neighborhoods, and other locations—on
an everyday level as well as during times of crisis—will reveal social dynamics that
are anything but inevitable.

The Place of Japanese Brazilians in Japan

It wasn't just anybody that was moving to Japan to work in the 1980s. Migrants primarily came from those Asian countries that had reciprocal visa treaties with Japan.
By 1990, tens of thousands of foreigners, notably from Iran and Pakistan, were living
and working in Japan. Most who came on tourist visas ended up working in construction and other industries, and they often overstayed their visas by many years. As
the economy slowed, however, the large number of irregularly employed foreigners
was framed as a social problem, and the Japanese government clamped down. In the
search for alternative sources of foreign labor, the government prioritized cultural
familiarity, as well as a pool that was not overwhelming in size. The government
found what it thought to be an ideal group in overseas Japanese, who were not too
numerous and were perceived to be culturally unthreatening. Beginning in 1990,
overseas Japanese—including Japanese Brazilians—became the only category of
foreigner to be granted special visas to work in Japan without any restrictions.

However, being eligible for special visas does not in itself explain what motivated
Japanese Brazilians to move to Japan in the 1990s. After all, many were completely
integrated into Brazilian society. While Japanese Brazilians are still prominent in the
agricultural sector in Brazil, where their grandparents had started many years earlier,
many more of the second, third, and fourth generations have gone on to universities,
entered prestigious professions, and enjoyed middle- and upper-middle-class status.
Still, Japanese Brazilians had cultivated an identity as "Japonês," which allowed

even those who could not speak the language to imagine Japan as an ancestral land. Thus, when an economic crisis hit Brazil in the late 1980s and triple-digit inflation decimated the life savings of the middle class, it wasn't too hard for many of them (including architects, geologists, bankers, teachers, and so forth) to imagine working in Japanese factories for a period of time. The employment conditions they faced in Japan, however, quickly reinforced the understanding of most Japanese Brazilians that they were Brazilian and not Japanese.

In the mid-1990s, when Joshua conducted dissertation research on Japanese Brazilian migrants in Japan, he noticed a growing divide between those who had a long-term perspective (*veteranos*) and those who had arrived more recently. It was during this time that Joshua became friends with Mariko, who is a second-generation Japanese Brazilian, and Luís, who is third-generation, both of whom had already lived in Japan for five or six years and were becoming *veteranos*. *Veteranos* were not trying to pass as Japanese. For many, "passing" was not an option because of their lack of fluency in Japanese and physical differences (depending on the degree of mixture in their ancestry). Rather, the divide was between those who had a long-term perspective and did what they could to gain acceptance as legitimate members of Japanese society, and those for whom acceptance was not a concern. *Veteranos*, who worked hard for acceptance, bridled at what they perceived as newcomers' disrespect for Japanese social norms.

Since the 1990s the differentiation has gradually increased between Japanese Brazilian *veteranos* and newcomers. This may in part be expressed in the decision of many *veteranos* to apply for and obtain permanent residency. Even as the total number of Brazilians in Japan declined dramatically—from 312,582 in 2008 to 190,581 in 2012—the number of those with permanent residency increased—from 78,523 in 2006 to 110,267 in 2008, and to 114,632 in 2013 (Ministry of Justice 2006-2013). The financial crisis and the 3.11 disasters have slowed, but not stopped, the increase in numbers of permanent residents.

Since the start of Brazilian migration to Japan in the late 1980s, most migrants have come and gone after stints of three, four, five, or more years working in Japanese factories. But both Luís and Mariko have been living in Japan for 20 years. They have made their lives there, and they do not have any intention of moving back to Brazil in the foreseeable future. Gradually, a growing contingent of Brazilians is settling in Japan. Some have raised families and sent their children to Japanese schools. While some children have had difficulties and dropped out, others have grown up speaking Japanese fluently and have completed the compulsory nine years of schooling and gone on to high school and even college.

In the months following 3.11, however, many Japanese themselves became very critical of the national government's response to the disasters, and of the collusion between the government and the nuclear industry. The movement led to large-scale protests that helped push the national government to temporarily shut down all of Japan's 54 nuclear power plants. More than two years after the start of the crisis, just one nuclear plant has reopened, despite the brownouts (especially in the first year) that affected train schedules and manufacturing, not to mention the constraints on energy availability for household use. Social movements within the Japanese population have helped local governments, which have the power to deny authorization to restart the plants, to stand firm against pressure from the national government and nuclear industry.

Reflecting on Luís's declaration of love for Japan following 3.11, Joshua wondered whether this solidarity made it difficult for Luís and other migrants to formulate the kind of critique that emerged among some Japanese. Even after 20 years of living in Japan, many Japanese Brazilians continue to depend on employment brokers for work and housing. Thus the *veteranos'* critique of newcomers and their expression of solidarity and love for Japan following the 2011 disasters could be interpreted as symptoms of their ongoing insecurity in an adoptive home where they still did not feel fully accepted. Joshua wondered whether this insecurity made it difficult for them to engage in any legitimate critique of the Japanese government and industry.

Different Experiences, Alternative Interpretations

To help think through this question, in the summer of 2013, two years after the 3.11 disasters, Joshua got in touch with his friend Mariko. He asked her to recall her experiences of 3.11 and to comment on Luís's posts. Like Luís, Mariko still lived in Hamamatsu, Shizuoka Prefecture, 150 miles southwest of Tokyo, and 300 miles from the Fukushima power plant. At that distance, Hamamatsu experienced little or no damage from the earthquake, but it was felt strongly enough to startle many of its residents. Here is a record of our initial discussion over e-mail about collaborating on this chapter:

JR: I wanted to ask you whether you would want to write an article with me about Japanese Brazilians in Japan. . . . What do you say?

MS: Josh, I say YES!! Let's start, about nikkeis [overseas Japanese], do you want something about their careers and success, dashed hopes, education, Brazilian fairy tale? Tell me what you need, and I will start on it today.

JR: Yay! Let's start! I wanted to frame the paper in terms of responses following the 3.11 disasters. Disasters are moments that force people to reflect on their lives and commitments. I'm sure you thought about whether to stay in Japan.. . . Can you write up an account of those days and weeks immediately following 3.11?. . . .

MS: I'm in, again. Luckily (for you) I'm at home with a cold, I'll take a nap for two hours and then start writing. . . .

One day later:

MS: Joshua I started writing, but it will take a little longer, because with the memories comes emotion. When I am able to stop crying I'll continue writing.

JR: Sorry to bring you back to that difficult time. . . .

MS: I think it was good to start writing. The account has to be honest. Today I'm feeling better, although I'm at home because I ended up with an ear infection, a bit of dizziness and nausea. I'll write a little more. I said yes, so it is YES. Let's turn in a super article. Yesterday I became emotional when I looked at the photos of Saemi's [Mariko's younger daughter] graduation, a couple of days after the tsunami. I felt the pain of the mothers who lost their children, of the children who could not graduate, of the emptiness which came into our lives. . . .

It struck Joshua from this initial exchange that Mariko's account would force him to reevaluate his interpretation of minority anxiety. His interpretation had dismissed the real empathy Japanese Brazilians expressed for the tragedy of 3.11. In Mariko's message, she represented herself not as an outsider precariously positioned in Japan, but as as a mother whose daughter was graduating from elementary school just days after so many Japanese mothers in northern Japan, expecting to celebrate their own children's graduations, had ended up losing them to the tsunami. This act of identification is not something easily felt by one who feels marginalized in Japan. Mariko's identification allowed her to empathize with Japanese mothers and feel their loss strongly.

The Digital Archive of Japan's 2011 Disasters (http://www.jdarchive.org/en/home), a project of Harvard University's Reischauer Institute of Japanese Studies, attempts to archive and widely disseminate all material, including social media, about the 3.11 Triple Disaster.

One week later, Mariko sent Joshua the following account of her experience of the moment of the earthquake on March 11, 2011:

Today I end my contract with the Fukude elementary school, where I have worked as Portuguese-Japanese translator and interpreter. . . .

In two hours I return home, closing one more chapter of my life. The day is tranquil and I have already prepared some words to take my leave of the teachers. After the crisis of 2008 [the global financial crisis], things were complicated, and I'm grateful to have gotten this temporary job. It has been a good year.

At the end of February, my younger daughter passed with merit the entrance exam for a private junior high school. My girls really worked hard during the 2008 crisis, never complained, only asked for money for materials for school. My husband and I are very proud of them, we spoke at home about the sacrifices we have had to make, we all agreed that they would proceed with their schooling, that all kids deserve the best education possible. We were very happy.

It was the end of the Japanese school year [which starts in early April and ends in mid March], there were just a couple of days left before spring break.

I was seated at my desk, putting away my things.

[A Japanese co-worker asked me,] "Do you know what you will do with your life? Do you have another job lined up?",

"No, at the end of the month I'll go to Hello Work [Japanese government employment office]."

"Tremor! Did you feel it?",

"No, I think you've been drinking too much tea, sensei!!"

"It's an earthquake!! Where is Suzuki-san?"

"He's outside pruning the trees."

"Suzuki-san! Stop!! Earthquake!!",

"Again, did you feel it?",

Now I felt it, it was the 11th of March, 2011, 2:46 p.m. A great earthquake followed by a tsunami struck the eastern coast of Japan; I sat on the floor during the tremors, some colleagues ducked under tables. The tremors seemed to last an eternity, with horizontal movements. Magnitude 5 [弱; weak].

The director of the school turned on the TV for information and we saw the worst—a live image of the Tsunami, houses, boats, cars engulfed and swept away by the giant waves. My heart froze. I looked at the director, tears streaming from his eyes, some professors shouted desperately as they watched the images of cars trying to flee the giant waves.

速く速く、神様助けて下さい！！[Quick, quick, please God help us!!]

I couldn't believe what I was seeing!! I felt cold in my stomach and on my back!!

The tsunami siren wailed, the school being an emergency evacuation site. There were many secondary shocks and the alert asked people to get away from the coast. The school is just 3 kilometers from the shore, my house 4.6 kms. The teachers started to prepare to receive the residents of neighborhoods near the shore, and the evacuation to the school site began at 18:00. I returned home at 17:00, and calmed down only when I saw my husband and daughters at home. We hugged each other tightly for several minutes. I looked at my husband. We were very fearful. My husband worked in an industrial complex just meters from the beach.

My older daughter was studying at a junior high school close to city hall, and was located on high ground far from the shore. On this day, they were seeing off the graduating seniors. After the earthquake the students stayed in the gymnasium awaiting the instructions of their teachers; the students heard their teachers say "yabai!! yabai!! [damn, damn]." Club activities were cancelled and students were sent home. My daughter saw the tsunami on TV; she didn't believe it. It looked like scenes from a Hollywood film.

My younger daughter was in the sixth grade of elementary school, located six kilometers from the shore. The school telephoned asking that I pick her up. As the teacher knew that I worked in another school and that it would be difficult for me to leave immediately, the teachers took groups of children and delivered them to集合場所 [a meeting place] very close to my home.

I remember my younger daughter, with tears in her eyes as she watched the news. She says that she doesn't remember anything of the day of the tsunami; my older daughter says that in truth, she doesn't want to remember the anguish and sorrow, thinking of the children the same age as her, preparing for their graduations, who died tragically on March 11.

I was worried about the size of the catastrophe, but also knew that my daughters, as well as Seiji [Mariko's husband] and myself, were well trained for this moment. For example, we knew not to panic and that we should meet at the emergency shelter if we were unable to get back home or to communicate with each other by phone.

We listened for information on TV and for guidance from the government on NHK [the public broadcasting channel], and also tried to get information on-line, but the principle source of information was the Japanese TV.

I posted the following on Facebook: "An 8.9 degree earthquake struck Japan, it was 5 degrees in my city. We are okay, but the tsunami was devastating and I am still without words."

We saw the problem with the nuclear reactors in Fukushima. I've never felt such fear in my life. This fear was not for myself, but for my girls.

That same night, my cell phone rang two times with earthquake alarms, magnitude 6 further within the prefecture and magnitude 4 in my region. We had provisions at home. My husband went to the store to buy a little more water in case supplies were cut. But to our surprise there wasn't any more water, nor any instant noodles, rice, nor frozen foods in any supermarket in the region. The shelves were empty. It took several days for the supplies to return to normal. I left the bath full of water for bathing and for the toilet, just as a precaution.

On the 12th of March, the Japanese government confirmed the leak at the Fukushima nuclear plant, and commenced isolating the area, first within a radius of 10 kilometers, then 20 kilometers, and the fear of radiation entered our lives. In the days following the catastrophe, insecurity gripped us all, and family and friends, fearful of radiation, asked that we return to Brazil.

My husband embraced me strongly with tears in his eyes:

"The girls, I don't know how to protect the girls. I don't know what to do!" There is no way to convey the sense of impotence that we felt.

Even with my chest pounding from such insecurity I knew that life must go on.

On March 16th I posted on Facebook: "Radioactive materials will reach Tokyo but not enough to be harmful to humans. . . . But I am so scared. Radiation and tsunami freak me out, a lot!",

March 19th was the day of my younger daughter's graduation ceremony. We felt gratitude and sorrow.

The children entered the gymnasium, bringing with them disaster hard hats, each hat representing a child lost to the tsunami, who should have graduated on this day. I couldn't keep back my tears. On this day I felt the pain of the families, the pain of the mothers who survived without their sons and daughters, the children of the same age who lost their lives so young.

Students gather for their junior high school graduation ceremony. *(Mariko Sikama)*

During the ceremony everyone honored the victims. Life was no longer the same, everything had changed.

After the graduation ceremony, the children, parents, and teachers walked once around the school, the ritual of leaving, and I kept looking the whole time at the roof, imagining the height of the waves that covered a school in Fukushima.

People who lost everything, except for their debts. . . .

My problems seemed small considering everything that had happened. In 2009 my husband and I lost our jobs. My husband was unemployed for almost a year, while I was able to get two temporary jobs, one from 8:30 am to noon, and the other from 1:30 to 5 pm. The contract for one ended on the day of the earthquake, and the other terminated ten days after that. At the end of 2009, my husband succeeded in getting a temporary job that was supposed to last just for three months but it has already been a year and three months since he started and he continues working. Once again we started economizing in order to afford the 500,000 yen [roughly U.S.$5,000] for matriculation and school uniforms. We did all that was possible so that the girls would not suffer in the crisis, and since 2008 we cut all that was superfluous. We did not want for food and were able to pay our bills on time.

The panic took its toll on foreigners; on TV we saw that all the international flights were packed with people, even with those who had nowhere to run to. There was a Brazilian demanding that the Brazilian air force send military planes to rescue them. The people no longer had any notion about what they were talking about. There was no longer any kikoku shien jigyoo [Japanese government financial assistance to return to home countries following the financial crisis], that had ended exactly a year previously.

Wherever you went there were groups asking for donations for the victims of the tsunami, at schools, supermarkets. Various Brazilian groups donated water, food, and blankets. But they insisted on placing signs on trucks written in Portuguese, saying that Brazilians were helping. Who did they suppose was going to read these signs?

Life must go on, but I had no idea how to go about it. My second job also came to an end. At this job I had been sent by the International Association in Iwata to work as an assistant teacher accompanying a six-year-old child with ADHD at a local elementary school.

On the good side, I now had more time to search for work!! I got up early, took my bicycle and went to Hello Work, 8 kilometers from home, thinking: Today I will get a job, whatever it takes!

Before arriving at Hello Work, I got a call on my cell:

"Are you working now?"

"Ah. .. no, why?"

Two hours later I was employed. This job fell to me from the sky.

It was the City of Iwata, offering me work as a tri-lingual interpreter for Japanese, Portuguese, and English.

Before too long, the government launched a measure to save energy, the factories would work on weekends and take Fridays off. Many factories reduced work schedules, and many workers clocked only five or six hours per day, just four days in a week. Some just worked one day per week. This motivated many Japanese Brazilians to go back to Brazil.

I perceived another collateral effect on migrants, since the global fiscal crisis was aggravated by the tsunami:

Those who still had work often preferred to leave their children with someone to look after them during the day rather than sending them to school. These sitters, many of them recently unemployed, would charge just 20,000 to 35,000 yen [$200-$350] per month per child, including three meals a day. Parents could drop off as early as 6:30 am, and pick up as late as 8 or 9 pm. But these sitters would just let the children watch TV the entire day. The children, without any education or activities, could turn into international ignoramuses and a social problem.

One person I knew said that "We are here temporarily. If they went to school, it would cause us trouble in the future [in the sense that the Japanese school curriculum is irrelavant for Brazilians later on], when we return to Brazil. God will matriculate them in school and college at the right time, etc. With this crisis, there is no way for me to pay for school and my husband doesn't want them to learn Japanese. He doesn't want them to plant roots here. The babysitter provides breakfast, lunch, dinner, and a bath. The kids just come home to sleep." [The child was out of school for two years.]

People became strange during the period of the crisis. People we knew would call me just to ask whether my husband was working overtime, what my salary was, etc. It was an annoying situation, and we decided to respond that he didn't have any overtime and that life was hard.

Another thing was that the tsunami accelerated the departure of factories from Japan, many to Thailand and Myanmar, the salary of one Japanese worker here was enough to pay for ten workers in Thailand.

My husband's factory had notified him that there would be no more overtime work from November 2011, but Thailand then experienced its worst flood at the start of that month, and my husband was "lucky" to continue doing three hours of overtime work every day.

In my city there had once lived 7,534 Brazilians (2008), and this number fell to 5,021 (2011), and then to just 3,879 (June 2013).

The tsunami did not just tell a tale of sorrow, death, and destruction; it told of the earthquake training done in schools. Many families were saved, for after the earthquake the children started to cry asking to be taken to higher ground, for they knew there would be a tsunami. In order to calm the children, they were taken to higher ground, just minutes before the gigantic waves.

After the tsunami the *Jieitais* [Japanese Self Defense Forces] rescued people and memories, gathering and restoring photographs and personal objects that they found in the debris, leaving them at the lost and found. It was slow and dangerous work due to the radiation.

I saw a man on TV gathering personal objects in the debris. There he found the knapsack of his six-year-old niece. She was going to enter first grade. He brought the knapsack back home and cleaned it, hoping that the niece who had been swept away by the tsunami would return home. Since then I see a lot of solidarity and also fear.

It is already two years since the catastrophe, and still my husband refuses to eat anything produced in Fukushima. No fish, no vegetables or meat from the contaminated region.

The fear of radiation is ever present.

There have been many job offers paying 30,000 yen [$300] for two hours of service in the contaminated region, helping to clear debris, etc. Many went, but few were able to endure it, so much suffering in the air.

I have been frustrated by those outside the area of risk lamenting their plight on the social networks, worrying people in Brazil for no good reason.

After the tsunami a woman from my hometown wrote to a TV program in Brazil saying that she was afraid of the radiation, afraid of the tsunami, that she was a victim of maltreatment, that she didn't have anything to eat. . . a lot of hot air floating over the actual pain that she never felt. She received free tickets back to Brazil for her entire family, jobs for herself and her husband, a scholarship for her children to go to school, and a HOUSE. The opportunists of tragedy.

The following e-mail exchange took place over several days after Mariko (MS) sent Joshua (JR) her reflections:

JR: Do you personally know any Brazilians who volunteered in some capacity or donated money or things?
MS: A group of Brazilian volunteers from the Kakegawa Praise Church went to Sendai. One of the members was depressed, went in order to feel better, and returned more depressed than ever.

Servitu [a Brazilian supermarket located in Hamamatsu] was collecting new blankets to send to the homeless, but I don't know how many they sent.

My family contributed donations at school, our workplaces (mine and Seiji's), the amount that was suggested by the company.

Sure there were people criticizing, who wanted the Brazilian government to repatriate them, and many left everything behind, abandoning their own homes and cars.

Sure there were many opportunistic politicians who took advantage for the purposes of their political campaigns.

JR: You mentioned that friends and family in Brazil asked you to leave Japan because of radiation fears immediately after 3.11. And you write that Seiji is still concerned about the safety of the food two years after 3.11. Do you have any reservations about staying in Japan with your daughters?

MS: Despite all the fear and insecurity about the future. . . my girls were born in Japan, and there was no way that we would turn our back on Japan in its moment of greatest need. Japan gave us the opportunity of our lives, the highest quality education for my girls, and received us with open arms. This is our home, but we are selective about the sourcing of the food that we eat, just in case.

JR: You say that the Japanese government received you with open arms, and that you couldn't turn your back on Japan in its moment of need. I can understand your feelings about this, but I also wonder whether you were at times angry with the Japanese government and industry for allowing the nuclear meltdown to happen in the first place, contaminating Fukushima for future generations, and threatening the food supply. Also, the Japanese government was very slow to evacuate a 20-kilometer zone around the nuclear plants, while the American government urged a more rapid evacuation of a 50-mile zone. Some were critical of the Japanese government for not acting more responsibly, both before the meltdown and after. Do you or other Brazilians have any criticisms of the Japanese government?

MS: . . . the reactors were well protected, it was believed that it was a safe region, and for this reason many companies opened new facilities in the vicinity. The reactor has a cooling system, when this system stops for some reason, back up generators are automatically activated to maintain the cooling function. They thought of everything except a tsunami of this size. The cooling system was knocked out as well as the backup generators, which allowed the heat and pressure to build until it exploded. The firefighters did everything they could to cool the reactors, but it was too late. We don't blame TEPCO [Tokyo Electric Power Company, which ran the Fukushima nuclear power plant]. Everything was done according to safety codes. The American government could pull out U.S. citizens to a safer area because there were few. How can you evacuate an entire population without roads, airport, no infrastructure, everything in chaos? The government did what was right, evacuating up to 20 kilometers, and went on evacuating as needed and as conditions allowed. This is not counting those residents who refused to leave their homes, principally the aged, which took a long time.

JR: When you say that everything conformed to the safety codes, I wonder who established those codes and why they were set so inadequately. I suspect that the Japanese government regulators wrote those codes, but that the regulators were completely influenced by the pressure put on them by the nuclear industry. I found a quote from Luís that includes some critique:

JAPAN IS THE LAND OF THE RISING SUN, ZINPAGU—THE GOLDEN LAND, THE LAND OF MY ANCESTORS, PRIDE OF ALL THE WORLD, EXAMPLE ALSO OF ERRORS FROM WHICH THEY HAVE LEARNED AND ALSO FROM WHICH THEY HAVE NOT LEARNED.

So I think it is possible to have an ambiguous feeling about Japan, to both love it and also recognize some of its faults. Do you sometimes have conflicting feelings like this?

MS: The problem is that everyone believed that the region offered low risk, based on earthquake registries. They protected the plant well. The damage was to the backup power station that furnished electricity for the cooling pumps. It was after the tsunami destroyed the station that the reactors melted down. Why not protect the power station? Learning from the past, now there is a sea wall 21 meters high. In my opinion, the accident was not caused by any failure in maintenance. It was the biggest recorded earthquake and tsunami in the history of Japan. Who is there to blame? Mother nature? The Mayans? Nostradamus? God? What I admire about human beings is their capacity to stand up and criticize. In the end "everyone is a good sports critic after the game is already over." You could have done this or that. . .

The plants can no longer keep up with the demand for energy. Industry has grown a lot in recent years. Another fact, economic pressure has caused Japanese factories to move to Thailand and other countries in Asia.

Luís drives me crazy!!

I am Brazilian, how can I criticize the country of others, when my own country is in chaos (and has been for a very long time, since the Imperial era). I am proud to be Brazilian, yes, but not to the point that I will sit on my tail and talk badly of others. It's easy to speak, and even easier to criticize; to conjure conspiracies and intrigues does not require practice or skill. But hatred does not change reality.

Look at how any foreigner, independent of the country within which they live, can criticize things, thinking that the locals are idiots. They feel themselves superior, and forget the bad side of their only beloved country, just comparing that which was good. I have seen this in Brazil, and I see this here in Japan when I speak to foreigners from other countries.

In the end, what government keeps the people happy? Bhutan?

Getting back to Luís, he does not know what he is writing. It's a lot of hogwash. . .

I have been working a lot in recent weeks, doing lots of overtime.

Today I'm sad, when I opened the site for the consulate of Canada to see what documents I needed for my daughter to apply for a visa I was greeted with this message:

THE PROFESSIONAL ASSOCIATION OF FOREIGN SERVICE OFFICERS (PAFSO) UNION IS CURRENTLY TAKING STRIKE ACTION.

It takes 13 weeks to get the Canadian visa, and I don't think there will be enough time for her to travel with her school, and she's very annoyed by this.

Concluding Thoughts

Social scientists often collect a wealth of data that allow for multiple interpretations, and sometimes they may not acknowledge the temptation to use those data selectively, focusing only on those that fit their preexisting theories. On his own, Joshua had interpreted Luís's expression of love for Japan following the 3.11 disaster as based on the anxiety of minorities living in an adoptive country that may not have fully accepted them. Disaster is a situation that makes demands of allegiance, and those who are insecure in terms of their belonging may feel the greatest pressure to express this allegiance in unambiguous terms. But working collaboratively with Mariko on this chapter forced Joshua to take alternate theories seriously. Indeed, Mariko's empathic response to the disasters was quite likely based on her integration into Japanese society, not on a marginal position within it. As a mother of children graduating from elementary and junior high schools in Japan in 2011, she felt the loss of those Japanese mothers whose children were lost in the tsunami. To force an interpretation of Mariko's reaction, attributing it to minority anxiety, would diminish the significance of her empathy. In the end, however, Mariko also positions herself as a Brazilian, and as such says she should refrain from flippant critiques of Japan. She is critical of those other foreigners who do not show such restraint. She turned the tables on Joshua, for her attitude here is very much that of the anthropologist—observing and trying to understand local culture, rather than engage in an overly hasty critique. Mariko wrote the following in a message she sent to Joshua some time after we had completed an initial draft of this essay:

> I invite everyone, whether or not they are temporary residents, to open their minds and their hearts to local communities, to get to know their joys, sorrows, dreams, and accomplishments, great and small, and to embrace ethnic, social and cultural differences. I promise that life will be much more animated, interesting, united, and surprisingly good.

If cultural relativism, a trait often exhibited by anthropologists, involves an appreciation of cultural differences, as well as a withholding of judgment based on one's own cultural perspective, Mariko exemplified the relativist stance.

Joshua's desire to focus on migrant anxieties also made him overlook the critique that was embedded in Luís's early posts. While his declaration of solidarity and love were most prominent and striking, he also included a recognition of the errors and faults of government workers. In addition, Joshua should have also taken note of the very Catholic idiom in which Luís had stated his love for Japan, conflating the resurrection of Jesus (the disasters occurred in the month leading up to Easter) and the resurrection of Japan (spring, the season of cherry blossoms, symbolizes renewal). This suggests that Luís was not expressing love out of anxiety. Indeed, it's most likely that he was not trying to become Japanese or deny his own cultural background. He expressed love for Japan in a way that expressed comfort in his own cultural difference, just as Mariko has insisted on speaking Portuguese to her children, who have grown up fluent in both Portuguese and Japanese. These expressions of difference may take place within the home or online in Portuguese-language contexts, but at other times they may take place in public spaces. Japanese Brazilians are comfortable speaking Portuguese to each other, and they have established restaurants, stores, and Catholic churches that make no effort to hide their difference. Solidarity with Japan does not require conformity.

Conventional studies of the social integration of migrants use surveys to ask how satisfied these individuals are with community support, with work, and with their lives more generally. These studies may also attempt to measure the degree of integration by asking migrants how many native friends they have, whether they participate in community or school events, and whether they have experienced discrimination. While responses to such questions provide some sense of migrant integration, anthropologists generally rely more on the method of participant observation to provide a fuller perspective, for it allows them to observe behavior and interact with people in multiple contexts over a period of time. However, many interpretive choices can result from the field notes and interview transcripts recorded through participant observation. In this case study, we have revealed the different interpretive stances of Joshua, Mariko, and Luís. A sense emerges not only of the diverging perspectives of the anthropologist and the two long-term migrants, but also of some of the differences among migrants themselves. While Luís expressed both love for Japan and a critique of Japanese government and industry, Mariko refused to critique Japan. This was not because of insecurity on Mariko's part arising from being less fully integrated into Japanese society. If anything, she was more integrated. But she was integrated in a manner that did not deny her Brazilian identity.

In the end, this disaster did not uncover a simple truth about the place of minorities in Japan today. The place of Japanese Brazilians is somewhat different from the place of other minorities in Japan. Japanese Brazilians are much more secure than undocumented migrants, for example, and yet they are perhaps less secure than third- or fourth-generation ethnic Koreans, or such "insider minorities" as Okinawans, Ainu, the disabled, *hibakusha* (victims of radiation poisoning), and *burakumin*. As we have seen, even among Japanese Brazilians, a divide exists between those *veteranos* with a long-term perspective on life in Japan and those who see Japan as an interlude in lives that are based elsewhere. And even among *veteranos* there are differences in stances between those such as Mariko and Luís. But one thing is clear. Attitudes toward difference in Japan have come a long way since 1923.

The subject of insider minorities in Japan is explored in Joshua Hotaka Roth's article "Political and Cultural Perspectives on Japan's Insider Minorities" (http://japanfocus.org/-Joshua-Roth/1723), published online in the *The Asia Pacific Journal: Japan Focus*.

References and Further Research

Allen, J. Michael. 1996. "The Price of Identity: The 1923 Kanto Earthquake and Its Aftermath." *Korean Studies* 20: 64–93.

Borland, Janet. 2006. "Capitalising on Catastrophe: Reinvigorating the Japanese State with Moral Values Through Education Following the 1923 Great Kantô Earthquake." *Modern Asian Studies* 40, no. 4 (October): 875–907.

Kingston, Jeffrey. 2012. *Natural Disaster and Nuclear Crisis in Japan: Response and Recovery After Japan's 3/11*. New York: Routledge.

Lesser, Jeffrey. 1999. *Negotiating National Identity: Immigrants, Minorities, and the Struggle for Ethnicity in Brazil*. Durham, NC: Duke University Press.

_____. 2007. *A Discontented Diaspora: Japanese Brazilians and the Meanings of Ethnic Militancy, 1960–1980*. Durham, NC: Duke University Press.

Linger, Daniel. 2001. *No One Home: Brazilian Selves Remade in Japan*. Stanford, CA: Stanford University Press.

Ministry of Justice. 2006-2013. Kokuseki chiiki betsu zairyuu shikaku (zairyuu mokuteki) betsu zairyuu gaikokujin [Resident foreigners by nationality, region of origin, and residency status]. Nyuukoku kanri kyoku [Immigration Bureau]. Available at http://www.moj.go.jp/housei/toukei/toukei_ichiran_touroku.html.

National Police Agency. 2014. Heisei 23 nen touhoku chihou taiheiyou okijishin no higai joukyou to keisatsu sochi [Damage Situation and Police Countermeasures associated with the Tohoku district Pacific Ocean Earthquake]. Keisatsu-cho kinkyuu saigai keibi honbu [Emergency Disaster Countermeasures Headquarters]. Available at https://www.npa.go.jp/archive/keibi/biki/higaijokyo.pdf.

Roth, Joshua Hotaka. 2002. *Brokered Homeland: Japanese Brazilian Migrants in Japan*. Ithaca, NY: Cornell University Press.

_____. 2003. "Urashima Taro's Ambiguating Practices: The Significance of Overseas Voting Rights for Elderly Japanese Migrants to Brazil." In *Searching for Home Abroad: Japanese Brazilians and Transnationalism*, edited by Jeffrey Lesser, 103–120. Durham, NC: Duke University Press.

_____. 2005. "Political and Cultural Perspectives on Japan's Insider Minorities." In *A Companion to the Anthropology of Japan*, edited by Jennifer Robertson, 73–86. London: Blackwell Publishing. Expanded version published online in *The Asia-Pacific Journal: Japan Focus* (http://japanfocus.org/-Joshua-Roth/1723).

_____. 2006. "A Mean Spirited Sport: Japanese Brazilian Croquet in São Paulo's Public Spaces." *Anthropological Quarterly* 79, no. 4 (Fall): 609–632.

_____. 2011. "Harmonizing Cars and Humans in Japan's Era of Mass Automobility." *The Asia-Pacific Journal: Japan Focus* 9, no. 45, http://japanfocus.org/-Joshua-Roth/3643.

Ryang, Sonia. 2004. "The Great Kanto Earthquake and the Massacre of Koreans in 1923: Notes on Japan's Modern National Sovereignty." *Anthropological Quarterly*. 76, no. 4 (Autumn): 731–748.

Schencking, J. Charles. 2006. "Catastrophe, Opportunism, Contestation: The Fractured Politics of Reconstructing Tokyo Following the Great Kantô Earthquake of 1923." *Modern Asian Studies* 40, no. 4 (October): 833–873.

Tsing, Anna Lowenhaupt. 2004. *Friction: An Ethnography of Global Connection.* Princeton, NJ: Princeton University Press.

Tsuda, Takeyuki. 2003. *Strangers in the Ethnic Homeland: Japanese Brazilian Return Migration in Transnational Perspective.* New York: Columbia University Press.

Weiner, Michael. 1989. *The Origins of the Korean Community in Japan, 1910–23.* Manchester, UK: Manchester University Press.

Yamaguchi, Tomomi. 2013. "Xenophobia in Action: Nationalism, Hate Speech, and the Internet in Japan." *Radical History Review* 117 (Fall): 98–118.

12

Society and Culture: Confucianism in East Asia Today

Jeffrey L. Richey

East Asia has been defined as a region in terms of its shared history of Western imperialism, its geopolitical importance as a set of linked nation-states, and its pivotal function as a fulcrum of global economic activity. Among all of the features that unite the countries of China (including Taiwan), Korea (North and South), and Japan as a region, perhaps the most striking is East Asia's common inheritance of Confucian ideology.

For millennia—beginning in the fifth century BCE, when the man now known as Confucius first gathered disciples to learn how Chinese antiquity could provide models for individual excellence and social flourishing in the present day, and continuing through the third and fourth centuries CE, when Confucius' teachings were adopted by Japanese and Korean elites—Confucianism has influenced personal, national, and regional life across East Asia. Although no one variety of Confucianism has ever prevailed throughout the entire region, and despite the serious criticism that the tradition has endured over the past century or so, over time it has become (arguably) the single greatest common thread that stitches together nations and peoples who otherwise are quite distinct from one another. Any ideology that has exerted such a profound and long-standing influence over the region where something like one out of four human beings now lives is worthy of our attention. Anyone who wishes to understand East Asia in either the past or the present, therefore, must know something about Confucius, Confucians, and Confucianism.

Defining Confucianism

The question of whether and how Confucianism ought to be classified—as a philosophy, as a religion, or as a deeply-embedded set of cultural values that is inseparable from East Asian identity—has occupied the attention of many participants in, and observers of, East Asian cultures. Because definitions of both "philosophy" and "religion" are notoriously diverse and contradictory, and because notions of "values" are even more nebulous, it is impossible to settle this question here. For the purposes of this chapter, let it suffice to say that Confucianism—like its neighbors, rivals, and partners, Buddhism, Daoism, and Shinto—is a system of ideas, institutions, and practices that provides ways for East Asian people to respond to three overlapping sets of concerns, which might be called "cosmological" (questions about the universe's origin, characteristics, and destiny), "anthropological" (questions about human beings' nature, potential, and purpose), and "ethical" (questions about norms, limits, and goals for living).

Buddhists usually address these concerns by focusing on the causes and effects of living in an impermanent and interdependent cosmos. Daoists tend to respond by working toward harmony with the fundamental powers and patterns of the universe. Devotees of Shinto typically seek answers by engaging what they see as the divine properties and personalities associated with the natural world. Although, historically, Confucianism has both shaped and been shaped by other East Asian traditions, Confucians differ from practitioners of Buddhism, Daoism, and Shinto by viewing cosmological, anthropological, and ethical concerns from a human-centered perspective that sees the universe as a morally patterned landscape to which sages and cultural heroes of the deep past have provided a clear map, represented by both scriptural texts and ritual institutions. For Confucians, the world is like a state, the human race is like a family, and the moral realm is like a farmer's field. A Confucian learns to see the universe in terms of political order, humanity in terms of social hierarchies and relationships, and moral development in terms of nurturing seeds of goodness planted deep in the soil of human nature. Because of Confucianism's primary emphasis on the political, social, and moral dimensions of human life, and because of Confucianism's historical interdependence with Buddhism, Daoism, and Shinto, the interaction of Buddhism, Daoism, and Shinto with such dimensions has tended to take on Confucian qualities, which is why these traditions will not be addressed separately in this volume.

Just as China, the Koreas, and Japan do not constitute one single, homogeneous cultural zone, neither does Confucianism exist as a monolithic, undifferentiated entity. Across East Asia, one may find various types and degrees of Confucian influence at work in politics, in social interactions, and in individual life. Historically, Confucianism has served as a source of authority for East Asian regimes. At a broader cultural level, East Asian communities consistently draw on Confucian traditions for resources that help to structure the family, village, and local society. East Asian individuals have also long relied on Confucianism as a resource for personal morality, intellectual development, and spiritual fulfillment. The different "faces" of Confucianism—state, cultural, and popular—sometimes function independently of one another, sometimes harmonize together, and sometimes fight against each other. Regardless of which "face" it happens to wear at any given moment in any particular sphere of East Asian life, however, Confucianism's role cannot be understood apart from its interaction with ruling powers. Given the focus of this volume, the remainder of this chapter will concentrate on the relationship of Confucian ideology to the state.

A translation of Confucius' works, including *The Analects*, *The Doctrine of the Mean*, and *The Great Learning*, is available at the Internet Classics Archive (http://classics.mit.edu/Browse/browse-Confucius.html).

Confucianism and East Asian Regimes

Although the modern governments of China, Taiwan, South Korea, North Korea, and Japan do not formally endorse Confucianism in quite the same ways as their predecessors, the legacy of centuries of state support for Confucian traditions in these nations can be seen in everything from official school textbooks to the behavior of politicians in moments of national crisis. Confucianism endures as a way for East Asian states to proclaim their authority, shore up their legitimacy, and advance their influence, both at home and abroad. At the cultural and popular levels, expressions of Confucianism often take their cues from how the tradition is treated by the regime in each country.

China

The government of China, although nominally Communist in orientation, annually spends large amounts of money promoting Confucian festivals and texts, paying for the renovation and upkeep of Confucian academies and temples, and generally borrowing the prestige associated with Confucius to enhance its international image. Students are once again committing Confucian teachings to memory in Chinese public schools and universities. Since the 1980s, hundreds of "Confucius Institutes" sponsored by the Chinese government have popped up all over the world, where their generous funding allows them to promote Chinese culture, often by providing Chinese language instruction to local schools. Today, there are over 50 Confucius Institutes in the United States alone. That Confucianism is so alive and well in China today is due both to the enormous legacy of Confucian traditions in Chinese history and to the recent backlash against more than a century of harsh anti-Confucian criticism in China.

Beginning in the late nineteenth century, when China was besieged by population pressures, political rebellions, and opium addiction within its borders, as well as Western and Japanese imperialism and a rapidly changing global economic and technological order beyond its borders, Confucianism's fortunes were altered radically. Long the favored ideology of Chinese rulers, Confucianism was now seen as a spent cultural, intellectual, and spiritual force that kept China backward, weak, and unjust. In the Republican era that followed the collapse of the Qing Dynasty in 1912, the most influential Chinese thinkers and leaders dismissed the tradition as yesterday's garbage, although some suggested that Confucianism was redeemable in modern times. After the triumph of the Communist revolutionary Mao Zedong and the establishment of the People's Republic of China in 1949, mainland China

Statue of Confucius at the Temple of Confucius in Beijing, China. *(Wikimedia Commons, Mr. Granger, http://tinyurl.com/o6pfkko)*.

became an especially inhospitable place for Confucianism. Intellectuals who sympathized with Confucian thought fled to Taiwan, Hong Kong, or the West, while those who remained behind often suffered public criticism, imprisonment, and even execution, especially during Mao's "Cultural Revolution" (1966–1976). Meanwhile, throughout the Chinese diaspora outside of mainland China, Confucian intellectuals who had escaped persecution by Mao spearheaded the revival of Confucianism as an academic field of study, a philosophy for modern times, an engine of economic progress and source of cultural strength for all East Asians, and a contemporary political ideology. This remains especially true in anti-Communist Taiwan, where there never was a "Cultural Revolution" to inhibit the embrace of Confucian traditions, which continue to exert a strong influence on both popular culture and personal values. While Confucianism's status as a religion often is questioned in the West, in Taiwan, "phoenix halls" (*luantang*) in which explicitly Confucian rituals are performed attract a steady stream of faithful Taiwanese, while the deeply Confucian new religious movement known as Yiguan Dao (the Way of Pervasive Unity) claims two million members and has become the third-largest faith community on the island.

The Chinese government's campaign against Confucianism was relaxed after Mao's death in 1976, but it did not abate entirely until the 1990s. The Communist regime began to "rehabilitate" the image of Confucius by sponsoring academic conferences and publications devoted to Confucianism, establishing the aforementioned Confucius Institutes, restoring Confucian texts to school and university curricula, and, beginning in 2013, awarding a Confucius Peace Prize to "promote world peace from an Eastern perspective." Popular culture in China has followed the government's lead. In twenty-first-century China, Confucius and Confucianism have become the subjects of best-selling books, popular television shows for children and adults, and multimillion-dollar movies. With the number of billionaires in China now second only to the number found in the United States, China's rising middle class has developed an appetite for self-help books, lectures, talk shows, and websites, many of which take inspiration from Confucian sources. In 2006 a version of Confucius' *Analects* produced by the university professor and media personality Yu Dan sold more than ten million copies in China. In rural areas, large-scale Confucian community rituals are now commonplace.

The most dramatic recent manifestation of Confucianism's reversal of fortune in China was the sudden appearance of a 31 foot bronze statue of Confucius in Beijing's Tiananmen Square, where it stood near Mao's tomb in early 2011. A few months later, the statue disappeared as mysteriously as it had appeared. The Chinese government has not yet provided any explanation, although it is speculated that the statue's comings and goings reflect internal power struggles within the Chinese Communist Party, which seems to be divided between conservatives who maintain the hard line against premodern culture and progressives who see Confucianism as a way to revive the regime's fortunes. The real test of any East Asian state's endorsement of Confucianism comes when its reliance on the ideology either protects it from collapse or helps bring it down. For the newly re-Confucianized Chinese government, that test is yet to come.

Korea

The most conspicuous sign of a modern Korean regime's association with Confucianism may be the South Korean flag, first used as the flag of the staunchly Confucian Joseon (also referred to as Choson or Chosun) Dynasty from 1883 to 1910. Each corner depicts one of four trigrams (three-line diagrams) found in the Confucian scripture and popular divination manual known as the *Yijing* (pronounced *Yeokgyeong* [or *Yŏkkyŏng*] in Korean), each of which represents a specific Confucian virtue (goodness, modesty, righteousness, or wisdom), family role (father, mother, son, or daughter), and cosmic element (wood, fire, metal, or water). In the center of the flag is the Confucian symbol of cosmic balance, the *Taegeuk* (or *Taegŭk*, the Great Ultimate), which illustrates the constant interaction of the paired opposites known as *yin* and *yang* in Chinese and *eumyang* (or *ŭmyang*) in Korean.

Despite the use of Confucian symbolism on its emblem, the Republic of Korea (as South Korea is known officially) has had an ambivalent relationship with Confucian traditions. Since 1945, when the Korean peninsula was liberated from Japanese control, only to be divided into a Soviet-controlled northern zone and an American-controlled southern zone, anti-Communist regimes in the South have made use of Confucian traditions as a way of underscoring Communism's threat to traditional Korean values. With the outbreak of armed conflict between North and South in 1950, persecution of Confucianism along with other traditional institutions intensified in the Democratic People's Republic of Korea (DPRK), as

Shrine at Confucian School in Gangneung, Korea. (Wikimedia Commons, http://tinyurl.com/lgwcql6).

the northern regime calls itself, and it seems unlikely that Confucianism receives much, if any, government support in that little-understood part of the Korean peninsula. South Korean governments have not always backed Confucianism, either, sometimes attacking it as an obstacle to the goals of modernization, such as economic development along capitalist lines, while relying on the Confucian tradition of authoritarianism during the country's period of rule by military dictatorships (1963–1987). While it is clear that North Koreans are expected to revile Confucianism as part of their unquestioning obedience to the Communist state, South Koreans often seem to value Confucian traditions as part of family and personal life, and visitors to the country frequently remark that it is the most Confucian society in East Asia.

In the early twenty-first century, official South Korean school textbooks both praise Confucianism (by highlighting Confucian values such as loyalty, social conscience, and self-improvement) and condemn it (by describing Confucianism as the ideology of a failed state—the Joseon (romanized as Choson or Chosun) Dynasty that was unable to resist Japanese aggression in the early twentieth century). North Korean sources, meanwhile, are uniformly harsh in their critique of Confucianism as an outmoded feudal ideology. Nonetheless, when South Korean president Park Geun-hye defends her policies by proclaiming her filial devotion to her father, the former dictator Park Chung-hee, assassinated in 1979—whom she credits for instilling her with a love of country—and when the North Korean dictator Kim Jong-un orders elaborate public rituals in honor of his deceased forebears, it may be said that Confucianism is never far from the Korean political scene, South or North. Indeed, Confucian heritage may be the one thing that truly unifies the otherwise divided peninsula.

Japan

Post-1945 Japan has proven to be a remarkable living laboratory for observing how Confucianism can survive, not only despite, but perhaps because of, modern capitalism and consumer society. Japan's defeat by the United States in World War II at first seemed to bring to an end almost a century of Confucian authoritarianism, which dated back to the Meiji emperor's promotion of "the family state" (*kazoku kokka*) as a way of uniting and disciplining his subjects under the umbrella of Confucian filial obedience. The Imperial Rescript on Education (1890) exhorted the Japanese people to be obedient to their parents, zealous in their self-improvement, harmonious in their relationships with others, and courageous in their self-sacrifice to the state, "to guard and maintain the prosperity of Our Imperial Throne coeval with heaven and earth." This document became required reading for Japanese schoolchildren and the fiftieth anniversary of its promulgation in 1940 was celebrated with great fanfare by the government. Five years later, the seven-year period of Japan's military occupation by the United States began, ushering in changes intended to remodel Japanese cultural, political, and social values along lines that were very much opposed to Confucian traditions.

However, Japan's rapid economic development during the 1960s and 1970s was often credited to its Confucian heritage of deferred gratification, selfless dedication to

Talisman of the Japanese deity Tenjin, a deified ninth-century Confucian said to grant academic success. *(Wikimedia Commons, Yuko Honda, http://tinyurl.com/m8q2hxr).*

group effort, and efficient social organization, even as it also was apparent that Japanese culture was undergoing a process of intense, if highly selective, Westernization. The historical reality is that those who governed Japan during the second half of the twentieth century mostly belonged to the generation that came of age during the peak of Japan's right-wing revival of Confucianism. Thus, the seemingly paradoxical qualities of contemporary Japan as both the land where "Confucius lives next door" (as T. R. Reid's best-selling 1999 book puts it) and the country that seems more modernized than many Western nations are due in large part to the policies and values of what may have been Japan's most Confucianized generation.

It was more commonplace to see modern Japan in Confucian terms during the late 1970s and early 1980s, when the country's postwar economic boom was peaking. After Japan's overheated "bubble economy" burst in 1990, followed by the Asian financial crisis of 1997 and the global recession of 2008, it seemed to many observers that Japan's Confucian heritage was on the brink of dying with its rapidly aging population, swiftly shrinking families, and dramatically curtailed corporate payrolls. Moreover, the association of Confucianism with the shrill and reactionary views of elderly politicians such as Tokyo mayor Ishihara Shintaro has done little to promote Confucianism as a contemporary Japanese ideology, much less one that upholds the authority and legitimacy of the state. Nonetheless, Confucian ideas, institutions, and practices still may be found throughout popular culture and personal life in Japan. Every Japanese household maintains family registers (*koseki*), which certify and record all marriages, divorces, births, adoptions, parental rights, and even deaths in terms of individual membership within a designated household (*ie*). Those older than their colleagues still can expect to be addressed as *senpai* (literally "of the earlier generation") and will use the term *kōhai* ("of the later generation") when addressing their younger counterparts.

As is the case elsewhere in East Asia, in Japan the culture of education may be the arena in which continuing Confucian influence is most obvious. Every January, hundreds of thousands of Japanese students visit Shinto shrines to pray for the assistance of deified Confucian scholars and other supernatural patrons of learning as they endure the grueling national university entrance examinations, themselves a legacy of traditional Confucian civil service qualification tests once required of prospective government officials across East Asia. Perhaps these students will become Japan's next generation of Confucian-minded leaders, finding inspiration in ancient tradition as East Asia's most developed nation faces an uncertain future.

Confucianism's Future(s) in East Asia

In the postmodern era, it still is possible to be "traditional," but participation in tradition has, paradoxically, become a personal choice rather than an ancestral mandate, as it generally was in premodern times. This is no less true of contemporary Chinese, Korean, and Japanese people than it is of Americans who champion "family values" or Europeans who protest the "Islamization" of continental culture. Thus, speculation on whether and how East Asia will continue to be Confucian must take into account the factors that may both encourage and discourage the persistence of state Confucianism, cultural Confucianism, and popular Confucianism as a vital force in East Asian societies. Among these are the ongoing "Asian values" debate, demographic changes related to increasing wealth and decreasing population, the apparent shift of global economic exchange, and military deployment to the East Asian region.

Since the 1970s, the claim that "Asian values" are "Confucian values" has rung out with regularity across East Asia and even beyond, especially in Southeast Asian countries with large ethnically Chinese populations, such as Singapore and Malaysia. Promoting a convergence of Confucianism and Asian regional identity has proven to be a useful way for Confucian- or Asian-identified regimes to protect themselves from criticism on issues such as human rights, and to highlight solidarity with other Asian nations against the West. At the same time, however, too close an identification of autocratic regimes with Confucianism may inspire eventual rebellion against both "Confucian" regimes and Confucianism itself as discontented East Asians throw out the Confucian baby with its political bathwater. Further, not everyone is convinced that Confucianism provides a way for East Asians to be both East Asian and modern.

Not only in Japan, but also in China, Taiwan, and South Korea, decades of economic development, rising standards of living, and increased educational attainment have resulted in wealthier households and falling birthrates, as women marry and bear children less frequently and at an older age, while marriageable men (especially in China) face much greater competition for mates due to sex-selective abortion and voluntary or mandatory limits on the number of children born in each family. By 2040, smaller families, improved health, and larger bank accounts are expected to result in an over-sixty-five population of 329 million people in China alone. Will it be possible to sustain Confucian values in cultures that define "family" in terms of two parents and one child, or among individuals who prize personal spending power and career satisfaction more highly than caring for relatives or subordinating themselves to the decisions and expectations of elders? Will a majority-elderly population take greater interest in a tradition that, at its heart, sees age as a social asset and a personal gateway to wisdom? It is possible that, in the undercrowded and overaged East Asia of tomorrow, Confucianism will be more valuable, but also less feasible, than ever.

As East Asian economies continue to elbow their way to the top of the global food chain, there is the question of whether and how Confucianism will survive what social critics call "affluenza," referring to the negative effects of consumerism. China and Japan are now the world's second- and third-largest economies, respectively, as well as the first- and fourth-largest exporters of goods across the globe. Confucianism, which developed under agrarian conditions in ancient China and later became the ideology of urban elites in highly bureaucratized monarchies, may not be well suited to adapt to an East Asia defined less by robes of state and more by Paris and Hollywood couture. On the other hand, popular Confucianism may be able to speak words of critical truth to commercial power when other modes of dissent, such as state Confucianism or cultural Confucianism, have been muzzled or disarmed by complicity with capitalism.

More worryingly, East Asia's current transformation into the primary global arena for military expenditure and territorial disputes may imperil the future of Confucianism in the state, cultural, and popular spheres. China and Japan—the world's second- and sixth-largest military spenders, respectively—now clash regularly over issues of access and control related to tiny but strategically important islands such as the chain known in Chinese as the Diaoyu and in Japanese as the Senkaku. In November 2013, China ruffled feathers in both Tokyo and Washington by declaring its sovereignty over what it calls an "air defense identification zone" in the East China Sea, a uni-laterally-imposed area of air traffic control that overlaps with airspace and territory claimed by Japan, South Korea, and Taiwan. North Korea's announcement in 2013 that United Nations sanctions against its government constituted a violation of the 1953 armistice that ended the Korean War, justifying nuclear missile strikes against South Korea and other targets, has elevated already high tensions across East Asia. The bulk of U.S. naval forces are now deployed to the Pacific, with special reinforce-ments dispatched to East Asia. The rekindling of old conflicts between historically Confucian cultures is occurring at the same time as the renegotiation of the balance of power in the region, which was established under American hegemony more than 60 years ago. What role, if any, will Confucian discourses about state responsibility, cultural solidarity, and popular morality play in East Asia's turbulent twenty-first century?

Confucianism is a multifaceted phenomenon in East Asian society and culture. It seems likely that its future, or rather futures, in East Asia will take a similarly var-ied course. Confucianism has proven useful to countless East Asian regimes, and it may retain its value for East Asian states as they consolidate and expand their power. Historically, Confucianism has been the cultural glue holding the diverse peoples of East Asia together, and elites across the region continue to share a Confucian vocabu-lary when addressing social wrongs and proposing ways to put things right. At the popular level, East Asians from Seoul to Sapporo and from Harbin to Hokkaido still live in a social world that is basically Confucian in terms of its dominant ideas, institu-tions, and practices. The complexity and diversity of Confucianism as a living legacy in contemporary East Asia is the best guarantee of its possible future in the region.

References and Further Reading

Angle, Stephen C. 2009. *Sagehood: The Contemporary Significance of Neo-Confucian Philosophy.* New York: Oxford University Press.

Bell, Daniel A., and Hahm Chaibong, eds. 2003. *Confucianism for the Modern World.* Cambridge: Cambridge University Press.

Bresciani, Umberto. 2001. *Reinventing Confucianism: The New Confucian Movement.* Taipei, Taiwan: Taipei Ricci Institute for Chinese Studies.

Elman, Benjamin A., John B. Duncan, and Herman Ooms, eds. 2002. *Rethinking Confucianism: Past and Present in China, Japan, Korea, and Vietnam.* Los Angeles: UCLA Asian Pacific Monograph Series.

Koh Byong-ik. 1996. "Confucianism in Contemporary Korea." In *Confucian Traditions in East Asian Modernity*, edited by Tu Wei-ming, 191-201. Cambridge, MA: Harvard University Press.

Liu, Shu-hsien. 2003. *Essentials of Contemporary Neo-Confucian Philosophy*. Westport, CT: Praeger.

Makeham, John. 2008. *Lost Soul: "Confucianism" in Contemporary Chinese Academic Discourse*. Cambridge, MA: Harvard University Press.

Reid, T. R. 1999. *Confucius Lives Next Door: What Living in the East Teaches Us About Living in the West*. New York: Random House.

Richey, Jeffrey L. 2013. *Confucius in East Asia: Confucianism's History in China, Korea, Japan, and Viet Nam*. Ann Arbor, MI: Association for Asian Studies.

Qing, Jiang. 2012. *A Confucian Constitutional Order: How China's Ancient Past Can Shape Its Political Future*. Translated by Edmund Ryden. Princeton, NJ: Princeton University Press.

Sun, Anna. 2013. *Confucianism as a World Religion: Contested Histories and Contemporary Realities*. Princeton, NJ: Princeton University Press.

Yu Dan. 2009 *Confucius from the Heart: Ancient Wisdom for Today's World*.

Zhang, Wei-Bin. 1999. *Confucianism and Modernization: Industrialization and Democratization of the Confucian Regions*. New York: St. Martin's Press.

13

The Korean Peninsula: Global Dimensions

JACQUES FUQUA

Imagine for a moment a nuclear winter, where the landscape is devoid of structures, people or life—a desolate wasteland. Or perhaps a hot war involving some of the world's most powerful nations, economies and militaries—the United States, People's Republic of China (PRC), Russian Federation, Japan, South Korea, and North Korea. The Korean peninsula stands as testament to our global past while indicating its possible future. On the one hand, it remains one of the final vestiges of a Cold War long abandoned by other nations, a visible reminder of how the global community of nations divided itself in the aftermath of World War II. On the other hand, it represents the proverbial finger on a trigger ready to be pulled, potentially hurtling the community of nations into global calamity.

For most of its existence, Korea was a unified state, beginning from the time of its establishment in 936 CE under the Goryeo Dynasty. By the end of World War II it would become a nation physically divided, with one foot in the Communist Bloc of nations and the other in the free world.

> The Communist Bloc included the former Soviet Union and other Eastern European countries that had Communist governments and were under Soviet influence.

This division was formalized politically in 1948 with the establishment of the Republic of Korea (ROK, or South Korea), which aligned itself with the United States, and the Democratic People's Republic of Korea (DPRK, or North Korea), which fell under the influence of the former Soviet Union (USSR) and, later, the PRC. The Korean peninsula has remained bisected for 60 years by the roughly 150-mile long, 2.4-mile wide Demilitarized Zone (DMZ) that was established in 1953 as a temporary political boundary and a condition of the armistice that brought the fighting associated with the Korean War (June 25, 1950–July 27, 1953) to an end. On either side of the divide, however, militaries still stand vigil and remain poised for war.

Learn more about the geography of the Korean peninsula by going to the Asia Society's website (www.asiasociety.org) and searching for "Geography of the Koreas."

The political division of the peninsula has had far-reaching and unintended implications for the two Koreas as well as the global community of nations. Because of decades of separation, the two nations have evolved diametrically and now occupy opposite ends of political, cultural, social, and economic continua. South Korea is a republic constructed on a foundation of capitalism, free elections, and recognition of individual rights and freedoms. Its citizens are permitted to freely pursue their educational, occupational, and leisure preferences. With the world's twelfth largest economy (2013), the nation is globally recognized not only for its leadership in commerce and technology (including companies such as Hyundai, Kia, Samsung, LG, and Lotte, to name just a few), but also for the increasingly significant roles it plays in multinational organizations (the current Secretary-General of the United Nations, Ban Ki-moon, is a citizen of South Korea).

Conversely, North Korea is a repressive dictatorship that often threatens war against South Korea and perpetrates acts of violence against it; practices "brinksmanship diplomacy" against other nations through its nuclear weapons and ballistic missile programs for the purpose of extracting economic and political concessions; and has demonstrated little regard for the human rights or well-being of its citizens. The nation is regarded as a global pariah characterized primarily by its hostile behavior. Since 1948 the country's leadership has been held by three successive generations of the Kim family: Kim Il-sung, Kim Jong-il and presently Kim Jong-un.

The Center for Arms Control and Non-Proliferation website includes a fact sheet on "North Korea's Nuclear and Ballistic Missile Programs" (http://armscontrolcenter.org/publications/factsheets/fact_sheet_north_korea_nuclear_and_missile_programs/).

Consequently, much of the world community's concern focuses squarely on North Korea and its regime, concerns that can be distilled into three basic concepts. First is the manifestation of North Korean miscreant behavior, which itself can be divided into four major types: (1) unpredictable brinksmanship diplomacy that centers on development of nuclear weapons and ballistic missile programs, (2) global proliferation of weapons of mass destruction, (3) direct threats against its southern neighbor, and (4) human rights abuses perpetrated against its own citizens. While each of these issues merits resolution to ensure global stability or recognition of fundamental human rights, the first issue is of particular global concern—so much so that it has resulted in five United Nations Security Council resolutions against North Korea since 2006, which have imposed increasingly harsh sanctions as a direct result of the regime's continued nuclear and ballistic missile testing programs.

Synopses of the five United Nations Security Council resolutions against North Korea, as well as selected excerpts from those documents, can be found on the website of the Arms Control Association (http://www.armscontrol.org/factsheets/UN-Security-Council-Resolutions-on-North-Korea).

Second is the probability of a unified peninsula—the likelihood that the two Koreas will in the future again become a unified nation. A final consideration is how major regional geopolitical players (the United States, Russia, China, South Korea and Japan) perceive a potentially unified Korea impacting their own national interests.

This case study focuses on several peninsular issues with broader global implications: (1) the root causes of and rationale underlying North Korea's brinksmanship behavior, (2) the global threat the regime represents, and (3) whether there appears to be a plausible way forward in resolving the North Korea issue.

Two Nations, One Beginning

Since the latter half of the nineteenth century, Korea has played an integral role in helping to shape global events, and has similarly been impacted by them, primarily because of its close historical connection with China and Japan, and later with several Western nations. Events occurring from the mid-1800s onward would not only become critical to mid-twentieth-century history, but they would also be important because of the role they would have in shaping contemporary global geopolitics.

After centuries of voluntarily submitting to China's tributary system and conducting most of its foreign affairs under the aegis of Chinese protection, by the 1870s Korea's sovereignty was being fully assailed by the incursion of Western nations and Japan. Western nations became increasingly interested in the East Asia region for purposes of expanded trade and commerce, and the competition among them became fierce. China was of greatest interest, but Japan was as well, particularly for the United States, because it provided a refueling point for ships traveling to China from America's west coast, and potentially offered a safe haven for shipwrecked sailors. Consequently, through the direct efforts of Commodore Matthew C. Perry and his employment of "gunboat diplomacy," the United States forced Japanese officials to conclude the Kanagawa Convention (1854), which led to similar treaties being signed with Great Britain (1854), Russia (1855), and the Netherlands (1856). These treaties were followed by a series of commercial treaties Japan was pressured to conclude in 1858 with the United States (the U.S.-Japan Treaty of Amity and Commerce), Great Britain, the Netherlands, France, and Russia, known collectively as the Ansei Commercial Treaties. These agreements provided for extraterritoriality for their respective citizens, opened numerous ports to trade, and allowed Western nations to post diplomats in Japan. In short, these treaties forced Japan to abandon its policy of national seclusion (*sakoku*), which had been established during the early seventeenth century. While signing these treaties led to the fall of the government headed by the shogun in Japan (*bakufu*), Western incursion also had the unintended effect of demonstrating to Japanese leaders that military might was the key to success in global geopolitics.

The full text of the Kanagawa Convention is available to read here: http://www. archives.gov/exhibits/featured_documents/treaty_of_kanagawa/.

After unsuccessful attempts to have the Ansei Treaties rescinded, Japan embarked on a course of action to establish itself as a colonial power, one able to stand on equal footing with Western nations. An integral first step included compelling another nation, in this case Korea, to abandon its own seclusion policy and submit to an unequal treaty, much as Japan had been forced to do. Contriving a military incident, Japan attacked and bested Korea, forcing Korean officials to conclude the Treaty of Kanghwa (1876), the major components of which were very similar to the treaties Japan had been forced to sign.

In 1866 the U.S. vessel *General Sherman* entered Korean territory, uninvited, by sailing up the Daedong (Taedong) River. The motivation for this was the expansion of U.S. commercial interests in the region. The vessel was ultimately attacked and destroyed, leading to punitive expeditions against Korea by the United States. With the assistance of Chinese diplomats, U.S. officials ultimately convinced Korean leaders to open the nation's doors via a commercial treaty—the Treaty of Chemulpo (1882), also known as the Schufeldt Treaty. Following earlier patterns, European nations soon joined the United States in full force on the Korean peninsula.

For Japan, however, issues on the Korean peninsula had become a national imperative, referring to the nation as a "dagger pointed at the heart of Japan." Wresting Korea from Chinese influence became a key domestic and foreign policy objective. After a number of near skirmishes between Japan and China, fighting erupted in 1894 between the two nations in what would become the First Sino-Japanese War (1894–1895), a war handily won by Japan. With this victory, Japan established itself as the preeminent East Asian power. The Treaty of Shimonoseki ended the fighting and, among other things, expressly established Korea's independence from China, providing Japan the opportunity to gain a stronger foothold on the peninsula.

The year 1905 proved particularly important in Korea's history, as its own future and world events became ever more intricately intertwined. With Japan's victory

Japanese soldiers victorious in 1895 in the First Sino-Japanese War. *(Wikimedia Commons, http://tinyurl.com/nvj5mfj).*

over Russia in the Russo-Japanese War (1904–1905), the first time an Asian nation defeated a Western power, Japan became a legitimate world power, one intent on exercising sole dominion over Korea. With Russia's defeat, it was compelled to abandon its interests on the Korean peninsula, and the Treaty of Portsmouth (1905) formally recognized Japan's prerogatives in Korea and southern Manchuria. That same year, secret negotiations were undertaken between the United States and Japan, evidenced by the Taft-Katsura Memorandum, which in effect called on Japan to recognize U.S. interests in the Philippine Islands while the U.S. recognized Japan's proprietary interests on the Korean peninsula. Such geopolitical maneuvering ultimately led to loss of Korea's sovereignty, manifested in the Eulsa Treaty (1905), which effectively rendered Korea a protectorate of Japan. This was followed by Japan's full annexation of the peninsula in 1910, reducing it to a colonial possession, a circumstance that would remain unchanged until the end of World War II in 1945.

The original archived version of the Taft-Katsura Memorandum, with handwritten edits, is available on the website of the Institute for Corean-American Studies (http://www.icasinc.org/history/katsura.pdf).

The full text of the Eulsa Treaty can be found on the website *Conservapedia* (http://www.conservapedia.com/Eulsa_Treaty).

The Soviet Union entered the war against Japan in the closing days of World War II, on August 8, 1945 (two days after the atomic bomb was dropped on Hiroshima), and quickly moved troops onto the Korean peninsula, occupying the northern cities of Nanam and Cheongjin. Concerned that Soviet troops could quickly occupy the entire peninsula, something the United States would have not been in a position to stop given its plans to invade the Japanese mainland, U.S. Army planners hastily developed a proposal that divided the peninsula in half along the 38th parallel. Bisecting the peninsula in this way recognized areas important to the Soviets in the north, which included ice-free ports, while ensuring that Seoul, the capital; Kaesong, a culturally important city; and sizeable prisoner of war camps remained in the southern half, over which the United States was to have control. Both nations agreed to the proposed partition, which in effect created two occupation zones on the peninsula, and proceeded with the broad understanding that the division was to be temporary in nature. These actions, however, came to represent the first steps toward the creation of a permanently divided Korea.

The ensuing three years (1945–1948) were characterized by the emergence of irreconcilable differences between the halves of the peninsula, leading to cross-border administrative, political and economic failures and further solidification of the peninsula's division. Such conditions were fueled by geopolitical maneuvering between the Soviet Union and the United States, political intrigue between the two halves of the peninsula, and internal fighting among factions within the northern and southern occupation zones. The peninsula's bisection was formalized in 1948 when UN-sponsored elections were conducted in the U.S. occupation zone in May, and on August 15, 1948, the newly elected National Assembly established the Republic of Korea. The Soviet Union, however, opposed such UN-sanctioned open elections within its occupation sphere. Rather, in the North, the Supreme People's Assembly ratified a constitution and elected Kim Il-sung as premier in September 1948. In the following month, the Soviet Union and other Communist Bloc nations officially recognized the Democratic People's Republic of Korea.

The final chapter of the newly split peninsula opened on June 25, 1950 when North Korea launched an unprovoked predawn attack on its southern neighbor, the opening salvo of the Korean War, in an effort to unify the peninsula under DPRK sovereignty. North Korea was aided significantly by the PRC in its efforts, primarily because North Korea's defeat would place the U.S. military directly on China's border with the Korean peninsula. On July 27, 1953, however, combatants—the United States, China, and North Korea—signed an armistice agreement; notable by its absence was South Korea. The armistice, which remains in effect today, recognized cessation of hostilities between militaries, not war between nations. Consequently, North and South Korea officially remain in a state of war to this day. The armistice also established the DMZ as we know it today, which is fairly close in configuration, but not precisely, to the peninsula's original division after World War II along the 38th parallel.

A South Korean child in Inchon after U.S. and South Korean forces invade the city in an attack against North Korean forces there; September 16, 1950. *(Wikimedia Commons, Pfc. Ronald L. Hancock/U.S. Army, National Archives and Records Administration, http://tinyurl.com/ohqvpud).*

The full text of the Korean Armistice Agreement can be found by searching for the "Armistice Agreement for the Restoration of the South Korean State" on the National Archives website (www.archives.gov).

Characterizing the North Korean Threat

Conceptually, nations typically have four potential implements of statecraft at their disposal when conducting affairs with other nations: diplomacy, military power, economic strength, and technological advantage. Consider the example of the United States. It has a strong corps of diplomats posted around the world in its embassies and consulates to engage other nations in pursuit of foreign policy, commercial, agricultural, and other objectives; it has a large, well-trained military capable of being rapidly deployed when needed (Iraq and Afghanistan serve as recent examples of this); its economy remains the strongest in the world; and its technological advantage in both the private and public sectors is notable (the information-gathering capability of Apple Inc. and the U.S. intelligence community' serve as just two examples). When these implements are considered *in toto*, the United States, comparatively speaking, is able to wield considerable influence in global geopolitics.

In the case of the North Korean regime, however, the full range of these implements is unavailable to its leadership. The nation has little economic or technological advantage at its disposal: it has a strong but inept central governmental, poor central planning, a disastrous agricultural policy, and an inability to develop its industrial sector. It also experiences frequent natural disasters (floods and drought) and lacks an entrepreneurial base. All of these factors have caused a substantial stagnation of its economy and thwarted the emergence of an independent technology sector. Consequently, its military and diplomatic implements, and to a much lesser degree its emerging nuclear capability, represent the remaining North Korean statecraft implements, and these have coalesced into a single geopolitical tool: *brinksmanship diplomacy*.

The strength of the regime's brinksmanship diplomacy, and its potential danger, rests on two pillars: its conventional military force and its nuclear weapons program. North Korea has a large conventional military force comprising 1.2 million active troops and another 7.5 million reservists, paramilitary personnel, and Red Guard and Red Youth Guard units. In addition to other armaments, the regime also has 12,000 field artillery pieces, a considerable number of which can easily target Seoul, the capital of South Korea, with a population of 10.4 million people and located only 31 miles from the DMZ. All of this is further underscored by the regime's policy of *seongun*, or "military first," which is used to rationalize spending 25 percent of the nation's gross national product (GNP) on military-related expenditures.

North Korea also has conventional weapons of mass destruction in its arsenal, such as biological and chemical weapons. While precise figures are difficult to establish because of the regime's opacity, estimates are that it possesses 250 to 5,000 tons of chemical agents (blister, nerve, blood, and choking agents) that could potentially be deployed against South Korea and its citizens. The regime has also pursued research of biological toxins (yellow fever, smallpox, cholera, anthrax, and bubonic plague) through its National Defense Research Institute and Medical Academy (NDRIMA). How advanced such research is at present is unknown. The greatest threat such conventional military forces and weapons present is to South Korea, because the North Korean regime has no real capability to project its conventional military strength beyond the peninsula. This, however, does not mean that employing its conventional forces in a peninsular war or skirmish could not have potential global implications.

Consider that the United States and South Korea operate under a mutual defense agreement (the Mutual Defense Treaty Between the United States and the Republic of Korea, signed in 1953), and as a result, the two nations have formally pledged to defend each other in the event of attack; thousands of U.S. military personnel are also deployed on the southern half of the peninsula for this purpose. Consequently, any conventional attack on South Korea could very quickly involve the United States. Retaliation against North Korea could also potentially invite Chinese involvement, much as it did during the Korean War. North Korea serves as a geographic buffer between China and South Korea (and its ally, the United States). A scenario that envisions the defeat and absorption of North Korea into South

Korea, thus placing the U.S. military on its immediate border, would likely be regarded as untenable by Chinese officials. Additionally, under such a scenario, U.S. military assets located in Japan would also likely be employed, and at least tangentially involve that nation as well. Thus, conceivably some of the world's largest economies—the United States (first), China (second), Japan (third), and South Korea (twelfth)—and advanced militaries could become embroiled in a hot war with immense geopolitical and global economic implications.

The full text of The Mutual Defense Treaty Between the United States and the Republic of Korea (1953) is available on the website of the Avalon project of the Yale Law School (http://avalon.law.yale.edu/20th_century/kor001.asp).

Considering the potential ramifications of North Korea's conventional military threat is not merely a hypothetical exercise. Indeed, the regime has launched two unprovoked attacks against South Korea in recent history. On March 26, 2010, the South Korean naval vessel *Cheonan* was sunk by a North Korean torpedo, causing the deaths of 46 sailors. Then, on November 23, 2010, North Korean ground forces attacked the South Korean island of Yeonpyeong using approximately 200 long-range artillery shells, killing four South Koreans. These events were not historical aberrations, for the decades-long history of inter-Korean polemics is filled with similar examples of unprovoked aggression by the North Korean regime.

Fire damage on the island of Yeonpyeong after the North Korean ground forces attack, November 2010. *(Wikimedia Commons, Woongjae Shin, http://tinyurl.com/ngfwjuv).*

The regime's nuclear capability, although still in a fledgling state, presents immediate global implications, particularly given its propensity for using brinksmanship diplomacy as a legitimate implement of statecraft. The nuclear program consists of two components: a ballistic missile program and a nuclear weapons program. Ballistic missiles function as a "carriage" for nuclear warheads—without them nuclear warheads could not be delivered against targets. North Korea has a well-developed and operational short- and intermediate-range missile program, with a capability of reaching distances up to 3,000 kilometers (approximately 1,865 miles), which represents a clear threat to the East Asia region. While the regime's long-range ballistic missile program remains in its infancy, it did conduct a successful rocket launch in December 2012, after several failed earlier attempts. This is an important first step toward developing an intercontinental ballistic missile capability, which could become a serious threat to the rest of the world.

With respect to its nuclear weapons program, experts estimate that the regime has approximately four to eight nuclear weapons on hand and has stockpiled roughly 30–50 kilograms of plutonium (66–110 pounds). As a point of reference, the atomic bomb detonated over Nagasaki (August 9, 1945) carried only 8 kilograms of plutonium (roughly 17 pounds). The regime also operates a highly enriched uranium (HEU) program. Unlike plutonium, which is man-made and a by-product of nuclear reactors, uranium exists naturally in the environment. Because HEU facilities can be hidden underground, no accurate estimates exist as to how much HEU the regime might have developed and possess. For comparative purposes, however, the uranium-based bomb detonated over Hiroshima (August 6, 1945) contained 60 kilograms of uranium, or just over 132 pounds. Although North Korean attempts to strengthen its nuclear program can be considered to be in a state of infancy, the regime has successfully conducted three separate nuclear test explosions since 2006, most recently in February 2013.

The North Korean regime represents a substantive threat to global peace and security through its potential indiscriminate use of conventional weapons as well as its advancing nuclear weapons and ballistic missile programs. When these two elements are considered together with the regime's propensity for exhibiting unpredictable behavior, the threat assumes a particularly dangerous hue. This is the construct of the regime's brinksmanship diplomacy model. Alternately employing vituperation, threats, and acts of aggression in exchange for some economic or political concession, or simply to garner world attention, is the single geopolitical card the regime has proven it is quite willing to play. Kim Jong-il once remarked, "I am the object of criticism around the world. But I think that since I am being discussed, then I am on the right track" (Fifield 2006). To discount the importance the regime places on being the center of global attention would be a mistake.

Understanding the parameters of the North Korean threat and how it manifests itself, however, is only a part of the equation. Equally important is understanding why the North Korean regime has come to rely almost exclusively on its diplomacy of brinksmanship as a means of engaging the world community.

Foundations of North Korean Brinksmanship Diplomacy

Since its creation in 1948, North Korea has transitioned from pursuing a militant path toward peninsular unification under its own sovereignty, most notably epitomized by its attack on South Korea in 1950, to one of belligerent survival, characterized by trying to wrest economic and political concessions from other nations through threats and aggressive behavior. This resulted from the coalescence of several factors: the end of the Cold War and former Communist Bloc nations rejoining the world community, primarily for economic benefit; the cumulative effect of decades of poor agricultural policies and practices; the loss of material support from China and the Soviet Union; the success of South Korea's *Nordpolitik* program of economic engagement with former Communist nations; and alternating natural disasters of drought and flood, leading to widespread famine and chronic malnutrition. While this transition represented a significant evolutionary degradation of circumstances for North Korea, which began taking shape during the 1990s, it shares an important commonality with both earlier periods in the nation's history and the present, but one that is often overlooked: its ideological and social imperative, *juche*.

The juche ideology serves simultaneously as a political framework and a philosophy for daily life. Its underpinnings are often perceived as being part of a larger whole, which leads to underestimating its importance in North Korean society.

Statue at the Juche Tower, Pyongyang, North Korea. *(Wikimedia Commons, Gilad Rom, http://tinyurl.com/nh5d2uc).*

The juche ideology, of course, does form the basis for how North Korea perceives and engages the rest of the world, and for how much or how little the regime permits outside access into its domestic affairs. But the ideology is much more than a political framework. Its tenets are also taught to school children from a very young age and reinforced throughout citizens' lives via local study groups, citizens spying on one another, and the threat of imprisonment. Not only is the nation's current leader, Kim Jong-un, treated in exalted fashion, but citizens are also required to revere the memories of his grandfather and father, Kim Il-sung and Kim Jong-il.

Juche is often defined as meaning "self-reliance." Although this is an important component of the ideology, it represents only a single factor. Juche is more accurately described as an autonomous self-identity that enables the regime to exercise independent action and not be impacted by the external influences of larger geopolitical powers—especially China, Russia, and the United States. This became particularly important to the nation's first leader, Kim Il-sung (1912–1994), as he played North Korea's two Communist guarantors, the Soviet Union and China, against one another in order to gain maximum benefit. Kim Il-sung described his interpretation of juche in a 1965 lecture he gave in Indonesia:

> The establishment of *juche* means holding fast to the principle of solving for oneself all the problems of the revolution and construction in conformity with the actual conditions at home, and mainly by one's own efforts. . . . This is an independent stand, discarding dependence on others, displaying the spirit of self-reliance and solving one's own affairs on one's responsibility under all circumstances. (Kim 1971, 87)

Key phrases in the above passage provide important guideposts as to the development of juche ideology. For example, "solving for oneself all the problems of the revolution" refers to the importance the regime places on its autonomy vis à vis other nations, particularly Communist nations. As originally conceived, it was most likely a reference to North Korea's relationship with the world's two largest Communist nations at the time, the Soviet Union and the China, which were waging an ideological war against each other. As this interpretation evolved over the decades, it has come to include the United States, China, Russia, and, to a slightly lesser extent, Japan. This concept is further reinforced by the phrase "discarding dependence on others." The phrase "mainly by one's own efforts" can be interpreted as an eschewal of external influences on domestic matters. Finally, the phrase "in conformity with actual conditions at home" underscored the need to refashion broader Communist doctrine to fit North Korea's domestic conditions through self-determination. In contemporary circumstances, however, the interpretation can be applied to the regime's unyielding pursuit of a nuclear weapons program as a means to achieving global legitimacy despite world condemnation.

The above passage provides an important segue into juche's major doctrinal elements—independence, pragmatism, flexibility, equality, and nationalism—each of which has real-world implications. Maintaining independence was always critical for Kim Il-sung. He felt strongly that although North Korea relied on support from China and the Soviet Union, the nation should be free to pursue its own brand of Communism, in this case juche, sometimes referred to as "Kim Il-sungism." Such thinking still forms the core of contemporary North Korean political ideology. Although China remains North Korea's single strongest ally, the regime continues to resist its influence. One case in point is North Korea's ongoing resistance to implementing genuine domestic market reforms in order to strengthen its economy, a path taken long ago by Chinese leadership. Another example is the reluctance of Chinese officials to exert too much influence and pressure on North Korean officials regarding the regime's nuclear weapons program, something that frustrates U.S. officials and representatives of other nations. Chinese officials fear that pushing the regime too hard might lead to unintended consequences, upsetting its own objectives of building the nation into an economic hegemon.

The regime's concept of pragmatism permitted the nation to accept support from its two feuding Communist benefactors with equal enthusiasm; the North Korean leadership did not feel doctrinally constrained despite its own ideological differences with both China and the Soviet Union. It did, however, take care not to alienate either nation. This sentiment is most accurately captured in a 1955 speech given by Kim Il-sung addressing internal party differences as to whether it was best to align the nation with the Chinese or Soviets: "It does not matter whether we eat our meal with the right hand or the left, whether you use a spoon or chopsticks at the table. No matter how you eat, it is all the same insofar as food is put into your mouth, isn't it?" (Kim 1973, 13).

Such a pragmatic approach to geopolitics reveals itself today in the regime's ability to castigate nations it considers enemies while also accepting economic, food and other assistance. A prime example of this is the Kaesong Industrial Complex (KIC) located in the North Korean city of Kaesong. Located just ten kilometers (6.2 miles) across the DMZ, the KIC is a collaborative venture between North and South Korea, relying largely on South Korean management and technology and inexpensive North Korean labor (roughly 50,000 workers) to manufacture labor-intensive products such as clothing, watches, and utensils. The regime benefits through the hard currency the venture brings into the country. Its willingness to cooperate with South Korea in such a venture, when juxtaposed against events like the sinking of the *Cheonan*, clearly illustrates not only its pragmatism but also its doctrinal flexibility. Whether assistance is received from an ally like the PRC or an enemy like the United States or South Korea, much like Kim Il-sung's reference to using a "spoon or chopsticks," the regime is still willing to bend its principles in order to reap any potential benefits.

The North Korean Economy Watch blog (www.nkeconwatch.com) has frequent posts about the Kaesong Industrial Zone. Go to the blog and search for "Kaesong Industrial Zone" to access these posts.

An old Korean proverb notes that "in a fight between whales, the back of a shrimp bursts." Geopolitically, Korea has largely been considered, and considered itself, in the role of a shrimp in comparison to other regional powers, because it has been unable to chart its own course. Thus the concept of equality is rooted in Kim Il-sung's aversion to what he called "big power chauvinism." Kim's objective was to have North Korea stand on equal footing with other nations and exercise self-determination. One means of ensuring that North Korea is not subordinated to other nations is by keeping those perceived as big powers "off balance" through surprise. A good example of this was the Six Party Talks (2003–2008), involving the United States, Russia, China, Japan, South Korea, and North Korea. The expressed purpose of the talks was to find a mutually agreeable way forward in dismantling North Korea's nuclear program. The talks were unsuccessful, however, in large measure because of North Korean intransigence and its unpredictable negotiating style. Four of its five negotiating partners in the Talks—the United States, China, Russia, and Japan—are perceived as big powers, and the fifth, South Korea, is a close ally of the United States. Demonstrating its equal status in the talks was imperative within the regime's ideological framework.

Learn more about the Six Party Talks on the Arms Control Association website (https://www.armscontrol.org/factsheets/6partytalks).

The final factor, nationalism, is resident in each of the foregoing determinants. This concept refers to the regime's belief that Korea, throughout much of its history, was unable to exercise full self-determination over its own affairs because of external influence and interference, with alternating circumstances of subordinating itself to or being subordinated by China, Japan, and various Western nations.

Understanding Korea's history, the global dimensions of North Korea's threat and its liberal use of brinksmanship diplomacy, and the ideological basis for its behavior, one important question remains: What can be done about North Korea?

Is Eliminating the North Korean Threat Possible, and at What Cost?

What options exist for eliminating the threat North Korea represents to global peace and stability? Fundamentally, there are only two: peaceful negotiation or hostile action. All other possibilities are variants of these basic choices. Let's briefly consider the ramifications of a forcible, or military, scenario. Approximately 21 percent of South Korea's population of 49 million live in the Seoul metropolitan area. The city is divided roughly in half by the Han River, the Gangnam section to the south and Gangbuk to the north. In the event of hostilities initiated by North Korea, citizens in the Gangbuk area would need to cross numerous bridges spanning the Han River, which are high-value targets for North Korean long-range artillery. Additionally, while Seoul boasts a modern highway system, it is not designed to handle millions of vehicles simultaneously. Hours-long gridlock is not unheard of, particularly on big holidays like Chuseok (Harvest Moon Festival), when many Seoul metropolitan residents return to their hometowns. Imagine the traffic gridlock and panic associated with millions of Seoul residents fleeing under a scenario of a North Korean attack. Then recall the thousands of field artillery pieces able to target Seoul from the vicinity of the DMZ—bridges, highways, and airports will be likely targets, and these places are precisely where most South Korean citizens will be. Also recall the regime's chemical weapons munitions capabilities, which could be employed using field artillery. Finally, consider that while a panicked citizenry will try to flee south, military units will be moving north to meet the attacking enemy, which at the very least could lead to significant confusion and impede military action. While there are many other factors to consider in this scenario that provide further cause for concern, the above factors make the point effectively enough—armed conflict on the peninsula would be both deadly and costly. Consequently, solutions other than war provide the most practical means for minimizing the regime's threat. Yet even these are not without challenges.

Negotiating with the regime has, over the past two decades, proven less than successful because of the central focus of negotiations: dismantling the North Korean nuclear weapons program. For regional powers specifically, and other nations more generally, the issue centers on the broader objective of global peace and security. Given North Korea's worldview and its supporting ideology, however, its nuclear weapons program represents its only lifeline. Loss of the nuclear program means loss of global legitimacy from its perspective, which in turn threatens survival of the regime. Consequently, well-meaning efforts to engage North Korean officials via meetings such as the Six Party Talks, which offer a menu of carrots and sticks in exchange for the regime abandoning its nuclear ambitions, have been largely unsuccessful. Conversely, what assistance the North Koreans do receive, whether it is support through the World Food Program or emergency assistance from China or South Korea, is attributed to the success of the regime's brinksmanship diplomacy and the superiority of the juche ideology, thus reinforcing its miscreant behavior. The regime thus has little motivation to moderate its tactics.

The United Nations has a long history of imposing sanctions against the regime in order to modify its behavior, all of which have proven ineffective, primarily for two reasons. First is what might be called the "rule of inversion," which points to the challenges of sanctions enforcement. Simply put, the longer sanctions remain in place, the greater the probability that a targeted nation will find workarounds to those sanctions, in the end rendering them toothless. In the case of North Korea, these workarounds come in the form of other illicit activities, such as drug smuggling, counterfeiting, and global arms proliferation. Second is the concept of fungibility. The humanitarian food assistance the regime receives for its citizens is instead siphoned off and used for the upper echelons of North Korean society and the military, in effect passing on the sanctions to its citizenry, the end result of which has been continued widespread starvation.

The North Korean regime has come to represent the Gordian knot of geopolitics. For decades, experts have predicted its imminent demise, only to be proven wrong time and again. The regime has evolved, adapted and aggressively protected its interests. Traditional means of engagement—negotiations, sanctions, and ostracism—have proven ineffective. Even the late South Korean president Kim Dae-jung's Sunshine Policy, which sought to ignore differences in inter-Korean politics while at the same time pursuing collaboration in economic and cultural ventures, proved unsuccessful— the regime pocketed the benefits while holding firm to its core issues. How and when the North Korea problem will be resolved is unknown, but one thing has become clear over the decades: traditional forms of engagement will not suffice. A new and bold way forward is required.

References and Further Research

Fuqua, Jacques L., Jr. 2007. *Nuclear Endgame: The Need for Engagement with North Korea*. Westport, CT: Praeger Security International.
———. 2011. *Korean Unification: Inevitable Challenges*. Washington, DC: Potomac Books.
Kim Il-sung. 1968. *Selected Works*. Vol. 2. Pyongyang, North Korea: Foreign Languages Publishing House.
———. 1971. *Revolution and Socialist Construction in Korea: Selected Writings*. New York: International Publishers.
———. 1973. *Selected Works*. Vol. 6. Pyongyang, North Korea: Foreign Languages Publishing House.

Internet Resources

Asia Pacific Connect. *Facts About South Korea*. http://www.anzbusiness.com/countries/south-korea0.html.
Center for Arms Control and Non-Proliferation. *Fact Sheet: North Korea's Nuclear and Ballistic Missile Programs*. http://armscontrolcenter.org/publications/factsheets/fact_sheet_north_korea_nuclear_and_missile_programs.
Central Intelligence Agency. *World Factbook: South Korea*. https://www.cia.gov/library/publications/the-world-factbook/geos/ks.html.
Federation of American Scientists. *Uranium Production*. http://www.fas.org/programs/ssp/nukes/fuelcycle/centrifuges/U_production.html.
Fifield, Anna. 2006. "N Korea Demands a Change of Political Heart." *Financial Times*, July 7. http://www.ft.com/cms/s/0/01e665c6-0dd4-11db-a385-0000779e2340.html#axzz2urfjAXqH.
North Korean Economy Watch. *Kaesong Industrial Complex: 2013 Crisis Timeline Compendium*. http://www.nkeconwatch.com/category/economic-reform/special-administrative-regions/kaesong-industrial-park.
United States Nuclear Regulatory Commission. *Backgrounder on Plutonium*. http://www.nrc.gov/reading-rm/doc-collections/fact-sheets/plutonium.html.
World Nuclear Association. *Supply of Uranium*. http://www.world-nuclear.org/info/Nuclear-Fuel-Cycle/Uranium-Resources/Supply-of-Uranium/.
World Population Statistics. *Seoul Population 2013*. http://www.worldpopulationstatistics.com/seoul-population-2013.

14

Reading "Kimigayo": The Japanese National Anthem in a Time of Postnational Transition

Junko Oba

March is graduation month on the Japanese school calendar. All over the country, people celebrate this rite of passage with special ceremonies, reflecting on their personal achievements, growth, and transition to new chapters in life. It is a festive occasion not only for students and their families, but also for their teachers. Planning and preparation often begin months before the ceremonies to ensure that they are properly executed. The process, however, is not always delightful, especially when government authorities interfere with political agendas to turn the personal rite of passage ceremonies into patriotic rituals.

In the first two months of 1999, Ishikawa Toshihiro, a Japanese high school principal from Sera, Hiroshima, found himself caught in a fierce conflict between his fellow teachers at Sera High School and the local board of education. In response to a series of mandates issued by the Ministry of Education, Culture, Sports, Science, and Technology and its subsidiary organizations at different levels since the summer of 1998, the board of education in Hiroshima had tried to implement a governmental order dictating the proper display of patriotic symbols, such as Japan's Hinomaru (Rising Sun) flag and "Kimigayo" (His Majesty's Reign) anthem, in school ceremonies, but the teachers adamantly opposed it. As negotiations dragged on between the school administrators, who tried to abide by the board's order, and the faculty, who refused to compromise, the pressure from both sides became unbearable. Exhausted by the situation, Ishikawa killed himself on February 28, 1999—the day before his school's graduation ceremony.

Although the emotional impact of the principal's death rendered this tragedy in Hiroshima particularly newsworthy, the dispute over Japan's national flag and anthem has been a long-standing political issue in post–World War II Japan, especially in the context of school education. As in the case of Sera High School, teachers have often reacted strongly against the governmental authorities' interference with school systems, especially their attempt to instigate patriotic education. For many teachers, as well as concerned citizens, such political intervention at school is a reminder of the Japanese government's totalitarian control of the education system

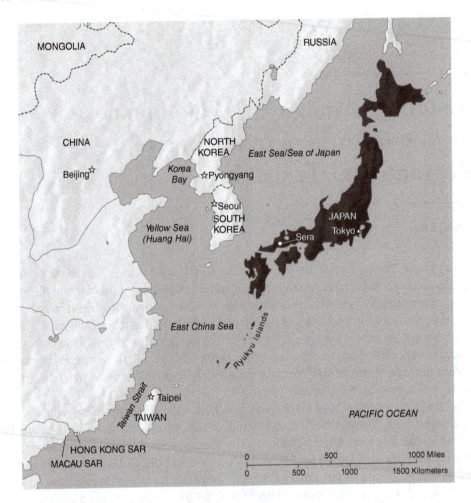

and its exploitation for the schooling of imperial subjects during World War II. It is also considered by some a forewarning of the resurgence of that era's distinctive nationalist ideology in contemporary Japan.

An English version of the details of the Law Regarding the National Flag and National Anthem (or the Act on National Flag and Anthem) is available on the website of the Cabinet Office, Government of Japan (http://www.cao.go.jp/en/flag_anthem.html).

Spurred on by the incident in Hiroshima, however, the conservative members of Japan's National Diet (the ruling Liberal Democratic Party, in particular) pushed for the passage of the Act on National Flag and Anthem in the following months.

The purpose of the legislation was to ratify Hinomaru and "Kimigayo" as agencies of official state representation, and to endorse national recognition of them as such. The government insisted that the official endorsement of the national flag and anthem would help avoid further disputes concerning their legitimacy and tragic situations like the one in Hiroshima. With the approval of the large conservative majority in the National Diet, the act was promulgated on August 13, 1999, after barely more than two months of deliberation and only half a dozen public hearings.

The NPR program *All Things Considered* reported on the Flag and Anthem controversy on July 22, 1999. The report is available on the program's website (http://www.npr.org/templates/story/story.php?storyId=1054382).

Despite the lack of legal endorsement prior to 1999, the Japanese people had tacitly approved Hinomaru and "Kimigayo" to represent their country in both formal and informal occasions for over a century. Their ubiquitous presence throughout Japan's modern history cultivated varying degrees of affinity and affection toward these de facto national symbols. While such feelings seemed to derive mostly from people's natural attachment to the familiar, some also acknowledged their "uniquely Japanese" aesthetic values as a source of national pride. Nevertheless, many people shared misgivings over the Act on National Flag and National Anthem because of the association of Hinomaru and "Kimigayo" with Japan's controversial imperialist past.

The Empire of Japan was established in 1868, when imperial control was restored—an event often referred to as the Meiji Restoration; it existed until the country's unconditional surrender at the end of World War II in 1945. With rapid industrialization, modernization, and militarization, it quickly rose to become a world power and expanded its territory and influence over many other Asian countries that it invaded, occupied, and colonized in the first half of the twentieth century. Although Japan's defeat in World War II dissolved the empire and the country was reconstructed as a democratic nation-state under a new constitution that came into effect in 1947, the imperial system escaped total obliteration, and the emperor kept his status as a ceremonial monarch and the symbol of the state and the unity of the nation. Hence, while Hinomaru and "Kimigayo" symbolically celebrate the antiquity and eternity of the Japanese imperial system, they are also painful reminders of the history of subjugation and forced Japanization in many countries and regions in East and Southeast Asia. In these countries, that history has never been forgotten. It was foreseeable that the official endorsement of Hinomaru and "Kimigayo" could elicit strong reactions, especially since imperial sovereignty (the legal recognition that the emperor holds sovereign political power and status) was repealed in postwar Japan under the current Constitution of the State of Japan. "Kimigayo," in particular, has constantly been a focus of debate, because its lyrics celebrate the eternity of His Majesty's reign.

MIT's Visualizing Cultures project puts the "Kimigayo" controversy into historical context in the online resource *Asia Rising*: *Japanese Postcards of the Russo-Japanese War (1904–05)*, written by John W. Dower and available on the Visualizing Cultures website (http://ocw.mit.edu/ans7870/21f/21f.027/asia_rising/ar_essay05.html).

Once the Act on National Flag and Anthem went into effect in August 1999, however, the main point of contention shifted from the interpretation of the lyrics of "Kimigayo" (its appropriateness as Japan's national anthem) to the importance of the public singing of it, although the two are essentially inseparable, since the singing replicates the lyrics. At the same time, public performances of "Kimigayo" themselves have become a political forum to renegotiate its significance performatively. In this case study, I examine two distinctive types of "Kimigayo" performances: *seishō* (斉唱, unisonous collective singing) and *dokushō* (独唱, solo singing), the latter featuring pop idols and famous professional singers as soloists. Although Japanese people had collectively sung "Kimigayo" in various public ceremonies over many decades, it was after the Act on National Flag and Anthem legislation that the governmental authorities more aggressively pursued the reinstatement of the patriotic ritual at school. I am particularly interested in the unisonous collective singing idealized and fetishized in this context. On the other hand, *dokushō* performances of "Kimigayo" are a fairly recent phenomenon. Inspired perhaps by the established ritual singing of "The Star Spangled Banner" at U.S. athletic events, which became more easily accessible via satellite TV and the Internet by Japanese viewers in the 1990s, solo vocal performances of "Kimigayo" by celebrities have become ubiquitous pre-event attractions at major athletic events in Japan since the mid-1990s.

Hinomaru, the Japanese national flag. *(photo courtesy of Erica Gullickson)*

Focusing on their different sonic textures and performance styles, I discuss what it means to sing "Kimigayo" in contemporary Japanese society against the backdrop of the changing global conditions of the twenty-first century. During this period, the political, economic, and cultural configurations of the world have altered dramatically. Although the nation-state as a geopolitical entity continues to exist, conventional national boundaries have blurred and the prestige of the nation-state as a referential frame of one's identity has diminished. While scholars such as Frederick Buell (1994), Arjun Appadurai (1999), Stuart Hall (1992), and Saskia Sassen (2002) have addressed the need for alternative theoretical frameworks to analyze the postnational global condition, the proper idioms to capture the new, postnational identities are not yet established. Many of them "are still entrapped in the linguistic imaginary of the territorial state" (Appadurai 1999, 166) and continue to use nationalized terms. To read and interpret nationalized signs in such transitional context requires extra caution. While these renewed interests in public performances of "Kimigayo" may seem to correspond to the country's resurgent right-wing nationalism in recent years, further close examination reveals some paradoxical elements that may defy such superficial interpretation. By analyzing such inconsistencies and discrepancies in their performances of "Japaneseness," I discuss complex significations of performing nationalized identities in a time of postnational transition.

"Kimigayo," A Nation's Anthem

Before analyzing "Kimigayo," it is helpful to delineate the functions of a national anthem as an apparatus of modern state nationalism. National anthems form a distinctive genre of music that evokes national consciousness, patriotism, solidarity, and a sense of belonging among a group of people. They celebrate the land, history, religion, cultural heritages, and ethnic identities that are perceived to unite a people as a nation. Although there are no formal musical specifications that define the genre, many national anthems adopt indigenous tunes, popular local folk songs, familiar hymns or military marches, resistance songs, and so forth associated with historic events important to each country. The same applies to the lyrics, many of which utilize ancient epics, folk tales, old poems, and legends and anecdotes of local heroes and historical figures for inspiration. In some cases, the use of "national" languages is highly significant.

Three views on the adoption of the flag and anthem can be found on the website of the Japan Policy Research Institute (http://www.jpri.org/publications/critiques/critique_VI_9.html).

Despite such pervasive historical references, the concept of a "national anthem" itself is a fairly new one. It was conceived as an apparatus of symbolic nation-state representation in late eighteenth- and nineteenth-century Europe, where a number of new nation-states emerged after the demise of the old feudal system and the dissolution of some of the most powerful European monarchies. As Eric Hobsbawm (1992) analyzes it, the peculiar archaism—the adoration of the ancient, traditional, and indigenous—prevalent in many newly invented "traditions" from this era was a reasonable reaction to the sweeping societal change from the traditional feudal states to modern nation-states, and the newly instituted states were thus eager to deploy time-honored cultural traditions, memories, and artifacts of the past to establish the historical authenticity and political legitimacy of the new nation-states. The idea of symbolic state representation through the agencies of national flags, anthems, and state rituals was transplanted to many countries in and outside of Europe as nationalism spread throughout the nineteenth and twentieth centuries. The history of "Kimigayo" as Japan's national anthem also goes back to this era.

The late nineteenth century was a time of turbulent transition for Japanese society. The feudal system, which had been rigidly controlled by the Tokugawa shogunate for centuries, was finally dissolved, and the emperor's rule was reinstated as a "new" constitutional monarchy in 1868. Although the emperors had always maintained honorable regal status throughout the course of Japanese history, their political influence was significantly diminished during the Edo period of feudal rule—a weakening led by the warrior class from the early seventeenth century until the late nineteenth century. Even after its restoration in 1868, the authority of the imperial monarchy was unstable and susceptible to internal power dynamics. Establishing its authority and legitimacy was therefore an urgent task for the new Meiji government. While earnestly pursuing Western-style modernization, the government skillfully used archaism to buttress its legitimacy by incorporating the antiquity and continuity of the imperial lineage into the historical narrative. "Kimigayo" was an integral part of this national political enterprise. It reflects the process of modern nation-state building mentioned above and the development of unique nationalist ideologies.

Lyrics

In search of proper lyrics to link the newly established nation-state to its ancient imperial history, Meiji officials turned to old *waka* poems for its source. Known as "Kimigayo"—it begins with the phrase "Kimigayo wa. . ." (May His Majesty's reign. . .)—the poem was chosen from the *Kokin Wakashū,* an imperial collection of short poems compiled in the heyday of aristocratic court culture in the early tenth century.

Waka is a form of short poetry that flourished in the era. Historical records, including poem anthologies and individual collections, indicate that poems consisting of 31 syllables (*tanka*) were particularly popular. The 31 syllables make up five short phrases, each with either five or seven syllables, and the five phrases are typically grouped into two asymmetrical sections: [5/7/5] + [7/7]. "Kimigayo" also follows this form, although it contains an extra syllable in the third phrase—a common minor variation resulting in a total of 32 syllables. However, the five phrases of "Kimigayo" are not organized in the typical two-section format, but are put together in the reverse asymmetry of [5/7] + [6/7/7]. As I will discuss later, this unusual division of the lyrics does not match the musical phrasing of the composition; this sometimes causes difficulty in properly singing the simple melody.

The Lyrics of "Kimigayo"

君が代は   *Kimigayo wa*
千代に八千代に   *Chiyo ni yachiyo ni*
さざれ石の   *Sazareishi no*
いわおとなりて   *Iwao to nari-te*
こけのむすまで   *Koke no musu made*

English translation of the lyrics

May His Majesty's reign
Live on for a thousand, nay, eight thousand generations
And for the eternity that it takes
For small pebbles to grow into a great rock
And become covered with moss.

While a variety of English translations are available from different sources, according to the Japan Information and Culture Center (JICC), Embassy of Japan, Washington, DC (contacted August 2008), there is no official English translation by the Japanese government. The translation above comes from a website (http://japanese.about.com/library/weekly/aa030400.htm) recommended by JICC, with modification in the first line.

The extemporaneous recitation of short poems like *waka* was customary practice in medieval Japan. People composed impromptu poems to express their feelings and emotions in response to tragic incidents as well as on happy occasions. "Kimigayo" is considered to have been either an ode to celebrate the longevity of a respectable lord on a happy occasion or a funeral eulogy at his (possibly her in rare cases) demise. Although there is no musical notation or historical record that refers to the musical aspects of the original "Kimigayo," the poem and its variants were "recycled" by later performers, who set the poem to different tunes in various musical styles. Given the lack of contextual information accompanying the poem, it is difficult to determine for what purpose the poem was used and who the word "kimi" (respectable lord) of "Kimigayo" referred to in each of these cases. There is no doubt, however, that "kimi" indicated the emperor when the poem was adopted with the clear purpose to authenticate the supremacy of His Majesty's reign on the occasion of its restoration.

Music

Extensive research on "Kimigayo" by Naitō Takatoshi, a Japanese composer and independent researcher, revealed that in addition to the song now known as Japan's national anthem, two other "Kimigayo" songs were composed at the end of the nine-teenth century to celebrate the longevity of the reinstated imperial reign. In contrast to the traditionalism reflected in the selection of the lyrics, the musical styles of these compositions indicate the country's strong aspiration for modernization through the adoption of Western models. Due to space limitations, I am not able to discuss each of these pieces in detail here (see Naitō 1999 for more information) but all three ver-sions "Kimigayo" incorporated elements of Western music in one way or another. The one now known as the national anthem is particularly unique, with its integration of Japanese *gagaku* (traditional imperial court music) melodies and Western harmonic accompaniment. The unique arrangement is a result of the "collaborative" work by Japanese court musicians and a German bandmaster. It demonstrates a confluence of "West and East" and "traditional and modern," and its artistic finesse renders this version an outstanding musical composition, not just an innovative experiment.

Melody

Although the composer of the *gagaku*-styled melody remained anonymous for a long time, it is most likely that Oku Yoshiisa and Hayashi Hirosue, two *gagaku* musicians affiliated with the Music Department of the Imperial Household Agency coauthored it in 1880. The melody is short and simple. It is contained in a somewhat unusual eleven-measure form, when notated in a Western staff notation (see Figure 14.3). While the piece is usually performed in a moderately slow tempo in a solemn atmosphere reminiscent of traditional court music, its playing time barely exceeds one minute.

The melodic contour follows the *ichikotsu-chō*, a traditional *gagaku* pentatonic mode (D-E-G-A-C in the setting in Figure 14.3). For those familiar with the terms of music theory and structure, the mode is laid out as three melodic motifs in the first three measures: D-C-D in the first measure, G-E-D in the second, and E-G-A in the third; the piece then develops on variations and different combinations of these motifs. The third motif, which marks the beginning of the second phrase in the third measure, also initiates each new phrase to follow. Either of the other two motifs, appearing in variations, concludes these phrases and anchors the melody to its tonal/modal center, while it gradually ascends to the climactic point in the last phrase (the ninth measure). These sophisticated melodic treatments, accompanied by a steady rhythmic structure, provide the composition with a sense of coherence and produce an overall effect of solemnity and calm.

Musical score of "Kimigayo."

As mentioned earlier, perhaps one shortfall of this composition is the mismatched phrasing of the melody and the lyrics. Semantically, the lyrics of "Kimigayo" are divided into two sections: the first two lines, "Kimigayo wa" and "Chiyo ni yachiyo ni," end in the fourth measure and are followed by the other three lines in measures five through eleven. Musically, however, the gradually ascending melody peaks at the end of measure six to conclude the first section, stretching into the beginning of the second section of the lyrics. This phrasing discrepancy could present a challenge to the proper delivery of the lyrics, which is presumably an important function of the national anthem.

The original score (without the romanized transliteration and phrasing marks) of "Kimigayo" was appended to the text of the Act on National Flag and Anthem and is available on the website of the Ministry of Internal Affairs and Communication (http://law.e-gov.go.jp/htmldata/H11/H11HO127.html).

Arrangement: "Japanische Hymne"

Although its full harmonic arrangement is not notated in the music appended to the Act on National Flag and Anthem, "Kimigayo" is typically performed with a Western-style harmonic accompaniment. The extraordinary arrangement was written by Franz von Eckert (1852–1916), a German music teacher and military band director who was employed by the Japanese government to help Japanese people learn Western music and to develop its own military bands between 1880 and 1889. Eckert was commissioned to write a military band arrangement of "Kimigayo" so that the military band could play the *gagaku*-style melody in various official state ceremonies.

Japan's national anthem can be heard on the VocalNationalAnthems channel on YouTube (https://www.youtube.com/watch?v=29FFHC2D12Q). This performance reflects an updated Western-style arrangement of the one attributed to Franz von Eckert. An instrumental version, performed by the United States Navy Band and faithful to Eckert's original version, is available on the band's website (http://www.navyband.navy.mil/Anthems/ANTHEMS/Japan.mp3).

The piece seems to have undergone several revisions before settling in the current arrangement in 1888. Once completed, however, the score of the final version was printed and distributed to Japanese governmental authorities as well as Japan's treaty countries. On the front cover of the music, the title of the piece appears in German as "Japanische Hymne nach einer alt japanischen melodie" (Japanese Hymn after an old Japanese melody) with the Japanese annotation that reads "Dainippon reishiki" (the ceremonial [music] of Great Japan). The cover is decorated with the imperial chrysanthemum flower insignia and an illustration of the rising sun, which also symbolizes the emperor according to ancient Japanese mythology. Despite the fact that no historical records suggest its official status as the "national anthem," the formality of the print score, the authority added to it by the imperial symbols, and the wide distribution rendered this particular arrangement more authoritative.

More importantly, the standardization of "Japanische Hymne" lent authenticity to the solemn military band arrangement (and later its more or less faithful orchestral and piano arrangements), as this became the only rendition of "Kimigayo" commonly heard. The introduction of sound recording technology and radio broadcasting in the early twentieth century furthered the process. The public has been repeatedly exposed to the recorded and mass-mediated performances of the same "Kimigayo." The particular sonority of the arrangement has thus been registered in people's auditory memory and become an integral part of their impression of "Kimigayo" and what it inspires in them.

"Kimigayo" thus embodies the politically constructed image of the newly established nation-state and its unique Japaneseness, symbolized by the antiquity and longevity of the imperial court cultures. Its pioneering musical arrangement reflects the distinctive political climate that surrounded Japan in the late nineteenth century, which propelled the country to pursue both progressive modernization and antiquarian cultural nationalism.

The "Unisonance" Singing of "Kimigayo" in School Ceremonies

Across the world, the singing of national anthems has played an important role in representing nations in various state rituals. The very art of collective singing has helped to inculcate the concept of the "nation." In his insightful critique contributed to *Mirror of Modernity: Invented Traditions of Modern Japan*, Dipesh Chakrabarty brings to our attention the importance of "sensuous practical activity" as a medium for instilling ideas and ideologies in individuals' minds and dictating their thoughts and behavior. "[Ideas] work not simply because they persuade through their logic," he states, "they are also capable, through a long and heterogeneous history of the cultural training of the senses, of making connections with our glands and muscles and neuronal network" (Chakrabarty 1998, 294–295).

Chakrabarty's insight into the repetitive multisensory process of ideological inculcation resonates with Benedict Anderson's argument on the effect of collective singing of national anthems as an "echoed physical realization" of the community imagined as a nation. Anderson states that what makes a national anthem a significant conduit for bonding people and driving them to die for such inventions as "nation" and "nationalism" is not the lofty idealism written in the lyrics or the beautiful melodies, but rather the physical, sensorial experience of selfless "unisonance" and a manifestation of simultaneity, anonymity, and uniformity experienced in this type of collective singing (Anderson 1991, 141–145).

The Act on National Flag and Anthem is a plain, straightforward law, comprising two unembellished provisions stating what Japan's national flag and anthem are; an illustration of the official Hinomaru flag, with precise measurements; and a basic melodic notation of "Kimigayo," with the lyrics but no accompaniment. As such, the law does not hold any legal authority responsible for dictating the observance of patriotic rituals and their protocols. Indeed, it does not stipulate the musical performance of "Kimigayo" at all. Despite this fact, the enactment of the act by the Japanese Diet has been misconstrued, often willfully and purposefully, as an official sanction of the nationalistic cause, of the reinforcement of patriotic rituals to honor "Kimigayo" and Hinomaru, and of governmental interference on the matter at different levels of administration.

One of the reasons behind the authorities' tenacious effort to incorporate the singing of "Kimigayo" and other nationalist elements into school ceremonies is the constitutional premise that forbids the restitution of patriotic rituals. The preamble declaring the popular sovereignty principle essentially prohibits the exercise of patriotic rituals in the way they were performed in Imperial Japan—as emperor worship. Deploying the preexisting framework of the rite-of-passage school rituals— that is, matriculation and graduation—is a way to negate the constitutional restriction and instigate patriotic rituals at school. Although the governmental authorities do not seem to have been conscious of this advantage, the recurrence of school ceremonies annually serves well to facilitate repetitive sensuous indoctrination, as theorized by Chakrabarty and Anderson (and discussed above).

The programs and procedures of school ceremonies vary in practical details from one school to another. However, the governmental authorities' strong aspiration to realize the "unisonance" ideal is quite prominent in the executive orders that they have issued to ensure the "proper" execution of the unanimous collective singing of "Kimigayo." For example, the directives issued by the Tokyo Metropolitan Government Board of Education on October 23, 2003, which is often referred to as the "October 23rd Order" by the media, is well known for its explicit methodical and procedural specifications for everyone's active participation in the singing in order to ensure the desirable unisonance performance. The order states that the ceremony should include "the collective singing of the national anthem by everyone in unison (*kokka seishō*)," and that it should be clearly annotated in the program; also, during the ceremony, the announcement should be made prior to the singing; all teachers and school staff should then rise from their seats and face the national flag, which should be displayed in the center of the stage at the ceremony venue, and sing the anthem with an accompaniment on the piano or like means. Later, officials more strongly insisted on live accompaniment on the piano, rejecting other "like means," such as sound recordings.

Unanimity and the October 23rd Order

The October 23rd Order, as well as other executive orders issued by different municipalities, does not specify the proper conduct of parents and other guests at the ceremony. However, a number of people who have tried to remain seated and refused to join the unisonous singing of "Kimigayo" have recounted feeling uncomfortable as a quiet minority in the singing crowd, and also feeling pressure from the humiliating atmosphere.

In addition, teachers are expected to educate their students to perform authentically on these ceremonial occasions. All school principals are required to submit a report with detailed information such as the teachers' participation rate in the singing and the names of those who did not sing. In some cases, board of education officials themselves have attended the ceremonies to monitor the observance of the order. The information collected pursuant to this order has been used to reprimand teachers who chose not to obey the order with involuntary transfers to other schools, salary cuts, suspension of their teaching licenses, and enrollment in reeducation workshops, among other disciplinary actions.

For many Japanese people, the issue of whether or not to sing "Kimigayo" is a politically charged question that prompts rigorous self-questioning of their political stand, moral integrity, and the repercussions of singing words celebrating the antiquity and longevity of the imperial monarchy. In other words, the singing of "Kimigayo" has an inherent potential for performative political actions. Public ceremonies involving the singing of "Kimigayo" have hence become ideational battlegrounds. Since the early 2000s, hostile confrontations at school have repeatedly garnered public attention, with some of them resulting in highly publicized lawsuits.

Although many of these court cases have revealed the authorities' outright totalitarian control, and the teachers' unbending opposition against it, "hostile" may not be the right word to describe these confrontations, since this may conjure the image of a violent encounter. On the contrary, the primary strategy adopted by the teachers to oppose the coercive singing of "Kimigayo" has been simply not to rise from their chairs to sing. However, many teachers have been subjected to punitive actions for their silent opposition. In response, a number of lawsuits have been filed by the teachers against their local board of education, seeking the acknowledgement of their constitutional right to exercise "freedom of thought and conscience" (Article 19 of the Constitution of the State of Japan). Although many of these court cases are still inconclusive, earlier rulings essentially rejected the teachers' appeals. In some recent cases, however, the plaintiffs won "partial victories" when the courts annulled the reprimand enforced on them by the authorities. While most of these rulings still dismissed or did not delve into the discussion of the unconstitutionality of the executive directives like the "10.23 Order," the ruling by the Tokyo High Court on November 7, 2012, is an important milestone. The court recognized that punishing the plaintiff, a female teacher at a metropolitan school for disabled children, because of her refusal to stand up and sing "Kimigayo" could infringe upon her constitutional right to exercise freedom of thought and conscience.

An English translation of the Constitution of Japan is available at the website of the prime minister of Japan (http://www.kantei.go.jp/foreign/constitution_and_government_of_japan/constitution_e.html).

It is important to note that in this recent development, despite the governmental authorities' insistence on the singing of "Kimigayo," the purpose of the coercive singing was no longer to facilitate the public adoration of the imperial monarchy or the inculcation of the distinctive nationalist ideology associated with it. What the authorities strive so hard to realize in the collective singing of "Kimigayo," however, seems to be the performance of an extreme form of "unisonance" or singing in one voice—a symbolic sonic realization of the selfless oneness of the community imagined as a nation. In such earnest pursuit of *oneness*, it is not difficult to identify an underlying nationalist ideology that resonates with a trope of the *nihonjinron* discourse, or the homogeneity myth of the Japanese nation. The view constructed on the imagined ethnic and cultural homogeneity of Japanese people and society as a foundation of its unique national identity systematically refutes the diversity of the country by marginalizing ethnic and cultural minorities and silencing "different voices."

Although the conscientious silence that the teachers exercise at school ceremonies may be inaudible in the collective mass singing of "Kimigayo," that does not mean that their voices are nonexistent. On the contrary, their quiet performance is a strong statement of refusal to partake in one collective voice. It is, in fact, an effective way to undermine the unisonance ideal and defy the concept of Japaneseness desired by the authority.

"Kimigayo" to Watch, Listen to, and (Perhaps) Sing Along With

While the collective participatory singing of "Kimigayo" at school became the focus of the national anthem debate following the passage of the Act on National Flag and Anthem in 1999, solo performances of "Kimigayo" have become an important feature of many athletic events in Japan since around the same time. Likely inspired by the established practice of national anthem singing in American sports events, whose broadcasts became more accessible for Japanese viewers via global satellite networks and affordable information technology services in the 1990s, high-profile professional (and some amateur) sports events began to adopt the ceremonial singing of the national anthem (including anthems of both countries in international matches) as a part of their pre-event attractions. Musicians of all genres, mostly young pop singers, but also some well-known opera singers, have since received the honor of singing "Kimigayo" to open various athletic events.

The primary motive behind this newly invented tradition, however, appears to be commercial rather than political. From the viewpoint of the event producers, "the celebrity effect" helps boost the popularity and prestige of the events, and highly recognized pop singers would in turn help the events get more media coverage and sponsorship. For the musicians, these events help to demonstrate their celebrity status, as gauged by the scale of the event: the more famous and popular they are, the bigger events they are invited to open. It is common practice for the organizers and artists' managements to make public announcements months before and set up press conferences prior to the events for publicity. The artists typically express how honored and thrilled they are to sing at such big events as the World Cup soccer championship and All-Star Game of the Japanese professional baseball league. By tacit rule, sensitive political questions surrounding "Kimigayo" are never asked.

As in most pregame attractions in the United States, solo acts dominate at these ceremonies. In addition the ceremonies rarely include instrumental accompaniment, live or recorded. Even when the featured artists are members of popular bands, the lead vocalists usually perform solo without the bands. The only exceptions are a cappella vocal groups, which are considered single units. The performances by the popular vocal groups Chemistry (at the FIFA World Cup in 2002) and Gospellers (at the Kirin Challenge Cup in 2000) were billed as solo singing (*dokushō*) acts, despite the fact that the former is a vocal duo and the latter is a quintet.

On YouTube and other online sources, many versions of "Kimigayo," including those by Chemistry (http://www.youtube.com/watch?v=XR96u1bVzjQ) and Gospellers (http://www.youtube.com/watch?v=USGBsF1Xu94), can be seen. The images accompanying the various versions illustrate many of the issues raised in this case study.

At a practical level, the preference for solo acts is to avoid the additional cost and technical challenge involved in performances by larger acts with bands and multiple performers. It does not necessarily reflect the artistic preference of the audience. In contrast to the nameless mass in the collective unisonance singing at school, however, the aura of the single corporeal presence of the singer at mass sporting events almost always overshadows the semantic meanings of the lyrics that they belt out of their bodies. In his insightful analysis of the meaning of "pop," Simon Frith states, "the meaning of pop is the meaning of pop stars, performers with bodies and personalities; central to the pleasure of pop is pleasure in a voice, sound as body, sound as person" (1998, 210). In this sense, these "Kimigayo" performances at athletic events are little different from regular pop music entertainment, whose primary focus is the pop star.

In most of these cases, the singing is technically accurate: the basic melody of the national anthem (as well as its lyrics) is followed. Without the constraints of instrumental accompaniment and co-performers, however, the singers have more freedom for self-expression. Transposing the original melody to different keys so the melody will better fit individual singers' voice ranges is very common. The resulting additional comfort allows for more personally nuanced vocal expressions. Similarly, the singer uses a comfortable tempo, which occasionally fluctuates at different points within the piece. Furthermore, they demonstrate their individual interpretations with peculiar vocal production techniques (such as vibrato, and nasal, raspy, and husky voices with extra "h" sounds in the long-held notes), rhythmic nuances (such as an unusually accentuated beat, prolonged notes and pauses, and "*ma*" spacing), and subtle ornamentations unique not only to their personal styles but also to the respective musical genres and traditions, be it in opera, rock, R&B, hip-hop, or sentimental ballads of *enka*, in which they trained professionally. Many singers opt to emphasize the melodic climax of the song by slowing down the tempo and adding little pauses—a *fermata* effect, so to speak—in the middle and at the end of the third line of the lyrics: "sazareishi no." Although the decision to make the most of the melody's dramatic effect might alter the phrasing of the words "sazareishi no" into "sazare (pause)/ishi-no (pause)," as well as disrupt the semantically proper phrasing of the lyric "Sazareishi no, Iwao to nari-te" (for the eternity that it takes for small pebbles to grow into a great rock), this would not elicit any criticism or controversy. The solo singing of "Kimigayo" is not about nationalism or any other political stand, but rather an occasion to showcase individual singers. Singers known for being politically outspoken and for their performative activism—such as the late punk rocker Imawano Kiyoshirō, whose sarcastic rendition of "Kimigayo" prompted major record labels to back off from issuing a CD release—would not be considered proper features for such occasions.

Although the audience's participation in the singing is not mandatory at these *dokushō* solo performances, congregational singing may voluntarily occur, especially in the context of international matches. For example, at the World Cup soccer championship cohosted by Korea and Japan in 2002, thousands of Japanese supporters demonstrated their national identity and solidarity by wearing their team color of "samurai blue" outfits, painting their faces the same color, and joining in the singing of "Kimigayo" in a massive unisonance chorus.

In my interviews, those who had joined similar massive collective singing of "Kimigayo" unanimously recounted their exuberant experiences of "singing with all those thousands of people" and *ittai-kan* (solidarity, unity)—the sensation that resonates with what Benedict Anderson conceptualized as "an echoed physical realization of the imagined community" (1991, 145). However, their responses were ambivalent when it came to the question of national consciousness behind their actions. They were mostly reluctant to articulate their experiences in nationalist, or any other political, terms, since they were not singing for those reasons. I typically got answers like the following: "I sing ["Kimigayo"] to express my support for the Japanese team, and to feel the oneness with everyone there [in the stadium]." Such remarks imply that the imagined community realized in the singing may be something much smaller and more ephemeral than a nation state. In this regard, it is significant that what the supporters symbolically identify themselves with was the team color of "samurai blue" but not the traditional red and white of the Hinomaru flag. The distinction is also reflected in the media's preference of the English word "Japan" (ジャパン) rather than "Nippon" (日本)—the men's and women's Japanese national teams, for example, are referred to as "Samurai Japan" (侍ジャパン) and "Nadeshiko Japan" (なでしこジャパン), respectively. While the traditional symbolism of *samurai* warriors and *nadeshiko* flowers for ideal masculinity and femininity (the *nadeshiko* flower symbolizes an idealized traditional Japanese femininity) suggests a trope of antiquarian spiritualism, when combined with the Anglicized country name their implications are exotic, superficial, and noncommittal, rather than profoundly ideological. This temporary community would naturally dissolve when thousands of supporters took off their "samurai blue" outfits, washed off their face paints, and resumed their life in ordinary time.

Conclusion: Doing it Differently—From *Seishō* to *Dokushō*

As noted in the opening of this essay, we live in a time of postnational transition in which the prominence of nation-states as a referential framework of one's identity has increasingly and significantly withered. In recent decades, it has been undermined and superseded by various alternative identities. More careful and sensible approaches and readings of nationalized signs in identity performances are needed, since such signs could very well be deceptive surface features of underlying complex identity formations and expressions. "Kimigayo" as the de facto national anthem of Japan has represented the unisonous voice of the nation throughout the country's modern period, since the late nineteenth century, but in contemporary Japanese society, despite the government's efforts to legislate the song as an official unified voice, Japanese people's attitudes towards "Kimigayo" vary, and many of them are ambivalent.

As noted above, some people's conscious choice to not join in the unisonous singing not only delivers a strong political message, but it also effectively unravels the homogeneity myth sonically realized in the unisonous singing. In addition, the normative practice set for this type of performance—solo performances by celebrities for appeal and entertainment—removes the essence of the conventional, solemn unisonous performance of "Kimigayo" by the anonymous collective. Except for the example of the silent performance in school ceremonies, the rejection and deviation in these alternative performances are not consciously subversive acts, but rather variations that result from the specific contexts and conditions of performance. However, by unraveling the sonorous aura of this particular arrangement, these cases provide opportunities to liberate "Kimigayo" from being the symbol of unanimity and uniformity desired for the nation. Multiple individual renditions of "Kimigayo" sung by celebrity artists to showcase their personal aura clearly indicate a critical shift in "Kimigayo" performance from *seishō* to *dokushō*. Furthermore, these kinds of settings allow audience members to observe their freedom not to make any choices, expressed by not participating in the singing of "Kimigayo." They are not punished for not singing "Kimigayo" (as opposed to those who choose not to sing in school ceremonies). For those who choose to participate in the singing, there is little fear that their voices will be heard or become the focus of attention. These conditions perhaps generate a much more inviting atmosphere for spontaneous collective singing at athletic events. This suggests that coercion is not the only way to draw the nation into singing. In this context, however, no matter how loudly and proudly "Kimigayo" is sung, the resulting congregational singing is not necessarily a nationalist pronouncement of the selfless unisonous community.

References and Further Research

Anderson, Benedict. 1991. *Imagined Communities: Reflections on the Origin and Spread of Nationalism.* Rev. ed. London and New York: Verso.

Appadurai, Arjun. 1996. *Modernity at Large: Cultural Dimensions of Globalization.* Minneapolis, MN: University of Minnesota Press.

Befu, Harumi. 1993. "Nationalism and *Nihonjinron.*" In *Cultural Nationalism in East Asia: Representation and Identity*, edited by Harumi Befu, 107–135. Berkeley: University of California, Institute of Asian Studies.

Buell, Fredrick. 1994. *National Culture and the New Global System.* Baltimore: Johns Hopkins University Press.

Chakrabarty, Dipesh. 1998. "Afterword: Revisiting the Tradition/ Modernity Binary." In *Mirror of Modernity: Invented Traditions of Modern Japan*, edited by Stephen Vlastos, 285–296. Berkeley: University of California Press.

Frith, Simon. 1998. *Performing Rites: On the Value of Popular Music*. Cambridge, MA: Harvard University Press.

Fujita, Tomoji, and Rekishi Tetsugaku Kenkyūjo. 2005. *"Kimigayo" No Kigen: "Kimigayo" No Honka Wa Banka Datta* [The origin of Kimigayo: It was a funeral eulogy]. Tokyo: Akashi Shoten.

Fukuoka, Yōko. 2005. *Ongaku wa Kokoro de Kanadetai: "Kimigayo" Bansō Kyohi no Hamon* [Play music with soul: "Kimigayo" accompaniment refusal and its aftermath]. Iwanami Booklet No. 657. Tokyo: Iwanami Shoten.

Hall, Stuart. 1992. "The Question of Cultural Identity." In *Modernity and Its Futures*, edited by Stuart Hall, David Held, and Tony McGrew, 273–325. Cambridge, UK: Polity Press, in association with the Open University.

Hall, Stuart, David Held, and Tony McGrew, eds. 1992. *Modernity and Its Futures*. Cambridge, UK: Polity Press, in association with the Open University.

Hobsbawm, Eric J. 1992. "Introduction: Inventing Traditions." In *The Invention of Tradition*, edited by Eric J. Hobsbawm and Terence O. Ranger, 1–14. Canto ed. Cambridge, UK: Cambridge University Press.

Ivy, Marilyn. 1995. *Discourse of the Vanishing: Modernity, Phantasm, Japan*. Chicago: University of Chicago Press.

Johnson, Shiela K. 1999. "Three Views of the Hinomaru and Kimigayo Vote: Flags and Anthems as National Symbols." *JPRI Critique* 6, no. 9. http://www.jpri.org/publications/critiques/critique_VI_9.html.

Kikkawa, Eishi. 1984. "Hôgaku-kyoku ni torareta 'Kimigayo'" ["Kimigayo" adopted in traditional Japanese music genres]. In *Nihon Ongaku no Biteki Kenkyu* [Studies of Japanese music aesthetics] 219-228. Tokyo: Ongaku no Tomo-sha.

Naitō, Takatoshi. 1999. *Mittsu no Kimigayo: Nihonjin no Oto to Kokoro no Shinsō* [Three Kimigayos: Depth psychology of Japanese sound and mind]. Tokyo: Chūō Kōron Shinsha.

Onishi, Norimitsu. 2004. "Tokyo's Flag Law: Proud Patriotism, or Indoctrination?" *New York Times*, December 16. http://www.nytimes.com/2004/12/16/international/asia/16tokyo.html?_r=0.

Sassen, Saskia. 2002 "Towards Post-National and Denationalized Citizenship." In *Handbook of Citizenship Studies*, edited by Engin F. Isin and Bryan S Turner, 277–292. London: SAGE.

Tanaka, Nobumasa. 2000. *Hinomaru, Kimigayo no Sengo-shi, Iwanami Shinsho 650* [Postwar history of Hinomaru and Kimigayo, Iwanami Shinsho 650]. Tokyo: Iwanami Shoten.

Tokoro, Isao. 2000. "'Kimigayo' kashi no Raireki" [Origin and history of the "Kimigayo" lyrics]. In the booklet accompanying the CD *Kimigayo no Subete* [All about Kimigayo]. Tokyo: King Records.

Tolbert, Kathryn. 2000. "A Pledge of Allegiance; Japan's Flag, Anthem take Greater Roles at School Graduations." *Washignton Post*, March 2.

Vlastos, Stephen, ed. 1998. *Mirror of Modernity: Invented Traditions of Modern Japan*. Berkeley, CA: University of California Press.

Yamada, Yoshio. 1956. *Kimigayo no Rekishi* [The history of Kimigayo]. Tokyo: Hōbunkan.

Yamazumi, Masami, ed. 1990. *Anata wa Kimigayo wo Utaimasuka: Hinomaru, Kimigayo Mmondai to Gakkō-kyōiku* [Would you sing Kimigayo? Hinomaru and Kimigayo disputes and school education]. Tokyo: Kokudo-sha.

15

Globalization and Deindustrialization in China's (Former) Porcelain Capital

Maris Gillette

In the first two decades of the twenty-first century, if you were to ask Americans about globalization, many would respond by talking about deindustrialization and China's economic rise. In 1950 more than one-third of all U.S. jobs were in manufacturing. By 2011 this figure had dropped to 9 percent, according to the economist Gary Becker. Abandoned factories and derelict neighborhoods bore witness to deindustrialization in the midwestern "Rust Belt," eastern seaboard cities, and, perhaps most famously, Detroit, which declared bankruptcy in July 2013. In Europe, manufacturing's share of the labor market also contracted significantly between 1965 and 2006, as reported by Jennifer Raynor in the *Monthly Labor Review*. As firm owners sought lower costs and gains in productivity, they closed plants in Europe and the United States and moved jobs to the developing world.

Although some experts disagreed, most Americans related deindustrialization in the United States and Europe to China's economic growth. On average, China's gross domestic product grew 10 percent per year from 1979 to 2012, states Wayne Morrison in a 2013 report for the U.S. Congress, meaning the size of the economy doubled every eight years. China replaced Japan as the world's second-largest manufacturer in 2006, and it overtook the United States in 2010, according to Morrison. From 1991 to 2007, Mubin Khan reports in *The Guardian*, U.S. imports from China grew by 1,156 percent, while the fraction of the U.S. working population who were employed in manufacturing fell by one-third. Particularly since 1992, when China's top leader, Deng Xiaoping, made his "southern tour" (*nan xun*) to support marketization and privatization, the Chinese government has actively encouraged non-Chinese companies to invest in Chinese operations or establish their own enterprises. Long Guoqing, deputy director general of the Department of Foreign Economic Relations in the Development Research Center of the State Council of the People's Republic of China, writes that about 70 percent of this foreign direct investment is in manufacturing. In 2010, 30 percent of China's total economic output came from manufacturing, according to the congressional advisor Marc Levinson, as compared with 12 percent in the United States and 10 percent in the United Kingdom.

Wages and compensation are one reason why European and American manufacturing jobs have gone to China. In 2011, Levinson reports, a manufacturing worker in the United States averaged $23.70 an hour, while a manufacturing worker in China averaged $1.60. Morrison's report to Congress states that the first decade of the twenty-first century saw a sharp increase in the average Chinese wage, from about $US100 per month in 2000 to $US600 per month in 2010, yet the cost was still far less than an American salary. Bonnie Kavoussi's *Huffington Post* article indicates that in 2012, for example, the average monthly wage for an American factory worker was more than $3,500 per month.

Ceramics, as a segment of manufacturing, follows the general trend. For example, Rörstrand is Sweden's most famous ceramics manufacturer, founded in 1726 to compete with Chinese porcelain from Jingdezhen, as well as newly established European manufacturers. Rörstrand manufactured in Sweden for more than 250 years and is credited with developing a distinctly Swedish style of ceramics. In the early 1970s, Rörstrand began downsizing. It was sold to a Finnish company in 1975 and resold several more times over the next three decades. In 2004 the owners closed the last Swedish factory, located in Lidköping. In 2013 the holding company that owned Rörstrand (Fiskars, Inc.) manufactured ceramics in China, Indonesia, Thailand, and Finland, as noted on the company's website.

The English ceramics giant Wedgwood was founded by the inventor and entrepreneur Josiah Wedgwood in 1759. Wedgwood, his factories, and his workers played a key role in transforming Stoke-on-Trent into the center of British ceramics production. Indeed, Rörstrand copied Wedgwood's designs for many years, as scholars like Eric Wettergren and Bo Lindgren have noted. Wedgwood began losing ground in the 1960s, was purchased by the Waterford Glass Group in 1986, and went bankrupt in 2009. Most Wedgwood ceramics are now made in Indonesia, as reported by Martin Arnold in the *Financial Times* and Helen Brown in *The Guardian*. In fact, almost all of Stoke's potteries have closed or downsized. Jennifer Rankin reports that in 1950 the city's ceramics industry employed more than 70,000 workers; in 2013, in contrast, it employed less than 7,000. A 2008 report on European ceramics industries written for the European Commission stated that European tableware output had fallen by 50 percent, and employment even more, over the previous two decades. Chinese ceramics "flooding the EU market" were identified as the cause. The European Commission responded by imposing new taxes on Chinese ceramics in November 2013.

Reports on the American ceramics industry also described the closure of U.S. factories and competition from China. Stephanie Strom reported in the *New York Times* that East Liverpool, Ohio, the "pottery capital of the United States," once had four dozen ceramics factories; in 2012, only two remained. Syracuse China, which produced fine china in upstate New York for 138 years, is another example. The company passed out of family hands in the 1970s, was resold several times, and was purchased by Libbey, Inc. in 1995. Libbey closed all of Syracuse China's North American plants in 2009 and moved production to China and Mexico, according to the journalist Rick Moriarty.

As of 2011, China was the world's largest producer of architectural tiles. About 70 percent of the world's household ceramics were made in China, according to a

Xinhua News Agency report in the *Global Times*. *The Guardian* reported in 2012 that 80 percent of the sales volume of ceramic tableware and kitchenware in Europe were wares from China. Gao Yuning writes in his 2012 book *China as the Workshop of the World* that Chinese sanitary porcelain was more than one-third of global production. The China Ceramic Industry Association forecasted continued growth, projecting that China's ceramics industry would grow by 10 percent a year until 2030.

In this story of globalization and China's domination—or more correctly, re-domination—of ceramics manufacturing, we might expect Jingdezhen to be the big winner. Well-known as China's "porcelain capital," Jingdezhen housed the imperial manufactory, produced the world's finest and largest quantity of blue and white porcelain (and many other wares), and, after the founding of the People's Republic of China (PRC), became the nation's premier ceramics production site. Yet when I first conducted ethnographic research in Jingdezhen in 2003, almost everyone I met was a laid-off porcelain worker. Why?

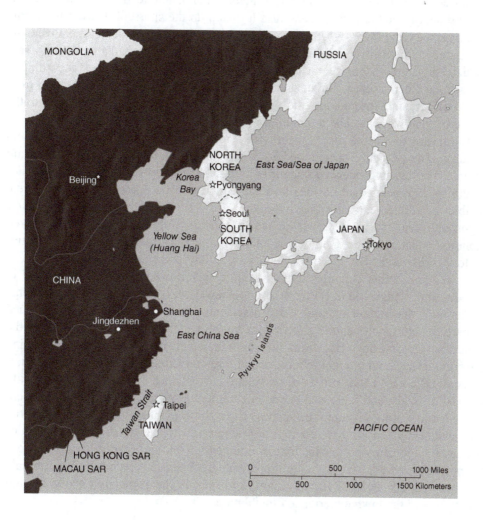

Jingdezhen's History

Jingdezhen first attracted the attention of China's emperor in 1004, during the Song Dynasty. Prior to then, the town was called Changnanzhen, "the town south of the Chang River." After encountering its porcelain, the emperor renamed the town after his reign name (Jingde), commissioned ceramics for the court, sent an official to supervise production, and began taxing its porcelain, according to the *Jiangxi Provincial Gazetteer*. He initiated central government management of, and investment in, Jingdezhen ceramics manufacturing that would last for centuries.

During the Yuan Dynasty, the government established a porcelain bureau in Jingdezhen to oversee production, taxation, and trade. The state first built a factory to make the court's wares shortly after the founding of the Ming dynasty. As Rose Kerr and Nigel Wood report in their monumental study of Chinese ceramics, the fifteenth- and sixteenth-century Ming emperors commissioned large quantities of wares, to the point that the imperial factory was unable to fill the orders and the government turned to private ceramists to make up the shortfall. During the Ming, and then the Qing Dynasty, Jingdezhen's porcelain production professionalized and expanded dramatically. By the eighteenth century the industry had an extremely specialized division of labor, requiring "seventy-two hands to finish a pot," according to the scholar Chen Yuqian. Jingdezhen dominated China's porcelain production from the mid-fourteenth through the mid-nineteenth century, and supplied ceramics to the world in what was basically a monopoly trade.

Europeans first came into contact with Jingdezhen porcelain in the late fifteenth century. They quickly succumbed to what Robert Finlay has called "porcelain disease," purchasing massive quantities through the early eighteenth century. For centuries, Europeans had no idea how the Chinese made porcelain, and they were unable to produce ceramics that were as white, hard, or durable. But in the early eighteenth century, the German alchemist Johann Böttger produced a high-fired stoneware that resembled porcelain and, with state patronage, founded a manufactory in Meissen. His fascinating story is vividly presented by Janet Gleeson in *The Arcanum*. Other ceramics industries quickly followed, including Rörstrand in Sweden and Wedgwood in England, and took away market share from Jingdezhen.

Through the eighteenth and early nineteenth centuries, Jingdezhen continued to receive significant central government investment, and markets in Asia and the Americas were strong. But from the mid-nineteenth century onwards, the Qing government suffered internal rebellions and foreign incursions, and the emperor dramatically decreased state orders of porcelain, gave management of the imperial kiln to local officials, and increased taxes on commercial wares. When the government conceded to Europeans and the Japanese the right to manufacture on Chinese territory, and also taxed foreign ceramics at low rates, European and Japanese ceramics overtook Jingdezhen porcelain, first in Southeast Asia, and then in China, as contemporary observers such as Jiang Siqing and later historians reported. Jingdezhen's economy shrunk as local firms struggled to outsell cheap machine-made foreign ceramics, and the town experienced social unrest.

The Qing collapsed in 1911, and the weak Republican (Guomindang) government replaced it. The new government—which never controlled the whole country, and spent much of its short reign fighting the Chinese Communist Party and local warlords—increased taxes on Jingdezhen porcelain. In the first half of the twentieth century, provincial-level officials made plans to "save" Jingdezhen, but none succeeded. By the end of the Chinese Civil War in 1949, most of Jingdezhen's porcelain manufactures were closed. In the eighteenth century, Jingdezhen's population had been over one million, and the city had more than 3,000 commercial kilns (in addition to the imperial kiln) and 100,000 skilled artisans. In 1948 a deglobalized, deindustrialized Jingdezhen had a population of 50,000, with fewer than 100 shuttered kilns and 1,000 unemployed ceramists, according to the Jiangxi Light Industry Bureau.

When the Chinese Communist Party arrived in Jingdezhen in the spring of 1949, officials immediately began restoring its ceramics industry. The economic historians Wang Zongda and Yin Chengguo document how the new government commissioned porcelain and opened the first nationalized ceramics factory within a year. Officials set up Jingdezhen's branch of the Bank of China in 1950, and issued low-interest loans to porcelain entrepreneurs. Next, the government encouraged local ceramists to form porcelain cooperatives. With official prodding, these became joint public-private enterprises and collectives. At the start of China's Second Five-Year Plan, officials combined Jingdezhen's factories and cooperatives into nine additional nationalized factories. Many of these state-run porcelain factories operated as collective factories, and the city government also ran four porcelain factories.

Traditional porcelain work in Jingdezhen. (*Wikimedia Commons, Ariel Steiner, http://tinyurl. com/kcyzuz3*).

With Jingdezhen's integration into China's planned economy in 1956, government officials managed every aspect of production and distribution. Officials provided factories with fuel and supplies, told them what wares to make, purchased or commissioned new technology, determined how many workers each factory could employ, and assigned jobs. According to the *Jiangxi Provincial Gazetter*, from the mid-1960s until 1995, the government managed 52 porcelain industrial sites, divided into 23 nationalized and 29 collective enterprises, that carried out every aspect of ceramics production. The state dramatically expanded the types of porcelain Jingdezhen made, to include industrial, architectural, sanitary, and electrical ceramics, in addition to dinnerware and art. By the 1970s, if not before, Jingdezhen was again the dominant force in Chinese ceramics manufacturing. Between 1976 and 1985, Jingdezhen porcelain won three international prizes, as well as five gold and three silver medals in national competitions. The industry received 12 honorable mentions from the China Light Industry Bureau and 23 from the Jiangxi provincial government. On average, the value of Jingdezhen porcelain production increased by 6 percent a year between 1979 and 1985. The *Jiangxi Provincial Gazetter* reports that in 1985 the value of Jingdezhen's exports in porcelain was $US20 million.

A One-Thousand-Year Anniversary as Porcelain Capital?

Jingdezhen officials designated 2004 as the year to celebrate Jingdezhen's one-thousand-year anniversary as China's porcelain capital—the very year that the China Ceramic Industrial Association and China Light Industry Association named Chaozhou, in Guangdong province, China's "porcelain capital." The deputy director of the China Light Industry Association explained that Chaozhou was awarded the title for its "market recognition, export volume, technological standards, and cultural values" (Na 2004). One of the judges, a member of the China Ceramic Industrial Association, stated, "it would be irresponsible if we gave the title to Jingdezhen, ignoring the changes and development within the industry. Jingdezhen is not what it was and is on the decline" (Jian 2004). Newspapers reporting Chaozhou's victory wrote that Jingdezhen was "besieged by new economic challenges" and "hard pressed for a market" (Jian 2004, Na 2004).

The city of Jingdezhen's website includes "A Brief Introduction of Jingdezhen" (http://eng.jdz.gov.cn/Brief/introduction/201112/t20111201_122542.htm), which offers information about the city's history and government. The website also includes tourist information and an online ceramics museum.

Sales and output figures confirm this analysis. In 2005 and 2006, competitor ceramics industries in China did not merely outpace Jingdezhen—they left the city far, far behind. The top four producers earned 10 to 40 times what Jingdezhen did in export ceramics (see Table 15.1). In total output value, Jingdezhen again ranked last (see Table 15.2). The value of Jingdezhen's export porcelain for 2005, $21.84 million, was only $1.86 million more than the value of its export porcelain had been 20 years earlier. According to the *China Statistical Yearbook*, prices in China rose 3.54 times between 1985 and 2005. This means that the dollar value of Jingdezhen's 2005 export porcelain, in 1985 dollars, was $5.65 million. In other words, over the 20-year period from 1985 to 2005—the period when China saw an average 15 percent growth a year in manufacturing exports, according to Cui Zhiyuan—the value of Jingdezhen's export porcelain fell by three-quarters.

By 2004, Jingdezhen's ten state-enterprise porcelain factories, four city-owned factories, and collective enterprises had been closed, sold off, or contracted out to private entrepreneurs. Manufacturing of architectural tiles, sanitary ceramics, and

Table 15.1

Export Value of Chinese Ceramics Industries, 2005 and 2006 ($US, in Millions)

City	2005	2006
Foshan, Guangdong	825.00	1,000.00
Chaozhou, Guangdong	709.22	860.00
Dehua, Fujian	423.75	480.00
Liling, Hunan	199.10	245.00
Yixing, Jiangsu	76.37	88.00
Zibo, Shandong	55.00	56.00
Jingdezhen, Jiangxi	21.84	36.00

Source: Xiao and Guo (2008), 24.

Table 15.2

Output of Chinese Ceramic Industries, 2005 and 2006 (Renminbi, in Billions)

City	2005	2006
Foshan, Guangdong	45.00	50.00
Chaozhou, Guangdong	20.25	24.00
Liling, Hunan	5.52	6.40
Yixing, Jiangsu	4.33	5.00
Dehua, Fujian	4.08	4.80
Zibo, Shandong	2.50	3.20
Jingdezhen, Jiangxi	2.46	3.20

Source: Xiao and Guo (2008), 24.

industrial ceramics was defunct. Most production took place in small, family-owned workshops that had fewer than five permanent employees. About 80 percent of ceramists made art porcelain, replicas of historic wares, or what locals called "new style" porcelain. Handicraft replaced industry, with slip-casting the dominant form of "mechanical" production. Most ceramists who did not have their own workshops worked on a freelance basis. They were paid by the piece, employed by the order, and had no benefits. Many former industrial workers were no longer employed in porcelain. A large number had no jobs at all.

Jingdezhen potters regarded slip-casting as mechanical production, although the process is not mechanized and requires a lot of labor. Locally, the important distinction was between wares that were hand-made, by throwing or pressing, and wares that were made by slip-casting or jigger-jolly machines. Two YouTube videos explain the slip-casting method: "Ceramic Artist Richard Notkin Demonstrates Slip Casting" is available on the Craft in America YouTube channel (http://www.youtube.com/watch?v=DGtoPAAFcyQ), and "Slip Casting at the Emma Bridgewater Factory at Stoke-on-Kent, England" is on the Emma Bridgewater factory YouTube channel (http://www.youtube.com/watch?v=W1YCRs6QtEY).

Why wasn't Jingdezhen the winner in the global competition for ceramics manufacturing? The city had a long history of porcelain production and plentiful natural resources, including its outstanding china stone. For more than four decades, the PRC government had invested heavily in Jingdezhen ceramics, mechanizing production, moving the city to cheaper energy sources, and ordering large quantities of wares. The city had tens of thousands of experienced workers, and wages were low. Transport was adequate: city officials had completed the railroad station in 1975, and they paved roads with concrete and asphalt. The airport, built in 1959, was expanded and improved in 1992. The Chang River, Jingdezhen's traditional means of transporting ceramics, was still used in the 1980s. In addition, Jingdezhen had the only institute of higher education devoted to training ceramics industry professionals. Why then did the state-owned factories and their subsidiary collectives close and/ or go bankrupt, leaving 70,000 ceramics workers without jobs? Why did competitor industries in Chaozhou, Foshan, Dehua, Zibo, and Liling expand, while Jingdezhen shrank and turned to handicraft production?

Market Reforms

Jingdezhen's deindustrialization resulted from the PRC's market reforms, as did the success of its competitor industries. After Mao died in 1976, Chinese leaders at the highest level decided to move China away from a planned economy and expand its international relations. The Chinese Communist Party had always taken China's modernization as its core mandate, but top political leaders had differed on the role of markets. Since its establishment in 1949, the PRC had achieved substantial development under successive Five-Year Plans (the first begun in 1953), but by the 1970s the economy was stagnant, living standards were low, and agricultural output was declining, as the sociologist Andrew Walder describes. Relations with the Soviet Union and Eastern Bloc countries were poor, leaving China with few allies or trading partners. When Deng Xiaoping returned to power in the late 1970s, the officials who believed markets could help China modernize could realize their vision.

Five-Year Plans: Terminology and Practice

From 1953 to the present, the Five-Year Plans adopted by the Chinese Communist Party have guided economic and social development. The most recent, as of this publication, the Twelfth Five-Year Guideline, covers the years 2011–2015 and uses the term "Guideline" as opposed to "Plan," an innovation adopted in 2006 in light of China's transformation to a market economy.

In this case study, and in other analyses, "on the plan" refers to an economic activity that is part of the government's central planning in what is sometimes called a "command economy" (in contrast to a "market economy"). While all economic systems in the modern era entail some level of government intervention and management, in a planned economy, the government determines the inputs and outputs for every sector, including by allocating employment to its citizens. Market forces are irrelevant, since no goods are bought and sold except as determined by the plan.

There are many online sources that outline the goals established by each plan. China's authorized government portal site, China Through a Lens, has a web page that outlines all of the Five-Year Plans, titled "Changes in Five-Year Plans' Economic Focus" (http://www.china.org.cn/english/2005/Nov/148163.htm).

As the economists Qian Yingyi and Carsten Holz detail, China's central leadership initially wanted to make China's state-owned enterprises profitable. They began the market reforms by creating dual-track pricing. The bulk of the economy remained on the plan, and the government continued to fix prices for manufactured commodities. Production levels were basically frozen. If a state enterprise produced beyond its quota, it could sell the rest on the market. In addition, private entrepreneurs were allowed to own and operate businesses. These private firms produced entirely for the market. Government officials did not regulate their pricing and were limited in their ability to tax private entrepreneurs, since the banks in China did not require identification to open savings accounts until 2000. Such "anonymous banking" allowed private entrepreneurs to hide wealth from the state and kept tax rates low and flat.

In Jingdezhen, the people who had been excluded from employment in state and collective enterprises—those with bad class labels or rural household registrations—were the first to go into private porcelain production. They made art porcelain using handicraft methods, since this required minimal capital investment. Such private entrepreneurs used their relationships with employees at state and collective factories to fire greenware, and to access supplies that they needed for production. They often hired state and collective workers as temporary labor, paying them cash for working after factory shifts. In 1992 the technology for small propane kilns came to Jingdezhen. Some private entrepreneurs purchased kilns and operated them as businesses, firing wares for local potters. Others bought kilns so they could complete wares in their own workshops.

At that time, almost all of Jingdezhen's ceramics were produced and distributed on the plan. A small fraction was art, and styles were limited. Local officials decided around 1984 that state and collective workers could not open private businesses and keep their factory jobs. If they wanted to be in private business, they had to forfeit their employment. Few state enterprise or large collective workers wanted to give up their "iron rice bowls" to "plunge into the sea" as private entrepreneurs. This meant Jingdezhen had few private firms and little competition for art porcelain. The 1980s and early 1990s were a seller's market, in Jingdezhen and all over the country. Jingdezhen residents said the people who went into private porcelain production in the 1980s "got rich." Particularly popular with consumers were replicas of historic wares made in the imperial kilns.

As the economist Qian Yingyi discusses, one early initiative of the reform period was allowing local officials to manage local government expenditures within broad guidelines set by the central government. In some areas, officials took advantage of this autonomy to found new public-private manufacturing ventures. Most of the enterprises founded between 1979 and 1993 were local government firms. The central government stipulated that officials should use the profits from such enterprises for reinvestment and public works. Most of the profits stayed local.

In Chaozhou and Foshan (in Guangdong Province), Dehua (in Fujian), Zibo (in Shandong), Liling (in Hunan), and Chongqing (in Sichuan), local officials built new ceramics factories and attracted foreign investment. For example, Chen Zhenghao describes in *Asian Ceramics* how Chaozhou officials encouraged state and collective workers to found new ceramics firms. They funded new equipment and renovated facilities, for example by replacing kilns. Together, municipal and provincial officials founded six research centers to promote technological advancement and innovative products. They invited experts to speak to local entrepreneurs, and built cooperative relationships with more than 100 universities, colleges, and scientific research institutes, to ensure that local porcelain manufacturers kept abreast of new developments. Officials also enacted policies to protect intellectual property rights and the integrity of brand names. By 2004, Chaozhou had more than 100,000 new ceramic enterprises, employing more than 400,000 workers.

Kathy Chen, writing in the *Wall Street Journal*, reports that the mayor of Foshan borrowed money to modernize factories, encouraged the founding of new plants jointly owned by the local government and private investors, and offered grants to new private businesses. The new ceramics manufacturers focused on architectural tiles and sanitary ceramics, which are growth areas in China's new economy. In Zibo local officials developed high-tech porcelain manufacturing for electronics, aerospace, and defense industries, according to Wang Qian of the *China Daily*. They invested large sums in research and development, founding 70 technology centers. The Ministry of Science and Technology rewarded their efforts by designating the city a center for the development of new materials in 2002.

China's central government developed a "managerial contract responsibility system" to give state-owned enterprise managers more decision-making power and incentives in the late 1980s. In his PhD dissertation, Wang Jifu describes how one manager of a state-owned ceramics enterprise in Chongqing used his new authority to develop a business plan that prioritized new technology and upgraded the factory's output. When local banks refused to issue credit, the manager went directly to Zhu Rongji, then-vice premier of the State Council and Governor of the Bank of China, who authorized a loan for $US4 million. The manager traveled to Jingdezhen in 1993 to recruit talent for the Chongqing factory, promising wages ten times higher than Jingdezhen salaries, as well as free housing. He found a Hong Kong investor to support expansion, and received a central government commission to make tableware for state dinners. Guo Yuning, in a 2012 book on Chinese manufacturing, describes how managers of the state-owned Third Ceramic Factory of Beilu City in Yulin, Guangxi, founded a joint venture ceramics manufacturing firm, Sanhuan, with private Hong Kong investors. After the central government legalized shareholding cooperatives in 1992, all of Sanhuan's employees bought shares in the company. By 1995 Sanhuan could purchase Beilu's largest state-run ceramics factory. The company became China's third-largest producer of household ceramics in 1998. In 2005 Sanhuan was selling to IKEA, the international furniture and home goods company based in Sweden, and outsourcing some production to Chaozhou.

The managers of Jingdezhen's state-owned porcelain factories did not take such bold measures. They began a system of bonuses for employees who did exceptional quality work, trained extra apprentices, or produced above quota. They hoped to foster higher production and competition within the factories. Managers and local officials did little to invigorate research and development, investigate other ceramics industries, or consult outside experts. Factories produced the same wares that they made under the plan, stockpiling the surpluses that they couldn't market.

Mr. Luo, a professor at a local ceramics institute, recounted an example of local conservatism. In the late 1970s Luo worked at the Light Industry Bureau Ceramics Research Institute, one of Jingdezhen's state-run research centers (which the government merged with the Jingdezhen Ceramics Institute in 1999). He traveled to Beijing to do research at the Palace Museum, and met a private exporter who told him there was an excellent market for high-quality replicas of antique porcelain. Luo realized that the Ceramics Research Institute was well situated to replicate Yuan, Ming, and Qing porcelain from the imperial manufactory. The institute had a small production site, where researchers tested their theories about historic porcelain and handicraft methods, and it did ceramic analysis. Luo approached his bosses when he returned to Jingdezhen, proposing that the Institute produce high-value replicas by throwing on stick-spun wheels, blowing on glaze by mouth, painting by hand, and firing in wood-burning kilns. Luo's superiors were uninterested. Luo explained to me in an interview, "This was the early 1980s. Reform and Opening [the official title for the market reforms] had just begun. We were recovering from the Cultural Revolution, with its extreme politics, and people weren't enthusiastic about private production. They didn't think about going into business."

So Luo and some associates founded their own antique replica workshop, which they ran in their off hours, until they had to choose between keeping their state-enterprise jobs or private entrepreneurship. Because no one knew how long the market reforms would continue, Luo and his compatriots decided to keep their jobs. They sold the workshop to Mr. Xiang, a young migrant from the countryside who had been their customer. I asked Xiang why he bought the workshop, and he explained it was because he couldn't get a good job in a state enterprise. In 2004, locals often cited Xiang as an example of the private porcelain entrepreneurs who got rich early. His firm, Hua Hong Ceramics, is a top producer of antique replicas in Jingdezhen.

The central government began reducing the planned track of the economy in the early 1990s. Local officials had to decide how to handle this shift. In 1994 the central government instructed banks to tighten credit to state and collective factories. China's Ninth Five Year Plan (1996–2000) stated that all of the PRC's state enterprises should be made into "modern enterprises." Exactly how was left up to local officials. In some areas, officials strengthened state-owned enterprises. In others, they closed, contracted out, or sold them. Jonathan Woetzel reports for *Forbes* that between 1994 and 2005, 3,658 of China's state enterprises went bankrupt. Jingdezhen officials let the city's state and collective porcelain enterprises fail. The Guangming Porcelain Factory was the last state enterprise to close, in October 1998.

One Family's Experience

Locals were utterly unprepared for deindustrialization. Many laid-off workers told me how they came to work one day and only then learned that the factory was permanently closed. Managers offered no explanations to workers after plants were shuttered. One retired official told me that, in some cases, the local government forced the factories to close, despite the managers' desires to remain open. Most workers had difficulty finding new jobs.

Members of a family often worked at the same factory, as factory employees used their connections to find positions for relatives when they had good jobs. For example, a man who worked at a large collective factory that made brushes for painting on porcelain found jobs for his son and daughter there. A married couple who worked at a state-enterprise porcelain factory helped two of their three sons find work there, and they managed to locate a job for the other son at a different state enterprise. A thrower with seven children got five of them jobs at the porcelain factory where he was employed. A sculptor at Jingdezhen's large collective sculpture factory found work for his son and daughter there. This employment strategy was beneficial under the planned economy, but it meant entire families were laid off simultaneously when their factories closed.

A 2009 story in the *China Daily* newspaper, titled "Molding Dreams" (http:// www.chinadaily.com.cn/showbiz/2009-10/22/content_8831581.htm) and written by Quan Ziaoshu and Shen Yang, explores the story of Sun Lixin, who "followed in the footsteps of his father Sun Tongxin and secured an 'iron rice bowl job' at the state-owned Hongqi Porcelain Factory in Jingdezhen, where his father had worked for more than 20 years."

Mr. Gong, his younger brother, his son, and his daughter worked for the Guangming Porcelain Factory, one of Jingdezhen's ten provincial-level state enterprises. Guangming was a large, vertically integrated site with 4,000 workers, specializing in blue-and-white dinnerware with a rice grain pattern. It managed two collective factories. When Guangming closed, Mr. Gong's job was hauling clay from the clay-making section to the assembly lines. He had begun his career as a porcelain worker in 1960 at the age of 13. He entered as an apprentice, and then performed several jobs, including glazing and operating the jigger-jolly machines, where the clay forms were made. Gong's varied work background was somewhat unusual. He explained that he got tired of doing the same work all the time and so regularly petitioned factory leaders to allow him to try something new. His daughter added that her father always tried to find the jobs that required the least amount of time at work. One reason Mr. Gong liked hauling clay was that the job required only two or three hours of work each day for a full salary. Because Mr. Gong's father was an official at the Labor Bureau, which allocated employment, Mr. Gong had more opportunities to change jobs than other workers.

Ethnographic Research in Jingdezhen: The Gong Family

Social and cultural anthropologists usually adopt the research method known as ethnography. Ethnographers conduct research in naturalistic settings, following people as they go about their daily lives and participating as much as possible in ordinary activities. Typically, ethnographic interviews, such as the ones Gillette conducted in Jingdezhen, are informal conversations between the anthropologist and local people in their homes, at their work places, or in other public or private settings where locals spend their time. Ethnographers stay in their field sites for long periods, often a year or more, in order to gain as much understanding as they can about how local people think and behave, and about the social, political, and economic circumstances in which they live. Gillette went to Jingdezhen to learn about the lives of ceramics workers in China's most famous porcelain industry.

Mr. Gong's younger brother was a barber in Guangming's barbershop. Like other state-owned porcelain factories, Guangming provided free haircuts and shower facilities on site. Each worker got a monthly ration coupon to redeem for a haircut. Mr. Gong's wife was a migrant from the countryside without a Jingdezhen residence permit, so she was barred from employment at Guangming. However, her husband helped her find work as a temporary laborer at a small collective factory that Guangming operated. She stamped or applied transfers to pots for surface decoration. Mr. Gong's son was part of the team at Guangming that placed greenware or unfired porcelain into saggars (protective containers) and loaded the kilns. Loading porcelain was strenuous, so three hours of labor was considered a full day. Working with Mr. Gong's son was Mr. Liu, who married Mr. Gong's daughter. Mr. Liu initially operated the jigger-jolly machines at the front of the assembly line, but he switched to the kiln-loading job, which required less work hours, with the help of his mother's connections. Mr. Liu met Ms. Gong at a dance that the factory hosted. Ms. Gong worked on the line as a decorator, where she stamped wares, applied transfers, or banded pots. Her job required an eight-hour day. She told me that the hardest part of her job was being unable to leave her position when she needed to use the toilet. She and her fellow decorators would drink as little as they could, and hold their bladders as long as possible, to avoid disrupting production. As a result, Ms. Gong got bladder stones, a common occupational illness among assembly-line workers.

The Gongs were happy working at a state-enterprise porcelain factory. State-enterprise workers were the aristocrats of the workforce. For most of Guangming's history, Jingdezhen's state-enterprise porcelain workers were the best paid and got the biggest bonuses of any industrial workers. Mr. Gong recalled his pride at being a worker, and the status it gave him. Even in the 1990s, when the earnings of some private porcelain entrepreneurs outstripped state-enterprise workers' wages, the Gongs preferred Guangming's job security, guarantee of cradle-to-grave welfare, and routine work hours. Ms. Gong worked briefly in private enterprise after she graduated from the factory's vocational high school in 1989, but she wanted state-enterprise employment. "Working at the porcelain factory was really orderly (*hen you guixu gan*)," Ms. Gong remembered. "It was like being in your own home (*gen ziji jia yiyang*). Your job was so stable, and the benefits were excellent."

Her husband recalled the layoffs. "We had no forewarning that the factory was closing," Mr. Liu said. "One day it was open and the next day it was shut. One day it was a state enterprise and the next day they were renting it out to private entrepreneurs." Ms. Gong agreed: "We were all standing outside by the gate, talking. No one knew what was going on, we were waiting to start work. Finally someone came out and told us that the factory was closed and we were laid off." Mr. Liu said, "We were all laid off at the same time, my brothers [who worked at another state-enterprise porcelain factory] too. We got to the point that we only had ten yuan (about $US1.20) between us. It was really tough." Ms. Gong continued, "At that point, we went out and bought some baby formula for our daughter [aged one year]. . . . Whatever happened, we wanted to make sure that she had enough to eat."

When Guangming shut its doors, Mr. Gong was 51 years old, and had worked in porcelain for 38 years. His initial thought was to work for one of the private entrepreneurs who were renting the factory's facilities. No one would hire him, however. They told him he was too old for manual labor. Mr. Gong never again found a permanent job, or even a long-term one, and he reached retirement age in 2007. Indeed, a large number of older male factory workers in Jingdezhen found themselves unemployable. Some purchased motorcycles and operated them as taxis, an activity that was illegal. Others became peddlers of porcelain shards, old books, or wares taken from factory storage facilities. Still others opened tiny food stalls, selling hand-made noodles or dumplings. Mr. Gong and his wife ended up getting emergency support from their neighborhood association, and relying on their children for money. Things improved when Mr. Gong finally received his retirement pension of 500 yuan per month in 2007.

Mr. Gong's son and daughter, and Mr. Liu, were in their late twenties and early thirties when the factory closed. One consequence of being state-enterprise employees was that they were eligible only for contract or temporary jobs at other sites. If they took regular employment elsewhere, they lost the right to any benefits that could result from their state-enterprise status (*bianzhi*), and they forfeited the right to a job should the Guangming Factory reopen. If Guangming were sold to real estate developers, as happened to other porcelain factories, only workers with active employee status had a claim on revenue realized after the factory's debts and expenses (such as retirement pensions) were paid off. Similarly, should surpluses result from renting the factory's facilities to private entrepreneurs, workers with active status would receive a share. A few years after Guangming closed, the factory leaders managed to sell part of its grounds. They notified the laid-off workers to bring receipts of any medical expenses since the factory closing for reimbursement. Unfortunately, the Gong family had not saved any medical receipts. Ms. Gong was fairly certain that none of the other Guangming Factory employees had any receipts either, as no one knew such a one-time benefit would become available.

Broken Pots, Broken Dreams (2009) is a documentary about the pottery industry in Jingdezhen by the author of this chapter. The website for the film (http://www. haverford.edu/anthropology/brokenpots/film/film.html) has links to a number of additional resources about Jingdezhen, as well as a link to the film's trailer.

After losing her job, Ms. Gong found work at private porcelain factories, but it was always short-term work. Initially, a private entrepreneur who rented part of another former state enterprise hired her, but he let her go after a few months when he had no orders to fill. She was briefly unemployed again, and then found work at the Hongguang Porcelain Factory. Hongguang had been a collective enterprise. It had closed and its facilities were rented to private entrepreneurs. The collective had produced a popular dinnerware line called Red Leaf, which a private entrepreneur took over. Ms. Gong worked for him for more than a year, and was required to take only a few months of mandatory unpaid leave, because Red Leaf dinnerware sold well and he had a lot of orders. Most other private entrepreneurs could not offer such regular employment. Her salary ranged from 300 to 800 yuan per month, depending on how many hours she worked. She had no other benefits. Still, Ms. Gong would have continued working for this firm, but the Chang River flooded in 2000 and forced the factory to close. At this point, Ms. Gong left the ceramics industry, and worked as a hotel maid. Later, she and her husband purchased a gambling parlor, which she was still running when I visited Jingdezhen in 2009 and 2010.

After a period of unemployment, Mr. Liu was hired as a kiln loader at Hongguang. He considered it a good job because he usually had work. However, loading was much harder than at Guangming. He and the other workers had to load until the job was done, rather than punching the clock as they did Guangming. When Hongguang was busy, this meant working late into the night. In the state porcelain factories, kiln loading had been exclusively male, since the work was considered too strenuous for women. In private enterprise, however, the loaders' wives often helped so that the men could go home earlier. Ms. Gong often loaded with Mr. Liu, which he found humiliating. The flood in 2000 also put an end to Mr. Liu's work at Hongguang. He briefly hauled coal for a state-enterprise hotel, and then found a contract labor job on an assembly line at a pharmaceutical factory. Having twice lost their jobs simultaneously, Ms. Gong and Mr. Liu agreed that they would never again work at the same enterprise.

Understanding Jingdezhen's Deindustrialization

Between 2003 and 2010, I frequently asked laid-off workers, government officials, and other residents to explain the porcelain industry closures and bankruptcies. Some people talked about the size of the porcelain factories and the burden of providing pensions, benefits, and permanent employment. Some complained that the enterprises collapsed because they had too many "waste people" (fei ren) who didn't work, especially managers.

Several former workers and officials blamed Jingdezhen's deindustrialization on bad management. Many said the managers did not adapt to the market economy. A number complained that the factories kept producing the old patterns, rather than looking for new designs. "We [workers] always said that we ate food that the ancestors had cooked [chi laozu zeng de fan]," one former decorator told me. "The styles, decorations, patterns, and forms of dinnerware in Jingdezhen haven't changed in years." Managers allowed the factories to produce wares that they couldn't sell, leaving large quantities in storage. "The managers were accustomed to being told what to make," a local official explained. "They didn't know how to respond to market demand, and they didn't know how to sell things. The result was that factories went bankrupt, shrunk, or were split up and contracted out to private entrepreneurs." However, one former manager pointed out that the problem was not simply that managers couldn't sell goods. "The government set the prices for everything the factory made, and kept prices artificially low. We couldn't earn enough from sales to support ourselves without a government subsidy. When the government quit subsidizing us, we went under."

Another complaint was that managers didn't invest in new technology (perhaps because they were denied loans to do so). "Competitor industries like Zibo and Foshan use powder clay and mechanical presses to make daily use porcelain," one private producer explained. "It's quicker and saves money because there is no clay-making stage. The porcelain comes out very neat, with highly standardized sizing. But those machines require a big up-front investment, and no one did that here. We use the same machines that we had in the 1960s." Firing technology was similarly outdated. "Jingdezhen used to be known for its dinnerware," a former gilder lamented, "but now people think Jingdezhen is inferior to Liling and Chaozhou. Those industries fire their wares at lower temperatures. Their pots are smooth, while Jingdezhen pots have a wave because they are fired at higher temperatures."

In Jingdezhen and elsewhere, state-enterprise managers were political appointees who got their jobs based on bureaucratic rather than business criteria. Some residents believed that the factory managers were corrupt. They talked about nepotism in hiring, though in fact many workers took advantage of family ties to find or improve their employment. Others speculated that managers were embezzling factory resources. "The managers all had a lot of money," one laid-off worker explained. "We knew it wasn't from their salaries. They were taking things from the factory. Stuff would disappear from storage, and people would say that they'd seen one of the managers' nephews removing things. The managers wouldn't steal things directly, they'd call up their relatives to come do it." One man who was a sales manager at a state enterprise admitted that he took the factory's clients to private porcelain workshops. If the clients bought dinnerware from a private entrepreneur, he got a commission on the sale. He got his factory salary too, of course.

Government decisions also caused problems. As one Jingdezhen official pointed out, it was the central government that told the banks to stop issuing credit to the state and collective enterprises, which meant they couldn't pay their bills. Another official said,

> You know we don't say that any of the factories went bankrupt [daobi] here. We say that they were structurally reformed [tizhi gaige]. We don't say that the workers lost their jobs [shiye], we say they left their posts [xiagang]. The idea is to keep things vague, so that no one protests. Look at the Jingxing Porcelain Factory [a large collective], for example. No one says it went bankrupt, they say it was structurally reformed. It closed its doors in 1996. Initially parts were rented out to private entrepreneurs. Then, in 2000, the Bureau of Industry and Commerce bought it. The sale price was ten million yuan. Money for the sale went to the factory leaders, and the workers never saw a penny. The site was demolished, and now it is a fruit and vegetable market.

Yet another official commented, "One of the strange features of the market reforms was that the state ceramics enterprises here closed, but stayed open elsewhere. Look at the difference between Zibo and Jingdezhen. Zibo's state-run ceramics industry remains active to this day, while here the market reforms were more damaging than the Cultural Revolution. Here the market reforms ended large-scale production and industry."

Government documents from the 1990s indicate that Jingdezhen officials were constrained by orders from government leaders at the provincial and higher levels. Shortly after the market reforms began, the city government was instructed that Jingdezhen should focus on producing high-quality daily-use porcelain, particularly dinnerware sets, rather than architectural tiles, sanitary porcelain, or porcelain for industry. Yet in the newly marketizing and privatizing PRC, architectural tiles and sanitary porcelain were growth markets, largely responsible for the success of ceramics industries in Guangdong and elsewhere. Dinnerware sets, by contrast, were not in demand, and in fact many of the famous European ceramics companies who produced dinnerware, such as Rörstrand and Wedgwood, also ran into serious difficulties because of declining markets.

Many Jingdezhen residents, including those who believed the market reforms were positive, felt that the government should redevelop the ceramics industry. Many ceramists complained that the government didn't care about porcelain workers and didn't invest in porcelain manufacturing. Articles reporting that Jingdezhen city officials had "selected helicopters, minivans, refrigerator compressors, building materials, and pressed salted chicken as [Jingdezhen's] pillar industries," as Cao Min wrote in China Business Weekly, supported their criticisms. Jingdezhen residents knew that China's porcelain industry flourished in other locations, while Jingdezhen had only small-scale enterprises making primarily art, and this provoked resentment. One laid-off state-enterprise worker, who now ran a private porcelain workshop, put it this way: "The government should protect, nurture, develop, and correct the ceramics industry. But the city officials get their salaries and eat out on public money, and they don't care if the workers live or die." Others complained that city officials took wrongheaded steps. Jingdezhen's annual ceramics festival provoked criticism as a superficial show that resulted in neither sales nor investment. Locals also complained that the government spent too much time looking for foreign investors who would come start new industries, rather than taking care of the industry that was already present. One potter gave this example of local officials' management:

> The city government doesn't pay attention to ceramics as long as the workshops pay their taxes. And the few steps they are taking are impractical. Fanjiajing [a neighborhood in the center of Jingdezhen that housed many antique replica makers] is a great example. There is a flourishing porcelain market there, and the government wants to get rid of it. They claim that making porcelain in town is unsafe. So they found some real estate developers, and got them to make the Ceramics Town [a new set of buildings across the Chang River in the western

suburbs] and other sites, and now they want the ceramists to move. The ceramists don't want to move, of course, and no one has. First of all, the customers already know where to come. Second, moving is expensive. It takes time, at least half a month, and while you are moving you cannot be producing. Third, you can't move everything. In particular, you can't move the kilns [in Jingdezhen, most private kilns were propane-fired fixed structures]. But the government isn't compensating people for their kilns. People are expected just to leave behind this investment worth thousands and thousands of yuan, and move across the river and buy a new one. No one is moving. So the real estate developers are complaining to the government that they haven't sold their property, and the government in turn pressures the potters. But at the same time most officials are pretty corrupt, so no one moves, and that's where it rests.

Jingdezhen's Reglobalization

Observers differed in how they evaluated Jingdezhen in the wake of its industrial decline, but they agreed that the city had shifted toward small-scale production of art ceramics. Many criticized contemporary ceramists for producing art that was "low end," "poor quality," "identikit goods," "kitsch," and "imitation," as reported in the *China Daily, Ceramics Monthly, CNN Travel*, and *Studies in the Sociology of Science*. Others believed Jingdezhen was undergoing a "creative renaissance" sparked by an influx of artists from other parts of China and abroad, as Violet Law of the *South China Morning Post* and curators at the China Institute put it.

Conceptual art and studio ceramics are global trends influencing Jingdezhen in the twenty-first century. Ai Weiwei is the best-known conceptual artist to produce art in Jingdezhen. Ai works with a local antique replica producer and has employed many Jingdezhen artisans to create ceramic art, including an installation of 100 million hand-painted ceramic sunflower seeds at the Tate Modern in London in 2010. Many other international artists have used local artisans for conceptual work. For example, British artist Clare Twomey commissioned 80 large vases from a Jingdezhen workshop for her installation piece *Made in China*, which was exhibited at the British Ceramics Biannual in 2013. Norwegian artist Ole Lislerud had Jingdezhen artisans produce silk-screened porcelain tiles for his Ignis Bybrann Monument in Aalesund, Norway. The American ceramist Barbara Diduk commissioned 101 blue-and-white vases from Jingdezhen for an installation project in which she reflects on industrial mass production and handicraft.

The Tate Modern web page for the exhibition "The Unilever Series: Ai Weiwei: Sunflower Seeds" (http://www.tate.org.uk/whats-on/tate-modern/exhibition/unilever-series-ai-weiwei-sunflower-seeds) offers images and information about the artist's work, including a film showing footage of the sunflower seeds being made in Jingdezhen.

By 2010 the list of international artists who had produced work in Jingdezhen was long. Many ceramics artists and studio potters listed a "Jingdezhen residency" on their resumes. Several sites offered artists facilities and access to artisans, including the Pottery Workshop (founded in 2005), the Sanbao Working Ceramics Village (founded 2000), and the studio of Liu Yuanchang at the Sculpture Factory (which started hosting visiting artists in 2004). The West Virginia University professor Bob Anderson ran study abroad programs in collaboration with the Jingdezhen Ceramics Institute, founding a summer program in 1995 and a fall program in 2004. These ceramics residencies, and visits from international artists hosted by the Jingdezhen Ceramics Institute, increased local exposure to international ceramics. Art students at the Jingdezhen Ceramics Institute, in particular, found inspiration from the works presented at these venues.

In the first decade of the twenty-first century, a form of studio pottery emerged in Jingdezhen. Jingdezhen's studio ceramics differed ideologically and practically from that found in Europe, the United States, and elsewhere. Jingdezhen has never had a tradition of studio pottery. The archaeological and textual evidence indicates the area once had farmers who were part-time potters, but this mode of production gave way to industrial manufacturing six centuries ago. Jingdezhen studio ceramists could not refer nostalgically to a small-scale community, therefore, or recent rural past, as typified studio pottery movements in the United Kingdom, Europe, Japan, and the United States. In fact, very few ceramists in Jingdezhen made wares from initial clay-making through final firing, as the phrases "studio ceramics" and "studio potter" imply. Most ceramists explained it was "too convenient" to employ others to help with various parts of production, such as throwing pots, making glazes, and so on.

Local officials sought to link Jingdezhen's new "studio potters" to cultural heritage tourism that exploited Jingdezhen's past as porcelain manufacturer for the court. Officials commissioned public ceramic art, which they sited all over the city. They hosted ceremonies to honor the traditional Ceramics God and commemorate the imperial kilns. They opened a museum on the site of the former imperial manufactory, operated a living history museum where visitors could see potters make bowls using handicraft methods, and rebuilt an "old street" in downtown Jingdezhen. According to a professor at the Jingdezhen Ceramics Institute, in 2003 the number of people working in tourism surpassed the number working in ceramics for the first time in the city's history.

Globalization and Manufacturing

Looking at China's former porcelain capital, we see that globalization is historically deeper than most popular accounts acknowledge. Jingdezhen was the world's most important ceramics manufacturing center at the turn of the eighteenth century, when China was the world's largest economy, as the economist Angus Maddison has shown. American and European ceramics industries developed as competitors to Jingdezhen. America's rise to become an economic powerhouse, and Britain's rise before that, occurred at China's expense. Media reports today suggest that American or European dominance should be taken as the natural or proper order. Many Americans feel threatened by reports that China has overtaken the United States as the world's largest economy. Yet the European and American position at the top of a global economic order is a relatively recent historical circumstance, and it should not be surprising if such dominance eventually ends or diminishes.

The University of Warwick's website for its Global Jingdezhen project (www2. warwick.ac.uk/fac/arts/history/ghcc/research/globalporcelain/) has links to reports and papers from a number of events on Jingdezhen, viewed from a global perspective.

Jingdezhen's deindustrialization demonstrates that economic trajectories come from political decisions. Deindustrialization is not an inevitable result of "the mechanical hand of the market." The policies of central and local government officials allowed Jingdezhen's ceramics industry to shrink and atrophy, while officials in Chaozhou, Foshan, and other locations committed to expanding ceramics manufacturing. Jingdezhen was capable of hosting a thriving ceramics industry, and markets for ceramics manufactured in China existed. Porcelain manufacturing in Jingdezhen rose and fell because of the steps that officials were willing, or not willing, to take.

Deindustrialization's human cost is enormous. Mr. Luo, who was a strong advocate of China's market reforms, put it this way: "The layoffs produced a lot of waste. Lots of people who worked in the porcelain factories had been trained in a particular skill. Then they were laid off and told that no one needed their skills anymore and they should find something else to do. It would be the same as if someone came to you and said, look, we don't need any professors any longer, find something else to do—here, go and farm." Deindustrialization affected every aspect of Jingdezhen's ceramic workers' lives. They faced both economic deprivation and social redundancy. By 2010 most families had recovered, or recovered enough, from deindustrialization's economic impact, but the psychic scars remained painful.

Heritage tourism and studio art are the latest forms of globalization to shape Jingdezhen. The new studio and conceptual art cannot employ the large numbers of workers that the porcelain factories did, but the sector does provide jobs for some. Recent moves to make Jingdezhen a center for hand-made art, creative production, and cultural tourism occlude the city's industrial past. We must wait to see how Jingdezhen residents manage this history, and whether the city's future will again include large-scale manufacturing.

Acknowledgment

I am deeply grateful to the people in Jingdezhen who participated in this research. Funding came from the American Council of Learned Societies, the National

Endowment for the Humanities, the Smithsonian Institution, Haverford College, the EURIAS Fellowship Program, and the Swedish Collegium for Advanced Study. I thank the 2013–2014 Fellows at the Collegium, and the participants in the British Ceramics Biennial Conference, for their comments on an early version of this work. I thank Carsten Holz and Charles Gillette for helping me understand the statistical measures of Jingdezhen's deindustrialization.

References and Further Research

Arnold, Martin. 2009. "Waterford Wedgwood to Hasten Overseas Production." *Financial Times*, March 27. http://www.ft.com/intl/cms/s/0/6ba056a2-1a6f-11de-9f91-0000779fd2ac.html#axzz-2lCEGXpDU.

Becker, Gary S. 2012. "Concern About the Decline in Manufacturing in the United States?" *The Becker-Posner Blog*, April 22. http://www.becker-posner-blog.com/2012/04/concern-about-the-decline-in-manufacturing-in-the-united-states-becker.html.

Brown, Helen. 2009. "How the Ceramics Industry Can Avoid Wedgwood's Fate." *The Guardian*, January 15. http://www.theguardian.com/artanddesign/2009/jan/15/ceramics-industry-waterford-wedgwood.

Cao Min. 1997. "Jingdezhen Reforming Enterprises." *China Daily*, March 2. http://www.chinadaily.com.cn/epaper/html/bw/1997/199703/19970302/19970302005_2.html.

Chen, Kathy. 1992. "Foshan Blends Capitalism and Socialism: China City's Market Savvy and Domestic Sales Fuel Civic Projects." *Wall Street Journal Asia*, September 28.

Chen Yuqian, ed. 2004. *Jingdezhen taoci wenhua gailun*景德鎮陶瓷文化概論 [A discussion of Jingdezhen's ceramic culture]. Nanchang, Jiangxi: Jiangxi Higher Education Publishers.

Chen Zhenghao. 2005. "Big Moves in China City: Chaozhou Assumes the Porcelain Mantle." *Asian Ceramics* 5:19–27.

China Institute. 2012. "New 'China': Porcelain Art from Jingdezhen, 1910-2012." http://www.china institute.org/cimain/wp-content/themes/chinainstitute/pdfs/gallery/New%20China_LARGE%20 PRINT%20TEXT_For%20Web.pdf. This is a description of an exhibition held September 21, 2012–February 17, 2013.

Cui Zhiyuan. 2003. "China's Export Tax Rebate Policy." *China: An International Journal* 1, no. 2 (September): 339–349.

Diduk, Barbara. 2012. "The Vase Project: Made in China—Landscape in Blue." *The Vase Project: Made in China—Landscape in Blue*, edited by Barbara Diduk with Zhao Yu. Easton, PA: Williams Center Gallery, Lafayette College.

ECORYS Research and Consulting. 2008. *FWC Sector Competitiveness Studies—Competitiveness of the Ceramics Sector: Final Report*. Rotterdam, Netherlands: ECORYS Nederland BV.

Feytis, Alexandra. 2011. "Chinese Ceramics Prepared for Further Growth." *Industrial Minerals* 526 (July): 26–27.

Finlay, Robert. 1998. "The Pilgrim Art: The Culture of Porcelain in World History." *Journal of World History* 9, no. 2:141–187.

Gao Yuning. 2012. *China as the Workshop of the World: An Analysis at the National and Industry Level of China in the International Division of Labor*. London: Routledge.

Gillette, Maris Boyd. 2010. "Copying, Counterfeiting, and Capitalism in Jingdezhen's Porcelain Industry." *Modern China* 36, no. 4: 367–403.

Gillette, Maris Boyd. 2014. "Labor and Precariousness in China's Porcelain Capital." *Anthropology of Work Review* 35, no. 1: 25–39.

Gleeson, Janet. 2000. *The Arcanum: The Extraordinary True Story*. New York: Warner Books.

The Guardian. 2012. "British Retail Consortium Criticises Tax on Chinese Crockery." *The Guardian*, November 15. http://www.theguardian.com/business/2012/nov/15/british-retail-tax-chinese-crockery.

Holz, Carsten. 2002. "Long Live China's State-Owned Enterprises: Deflating the Myth of Poor Financial Performance." *Journal of Asian Economics* 13, no. 4: 493–529.

Holz, Carsten. 2011. "The Unbalanced Growth Hypothesis and the Role of the State: The Case of China's State-Owned Enterprises." *Journal of Development Economics* 96, no. 2: 220–238.

Imkamp, Laura. 2011. "The Future of China: Jingdezhen Struggles to Maintain its Porcelain Fame." *CNN Travel*, July 20. http://travel.cnn.com/shanghai/shop/future-china-jingdezhen-struggles-keep-its-porcelain-fame-835545.

Iittala. n.d. "Meet the Company." https://www.iittala.com/about-us-meet-the-company.

Jian Fa. 2004. "The Glory of China: A Change of Guard in the Porcelain Kingdom." *Beijing Weekly* 47, no. 38: 40–43.

Jiang Siqing. 1936. *Jingdezhen ciye shi*景德鎮瓷業史 [A history of Jingdezhen's porcelain industry]. Shanghai: Zhonghua Shuju.

Jiangxi Light Industry Bureau Ceramics Research Center. 1959. *Jingdezhen tao ci shi gao* 景德鎮陶瓷史稿 [A draft history of Jingdezhen ceramics]. Beijing: Sanlian.

Jiangxi Provincial Gazetteer Editorial Committee, eds. 2005. *Jiangxi Sheng tao ci gong ye zhi* 江西省陶瓷工業志 [A record of the ceramics industry in Jiangxi Province]. Jiangxi: Jiangxi Province Gazetteer Publishing.

Kavoussi, Bonnie. 2012. "Average Cost of a Factory Worker in the U.S., China and Germany." *Huffington Post*, March 8. http://www.huffingtonpost.com/2012/03/08/average-cost-factory-worker_n_1327413.html.

Kerr, Rose, and Nigel Wood. 2004. *Science and Civilization in China.* Vol. 5, *Chemistry and Chemical Technology*; Part 12, *Ceramic Technology*. Cambridge: Cambridge University Press.

Khan, Mubin. 2013. "US Manufacturing and the Troubled Promise of Reshoring." *The Guardian*, July 24. http://www.theguardian.com/business/2013/jul/24/us-manufacturing-troubled-promise-reshoring.

Kollewe, Julia. 2009. "Waterford Wedgwood, 250 Years of History." *The Guardian*, January 5. http://www.theguardian.com/business/2009/jan/05/waterford-wedgwood-history.

Law, Violet. 2013. "Intelligent Design: A Ceramic Renaissance in Jiangxi." *South China Morning Post*, September 29. http://www.scmp.com/magazines/post-magazine/article/1316624/intelligent-design-ceramic-renaissance-jiangxi.

Lawrence, Robert Z., and Lawrence Edwards. 2013. *US Employment Deindustrialization: Insights from History and the International Experience*. Policy Brief 13-27 Washington DC: Peterson Institute for International Economics. http://www.iie.com/publications/interstitial.cfm?ResearchID=2500.

Levinson, Marc. 2013. *US Manufacturing in International Perspective*. CRS Report 7-5700. Washington DC: Congressional Research Service. http://www.fas.org/sgp/crs/misc/R42135.pdf.

Liang Saiyu. 2013. "Ancient Chinese City's Burning Desire for Past Glories." *Xinhua*, October 23. http://english.sina.com/2013/1023/639513.html.

Lind, Daniel. 2011. "A Deindustrialized Europe." *Social Europe Journal*, November 11. http://www.social-europe.eu/2011/11/a-deindustrialized-europe/.

Lindgren, Bo. 1959. *Three Centuries of Swedish Pottery: Rörstrand 1726–1959 and Marieberg 1758–1788*. London: Victoria and Albert Museum.

Long Guoqing. 2005. "China's Policies on FDI: Review and Evaluation." In *Does Foreign Direct Investment Promote Development?*, edited by Theodore Moran, Edward Graham and Magnus Blomström, 315–336. Washington DC: Institute for International Economics.

Maddison, Angus. 2007. *Chinese Economic Performance in the Long Run*. 2nd ed. Paris: OECD Publications.

Martin, Colin. 2012. "International Ceramic Artists Working in China." *Craft Arts International* 86: 97–99.

Moriarty, Rick. 2008. "Syracuse China: Made in China?" *Syracuse.com*, December 10. http://www.syracuse.com/news/index.ssf/2008/12/syracuse_china_to_close.html.

Moriarty, Rick. 2009. "Syracuse China plant clatters to a close today." *Syracuse.com*, April 6. http://www.syracuse.com/news/index.ssf/2009/04/syracuse_china_plant_clatters.html#more.

Morrison, Wayne. 2013. *China's Economic Rise: History, Trends, Challenges, and Implications for the United States*. CRS Report 7-7500. Washington, DC: Congressional Research Service. http://www.fas.org/sgp/crs/row/RL33534.pdf.

Na Lan. 2004. "Jingdezhen: Still China's Porcelain Capital?" *CRI Online*, August 7. http://english.cri.cn/1174/2004-8-7/103@139250.htm.

PRN Newswire. 2013. "Jingdezhen Holds Kiln Reactivation Ceremony for Ming and Qing Dynasty Royal Kilns." *PRN Newswire*, October 30.

Qian Yingyi. 2003. "How Reform Worked in China." *In Search of Prosperity: Analytic Narratives on Economic Growth*, edited by Dani Rodrik, 297–333. Princeton, NJ: Princeton University Press.

Quan Xiaoshu, and Shen Yang. 2009. "Molding Dreams." *China Daily*, October 22. http://www.chinadaily.com.cn/cndy/2009-10/22/content_8829396.htm.

Rankin, Jennifer. 2013. "Ceramics Firms Get Fired Up over Budget Tax Break." *The Guardian*, March 22. http://www.theguardian.com/business/2013/mar/22/ceramics-firms-fired-up-budget-tax-break.

Raynor, Jennifer L. 2007. "Comparative Civilian Labor Force Statistics, 10 Countries." *Monthly Labor Review* 130, no. 12 (December): 32–37. http://www.bls.gov/opub/mlr/2007/12/art4full.pdf.

Rörstrand Museum. n.d. "History." http://rorstrand-museum.se/en/history/.

Strom, Stephanie. 2012. "For Ohio Pottery, A Small Revival." *New York Times*, June 11. http://www.nytimes.com/2012/06/12/business/starbucks-turns-to-ohio-not-china-for-coffee-mugs.html?_r=0.

Walder, Andrew. 1989. "Social Change in Post-Revolution China." *Annual Review of Sociology* 15: 405–424.

Wang Jifu. 2001. "Strategic Challenge, Strategic Responses, and Strategies: Study of Chinese State Owned Enterprises." PhD diss., Auburn University.

Wang Qian. 2011. "From Local Ceramics to High-Tech Goods Exporter." *China Daily*, December 9. http://www.chinadaily.com.cn/cndy/2011-12/09/content_14236875.htm.

Wang Qian. 2012. "Expo Revitalizes Age-Old Ceramics Industry." *China Daily*, August 22. http://usa.chinadaily.com.cn/epaper/2012-08/22/content_15697125.htm.

Wang Zongda, and Yin Chengguo, eds. 1994. *Xiandai Jingdezhen tao ci jing ji shi, 1949-1993 nian* 现代景德镇陶瓷經濟史 [Modern economic history of Jingdezhen, 1949–1993]. Beijing: Zhongguo Shuji Publications.

Wettergren, Eric. 1943. "Swedish Pottery: Rörstrand and Marieberg—I." *Burlington Magazine for Connoisseurs* 83, no. 489: 308–311.

Wettergren, Eric. 1944. "Swedish Pottery: Rörstrand and Marieberg—II." *Burlington Magazine for Connoisseurs* 84, no. 490:16–21.

Woetzel, Jonathan. 2008. "Reassessing China's State-Owned Enterprises." *Forbes*, July 8. http://www.forbes.com/2008/07/08/china-enterprises-state-lead-cx_jrw_0708mckinsey.html.

Xiao Gongduo, and Guo Guo'an. 2008. "Jingdezhen Rising: The Return of a Porcelain Major." *Asian Ceramics* 2: 18–26.

Xinhua News Agency. 2013. "Competition and Protectionism Dim China's Ceramic Industry." *Global Times*, October 5. http://www.globaltimes.cn/content/815645.shtml.

Zhang Yansheng, and Li Longji. 2009. "The Study of Independent Innovation on Foshan Ceramics Industry 'China.'" Paper presented at the International Conference on Management and Service Science. Wuhan: IEEE.

16

Butō: The Birth and Maturation of a New Global Art Form

BRUCE BAIRD

Dance comes from the most elemental part of human existence, from the intersection of bodies and minds. As circumstances and surroundings change, bodies respond and dances change. As people's bodies react to the new conditions in which they live, new kinds of dance may emerge. One such development in dance is butō (also romanized as butoh), which sprang from the turbulence of postwar Japan but astounded the wider performance world with its achingly beautiful and raw performances. Today there are practitioners all over the world, as well as many performers (both in theater and dance) who have been influenced by butō, and this dance form has taken its place among the most important developments in performing arts in the latter half of the 20th century. This case study will trace the growth of butō as it has traveled out of Japan and into world. It will explore how butō has evolved, molded by the geopolitical pressures of contact with other cultures around the world.

The Foundations of Butō: Hijikata Tatsumi

Although it was not called butō until the late 1960s, Hijikata Tatsumi (born Yoneyama Kunio, 1928–1986) is acknowledged as its founder. Hijikata grew up in the countryside, and after World War II he moved to Tokyo, where he studied German Expressionist dance (*ausdruckstanz*, but known to the Japanese as *neue Tanz*), as well as mime, tap, ballet, flamenco, and jazz dance. During the mid-1950s he was increasingly in demand as a dancer, but he shocked the Tokyo dance world with his own choreography in a dance called *Forbidden Colors* (*Kinjiki*, 1959). This dance portrayed an older male having sex with a younger male, and then supervising the young man as he suffocates a chicken. Some of Hijikata's other early dances also loosely told stories using representational movements. For example, *Banzai Woman* (1959) told the story of a mother sending her son to war, and *Bride* (1960) depicted the story of a bride being passed from one family to another as one might hand over a piece of luggage. Although no film remains of these dances, written sources describe them as sharing qualities with the German Expressionist pioneer Kurt Jooss's dance-theater work *The Green Table*, which depicted futile peace negotiations leading to the horrors of war. However, Hijikata soon turned away from this style of dance.

For the next decade, Hijikata surrounded himself with a small group of dancers, artists, and writers. These included artists in the Neo-Dada, Happening, and Fluxus movements, such as Akasegawa Genpei, Nakanishi Natsuyuki, and pop artist Yokoo Tadanori, as well as the surrealist Takiguchi Shūzō. All of these people shared a distaste for both Japanese and Western customs and social constraints, which they assumed were so much a part of us that they controlled our thoughts, feelings, and speech. They supposed that the world was more complex than anyone could imagine, and they searched for a way around conventions and socialization by trying to trigger unconscious processes through the use of randomness or shock.

Within this movement, Hijikata's material was the body, and he led a group of dancers (including Ōno Kazuo, Ōno Yoshito, Kasai Akira, Ishii Mitsutaka, Nakajima Natsu, Takai Tomiko, Maro Akaji, and his partner, Motofuji Akiko) in experimenting with new bodily "languages" and questioning all ideas about dance. Experiments—in such dances as *Three Phases of Leda; Masseur: A Story of a Theater that Sustains Passion; Rose-Colored Dance: To M. Shibusawa's House;* and *Instructional Illustrations for the Study of Divine Favor in Sexual Love: Tomato*— included all of the performers leaving the stage and running a lap around the theater, pretending to throw baseballs across the universe, bicycle riding, photographing the audience, painting the inner anatomy of dancers on their bodies, lighting lanterns, and playing trumpets on stage. Larger themes such as eroticism (including homoeroticism), pain, madness, violence, disease, and the relationship of humans to technology always showed through.

Kasai Akira and Ishii Mitsutaka, *Rose-Colored Dance* (Sennichidani Public Hall, Tokyo, November 1965). (*Photo by Nakatani Tadao, courtesy of Morishita Takashi Butoh Materials, NPO, and the Keio University Arts Center*)

Hijikata and the other dancers initially called their performances "dance experiences," or "terror dance," and then *ankoku buyō* (dark black dance), and even later still *ankoku butō*. *Butō* is the general word for "dance." The word *butō*—composed of two Chinese characters meaning "dance" and "tread/stomp"—usually indicates Western-style dances such as flamenco, ballet, and waltz. So *ankoku butō* means something like the "foreign dance of darkness" where the word *foreign* means "unrelated" or "not belonging," as opposed to the lightness (both metaphorical and literal) of ballet and much modern dance.

Transformation to the Generative Body-Mind

In the late 1960s, Hijikata began a meticulous and comprehensive study of the countless conventions and habits that had shaped and socialized both his body and mind. Through this research, which was at the same time an experiment, he was simultaneously trying to vastly increase the productivity of the body and the mind. His program was based on the idea that he could use elements from his past as material for new dances, and on the assumption that being aware of all the conventions that had molded him would enable him to free himself from unconscious bodily and mental structures. In addition, he assumed that if he could neutralize the conventions, habits, and customs that had been controlling him, he would be more sensitive to the world around him, and thus be able to respond to it in new ways and further generate new movements and ideas.

A dance from this time, *Hijikata Tatsumi and Japanese People: Rebellion of the Body* (1968), shows the scope of his project. This dance was about Hijikata himself,

Hijikata Tatsumi, *Hijikata Tatsumi and Japanese People: Rebellion of the Body* (Nihon Seinenkan, Tokyo, October 1968). (*Photo by Nakatani Tadao, courtesy of Morishita Takashi Butoh Materials, NPO, and the Keio University Arts Center*)

about the ethnicity that shaped him, and about how he might free his body from prior constraints. In this collection of solos, Hijikata danced a bride, an old woman, a male burlesque dancer, a flamenco dancer, a scoliosis patient, a nattily dressed sailor, and a young girl. One interpretation of this dance is that Hijikata was enacting various people from his past, and another interpretation is that he was portraying several aspects of himself that normally were not allowed to come to the surface because of prevailing norms, including those of gender.

The detailed nature of the project translated into a new comprehensive approach to choreography and dance training. Hijikata even dictated the imagery performers should visualize to achieve their performance. He started by studying people and things not usually seen on stage. These included animals, people from lower classes or the periphery of Japan (prostitutes, farmers, diseased people), or even figures in paintings and sculptures. From these, he created poses or dance steps, which he would then alter using imagery prompts. The dancers might be asked to envision a specific person doing the step, so that if a young girl were imagined doing the step, it would be different from if an old woman were imagined doing it. Or Hijikata might require the dancers to imagine differing media in which the step occurred. For example, water would create a drag on the movements that would not appear if the medium was simply air. Hijikata also experimented with modifying the scope of a movement. For example, insisting that dancers imagine the movement filling the air around a dancer, or transferring a movement from one limb to another. Finally, Hijikata would have the dancers imagine many different things in order to transform the underlying pose or step. These might include being eaten by a certain number of bugs, or being shocked by a certain number of volts of electricity, or having imaginary liquid dribble down parts of their bodies.

Hijikata had studied surrealism, and he was likely aware of the famous saying by Comte de Lautréamont (an alias for Isidore-Lucien Ducasse)—"As beautiful as the chance encounter of a sewing machine and an umbrella on an operating table"—which the surrealists took as emblematic of their attempt to find new ways of thinking by putting together dissimilar ideas, images, or objects. In his new dance experiments, he probably wanted to find out what would happen when he combined very different things. Perhaps he thought that people's usual conventions and habits could not control the movement that came from simultaneously imagining these various things. The use of imagery also allowed him to create new movements by modifying any dance step through several imagery exercises. Moreover, when the dancers practiced imaging all these things, they had to observe all the parts of their bodies. They even had to be aware of the spaces around their bodies. As they became better at doing this, they became increasingly able to alter their bodies in minute ways. Moreover, they became progressively more sensitive to the things and people that surrounded their bodies.

When Hijikata choreographed a dance, first he created the steps, which were individually modified with whatever imagery he thought necessary. He then put the steps in sequence with other steps, in order to enact a narrative. However, he did not tell the audience about the story. One sequence, such as the one in *Susamedama* (1972), portrayed a prostitute waiting for an abortion in a bathroom while daydreaming about peeling cabbages. The technique of connecting movements allowed Hijikata to portray a wide range of content, but he generally focused on bodies that were disposed, diseased, senile, mad, or in pain.

The Splintering of Butō

In the late 1960s, the small community involved in Hijikata's dance began to fracture. One of the first people to declare his independence was Ishii Mitsutaka (b. 1939). In 1959 Ishii began studying ballet and modern dance with the Ishii Baku. He then switched to studying avant-garde dance with Hijikata in 1961. He appeared in Hijikata's performances and in two recitals specially choreographed for him by Hijikata: *Butō Genet* in 1967 (based on Shibusawa Tatsuhiko's translation of Jean Genet's *Querelle of Brest*), and *Genetarianne* in 1968. These dances were experimental, like the other performances in the 1960s. *Butō Genet* featured scenes such as Hijikata shaving Ishii's head and drawing blood, which dripped onto a long white barber's cape; spreading rice on the dance floor; impersonating female dolls, and placing a statue of the Victor RCA Nipper dog in the center of the stage and parading around it. In *Genetarianne*, Ishii danced with a fan made from feathers and ate dirt.

In 1969 Ishii gave his first autonomous performance, title *Butō City: Blind Thief Version*. The stage was set in the middle of the spectators. A man crawled out from under a huge pile of weeds, which were attached to his waist like hair. Then Ishii appeared as a girdled grim-reaper wielding a giant sickle. He cut the man free from his weed-hair, mounted the stage, and danced wildly. In another scene, an elderly woman played the samisen while Ishii danced solemnly. In yet another scene, Ishii used a grinder to send sparks from a Mongolian barbecue pot that a dancer wore as a hat. In 1970 Ishii and two collaborators staged a performance in a Tokyo gymnasium. They used a slingshot to repeatedly smack a suspended 50 kilogram bag of flour so that flour billowed everywhere. They rolled around in the clouds of flour and ran about glaring menacingly. Then, thoroughly covered with flour, they jumped into a tub of water to make the flour gooey on their skin. At this time, Ishii dressed in drag and wore his hair in modern women's styles. He also started an artists' commune. There were rumors that the group used graveyards for rehearsal space and ate ceremonial food offerings from gravestones.

In 1971, Ishii moved to Europe. He was first based in Paris, then Amsterdam, and finally in Germany beginning in 1975. He traveled the continent and the Middle East performing and teaching dance classes. His activities in Europe are not well recorded, but a visitor gave a report about a 1975 performance in Worpswede, Germany, writing that, "without exception, the Germans were impressed by his bodily art that speaks to us from the fundamental level of gentleness and violence of a soul living directly in nature and the universe" (Harada 2004, 141). Based on this description, the performance must have contained a similar mixture of wild and serene moments that characterized his previous dances. However, the focus on Ishii responding to nature and the cosmos makes it sound as though Ishii's dances were changing. In 1977 Ishii started the series *MU-dance*. The title referred to the fictional continent of Mu, but with a likely allusion to the Buddhist concept of *mu* (nothingness or formlessness). The possible appearance of a Buddhist term is strange considering the nature of Ishii's dances in Japan. But it turns out that in Europe at the time, no one knew the word or genre *butō*, so at some point he took to advertising his performance as a "pantomime portraying a being imbued with Eastern philosophy and Buddhist sutras" (Harada 2004, 132). Additionally, a character modeled after him in a contemporary Japanese novel complains, "If I don't call [my performance] something like 'The Miracle of the Buddha'. . ., I cannot stimulate the deep psychology of people who come to the theater for the usual fare" (Harada 2004, 140). Statements like this make it seem that Ishii's dance transformed over time in response to the expectations of his European audience. In 1979 Ishii returned to Japan, where he became known for structured improvisations in performance and unstructured improvisations in natural environments such as forests, fields, and streams. He also experimented with a butō version of therapy at a mental health institution. Both the use of improvisation and experiments with butō dance therapy were likely related to a deeper understanding of dance as self-expression.

Another early performer was Kasai Akira (b. 1943). He studied mime with Jean Nouveau (stage name of Ōta Junzō), classical ballet with Chiba Akinori, and modern dance with Eguchi Takaya and Miya Soko. In 1963, he began to study with Ōno Kazuo. Sometime in 1963 he held a recital of a piece called *Sacrificial Ceremony*, which included a solo danced in a glass box into which 5,000 yellow chicks were dropped from the fly loft. The chicks fluttered down chirping, reflecting the light, and gradually filled the box. Kasai kept on dancing, crushing some of them, which caused an outcry (and caught Hijikata's attention). Kasai appeared in several of Hijikata's dances through 1966. He then parted company with Hijikata and began to stage his own recitals. In 1971 he formed a studio/company named Tenshikan (Angel hall) as a center for nonhierarchical anarchic bodily experimentation. In 1979, he closed Tenshikan, and traveled to Stuttgart, Germany, to study the eurythmy and anthroposophy of Rudolf Steiner.

There are 70 branches worldwide of the General Anthroposophical Society founded by Rudolf Steiner, including the Anthroposophical Society of America (http://www.anthroposophy.org/).

The Eurythmy Association of North America (http://www.eana.org) explains that "eurythmy brings the essence of music and language to visible manifestation. We not only hear the words and music but they become visible to our eyes. Through deliberate, sculptured gestures sounds take physical form. . . . It is true sounding or singing through the body as an instrument."

Kasai Akira, *Tannhäuser* (Kōseinenkin kaikan, Tokyo, June 1969). (*Photo by Nakatani Tadao, courtesy of Morishita Takashi Butoh Materials, NPO, and the Keio University Arts Center*)

After graduation from the Eurythmeum in Stuttgart in 1983, Kasai joined a eurythmy stage group for two years. He then returned to Japan, where he taught eurythmy and anthroposophy and presented airy, flowing, and colorful eurythmy-based performances. He resumed butō activities in 1994 with a performance of *Séraphîta: My Girl with the Mirror Genitalia*. The title was taken from Balzac's novel about an androgyne beloved by both a man and a woman. The dance depicted black-clad Yamada Setsuko and Sugita Josaku bringing ethereally white-clad androgynous Kasai out of a mirrored coffin at the back of the stage. Meanwhile, two other young girls in ballet tutus danced around, seemingly unaware of the three. In the second half, Kasai came into physical contact with Yamada Setsuko and suddenly came down to earth, where he danced both humorously and violently, pulling faces and sidling up to the girls. This dance demonstrates a typical butō concern for mixing disparate elements together. In time, Kasai also introduced hip-hop and kabuki dance into his butō dances (such as the dance *Pollen Revolution*, in 2001).

In his dance and training exercises, Kasai has dancers enunciate sounds or move in tune with music or poetry. The dancers try to feel the reverberations of the sounds through the body and allow the sounds to dictate movement. He also practices fine-tuning his perception of the body to be aware of the different responses of the body to different outer stimuli. It is difficult to assess Kasai's motivation for leaving the world of butō for 15 years and studying eurythmy. However, a focus on the connection between words, sounds, and bodily movements has remained in his butō practice. Over time, Kasai has promoted an understanding of dance and butō as striving for a kind of atheistic mysticism that incorporates the body, language, music, community, and history into one unified whole.

The very fact that he wanted to study eurythmy and anthroposophy may indicate that the experiences of the founders of butō in studying with German Expressionist–trained dancers fundamentally shaped the origins of butō and continue to guide it today. Of course, butō and German expressionism differ significantly, but they share many core concerns, such as a focus on individual experience and its expression, and an attempt to find or create a universal bodily vocabulary. The similarities between butō and German Expressionist dance likely dictated the direction many butō performers would take and specifically lead Kasai out into the world to seek out other parallel sources for the task of articulating individual expression in both verbal and bodily ways.

Butō Gains a Foothold in Europe and Beyond

The artist who has been single-handedly most responsible for the worldwide longevity of butō is undoubtedly Maro Akaji (b. 1943). Maro had studied with Hijikata from 1964 to 1971 and also performed in the Situation Theater of Kara Juro (b. 1940). He brought to butō an even greater sense of theatrics than any of his predecessors, and he became known for the use of complex stage devices and props. In 1972 he established the troupe Dairakudakan (translated as Great camel battle ship). Early dances such as *Myth of the Phallus* (1973) and *The Emperor's Testicles* (1974) show antisocial themes typical of the style. They can be seen to mock, respectively, male-dominated society and the Japanese imperial system.

Maro Akaji, *Ivory Order* (Suzuran Minami-za, Nagoya, May 1977). (*Photo by Miyauchi Fumio, courtesy of Miyauchi Fumio and Dairakudakan*)

For more insight into the work of Maro Akaji, read the Artist Interview on the Performing Arts Network Japan website (http://performingarts.jp/E/art_interview/0506/1.html).

As important as Maro's style is for the history of butō, his ability to nurture new performers has also been important. Maro has expressed the philosophy of "One Person, One Troupe." From 1974 onward, one by one, performers left Dairakudakan and started their own companies. In 1974 Furukawa Anzu (1952–2001) and Tamura Tetsurō (1950–1991) started Dance Love Machine, and Carlotta Ikeda (Ikeda Sanae, b. 1941) started Ariadone Dance Company. In 1975 Murobushi Ko (b. 1947) established Butō-ha Sebi (Butō-faction back-fire), and Amagatsu Ushio (b. 1949) founded Sankai Juku (Mountain-ocean school). In 1976 Ōsuka Isamu (b. 1943) created Byakkosha (White tiger company).

These companies spread out over Japan, and then to Europe and around the world. After Ishii's various activities across Europe, in January 1978, Carlotta Ikeda and Murobushi Kō presented the first recorded butō performance in Europe, a dance called *Last Eden—Gate of the Beyond*. This performance touched off a frenzy of interest in butō and was extended for a month. A reviewer for the French weekly news magazine *L'Express* called the dance "a disturbing plunge into the metamorphoses and questionings of the human body, going to the very roots of anguish," and noted that nothing like it had ever been seen before (*L'Express*, 22). In October 1978 Hijikata presented *Twelve Phases of the Terpsichore of Darkness: Fourteen Nights for the Louvre Palace*. This dance was choreographed for Hijikata's principle danseuse, Ashikawa, and sponsored by the Festival d'Automne in connection with the MA: Space-Time of Japan exhibition at the Museum of Decorative Arts, which featured sections on classical Japanese aesthetics and was accompanied by various kinds of classical and contemporary Japanese performance. The Parisian audience was so astounded by what they saw that they demanded repeat performances up to five times a day. Also at the *MA* exhibition, an outsider to the butō community, Tanaka Min, performed. He was later to collaborate with Hijikata and become known for a time as part of the butō community. Soon, several dancers relocated to Europe (Murobushi and Ikeda in 1979, Amagatsu in 1980, and Furukawa Anzu to Berlin in 1989), and the European butō boom swung into gear. For dancers who were used to presenting roughly one show a year (and paying for the theater), the interested producers, packed crowds, dancers eager to take lessons and workshops were a dream come true.

The artist who had the most success in Europe was Amagatsu Ushio. He trained in ballet and modern dance before joining in the cofounding of Dairakudakan. He broke out on his own in 1975. He toured Europe with Sankai Juku in 1980, and then in 1981 he relocated to Paris. Sankai Juku became one anchor in the butō rage. Between 1981 and 2013, Amagatsu premiered new works on an biannual basis at the Theatre de la Ville Paris, which has also acted as a coproducer for the shows. On the alternate years, the troupe tours the outlying French provinces and also tours extensively through the rest of Europe, North and South America, and Asia. Sankai Juku has become internationally famous for lyrical and achingly beautiful shows, enacted with supreme control and touched with a tinge of the grotesque.

Ōno Kazuo, Embodiment of the World of Butō

Undoubtedly, the person who became the most famous in the history of butō, and an iconic expression of its global roots and reach, was Hijikata's long-time collaborator Ōno Kazuo (1906-2010). In 1929 Ōno saw the Spanish folk and neoclassical dancer Antonia Mercé y Luque (La Argentina) perform. In the 1930s he took dance lessons from three of the Japanese pioneers of German Expressionism, Ishii Baku, Eguchi Takaya, and Miya Sōko, the latter two both pupils of Mary Wigman, a leader of German expressionist dance. He also saw Harald Kreutzberg perform. After graduation from Japan Athletic College, Ono became a physical education teacher (and subsequently a janitor) at the Catholic High School in Yokohama, and converted to Christianity. In 1938, World War II called him away from dance for nine years. He was initially a supply soldier, and later he became a war prisoner in New Guinea. Upon his return to Japan in 1947 he resumed his dance career. He debuted with the Ando Mitsuko Dance Company, after which he appeared in a series of solo recitals (three of which contained a dance entitled *Tango*). He caught Hijikata's attention, and danced for him from 1960 to 1968. He then turned his attention to acting in a series of experimental movies by Nagano Chiaki, such as *The Portrait of Mr. O*.

In 1977 Ōno returned to the stage at the age of 71 in a solo piece titled *Admiring La Argentina*. The dance was a retrospective of his own life, and also a homage to the dancer he had seen 47 years before. The first two scenes were taken from Hijikata's 1960 revised version of *Forbidden Colors*. They showed the aged male prostitute Divine (in a ratty shawl and soiled dress) from Jean Genet's *Our Lady of the Flowers*. Ōno appears to have been expressing the painful life of the poor male prostitute. At one point he hung, almost as if impaled, on the back wall, with his arms and head hanging down. Then, perhaps miming the tuberculin Divine retching into a toilet, Ōno knelt and died. In the scene "Daily Bread," Ōno, naked save for a pair of black trunks, engaged in daily activities such as stretching his neck and cleaning. The "Marriage of Heaven and Hell" featured Ōno leaning against a grand piano, mouth agape and looking up, with his arms splayed out to the sides, as if the hard years pressed on him and threatened to squeeze out any remaining life. The second half was the homage to Mercé, in which Ōno danced impressionistically flamenco/ tango movements to tango music. In the final section Ōno appeared in a yellow dress to the accompaniment of Maria Callas singing Puccini. The section consisted of off-balance tiptoeing in rightward arcs, menacing attacks, kneeling and miming drinking, and covering his mouth and bending over in grief. Ōno reappeared for a curtain call without the hat and looking very frumpy. Finally, after a second curtain call and still in the dowdy dress, he raised his hand in military salute to end the dance.

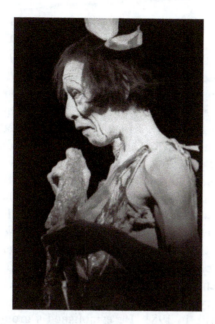

Ōno Kazuo, *Admiring La Argentina* (Dai-ichi Seimei Hall, Tokyo, November 1977). (*Photo by Nakatani Tadao, courtesy of Morishita Takashi Butoh Materials, NPO, and the Keio University Arts Center*)

The 1977 version of *Admiring La Argentina* was not yet epoch-making in the history of butō. It needed to detour through France in order to become historically significant. Capitalizing on the recent success of butō performers, in 1980 Ono was invited to the Nancy International Theatre Festival, in Nancy, France. He also performed in London, Paris and Stockholm. As with other butō artists, in time Ōno danced to packed houses all over Europe, the Americas, and Japan. Over the first 30 years of his career, Ōno had performed approximately 25 times, but during the next two decades he performed about 125 times. However, Europe was changing Ōno's dances as well. The original performance of *Admiring La Argentina* had been rather heavy and contained specific hints about Ōno's life, such as janitorial duties, stretching exercises, and wartime experiences (along with a depiction of a dying prostitute and the homage to Mercé). Over time, however, the dance (and his dances in general) became more abstract, much lighter in tone, and more sacral, humorous, and campy. One reviewer referred to him as a "glittering old hag" (Dunning), and it is hard to escape the impression that there was something quite powerful but unchallenging in his later dances. There was a gap in the European understanding of Ōno as well, because although he also did some site-specific improvisations, in general he kept careful notations of his work for performances, and he used Hijikata's late-era imagery work to create and reproduce movements. Publicly, however, he talked and wrote about dance is if it stemmed from deep inner urges, which led many people to assume that his dances were strictly improvisational self-expression.

These dancers were joined by relative outsiders such as Tanaka Min (b. 1945). Tanaka was a basketball player, and he trained from 1963 to 1973 in classic ballet and modern dance at the Hiraoka Shiga Dance Academy. In 1973 he began his own dance experimentation. Early dances were usually entitled *Subject* (sometimes with a subtitle) or *Butai* (Dance state). They almost invariably featured Tanaka dancing naked (often to a soundscape provided by Noguchi Minoru). In one early version of *Subject* (June 22, 1974), Tanaka seated his naked wife and child on the lawn outside OAG Hall in Tokyo. There he did things such as lie on his back on the lawn, or jump into the air over and over and pull his knees to his chest and then shift his weight to send himself toppling back to the earth on his side. Inside the hall, he crawled on the ground—seeming to examine the tiles on the floor—or crouched on half-point with his elbows and hands tucked close to his chest, but his face turned sideways to look up. Another dance, *Subject: Dead* (October 4–5, 1974), featured Tanaka dancing on wires strung in the performance space. Each dance was intended to be site specific, and Tanaka performed like this all over Japan. Sometimes he danced as many as five times a day. In 1978 he established Body Weather Laboratory, where he conducted workshops to explore the body as one part of a wider world. In 1981, He established a group named Maijuku as a compliment to his solo work.

In 1983 Tanaka joined forces with Hijikata for the *Hook Off 88: One Ton of Hairstyles for the Scenery*. Again in 1984, Hijikata choreographed Tanaka in the *Performance for the Establishment of the Pure Love Butō School*. In both of these performances, Hijikata gave Tanaka an extensive number of images to realize. However, Tanaka came to feel that the 'butō' label was paradoxically being used to limit the

Tanaka Min, date and location unknown. (*Photo by Nakatani Tadao, courtesy of Morishita Takashi Butoh Materials, NPO, and the Keio University Arts Center*)

possibilities of bodily experimentation. So, after being known internationally as a butō performer for several years, Tanaka repudiated the term. After his association with Hijikata, Tanaka took up farming as a way of invigorating his performance. He has broken new ground in understanding the nature of improvisation, collaboration (often with artists from the free jazz or free improvisation movement), and the relationship between bodies, spaces, and other bodies. And he has continued to work toward minute discernment and control of all parts of the body. In many respects, Tanaka can be considered an early proponent of postmodern dance as it would be defined in America in the works of the Judson Dance Theater, such as the use of slow and pedestrian movements and the exploration of everyday spaces as theatrical venues, and he worked directly with Anna Halprin and danced for Elaine Summers.

Global Influences

By the turn of the century, butō had blossomed worldwide, but it should be clear that as the dance form expanded, it was also changing as the various artists encountered Europe and the Americas. In part, this happened because the dancers (such as Kasai with Eurythmy, and Tanaka with Judson Dance Theater) specifically reached out to their counterparts in Europe and America to share ideas and learn things, thereby bringing themselves into dialogue with other currents of dance. In part, contact with Europe may have cultivated the aspects of butō already present in its roots in German Expressionist dance. The changes in butō may also have happened as Japanese artists conformed to Western expectations of what an art from Japan should look like.

The transformations in butō were possibly linked to misunderstandings about butō itself. Indeed, artists with different aims and methods all called their work butō. The artists can be categorized on three different continua. One ranges from improvisation to minute choreography (including choreographing what a dancer should think about while performing). Another ranges from pure personally meaningful emotional expressivity to theatrical spectacle or politically engaged narrative content. A third stretches from seeing movements as inextricably connected to emotional content and meaning to employing arbitrary movements to express underlying themes.

However, for much of butō's short history, not all these continua were equally visible in Europe and America. Many viewers, dancers, and dance critics knew butō mainly through the activities of Ōno, Amagatsu Ushio, and relative outsiders who did not call their work butō (or called it butō for some period of time, but then repudiated the term), such as Tanaka. However, Ōno always maintained that he did not have anything to teach others, because they should discover their own dance inside themselves. Amagatsu seldom talked about the techniques of his highly structured imaged-based choreography, and instead spoke of his dance as a dialogue between universals and particulars. So much of the detail about the actual techniques used in the performances, and particularly the use of the body and mind in Hijikata's branch, was missing in the discourse surrounding butō. A great number of people thought that butō was only concerned with improvisation and was a direct response to the atomic bomb, rather than seeing it as a product of an urban-inflected international avant-garde. So not only did Europe change butō, but the current European under-standing of butō also provides a filter that colors any attempt to understand butō more completely. Moreover, this misunderstanding may have acted as a feedback loop that exacerbated the problem of the pressure to conform to Western expectations, as art-ists felt some pressure to conform not just to what a Japanese art should look like, but also to what their audiences already knew (or thought they knew) about butō.

Despite the differences in the various branches of butō, there are some similarities that allow them to be coherently categorized together. These include attention to and receptivity of detail, fragmentation and precise control of the body, and a continued predilection for shocking images. Many performers share an emphasis on increasing the powers of concentration and focus (and spreading them ever wider—whether to account for something within the body or in the space surrounding the body). Considering these similarities as a whole, butō reflected and anticipated Japanese (and global) attitudes toward the body-mind.

To see a six-part online documentary by Edin Velez about butō, go to the website Dailymotion (www.dailymotion.com) and search for "Butoh Dance of Darkness Edin Velez."

A brief history of the recent Japanese philosophies of the body-mind starts with World War II. During the war, the militaristic government of Japan demanded that the Japanese populace suppress the needs and desires of their own bodies in the name of the emperor and what was called the "national body" (kokutai). After the war, Japanese people suddenly felt free to satisfy the desires of their own bodies. This was memorably manifest in the decadent and carnal literature of Sakaguchi Angō and Tamura Taijirō. The open eroticism of butō is certainly related to these larger social movements. The many references to sport and athletics in butō have parallels in the 1950s' "Sun Tribe" novels and cinema (celebrations of the youthful suntanned body sailing, waterskiing, and boxing). There were also athletic booms occasioned by the 1964 Tokyo Olympics. In the late 1960s and 1970s, Japanese society shifted into a high-growth economic era. The foundation of this era was the concept of flexibility in physical and mental production, reflected in the economic realm in "Toyotaism" or just-in-time production. Similarly, the butō-sphere artists (each in his or her own way) were striving for a body and mind that are physically and mentally as flexible and sensitive as possible.

Moreover, butō's body-mind experiments can be understood as prefiguring the robotic or cyborg body of Japanese pop culture in the 1980s and 1990s. The body and brain prosthetics of a cyborg enable it to be stronger and faster than normal humans. But the cyborg also has access to all the databases and information of the Internet, which it can process at lightning speed. So the cyborg is more aware than normal humans. Of course, butō artists were not really cyborgs. But they were training their body-minds to tolerate more tension, to be more twisted and contorted, and to be more out of balance than those of normal people. And they were expanding the scope of their concentration further and further and seeking to be increasingly sensitive to stimuli. Thus Japanese scholars such as Kuniyoshi Kazuko and Takeda Ken'ichi have fruitfully characterized butō as a dance appropriate to the increasingly globalized information age (Kuniyoshi 1989, 81; Takeda 1985, 106–108).

Butō Today

Butō has grown so large that it would be impossible to include here everyone who now uses this idiom. Focusing on select contemporary performers can give a taste of what butō has become as people have continued to bend and use it in new ways. The Swedish performer SU-EN (Susanna Akerlund) studied with Hijikata's principle danseuse, Ashikawa Yoko, from 1988, and learned improvisation techniques from the guitarist-turned-butō dancer Tomoe Shizune. In 1994 SU-EN moved to Sweden, and created SU-EN Butoh Company. She operates from the double assumption that the practice of butō should properly be an investigation into what it means to be a human being, but also that nature preceded human life, so that the environment shapes the organizations that people create in it. Thus an examination of the environment is at the same time an examination of oneself. After leaving Japan, SU-EN primarily forsook the worlds of theater and dance, and instead participated in the worlds of performance art, action art, sound art, and visual art. In the 2010s her works feature multimedia collaborations often performed to live experimental improvisational

Yoshioka Yumiko, i-ki: an Interactive Body Dance Machine, Schloss Broellin, Germany. *(Courtesy of Klaus Rabien and the artist.)*

music, with some structured improvisational solos and sections within larger carefully choreographed works. Her stages are strewn or framed with lots of organic matter (dried grasses, stones, or close-ups of maggots in the multimedia behind the dancers), and also lots of scraps and junk that are the residue of civilization.

Yoshioka Yumiko (who used the stage name Hanaoka Mizelle for a period of time) danced for Murobushi Ko and Carlotta Ikeda in 1978 in some of the first butō performances in France, and she continued to dance with Ikeda through 1981. Then she spent several years as a full-time burlesque dancer, before moving to Berlin in 1988 and joining forces with another Maro-lineage dancer, Minako Seki, in Tatoeba Theatre Danse Grotesque. There they focused on creating dance out of everyday movements, which they deformed slightly, and they also explored improvisation. In 1995, she founded TEN PEN CHii art labor with the visual artist Joachim Manger. The title TEN PEN CHii is a romanization of the term for "natural disaster," but it literally means "heaven moves, earth changes." Yoshioka intends it to indicate the interconnectedness of the environment with society and culture, so when they change, the earth necessarily changes also. Yoshioka and Manger have explored the relationship between dance and installation art, as well as the interactions between bodies and technology, in pieces featuring dancers caught up in complex machinery. Her choreography is a mix of structured improvisation and minutely crafted dances using imagery work. She also does valuable production work at Schloss Broellin in northeastern Germany, bringing together butō dancers for collaborations with each other and with other non-butō artists. As well, she maintains a grueling schedule teaching workshops worldwide. She thus contributes in three ways to expanding the future possibilities of butō: through her own dances, through her work producing shows and bringing other artists together to experiment with new directions in butō and dance, and through educating others around the world.

The activities of these two third-generation dancers demonstrate that butō has reached a stable place within the world's art forms. Some artists claim that they practice butō and call themselves butō dancers, while others study it for a time as one item in a smorgasbord of dance techniques, but do not self-identify as either butō artists or as doing butō. Even among those who do claim to belong within the butō circle, there are various approaches grounded in the different ideas of the early dancers. Perhaps the different directions that artists have taken with butō's idioms or themes paradoxically ensure the continued vitality of the dance form. They also demonstrate that it has gone beyond its roots in Japan and can address the needs of people in the globalizing world.

References and Further Research

Baird, Bruce. 2011. "Embraced by the (Spot) Light: Ōno Kazuo and the Postmodernism of Butō and *Admiring La Argentina*." In *Postmodernism: Style and Subversion, 1970-1990*, edited by Glenn Adamson and Jane Pavitt, 208–211. London: Victoria and Albert Museum.
———. 2012. *Hijikata Tatsumi and Butoh: Dancing in a Pool of Gray Grits*. New York: Palgrave Macmillan.

Candelario, Rosemary. 2012. "Eiko & Koma: Choreographing Spaces Apart in Asian America." PhD diss., UCLA.

Dunning, Jennifer. "The Dance: Kazuo Ohno." *New York Times*, July 31, 1981.

Fraleigh, Sondra Horton. 2010. *Butoh: Metamorphic Dance and Global Alchemy*. Urbana: University of Illinois Press.

Fraleigh, Sondra Horton, and Tamah Nakamura. 2006. *Hijikata Tatsumi and Ohno Kazuo*. New York: Routledge.

Harada, Hiromi. 2004. *Butō Taizen: Ankoku to Hikari no ōkoku*. Tokyo: Gendai Shokan.

Hijikata Tatsumi. 2004. "From Being Jealous of a Dog's Vein." Translated by Elena Polzer. MA diss., Humboldt University of Berlin.

Hoffman, Ethan, and Mark Holborn. 1987. *Butoh: Dance of the Dark Soul*. New York: Aperture.

Iwana Masaki. 2002. *The Intensity of Nothingness: The Dance and Thought of Masaki Iwana*. Réveillon, France: Iwana Masaki and La Maison du Butoh Blanc.

Kuniyoshi Kazuko. 1989. "Shômetsu suru kôzô: Butôka no rôgo no tame ni" [Perishing structure: In order that a dancer can grow old]. *Kikan shichō* 4 (April 1989): 81.

Kurihara, Nanako. 1996. "The Most Remote Thing in the Universe: A Critical Analysis of Hijikata Tatsumi's Butoh Dance." PhD diss., New York University.

———. 2000 "Hijikata Tatsumi: The Words of Butoh." *TDR: The Drama Review* 44.1 (Spring): 10–28.

L'Express Magazine, Agenda: Danse (Feb. 6-12, 1978): 22.

Mikami Kayo. 1993. *Utsuwa toshite no Shintai: Ankoku butō gihō e no apurōchi* [Body as receptacle: An approach to the techniques of ankoku butō]. Tokyo: ANZ-Do.

Morishita Takashi, ed. 2004. *Hijikata Tatsumi no butō: Nikutai no shururearisumu, shintai no ontorojī* [Tatsumi Hijikata's butō: Surrealism of the flesh, ontology of the "body"]. Tokyo: Okamoto Museum of Art, and Keio University Research Center for the Arts and Arts Administration. Includes a DVD with clips of Hijikata's *Hijikata Tatsumi and Japanese People: Rebellion of the Body* (1968) and *Story of Smallpox* (1972).

Nakamura, Tamah. 2007. "Beyond Performance in Japanese Butoh Dance: Embodying Re-creation of Self and Social Identities." PhD diss., Felding Graduate University.

Ohno Kazuo, and Ohno Yoshito. 2004. *Kazuo Ohno's World: From Without and Within*. Introduction by Mizohata Toshio. Translated by John Barrett. Middletown, CT: Wesleyan University Press.

Pages, Sylviane. 2009. "La réception des butō(s) en France: Représentations, Malentendus, et Désirs." PhD diss., Université Paris 8.

Rothfuss, Joan, ed. 2011. *Eiko and Koma: Time Is Not Even, Space Is Not Empty*. Minneapolis, MN: Walker Art Center.

Sas, Miryam. 2011. *Experimental Arts in Postwar Japan: Moments of Encounter, Engagement, and Imagined Return*. Cambridge, MA: Harvard University Asia Center.

———. 1999. *Fault Lines: Cultural Memory and Japanese Surrealism*. Stanford, CA: Stanford University Press.

Schwellinger, Lucia. 1998. *Die Entstehung des Butoh: Voraussetzungen und Techniken der Bewegungsgestaltung bei Hijikata Tatsumi und Ono Kazuo*. Munich: Iudicium.

Takeda Ken'ichi. 1985. "Yôzumi to natta nikutai to shintai no rika" [The flesh that has lost its usefulness and the parting song of the body]. *Gendaishi Techô* 28, no. 6 (May): 106–108.

Uno Kuniichi. 2012. *The Genesis of an Unknown Body*. Translated by Melissa McMahon. Sao Paolo: N-1 Publications.

Viala, Jean, and Nourit Masson-Sekine. 1988. *Butoh: Shades of Darkness*. Tokyo: Shufunotomo.

Waguri Yukio, ed. 2005. *Butoh kaden*. DVD-ROM and booklet. Tokyo: Nousite.

Wurmli, Kurt. 2008. "The Power of Image: Hijikata Tatsumi's Scrapbooks and the Art of Butoh." PhD diss., University of Hawai'i at Manoa.

Films

Beauty and Strength. 2000. Directed by Ōno Kazuo. DVD. Tokyo: NHK Software, 2000.
Butoh: Body on the Edge of Crisis. 2006. Directed by Michael Blackwood. DVD. New York: Michael Blackwood Productions.
Butoh: Piercing the Mask. 1991. Directed by Richard Moore. DVD. New York: Incite Media.
Cine Dance: The Butoh of Tatsumi Hijikata: Anma (The Masseurs) + Rose Color Dance. 2005. Directed by Iimura Takahiko. DVD. Tokyo: Takahiko Iimura Media Art Institute.
Goten, Sora wo Tobu. 2007. Directed by Ōno Kazuo. DVD. Tokyo: Quest.
Oh Kind God. 2002. Directed by Ōno Kazuo. DVD. Canta Ltd.
Summer Storm. 2010. Directed by Hijikata Tatsumi. DVD. San Francisco: Microcinema.

Online Video Sources

Ashikawa Yoko (performance). http://www.youtube.com/watch?v=Lb7nSr8BnGs&feature=relmfu.
Carlotta Ikeda (performance). http://www.youtube.com/watch?v=opaS-W7b6GI&list=PL9A932CB0C 1499FEE&index=26&feature=plpp_video.
Dance of Darkness:A Documentary on Butoh (online documentary in six parts). Directed by Edin Velez. http://www.dailymotion.com/video/x9cj0v_dance-of-darkness-a-documentary-on_creation.
Histoire du Butoh (French documentary). Directed by Jean Monnet. http://34francar.free.fr/histbutoh.html.
Japan Society YouTube Channel (features clips from past performances by contemporary butoh performers). http://www.youtube.com/user/JapanSocietyNYC/videos?query=butoh.
Kazuo Ohno Dance Studio YouTube Channel. http://www.youtube.com/user/kazuoohnodancestudio/videos?sort=p&view=0.
Nakajima Natsu (performance). http://www.youtube.com/watch?v=aKj6uxm_EH4&feature=related
Sankai Juku YouTube Channel. http://www.youtube.com/user/sankaijukumedia.

17

China's One-Child Policy and the Empowerment of Urban Daughters

Vanessa L. Fong

In 1998, when I first started tutoring Ding Na, the daughter of two factory workers in Dalian City, China, I thought her father's attitude exemplified the parental bias against daughters portrayed in many studies of Chinese family life. Although studious and well behaved, Ding Na was often criticized by her father, who liked to remind her that he had always wanted a son. He worried that she might not score high enough to get into a good four-year college, even though she usually ranked in the top 20 percent of her high school class on practice exams. "What will you do if you don't get into a good college?" he lamented. "If you were a boy, you could study abroad while supporting yourself as a laborer, but what can a girl do abroad besides sit around waiting for remittances I can't afford?" Her mother praised her for being more willing to help with chores than most other teenagers, but whenever Ding Na had trouble helping her father carry groceries or move furniture, he snapped, "Girls are so useless. A boy would have no trouble with this."

When Ding Na's college entrance exam scores were released, however, I began to see the relationship between Ding Na and her father in a different light. I stayed up with Ding Na and her parents well past our bedtimes as we waited for her scores to become available through an automated phone hotline at midnight. After her call finally went through, she wrote down her subject scores, checking and rechecking her arithmetic, her eyes wide. "Are you sure you heard correctly?" her mother asked. Ding Na was sure. She had scored higher than she had ever scored on a practice exam in high school, and well above the likely cutoff for her top-choice four-year college. She shouted with joy as we congratulated her. Her father beamed at her with tears in his eyes and said, "I was wrong to have wanted a son. A daughter like you is worth ten sons."

The experiences of girls like Ding Na are quite different from those of daughters who grew up in the patrilineal, patrilocal, and patriarchal world described in classic studies of gender in Chinese societies. The devastating effect of gender norms on daughters of that world is evident in the life stories of women born prior to the 1950s,

Note: This chapter is adapted from and reproduced by permission of the American Anthropological Association from *American Anthropologist*, Volume 104, Issue 4, December 2002, pages 1098–1109. Not for sale or further reproduction.

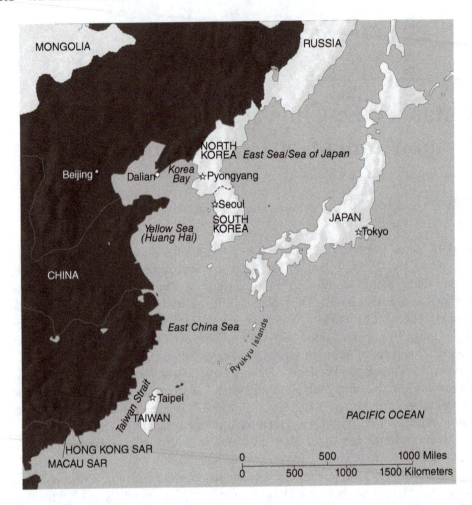

and to a lesser extent in those of women born in the 1950s and 1960s. Girls born after China's one-child policy began in 1979, however, have more power to challenge detrimental gender norms and take advantage of helpful ones than ever before, thanks to the decline of patriliny and the absence of brothers for their parents to favor.

A Note on Gender Norms

The degree to which any given gender norm is detrimental or helpful depends on the characteristics of the individual. The norm associating women with gentleness, for instance, might help a vocational high school graduate win a secretarial job and avoid the unemployment that plagues her male counterparts, but it could also prevent a female college graduate from obtaining a managerial position (since managers are not supposed to be gentle).

China's one-child policy is described in a narrated slideshow, "China: 1-Child Policy," produced by American Public Media's program *Marketplace* (http://www.marketplace.org/topics/world/china-1-child-policy).

Urban daughters born under China's one-child policy have benefited from the demographic patterns produced by that policy. A comparison of the experiences of Chinese daughters born in the 1980s with the experiences of their mothers and grandmothers suggests that singleton (only-child) daughters have unprecedented power to deal with gender norms in ways that benefit them. Although low fertility has been a key factor in the empowerment of urban Chinese daughters, it is not the only necessary and sufficient factor. Low fertility can empower daughters in areas where opportunities for employment and education are already available to women, and such opportunities are less likely to be available in rural areas of China than in urban areas. In cities like Dalian, however, it is clear that daughters would have been less able to take advantage of available opportunities if they had to compete with brothers for family resources, or if their mothers had not demonstrated that women can support their parents in old age.

Important Concepts

- Fertility transition: The transition from high to low fertility experienced by all developed countries and many developing countries after effective birth control technologies became widely available in the twentieth century.
- Filial duty: A child's lifelong duty to maintain social and emotional bonds to parents and, when necessary, to provide financial support and nursing care, to parents.
- Hypergamous marriage: The tendency for women to marry men of higher socioeconomic status their own.
- Patrilineal: Describing a kinship system in which wealth, investment, loyalties, and ritual continuity are passed from fathers to sons to grandsons in a lineage, while daughters are lost to their parents' lineage upon marriage when they join their husband's lineage.
- Patrilocal vs. neolocal: A patrilocal system is one in which men are supposed to continue living in their fathers' households after marriage, while women are supposed to leave their parents' households to join their husbands' fathers' households upon marriage. In a neolocal system, however, both men and women are supposed to leave their parents' household upon marriage and establish new households consisting only of the husband, wife, and any children the couple has.

Theoretical Considerations

Studies of developed and developing societies worldwide have documented a high correlation between low fertility and women's empowerment. Although these studies have focused on low fertility as both a cause and effect of mothers' empowerment, my findings suggest that more attention should be paid to how low fertility affects daughters. The effects of China's one-child policy on mothers are equivocal. On the one hand, it has freed mothers from heavy childbearing and child-rearing burdens; on the other hand, it has deprived mothers of the freedom to choose their family size and subjected them to state surveillance and enforcement tactics. The policy's effects on urban daughters, however, have been largely beneficial.

Low resistance to the one-child policy in cities like Dalian can be attributed to the rapid pace with which people in such cities have internalized the same cultural model of modernization that has caused fertility decline in many societies worldwide. A society's fertility rate usually correlates with the degree to which it has adopted a modern economy in which child mortality is low, most people live in urban environments where children consume a lot more than they produce, most mothers as well as fathers work at jobs incompatible with child rearing, and extensive education is widespread for both genders and seen as the road to socioeconomic success. All of these factors are likely to be both causes and effects of low fertility.

Parents are likely to want few children in a modern economy, where children cannot contribute much to family income, even though they require a lot of time and money to raise and educate. Daughters without brothers are more likely to be encouraged to pursue advanced education and demanding careers that tend to reduce fertility. Highly educated daughters have significant incentives to use their time to pursue prestigious and well-compensated work rather than using it to bear and rear large numbers of children. Fertility is especially low when most women are expected to work at jobs incompatible with child rearing. A high rate of female employment is one of the strongest correlates of low fertility. Schooling is also likely to cause women to learn child-rearing practices that reduce infant mortality and thus reduce the need to have large numbers of children.

Only children in China are often referred to as "little emperors." Louisa Lim's story "China's 'Little Emperors' Lucky, Yet Lonely in Life," from NPR's *Morning Edition* (http://www.npr.org/2010/11/23/131539839/china-s-little-emperors-lucky-yet-lonely-in-life), looks at the lives of some of these children.

The adoption of a modern economy tends to increase women's employment rates. Parental bias against daughters tends to decrease when daughters are seen as capable of earning money. When accompanied by modernization, the fertility transition enables and compels women to devote themselves to work and education rather than motherhood. This is not always beneficial to the first generation of women to experience the fertility transition, since they tend to have been socialized to desire large numbers of children, and they may suffer when they cannot realize this desire. It is much more beneficial, however, for daughters born to low-fertility mothers, since these daughters tend to be socialized from childhood to value the educational and career success that the modern economy and the fertility transition enable them to pursue. Among my 1999 survey respondents, 32 percent of the females (383 out of the 1,215; $N = 1,215$) who responded to a survey question about whether they wanted children indicated that they hoped to remain childless all their lives (they were between 13 and 20 years old at the time). The fertility transition has also enabled urban Chinese daughters to receive heavy parental investment and for all their lives to remain filial—an ideal relating to children's ability and willingness to remain close to and care for their parents that has been long been valued by Chinese people of both genders, but was usually only attainable by men.

Survey Details and Statistical Notation

This survey was administered in 1999 to most of the students in grades 8 and 9 at a junior high school, grades 10 and 11 at a vocational high school, and grades 10 and 12 at a college-prep high school. Of the 2,273 respondents, 738 were from the junior high school, 753 were from the vocational high school, and 782 were from the college-prep high school. The junior high school and college prep high school had balanced gender ratios, while the vocational high school was 71 percent ($N = 752$) female because it specialized in female-dominated majors such as business and tourism.

The percentages cited in this case study sometimes includes the notation "$N =$" to convey what the denominator is in the calculation, which is a standard practice in reporting statistics of survey responses. In the case above, the 71 percent female ratio is based on a total of 752 students. In the figures in the body of the chapter relating to females who responded that they wanted children, $N = 1,215$ means that 383 women out of the 1,215 who responded (or 32 percent) wanted children.

Methods and Representations

Ding Na is one of the students I tutored in English during over three years of participant observation conducted in Dalian, a large coastal city (1999 urban population: 1,977,214) in Liaoning Province in northeastern China, between 1997 and 2014. To learn about the experiences of singletons, I conducted participant observation in a junior high school, a vocational high school, a college-prep high school, and the homes of 107 families that invited me to tutor their children in English or provide information about going abroad. I established long-term relationships with 31 of these families and participated in their social lives, leisure time, and everyday activities. In 1999 I also conducted a survey of 2,273 students at the schools I where I taught English. Only 2 of the 31 families I befriended had more than one child. Only 6 percent of my 2,167 survey respondents had siblings (that is, 134 out of the 2,167 who answered the survey question about siblings had siblings).

The schools where I conducted my survey enrolled students from a wide variety of socioeconomic backgrounds, although the most disadvantaged teenagers (such as those who were disabled or lacked urban citizenship) and the most elite teenagers (who were more likely to attend private schools, highly selective keypoint, or top-ranked, high schools, or study abroad programs) were underrepresented. Because of the midlevel status of the schools I studied, my survey results seem unlikely to deviate too far from the norms that might be found by a census or random sample of Dalian City teenagers. Dalian City's educational system divided high schools into six ranks of prestige. The non-keypoint college-prep high school I studied belonged in the second most prestigious category, and the vocational high school I studied belonged in fifth most prestigious category. The junior high school I studied had the widest range of achievement levels and socioeconomic statuses, since it admitted all primary school graduates in its district without considering their exam scores or ability to pay. Almost all Dalian City teenagers attended primary and junior high school, and most went on to secondary education as well.

The tutoring and information I provided was only useful to those who believed they had some chance of getting high school or college degrees, going abroad, or getting work that required English skills. I suspect that most urban singletons held this belief, since 94 percent of the 2,192 survey respondents indicated that they were tutored or took private classes at some point in their lives, and I seldom heard of urban singletons who thought they had no possible chance of upward mobility. Still, I cannot claim to have known families from all areas of China's socioeconomic pyramid. Like my survey sample, my ethnographic sample does not include youth from the narrow, ultra-rich top or the wide, impoverished, rural bottom of that pyramid. Therefore, my findings are not representative of the experiences of the highest-ranked university graduates who dominate intellectual discourse, or of the rural citizens that constituted the majority of the Chinese population in 2000.

The One-Child Policy

The primary aim of China's one-child policy is not to empower women, but rather to promote modernization by reducing the number of people who must compete for resources, both in the family and the nation. While the goal of emancipating women from the burdens of high fertility was prominent in campaigns to promote the use of contraceptive technology during the 1950s and 1960s, government propaganda promoting the one-child policy that began in 1979 tended to mention women's empowerment only as an auxiliary benefit of the policy. Contraceptive technology has enjoyed official approval in the People's Republic of China (PRC) since 1954, although it did not become widely available until 1962. Family planning was voluntary until 1970, when a limited population control campaign began. This campaign encouraged families to have no more than two children, but it was frequently ignored. Strictly enforced fertility limitation began in 1978, when government officials set a population target of no more than 1.2 billion people by the year 2000, and decided that a nationwide one-child policy was the only way to avoid exceeding this target. Despite widespread rural resistance that led to a de facto two-child policy in the countryside, China had close to its target population in 2000, when a nationwide census counted a population of 1.27 billion. In 1970, when population control policies began, China's total fertility rate was six births per woman; in 1980, two years after the start of the one-child policy, China's total fertility rate was down to two births per woman. Farmers had higher fertility than urban residents even before the one-child policy, and two-child families are the norm in rural areas, where farmers' overwhelming desire for sons who can serve as labor resources and old-age insurance has made the one-child policy difficult to enforce. In urban areas, however, the vast majority of women who married after 1978 have only one child. Compliance with the policy has remained high in cities like Dalian, even during the 1990s and 2000s, when the costs of violating the policy were reduced by rising incomes and the decline of the state sector and its surveillance and enforcement mechanisms.

China announced in November 2013 that it would relax the one-child policy in 2014. Two *Marketplace* stories explore how this may—or may not—change the number of children in China: "China Eases One-Child Policy, But Don't Expect More 'Little Emperors'" (http://www.marketplace.org/topics/world/china-eases-one-child-policy-dont-expect-more-little-emperors); and "China Eases One-Child Policy" (http://www.marketplace.org/topics/world/china-eases-one-child-policy).

While medical techniques for detecting the sex of fetuses have been available (though illegal) in China since the 1980s, the mothers of boys I tutored denied ever having used abortion to avoid having daughters, maintaining that only farmers would do this. Most Dalian parents I knew told me that it was acceptable to have just one child, even if that child was female, and some even told me they were glad they had daughters instead of sons. They knew from their own experience that daughters could fulfill the filial obligations once reserved for sons. Unlike their rural counterparts, Dalian parents were not desperate to have sons at any cost.

The Legacy of Low-Fertility Mothers

The first generation of mothers affected by the one-child policy was able to begin the transformation of their society's kinship system from a patrilineal, patrilateral, and patrilocal one to a bilineal, bilateral, and neolocal one. This was at least partly because of the paid work they could perform because of their low fertility. Paid work enabled women to provide their own parents with financial support in old age, and thus prove that daughters could be as filial as sons.

Studies conducted before mine attribute much of the male dominance in Chinese societies to parents' preferential treatment of sons over daughters. Grandparents of singletons told me that, in their youth (in the 1930s and 1940s), daughters could not live with their parents after marriage or provide nursing care or economic support for their elderly parents. A significant obstacle to equality between daughters and sons in previous generations was the assumption that daughters would not be able to support their parents in old age. Because of this assumption, parents avoided investing family resources in daughters.

Because most of the singletons' grandmothers lacked the financial resources to support their own parents, they could not contest the cultural expectation that daughters would be less filial than sons. As early as the 1920s, leading Chinese feminists of both genders advocated paid work as a key to women's emancipation. Motivated both by feminist ideals and by a desire to mobilize women's labor for national development, the Communist government began providing women with employment opportunities soon after it took control of China in 1949. Yet many singletons' grandmothers told me that they were too busy bearing and rearing children to take advantage of these opportunities. "I got up at dawn, and by the time I had shopped, cooked, cleaned, and sewed clothes for my five children, the sun would be down," one such grandmother told me. "Who would have done these things if I had gotten a job?" Grandmothers were far more likely than their husbands or children to remain unemployed all their lives.

The maternity leaves and medical problems caused by frequent childbearing also hindered the careers of those women who did paid work during the 1950s and 1960s. "I got to work upstairs in the factory office because I had gone to school, but I couldn't take a position of responsibility because I always had to take time off when I got pregnant," a singleton's grandmother told me. "After my fourth child, my health was bad all the time, and I had to quit my job." These women were far less likely than their husbands or children to work as officials, managers, or white-collar workers at any point in their lives.

Because most available apartments had only two bedrooms and were considered too small to accommodate joint families, most urban married children lived neolocally but in close proximity to both sets of parents by the end of the twentieth century. Only 17 percent of my survey respondents indicated that at least one grandparent lived in their home in 1999. Neolocality allows couples considerable flexibility in the negotiation of relationships with both sets of parents. In the flexible kinship system enjoyed by urban families, paid work gave women the leverage they needed to maintain ties to their own parents. As a junior high school student's mother told her husband when he complained that she was giving too much money to her parents, "Why shouldn't I give them the money I've earned? You should be grateful that I don't give all my wages to them!"

In the 1990s and 2000s, elderly parents who were widowed or disabled usually moved into an adult child's household. Which child they ended up living with depended less on gender than on interpersonal dynamics and on the amount of time and living space each child's household could spare. In many families, elderly parents rotated among all their children, staying a few weeks to a few months in the household of each son or daughter. Regardless of their gender, adult children tended to contribute as much in care, companionship, money, and gifts to their parents as they could afford. Many singletons' mothers provided monetary support and nursing care for their own elderly parents (often getting their husbands to help); most who performed annual worship rituals for their husbands' deceased parents also did so for their own deceased parents, and some inherited money, goods, and housing from their parents. While 12 percent of my survey respondents ($N = 2,187$) were living with at least one paternal grandparent in 1999, 5 percent ($N = 2,188$) were living with at least one maternal grandparent. Because of these singletons' mothers' success in diverting resources to their own parents, their families accept that daughters can be as filial as sons.

A short video report from CNBC, titled "How China's One-Child Policy Hurts the Elderly" (http://www.cnbc.com/id/101130958), looks at the cultural and economic effects of the one-child policy on the elderly in China.

Singletons' mothers were not able to completely obliterate patrilineal assumptions. Because women tended to earn less than men, they also tended to contribute less to their parents than their brothers could. This became especially apparent in the 1990s, after the economic reforms caused layoffs and early retirements that disproportionately targeted women. According to survey respondents, 25 percent of their mothers ($N = 2,190$) and 12 percent of their fathers ($N = 2,190$) were in compulsory retirement or unemployed due to layoffs at the time of the survey in 1999. Men and women who lost their jobs tended to reduce the financial support they provided their parents, letting wealthier siblings pick up the slack. Because most men earned more than most women, these wealthier siblings were more likely to be brothers rather than sisters. Still, singletons' mothers had at least proven daughters were capable of providing financial support for their parents. This reassured singletons' parents that their daughters could have the same capability, especially if they were given the resources to take full advantage of socioeconomic opportunities.

Dealing Strategically with Gender Norms

The strategy of raising a brotherless daughter to fill the kinship role usually reserved for sons was occasionally practiced even in pre-revolutionary China. The appropriateness of such a strategy was proclaimed by legends like that of Mulan, a girl who took her father's place in the army because he had no son old enough to do so. As a rare and difficult last resort, the strategy of "raising a daughter as a son" (*guniang dang erzi yang*) had little influence on dominant Chinese cultural models or the scholars who studied them. But this strategy gained popularity after the one-child policy made it a necessity for almost half of the families in most Chinese cities.

The Ballad of Mulan

The Mulan ballad is said to have originated in China in the fifth or sixth century CE. The legend of Mulan has inspired many novels, plays, and poems, as well as a Disney animated movie. Mulan Girls' High School is an expensive private girls' school established in Dalian during the 1990s.

Parents whose love, hope, and need for old-age support are all pinned on just one child tend to do whatever is necessary to make that child happy and successful, regardless of the child's gender. Daughters and their parents have faced the extra challenge of winning happiness and success in a society structured by gender norms that have long disadvantaged women. My study and others show that they have met this challenge with a strategic combination of conformity and resistance.

For academically unsuccessful daughters of poor parents of the late twentieth and early twenty-first centuries, gender norms provided a means of upward mobility through marriage and job markets unavailable to their male counterparts. Women faced a glass ceiling produced by their extra burden of domestic responsibility, by gender norms that favor men in elite professions, and by inequalities between elite husbands and their less elite, hypergamous wives. But women also enjoyed the protection of a glass floor created by hypergamy, by gender norms that favored non-elite women in the educational system, and by the rapidly expanding market for feminine jobs in the service and light industry sectors. This "glass floor" made it less likely that women would sink to the bottom of society, into poverty, crime, and unemployment. Men had neither the obstacle of the "glass ceiling" nor the protection of the "glass floor." While elite men were more likely than their female counterparts to rise to the top of their society, non-elite men were also more likely than their female counterparts to fall to the bottom.

I also found that singletons and their parents often talked about people's expectations of how males and females would behave. They were not interested in debating the extent to which such expectations corresponded with the way people actually behaved. Rather, they focused on weighing the costs and benefits of disregarding, invoking, transforming, or conforming to particular expectations on particular occasions. I translate these expectations as "gender norms."

Because they have had more support from their parents than previous generations, singleton daughters have unprecedented freedom to challenge gender norms. At the same time, however, their freedom has been limited by a system that remains structured by socioeconomic and gender inequalities. While more elite women might have had the wherewithal to seek the liberation that many elite feminists emphasize, the mostly non-elite singletons in my study (and their parents) found that they had to choose their battles. Therefore, they did not try to eradicate all gender norms. Rather, they only tried to do away with ones most likely to hurt their own interests, such as those that portrayed daughters as less filial and less worthy of parental investment than sons. At the same time, they conformed to other gender norms, such as those that portrayed women as more patient and meticulous than men, when they felt that such norms may further their interests. They sought happiness and success, not liberation per se. While previous generations also did this, daughters born after the establishment of the one-child policy have had more familial support for their strategies than previous generations.

Education and Work

Parents of both daughters and sons believed that success in education and work would be the key determinant of their children's (and thus their own) future happiness. Like sons, daughters were their parents' only hope for the future.

Girls who conformed to gender norms were more studious and obedient than their male counterparts, and thus more successful in the educational system at all levels but the very highest. The greater studiousness of girls was of limited use in previous generations because parents were reluctant to spend money on daughters' education, and sometimes even made daughters drop out of school to do work that would fund their brothers' education. Brotherless daughters, however, were encouraged to make full use of their academic talents, because they were their parents' only objects of investment, and their only hope for old-age support.

In the educational systems of many developed countries, girls from stigmatized minority backgrounds have tended to outperform their male counterparts, who were more likely to rebel against school discipline, which is identified with their ethnic oppressors. Though they were not ethnic minorities, economically disadvantaged teenagers in Dalian have experienced a similar phenomenon. Girls at the schools I studied tended to have higher overall scores than boys. This advantage, however, was balanced out by elite schools' emphasis on math and science, which boys favored, over the social sciences and humanities, which girls favored. High school entrance exams tested students more on science and math than on humanities and social science, and four-year colleges accepted more science and math majors than humanities and social science majors. These factors constituted a significant bias against girls at the highest levels of academic achievement, but not at the middle and lower levels, where the majority of students found themselves.

The Asia Society has compiled a series of short articles on the top school systems in the world, including Shanghai. These articles can be accessed at the society's website (http://asiasociety.org/global-cities-education-network/school-systems-around-world).

Gender norms structured Dalian's job market, but not always to women's disadvantage and men's advantage. Rather, they worked in favor of younger women and academically unsuccessful women from lower-class families even as they worked against older women, elite women, and poor, academically unsuccessful men. Stereotypically feminine traits were seen as ideal for most jobs in light industry and the service sector. Stereotypically masculine traits were seen as ideal for most jobs in the rapidly shrinking heavy industry sector and in some high-status professions open only to a tiny elite. This meant that elite women were less likely to get elite work than their male counterparts, but also that non-elite women were more likely to avoid unemployment than their male counterparts. Daughters were therefore counseled to conform to gender norms that could give them an advantage in the general job market, and to disregard those that might exclude them from elite professional work.

Women were rare in the most prestigious and best-paid professions, partly because they were hindered by their "second shift" of domestic work and partly because of many employers' belief that women do not have enough daring and creativity to do elite work. Focusing on biases against older women and elite women, some studies have argued that post-Mao economic reforms have intensified discrimination against women. I found, however, that the consequences of those reforms are more complicated for the majority of youths, who are of average or below-average education and family background. The same economic reforms that encouraged state enterprises to discriminate against middle-aged women also created service and light industry jobs that favored young women. Physical attractiveness and stereotypically feminine positive traits could compensate for a woman's lack of education and family connections, but the poorly educated son of powerless parents was simply out of luck.

Recognizing the midlevel job market's greater demand for female workers, Dalian's educational system admitted more girls than boys at the high school level. Greater educational opportunities for girls were reflected in the materials published by Dalian's Bureau of Education and given to Dalian's graduating junior high school class of 1999. At the technical school level, there were 1,346 places open to both boys and girls and 4,492 places reserved for girls, but only 4,301 places reserved for boys. At the vocational school level, there were 2,949 places open to both boys and girls and 5,189 places reserved for girls, but only 3,849 places reserved for boys. According to teachers, students, and education officials, only the small minority of schools classified as keypoint college-prep schools had more boys than girls. Most of the boys and about a quarter of the girls in my 1999 survey sample indicated that girls had an easier time getting jobs than boys did.

The gap between male and female statuses is much narrower in the singleton generation than in their parents' and grandparents' generations. Though they still face a glass ceiling perpetuated by symbolic structures of masculine domination, singleton daughters are not hindered by the parental discrimination that disadvantaged their mothers and grandmothers. The removal of this disadvantage has enabled singleton daughters to make the best use of their glass floor, and in some cases push the limits of their glass ceiling.

Marriage

Many parents told me that girls are more fortunate than boys because girls have more paths to upward mobility. Family background, career success, and educational attainment are important criteria for both men and women in selecting a spouse, but women who fall short by these standards can compensate with pleasant personalities, physical attractiveness, and the ability and willingness to do housework. Men can use these qualities to compensate as well, but not nearly to the extent women can. (Although it was important in young people's choice of marriage partners in 1990s urban China, romantic love was still often influenced by—and sometimes outweighed by—socioeconomic factors.)

In the marriage market created by the one-child policy, women enjoy several advantages. As in the past, grooms are expected to provide marital housing. The ability to live up to this expectation remains an important determinant of whether a man can win a bride. Thus a son and his parents must try to buy a neolocal apartment that is as large and conveniently located as possible by the time the son is ready to marry. A daughter and her parents, on the other hand, can consider the ability to provide or contribute to the purchase of marital housing an extra bonus to enhance the daughter's marriageability and comfort, rather than a requirement. Brotherless daughters and their parents see this as an advantage, rather than a sign that daughters are valued less than sons. Singletons of either gender face no competition for parental investment or inheritance. They and their parents just have to decide what form the wealth transfer will take. Unlike sons' parents, daughters' parents can invest all their savings in their daughters' education, rather than saving part of it for the purchase of marital housing. The need to purchase housing to attract a spouse is thus a disadvantage for sons and their parents. This disadvantage became particularly onerous after the housing reforms of the late 1990s, which created a private market for real estate instead of having the state assign housing to workers in exchange for low, subsidized rents, which was the situation previously. A male vocational high school student told me that he could have gone to a college-prep high school if his parents, who ran a small shop, had spent all their savings on the extra fees and bribes that would have gotten him in despite his low exam score. He said, "They gave me a choice. Either they could use their savings to send me to the college-prep high school, or they could use it to buy an apartment for me so that I'll be able to get a wife when the time comes. I don't like to study, and I didn't think I could make it to college even if I went to a college-prep school, so I chose the apartment."

In Dalian, women prefer to marry men of higher status, while men prefer to marry women of the same status. Thus, women can gain upward mobility through hypergamous marriage, while men are often forced to choose between permanent bachelorhood and marriage to someone of lower status. Although it produces inequality between husbands and wives, hypergamy is in some ways more favorable to women than to men. Unlike women, men seldom gain upward mobility through marriage.

Because of women's preference for marrying up, men have had difficulty obtaining brides of similar socioeconomic status as themselves. I often heard boys and their parents complain about how difficult it will be to find brides. This was partly because of China's skewed gender ratio, which has increased since the implementation of the one-child policy. In addition, young Dalian men feared that there would be a shortage of urban women willing to marry men of equal status, since women already at the top of Dalian's socioeconomic hierarchy may aspire to marry even higher-status men from wealthier cities or foreign countries. Urban men who could not find local brides could marry women from the countryside, where women were eager to gain urban residency through marriage. Many urban men and their parents, however, considered marriage to rural women less desirable and more likely to lead to downward socioeconomic mobility than marriage to urban women.

Changing Domestic Roles

In singletons' parents' generation, men were expected to earn more, have better jobs, and do less housework than their wives, who were expected to take primary responsibility for domestic work, usually at the expense of their careers. Indeed, my 1999 survey respondents' mothers were far more likely than their fathers to do household chores.

According to respondents who answered my survey questions about which chores their parents did,

- 94% of mothers ($N = 2,198$) and 41% of fathers ($N = 2,199$) cleaned,
- 94% of mothers ($N = 2,195$) and 42% of fathers ($N = 2,194$) did laundry,
- 94% of mothers ($N = 2,196$) and 54% of fathers ($N = 2,196$) shopped for groceries,
- 88% of mothers ($N = 2,194$) and 59% of fathers ($N = 2,194$) cooked.

Still, respondents' fathers were far more likely to help with housework than respondents' grandfathers, many of whom told me that they did no housework at all even when they were young fathers.

However, in the families of a few singletons I tutored, husbands did even more domestic work than their wives. This was particularly likely when the mother worked or earned more than the father. The mother of a family I lived with cheerfully did all the housework while she and her husband both worked at nine-to-five jobs. But things changed when she rented a fruit stall, where she sold fruit from 8:30 a.m. to 7:30 p.m., seven days a week, while his factory increasingly sent him home with no work and no pay, and eventually laid him off. Suddenly, she was making more money and doing more hours of paid work than he was. Though she took pride in being a "good wife and virtuous mother," she realized that her time had become a lot more valuable than her husband's time, and she started pressuring him to do more housework. He reluctantly agreed, and from then on had dinner waiting for her when she got back home at 8 p.m.

> The website of the All-China Women's Federation (http://www.womenofchina. cn/) is a good resource for exploring many gender-related issues in China.

Survey respondents expect the division of domestic work in their own marriages to be more egalitarian than in their parents' marriages, as demonstrated by their responses to a question about how much housework they want to do after marriage. According to the 1,159 girls and 842 boys who responded to the my survey questions about housework in 1999,

- 25% of girls and 17% of boys intend to do more housework than their spouse,
- 63% of girls and 48% of boys intend to do half the housework,
- 12% of girls and 35% of boys intend to do less housework than their spouse.

The percentage of male respondents who indicated that they wanted to do at least half the housework after marriage was somewhat higher than the percentage of respondents who indicated that their fathers did any housework at all. The percentage of female respondents who indicated that they wanted to do more housework than their husbands, however, was a lot smaller than the percentage of respondents who indicated that their mothers did more housework than their fathers.

When I asked boys who indicated that they wanted to do more housework than their wives why they chose that response, some said they would have to do a lot of housework to win and keep wives, since they are not likely to get good jobs or neolocal housing in time for their marriages. Others who already had girlfriends pointed out that their girlfriends are unlikely to do much housework after marriage. As one college-prep high school student said, "my girlfriend is too lazy to even buy her own snacks, so I have to run down to the shop and get them for her during lunch. How can I expect her to do even her fair share of the housework?"

Boys and girls alike recognized that greater gender equality in the distribution of housework is expected for their generation than for previous generations. As a junior high school student replied when her mother, a retired factory worker, asked what she will do after marriage if she never learns to cook, "My husband will cook! Who says women have to be the ones to cook?"

Conclusion

The benefits enjoyed by singleton daughters result from the demographic pattern produced by China's one-child policy, and not necessarily from the compulsory nature of that policy. Global processes of industrialization, modernization, and urbanization have led to low fertility in all developed countries and many developing countries worldwide. These processes would probably have caused a fertility transition in cities like Dalian even without a one-child policy. Such a transition would have occurred more slowly, and produced fewer brotherless daughters, than the transition mandated by the one-child policy. Still, even a daughter with one brother is likely to enjoy more resources than a daughter with several brothers.

Singleton daughters have dealt with gender norms in ways that seem likely to further their own interests. People of every generation have tried to use gender norms to attain their own desires (whether they involve socioeconomic success or the maintenance of strong ties to one's parents), but the efforts of Chinese daughters born prior to the one-child policy were severely hindered by a patrilineal system that overwhelmingly favored sons at the expense of their sisters. In contrast, urban singleton daughters have enjoyed unprecedented support for their efforts to challenge norms that work against them, while utilizing those that work in their favor. When daughters are not systematically excluded from familial resources, norms that once went hand in hand with patriarchy become tools that girls can use as well as boys.

China's social structure is still characterized by gender inequality, particularly at the upper levels of the academic and socioeconomic hierarchies. But brotherless daughters have the power to make the best use of their glass floor and push the limits of their glass ceiling, thanks to the parental support once denied to their mothers and grandmothers. Daughters empowered by the support of parents with no sons to favor are able to defy detrimental norms while strategically using ones that give them advantages in the educational system and the job and marriage markets. Parents of singletons complained about their children's gender when they believed their children were conforming to disadvantageous gender norms, but not when their children were conforming to advantageous ones. Complaints like those of Ding Na's father can thus be seen as strategies adopted on specific occasions to exhort a beloved child to challenge gender norms that could harm them.

Despite his moment of epiphany upon learning his daughter's excellent college entrance exam scores, Ding Na's father continued to remind her that he always wanted a son whenever he found fault with her. He continued to fret about her future, demanding that she succeed in college and worrying that she would not be able to find a good job afterwards, especially since she chose to major in computer programming despite his misgivings. Yet Ding Na took her father's commentaries in stride. "He criticizes me only because he wants to push me to do better," she told me. Indeed, I noticed that, though he criticized her in her presence, he also boasted about her in her absence.

While Ding Na was away at college, I had dinner with her parents and paternal uncle, whose singleton daughter was still in high school. Ding Na's father's brother talked about his fear that his own daughter would not succeed in the science major she had chosen, since "science is harder for girls." Ding Na's father, however, reassured him by quoting a famous line from *The Red Detachment of Women* (*Hongse Niangzijun*), a revolutionary model opera about Communist women soldiers: "In ancient times there was Hua Mulan; in modern times there is the Red Detachment of Women." He then raised his glass of beer in a toast and added, "in the future it will be up to our daughters."

References and Further Research

Chen, Xinyin, Kenneth H. Rubin, and Bo-shu Li. 1994. "Only Children and Sibling Children in Urban China: A Re-examination." *International Journal of Behavioural Development* 17, no. 3: 413–421.

Falbo, Toni, and Dudley L. Poston Jr. 1993. "The Academic, Personality, and Physical Outcomes of Only Children in China." *Child Development* 64, no. 1:18–35.

Fong, Vanessa L. 2004. *Only Hope: Coming of Age Under China's One-Child Policy*. Stanford, CA: Stanford University Press.

Goh, Esther. 2011. *China's One-Child Policy and Multiple Caregiving: Raising Little Suns in Xiamen*. New York: Routledge.

Greenhalgh, Susan. 2008. *Just One Child: Science and Policy in Deng's China*. Berkeley, CA: University of California Press.

Hannum, Emily, Peggy Kong, and Yuping Zhang. 2009. "Family Sources of Educational Gender Inequality in Rural China: A Critical Assessment." *International Journal of Educational Development* 29, no. 5: 474–486.

Hesketh, Therese, Li Lu, and Zhu Wei Xing. 2005. "The Effect of China's One-Child Family Policy after 25 Years." *The New England Journal of Medicine* 353, no. 11: 1171–1176. http://www.nejm.org/doi/full/10.1056/NEJMhpr051833.

Jing, Jun, ed. 2000. *Feeding China's Little Emperors: Food, Children and Social Change*. Stanford, CA: Stanford University Press.

Kim, Sung won, and Vanessa L. Fong. 2014. "A Longitudinal Study of Son Preference and Daughter Preference among Chinese Only-Children from Adolescence to Adulthood." *China Journal* 71: 1–26.

Kipnis, Andrew B. 2011. *Governing Educational Desire: Culture, Politics, and Schooling in China*. Chicago: University of Chicago Press.

Liu, Fengshu. 2006. "Boys as Only-Children and Girls as Only-Children—Parental Gendered Expectations of the Only-Child in the Nuclear Chinese Family in Present-Day China." *Gender and Education* 18, no 5: 491–506.

Milwertz, Cecilia Nathansen. 1997. *Accepting Population Control: Urban Chinese Women and the One-Child Family Policy*. Richmond, UK: Curzon.

Murphy, Rachel, Ran Tao, and Xi Lu. 2011. "Son Preference in Rural China: Patrilineal Families and Socioeconomic Change." *Population and Development Review* 37, no. 4: 665–690.

Seeberg, Vilma. 2011. "Schooling, Jobbing, Marrying: What's a Girl to Do to Make Life Better? Empowerment Capabilities of Girls at the Margins of Globalization in China." *Research in Comparative and International Education* 6, no. 1: 43–61.

Shi, Lihong. 2009. "'Little Quilted Vests to Warm Parents' Hearts': Redefining the Gendered Practice of Filial Piety in Rural North-Eastern China." *China Quarterly* 198: 348–363.

Short, Susan E., Zhai Fengying, Xu Siyuan, and Yang Mingliang. 2001. "China's One-Child Policy and the Care of Children: An Analysis of Qualitative and Quantitative Data." *Social Forces* 79, no. 3: 913–943.

Xie, Yu, and Haiyan Zhu. 2009. "Do Sons or Daughters Give More Money to Parents in Urban China?" *Journal of Marriage and Family* 71, no. 1: 174–186. http://www.ncbi.nlm.nih.gov/pmc/articles/PMC2749496/.

Yan, Yunxiang. 2010. *The Individualization of Chinese Society*. Oxford, England: Berg.

Zhang, Hong. 2007. "China's New Rural Daughters Coming of Age: Downsizing the Family and Firing Up Cash Earning Power in the New Economy." *Signs: Journal of Women in Culture and Society* 32, no. 3: 671–698.

Zhang, Weiguo. 2009. "'A Married Out Daughter is Like Spilt Water'? Women's Increasing Contacts and Enhanced Ties with Their Natal Families in Post-Reform Rural North China." *Modern China* 35, no. 3: 256–283.

Zhang, Yuping, Grace Kao, and Emily Hannum. 2007. "Do Mothers in Rural China Practice Gender Equity in Educational Aspirations for Children?" *Comparative Education Review* 51, no. 2: 131–158.

About the Editor and Contributors

Anne Prescott is the director of the Five College Center for East Asian Studies in Massachusetts and a national director for the National Consortium for Teaching about Asia, a leading provider of professional development training on East Asia. Trained as an ethnomusicologist specializing in traditional Japanese music, she spent eight years in Japan. She has been an administrator at area studies centers since 2002.

Bruce Baird is an associate professor of Asian languages and literatures at the University of Massachusetts Amherst; he is interested in Japanese theatre, philosophy, and new media studies. He is the recipient of two Fulbright fellowships, author of a book about the founder of butō titled *Hijikata Tatsumi and Butoh: Dancing in a Pool of Gray Grits* (Palgrave Macmillan, 2012), and working on a general history of butō.

Jerry P. Dennerline began studying Chinese history and Confucian thought at Wabash College, and received his PhD in history at Yale in 1973. He has done archival and oral history research in Taiwan, China, and Japan, focusing on local communities in the Yangtzi delta between the seventeenth and twentieth centuries. He has taught Chinese history at Amherst College since 1981 and is currently engaged in research on Chinese overseas in Singapore and Malaysia. He is the author of *Qian Mu and the World of Seven Mansions* (Yale University Press, 1988).

Vanessa L. Fong is an associate professor of anthropology at Amherst College. She is the author of *Only Hope: Coming of Age Under China's One-Child Policy* (Stanford University Press, 2004), which won the 2005 Francis Hsu Book Prize from the Society for East Asian Anthropology, and *Paradise Redefined: Transnational Chinese Students and the Quest for Flexible Citizenship in the Developed World* (Stanford University Press, 2011). Since 1998, she has been engaged in a longitudinal project that will follow a cohort of Chinese only-children and their families throughout their lives. Information about her publications can be found at www.vanessafong.blogspot.com.

Jacques Fuqua is a retired U.S. Army officer who served the last 12 years of his career as a foreign area officer in Japan and South Korea involved in various international security negotiations. Since his retirement in February 2000, he has served in various capacities as an international affairs officer at some of the nation's leading universities and taught Japanese and Korean history and diplomatic history courses, including The History of East Asian Diplomacy (1844–Present); History of Korean Diplomacy (1392–Present); and Japanese History. He is the author of *Nuclear Endgame: The Need for Engagement with North Korea* (Praeger Security International, 2007); *Korean Unification: Inevitable Challenges* (Potomac Books, 2011); and *A Destiny Between Two Worlds: An Historical Novel of Okinawa* (Top Hat Books, 2015).

Maris Gillette is the E. Desmond Lee Professor of Museum Studies and Community History at the University of Missouri–St. Louis, where she directs a graduate program in museum studies. She is a sociocultural anthropologist and filmmaker who has studied porcelain workers and entrepreneurs in Jingdezhen (southeast China) and urban Chinese Muslims in Xi'an (northwest China). Gillette codirected the planning phase of the community history project Muslim Voices of Philadelphia, and she has facilitated several community-based documentary shorts in the Philadelphia area. She has curated and cocurated exhibits and installations at the Philadelphia Museum of Art, the Peabody Museum of Archaeology and Ethnology, and Haverford College.

Thomas Gottschang is a professor of economics at the College of the Holy Cross in Worcester, Massachusetts. He received a master's degree in Asian studies from Yale University and a PhD in economics and history from the University of Michigan. His research interests include Chinese economic history and the economics of transition. His publications include *Swallows and Settlers: The Great Migration from North China to Manchuria* (Center for Chinese Studies, University of Michigan, 2000, with Diana Lary), and "Viet Nam's Economy in Transition: Successes and Challenges," in the journal *Education About Asia* (Spring 2010). He was a visiting professor at National Economics University, Hanoi, Vietnam, in the spring semesters of 1993 and 1996.

Jina E. Kim's research focuses on the cultural history of early twentieth-century East Asia, with primary concentrations in Korean and global modernisms, urban literature and history, and comparative colonialism and postcolonialism. Her other research interests include material and popular culture from the late nineteenth century to the present. Her book *Urban Modernity in Colonial Korea and Taiwan* is forthcoming.

Beth E. Notar is an associate professor and the chair of the Anthropology Department at Trinity College in Hartford, Connecticut. After graduating with a degree in Chinese studies from Wellesley College, she spent three years in China and Taiwan—studying Mandarin at Beijing University, working as a translator at the

National Palace Museum in Taiwan, and studying Chinese economy and history at the Johns Hopkins–Nanjing Center for Chinese and American Studies. It was then that she became fascinated with the astonishing changes of China's reform era and decided to pursue research there. She is the author of *Displacing Desire: Travel and Popular Culture in China* (University of Hawai'i Press, 2006).

Junko Oba trained as ethnomusicologist and sound recordings archivist at Wesleyan University. Her research interests include traditional and contemporary Japanese popular musics; Asia and the Asian diaspora, especially Nikkey Brazilian expatriate communities in Japan; music and collective memory construction; and national identity in the trans- and postnational world orders. She is an assistant professor of music at Hampshire College, teaching ethnomusicology, popular music studies, and Asian studies courses.

Jeffrey L. Richey chairs the Asian Studies Program at Berea College, where he is an associate professor of religion and Asian studies. He is the author of *Confucius in East Asia: Confucianism's History in China, Korea, Japan, and Viet Nam* (Association for Asian Studies, 2013) and *The Patheos Guide to Confucianism* (Patheos Press, 2012), as well as the editor of *Teaching Confucianism* (Oxford University Press, 2008) and the co-editor (with Kenneth J. Hammond) of *The Sage Returns: Confucian Revival in Contemporary China* (State University of New York Press, 2015). Richey also serves as Chinese Philosophy area editor for the *Internet Encyclopedia of Philosophy* (http://www.iep.utm.edu/). Presently, he is editing *Daoism in Japan: Chinese Traditions and Their Influence on Japanese Religious Culture,* to be published by Routledge in 2015.

Joshua Hotaka Roth is a professor of anthropology and Asian studies at Mount Holyoke College. His book *Brokered Homeland: Japanese Brazilian Migrants in Japan* (Cornell University Press, 2002) won the 2004 Book Award for Social Science from the Association for Asian American Studies. More recently, he has been working on a book about Japanese automobility. "Heartfelt Driving: Discourses on Manners, Safety, and Emotion in Japan's Era of Mass Motorization," an article based on this recent research, appeared in *The Journal of Asian Studies* in 2012.

Index